SCIENCE AND RELIGION

The idea of an inevitable conflict between science and religion was decisively challenged by John Hedley Brooke in his classic *Science and religion: Some historical perspectives* (Cambridge, 1991). Almost two decades on, *Science and religion: New historical perspectives* revisits this argument and asks how historians can now impose order on the complex and contingent histories of religious engagements with science.

Bringing together leading scholars, this new volume explores the history and changing meanings of the categories 'science' and 'religion'; the role of publishing and education in forging and spreading ideas; the connection between knowledge, power, and intellectual imperialism; and the reasons for the confrontation between evolution and creationism among American Christians and in the Islamic world. A major contribution to the historiography of science and religion, this book makes the most recent scholarship on this much misunderstood debate widely accessible.

THOMAS DIXON is Senior Lecturer in History at Queen Mary, University of London. He is the author of *The invention of altruism* (2008) and *From passions to emotions* (Cambridge, 2003).

GEOFFREY CANTOR is Professor Emeritus of the History of Science at the University of Leeds and Honorary Senior Research Fellow at University College, London. He is the author of *Quakers, Jews, and science* (2005).

STEPHEN PUMFREY is Senior Lecturer in the History of Science at the University of Lancaster. He is the author of *Latitude and the magnetic earth* (2002), winner of the British Society for the History of Science Dingle Prize.

SCIENCE AND RELIGION

New Historical Perspectives

EDITED BY

THOMAS DIXON, GEOFFREY CANTOR, AND STEPHEN PUMFREY

CAMBRIDGE
UNIVERSITY PRESS

CAMBRIDGE UNIVERSITY PRESS
Cambridge, New York, Melbourne, Madrid, Cape Town, Singapore,
São Paulo, Delhi, Dubai, Tokyo

Cambridge University Press
The Edinburgh Building, Cambridge CB2 8RU, UK

Published in the United States of America by Cambridge University Press, New York

www.cambridge.org
Information on this title: www.cambridge.org/9780521760270

© Cambridge University Press 2010

First published 2010

Printed in the United Kingdom at the University Press, Cambridge

A catalogue record for this publication is available from the British Library

Library of Congress Cataloging-in-Publication Data

Science and religion : new historical perspectives / [edited by] Thomas Dixon,
Geoffrey Cantor, Stephen Pumfrey.
p. cm.
ISBN 978-0-521-76027-0 (Hardback)
1. Religion and science–History. I. Dixon, Thomas (Thomas M.) II. Cantor, G. N., 1943–
III. Pumfrey, Stephen. IV. Title.

BL245.S38 2010
201′.65–dc22

2009047386

ISBN 978-0-521-76027-0 Hardback

Dedicated with admiration and affection
to Professor John Hedley Brooke

Contents

Contributors

GEOFFREY CANTOR is Professor Emeritus of the History of Science at the University of Leeds and Honorary Senior Research Fellow at University College, London. His publications on science and religion include *Michael Faraday: Sandemanian and scientist* (1991) and *Quakers, Jews, and science* (2005). He co-authored *Reconstructing nature* (1998) with John Brooke and co-edited *Jewish tradition and the challenge of Darwinism* (2006) with Marc Swetlitz. He is currently researching the role of religion in the Great Exhibition of 1851.

THOMAS DIXON is Senior Lecturer in History at Queen Mary, University of London. He has pursued three related strands of research: the history of theories of passions and emotions; the history of debates about 'altruism', especially in Victorian Britain; and, more generally, the history of relationships between science and religion. Previous publications include *From passions to emotions: The creation of a secular psychological category* (2003), *The invention of altruism: Making moral meanings in Victorian Britain* (2008), and *Science and religion: A very short introduction* (2008).

NOAH EFRON chairs the Program in Science, Technology and Society at Bar-Ilan University. He is President of the Israeli Society for History and Philosophy of Science and a member of the executive committee of the International Society for Science and Religion. He has been a member of the Institute for Advanced Study in Princeton, the Dibner Institute for History of Science and Technology at MIT, and a Fellow at Harvard University. He is the author of *Judaism and science: A historical introduction* (2007).

JAN GOLINSKI is Professor of History and Humanities at the University of New Hampshire, USA. He is the author of *Science as public culture:*

Chemistry and Enlightenment in Britain, 1760–1820 (1992) and *Making natural knowledge: Constructivism and the history of science* (new edn, 2005). His latest book is *British weather and the climate of Enlightenment* (2007).

SALMAN HAMEED is Assistant Professor of Integrated Science and Humanities at Hampshire College, Massachusetts. He is currently working on the rise of creationism in the Islamic world and how Muslims view the relationship between science and religion. He is also analysing reconciliation efforts between astronomers and Native Hawaiians over telescopes on top of sacred Mauna Kea in Hawaii. At Hampshire College he teaches courses on 'History and philosophy of science and religion' and 'Science in the Islamic world'.

PETER HARRISON is Andreas Idreos Professor of Science and Religion at the University of Oxford. A Fellow of Harris Manchester College, he is also Director of the Ian Ramsey Centre at Oxford. He has published extensively in the area of cultural and intellectual history, with a focus on the philosophical, scientific, and religious thought of the early modern period. His most recent book is *The fall of man and the foundations of science* (2007), and he is currently editing the *Cambridge companion to science and religion*.

B. HARUN KÜÇÜK is a doctoral candidate at the University of California, San Diego, where he is writing his dissertation on the philosophical and scientific exchange between Europe and the Ottoman Empire during the early Enlightenment. He has contributed a chapter on the same subject to a recent volume entitled *Wahrnehmung des Islam zwischen Reformation und Aufklärung* (2008).

RONALD L. NUMBERS is Hilldale Professor of the History of Science and Medicine at the University of Wisconsin. His publications include *The creationists* (1992; new edn 2006), *Darwinism comes to America* (1998), and *Science and Christianity in pulpit and pew* (2007). With David Lindberg he has co-edited *God and nature: Historical essays on the encounter between Christianity and science* (1986), *When science and Christianity meet* (2003), and, with John Brooke, *Science and religion around the world* (2010). He is editor of *Galileo goes to jail and other myths about science and religion* (2009).

MARGARET J. OSLER is Professor of History and Adjunct Professor of Philosophy at the University of Calgary. Her research has focussed on the relationship between theology and natural philosophy in the early modern period, especially in the work of Gassendi, Descartes, Boyle, and Newton. Her publications include *Divine will and the mechanical philosophy: Gassendi and Descartes on contingency and necessity in the created world* (1994). She co-edited *Science in theistic contexts* (*Osiris* 16 (2001)) with John Brooke and Jitse van der Meer.

STEPHEN PUMFREY is Senior Lecturer in the History of Science at the University of Lancaster. His research mainly concerns early modern natural philosophy, including debates over Copernican, experimental, and magnetic philosophies. Recent publications include *Latitude and the magnetic earth* (2002) and 'Science and patronage in England, 1570–1625' in *History of Science* 32 (2004). He is co-producing an edition and translation of William Gilbert's *De mundo nostro sublunari*.

ADAM R. SHAPIRO is a Dibner Fellow in the History of Science at the Huntington Library. He has recently completed a project on the Scopes trial, biology education, and biblical literalism. His current research examines William Paley and the political economy of the natural theology movement from the nineteenth century to the present day.

SUJIT SIVASUNDARAM is a Lecturer in International History at the London School of Economics. He will be taking up a new position as Lecturer in World and Imperial History since 1500 at the University of Cambridge in 2010. His first book was *Nature and the godly empire: Science and evangelical mission, 1795–1850* (2005). He has also written on the relationship between science and religion in South Asia, and is currently working on a book on British colonialism in Ceylon, which will discuss Buddhist traditions of natural knowledge.

BRONISLAW SZERSZYNSKI is Senior Lecturer in the Department of Sociology, at the University of Lancaster. His research is primarily concerned with developing new understandings of the changing relations between humans, environment, and technology, drawing on social theory, qualitative sociological research, philosophy, and theology. He is the author of *Nature, technology and the sacred* (2005) and co-editor of several books, including *Risk, environment and modernity* (1996), *Re-ordering nature: Theology, society and the new genetics* (2003), and *Nature performed: Environment, culture and performance* (2003).

JONATHAN R. TOPHAM is a Senior Lecturer in the History of Science at the University of Leeds. Among his co-publications are *Science in the nineteenth-century periodical: Reading the magazine of nature* (2004), *Culture and science in the nineteenth-century media* (2004), and *Science in the nineteenth-century periodical: An electronic index* (HRI Online, 2005). His current research combines an ongoing project concerning the *Bridgewater treatises* and natural theology in early nineteenth-century Britain with a wide-ranging study of science and print culture in the same period.

FRANK M. TURNER is John Hay Whitney Professor of History and Director of the Beinecke Rare Book and Manuscript Library at Yale University, where from 1988 to 1992 he served as Provost. He is author of *John Henry Newman: The challenge to evangelical religion* (2002), *Contesting cultural authority: Essays in Victorian intellectual life* (1993), *The Greek heritage in Victorian Britain* (1981), and *Between science and religion: The reaction to scientific naturalism in late Victorian England* (1974).

Preface

In July 2007 a conference was held at the University of Lancaster to mark the retirement of John Hedley Brooke. The original idea for the conference came from Stephen Pumfrey, who had started his career under John's mentorship at Lancaster. Thomas Dixon, who was at that time also at Lancaster, took the lead in organizing the event. Both the Lancaster organizers were extremely grateful for the advice and support of Geoffrey Cantor, who assisted with the planning of the original conference.

The 2007 conference was attended by many of John Brooke's friends, colleagues, and students who were keen to acknowledge his substantial contributions to the historical study of science and religion, and particularly the influence he has had on a whole generation of scholars and students through his book *Science and religion: Some historical perspectives*, published in 1991, and his other publications, as well as through personal contact and encouragement. John taught in the History Department at the University of Lancaster from 1969 to 1999 and then moved to the Andreas Idreos Chair in Science and Religion at the University of Oxford until his retirement in 2006.

Over a hundred and fifty people attended the Lancaster conference. Dozens of excellent papers were given on that occasion, which could together have provided material for several edited books offering a range of historical and contemporary perspectives. The editors of this volume selected thirteen of those contributions to illustrate both the impact of John Brooke's work on the field and also major recent trends in the historiography of science and religion. The chapters collected in this volume together show how new understandings of the past continue to enrich our appreciation of how science and religion can affect one another. Most importantly, the editors intend this volume to be a companion to *Science and religion: Some historical perspectives* and, following Brooke's lead, to open up new and fruitful ways of understanding science–religion interrelations through the close study of history.

The editors would like to express their sincere thanks to Angus Winchester and Ghil O'Neill of the Department of History and to Hilary Barraclough and Tina Warren of the Conference Office at the University of Lancaster; and to the John Templeton Foundation, who generously provided a grant towards the costs both of the Lancaster conference and of the publication of this book. At Cambridge University Press, Kate Brett, Laura Morris, and Jodie Barnes guided us through every stage of the production process with great efficiency, and we are very grateful to Aline Guillermet for finding such an appropriate cover image. The final text benefited greatly from Chris Jackson's meticulous copy-editing. We thank the University of Chicago Press for permitting us to reprint Peter Harrison's article, '"Science" and "Religion": Constructing the boundaries', which first appeared in the *Journal of Religion* 86 (2006), 81–106.

The editors are deeply indebted to the other contributors to this volume for their considerable efforts in turning their original conference presentations into extended essays that address the key historiographical themes of this book.

CHAPTER I

Introduction

Thomas Dixon

John Hedley Brooke is well known to students of science and religion as
the slayer of the 'conflict thesis' – the hackneyed but popular idea that,
ever since the Scientific Revolution, 'science' and 'religion' have been
locked in a deadly battle in which science emerges triumphant. In his
Science and religion: Some historical perspectives (1991) and other writings,
Brooke has used historical scholarship to show how wrong this picture is.[1]

The systematic dismantling of received ideas about the nature of the
scientific enterprise was one of the starting points for this reappraisal of
scientific and religious relations. In the 1950s and 1960s historians and
philosophers of science began to criticize the 'Whig' view of history,
according to which science in the past should be seen as slowly but surely
approaching the truths put forward by science in the present.[2] The new
anti-Whig conception of science underpinned Thomas Kuhn's *The structure of scientific revolutions*, first published in 1962, which helped set the
agenda for future generations of scholars. In Kuhn's picture, the history of
science was a discontinuous series of traditions or paradigms dedicated to
solving particular puzzles with greater empirical accuracy, but not necessarily approaching some unseen objective reality in the process.[3] This shift
in the history of science also inaugurated a new ideal of the historian of
science as an observer of the science of past ages, rather than an advocate
for modern science. In other words post-Kuhnian historians of science
have tried to approach past science on its own terms and not as a curious
but unsuccessful attempt to deliver the scientific truths of the present.

Histories of the relationship between science and religion written in
this spirit started to appear in the 1970s. This new history of science and
religion would replace over-simple master-narratives with a richer sense of
the complexity of past engagements between science and religion; it
would place those intellectual engagements firmly in their proper social
and political contexts; and it would undermine the very idea that 'science'
or 'religion' could be reified as entities with timeless essences.[4] Brooke by

I

no means achieved the ascendancy of this new historiography single-handedly.[5] However, his *Science and religion* and his 1998 book with Geoffrey Cantor based on their Gifford Lectures, *Reconstructing nature: The engagement of science and religion*, have been particularly influential.[6] The present volume offers an opportunity for a group of scholars actively developing new historical perspectives on the history of science and religion to take stock of Brooke's landmark contributions to the field and also to map out the new directions being taken by historians of science and religion almost two decades after the publication of Brooke's classic study. In the rest of this introduction I engage briefly with each of these tasks, highlighting what I take to be the most important themes that run through the contributions to this volume and sketching out the agenda for future research that they collectively suggest.

JOHN BROOKE AND THE HISTORIOGRAPHY OF SCIENCE AND RELIGION

Noah Efron's chapter includes a vivid account of the impact that Brooke's 1991 book had on him personally as a young historian at the start of his career. Efron was certainly not alone in finding himself forced by Brooke's work to rethink his assumptions about the history of science. But, as any reader of Brooke will know, 'forced' is not quite the right word. The persuasive effect of Brooke's writings arises from a very subtle combination of factors: sophisticated and sympathetic readings of published and unpublished historical documents, a palpable delight in the richness and intricacy of the intellectual histories he unfolds, and a rhetorical style which manages to convey caution and modesty at the same time as a certain steely resolve.

These techniques were deployed by Brooke in the pioneering course materials he developed for the Open University in the 1970s and subsequently in his studies not only of European natural theology and of the religious commitments of notable English men of science, including Isaac Newton, Joseph Priestley, William Whewell, Robert Owen, and Charles Darwin, but also in a series of studies on the history of chemistry, and in his work in editing and contributing to many collections of essays, including recent volumes on *Heterodoxy in early modern science and religion* (2005), *Religious values and the rise of science in Europe* (2005), and *Science and religion around the world* (2010).[7] Brooke's writings are marked not only by elegance and erudition but also by a fondness for nuance and even occasional wordplay. Brooke suggests, for example, when writing of Priestley's utilitarian interest in science that 'it was through salt that he came to Bacon'.[8] He writes of the difficulties that confronted the mathematician Mary Somerville in her bid to become 'a queen of the sciences'.[9] And Charles Darwin, Brooke concludes, cannot be easily pigeon-holed at the various stages of his intellectual development: 'On reflection it would be surprising if the man who showed us that we cannot pigeon-hole pigeons could be pigeon-holed himself'.[10]

There is more to this last remark, though, than mere wordplay. The refusal to pigeon-hole is central to Brooke's project. He has repeatedly emphasized the complexity of individuals and their intellectual commitments and warned us of the distortions involved in lumping them together. He particularly cautions historians against trying to group people or ideas into pigeon-holes labelled 'science' or 'religion', or historiographical ones labelled 'conflict' or 'harmony'. Brooke famously wrote in his 1991 book: 'Serious scholarship in the history of science has revealed so extraordinarily rich and complex a relationship between science and religion in the past that general theses are difficult to sustain. The real lesson turns out to be the complexity'. And again: 'Much of the writing on science and religion has been structured by a preoccupation either with conflict or with harmony. It is necessary to transcend these constraints if the interaction, in all its richness and fascination, is to be appreciated'.[11]

Some might wonder whether in the midst of all this richness and fascination, however, any historical generalizations can be sustained at all. It sometimes seems not. One reviewer of Brooke's *Science and religion* described it as 'a very cautious book, a detailed, nuanced description of complexity and diversity that lacks an argument of its own'. That reviewer went on to say that, in his view, the 'almost astonishing balance' on display was a sign of 'historiographical maturity rather than lack of nerve'.[12] Brooke himself has been aware of the danger of over-complexification as an issue in the history of science. In his Presidential Address to the British Society for the History of Science in Leeds in 1997, speaking about whether the history of science was a unified field with a unified subject matter, Brooke asked his fellow historians of science: 'if we stress the permeability of the boundaries with which the word "science" has been ringed, does the subject not simply dissolve into fragments of socio-cultural history?' Such a prospect, Brooke admitted, would worry many. 'But if *the* history of science has no future', he went on, 'histories of different sciences in their different local contexts surely still have a bright one. As scholars in the field we can map the multiple spaces in which the sciences have taken shape and we can relish the differentiation'.[13]

That final phrase could serve very well as a motto to encapsulate Brooke's approach to history: 'Relish the differentiation'.

In that same talk Brooke spoke of the 'dissonance between simple narrative forms that have proven public appeal and the complexities disclosed by serious scholarship'.[14] This moves us from the dangers of reifying the categories 'science' and 'religion' to the harm that can be done by misleading historical master-narratives. Brooke's own solution to the problem of how to popularize the history of science without falling prey to misleadingly simplistic narratives, in his 1991 book, was to use the simplistic narrative as a foil for his own more complex and scholarly account. The wrongness of the conflict narrative motivated Brooke's whole book. A comparable historiographical ploy can be found in Jim Endersby's 2007 book, *A guinea-pig's history of biology*.[15] The historiographical villain for Endersby is the narrative of the lone scientific genius. As one reviewer put it, Endersby 'explodes the persistent myth that science is a series of eureka moments by heroic individuals, instead revealing a complex reality of social interaction and interdependence'.[16]

Drawing attention to this relationship between simplistic popular narratives and academic complexification, Richard Olson has written: 'There is a serious question about whether the forceful presentation of simple master narratives precludes or is a necessary prerequisite to more subtle investigation. Brooke seems to assume the former; I am inclined to believe the latter'.[17] Olson is right that the craft and rhetoric of the academic historian frequently makes use of a contrast between scholarly rigour on the one hand, and sweeping generalizations, overly simple narratives, popular misconceptions, and one-sided explanations on the other. But, as Olson implies, such complexification cannot be an end in itself. The success of Brooke's work should not mean that conflicts or generalizations are forever banned from the historiography of science and religion. The traces left by past individuals and societies impose upon the historian neither clear narratives, nor self-evident categories. But neither are they entirely without pattern. Several chapters in this volume, especially those by Peter Harrison, Geoffrey Cantor, and Ronald Numbers, directly address this question of how to find legitimate places for both conflict and generalization in a post-Brookean historiography.

I have discussed two of the most salient points of the new historiography of science and religion: its aversions to reification and to master-narratives. A third important feature is the idea that this new approach to the subject is less partisan than what went before. Brooke and Cantor have written of their desire to approach their subject as an 'impartial observer' would.

Historians, on this view, should 'strive not to be partisan but instead should seek to understand all the protagonists and the historical nexus in which they operated'.[18] Likewise, in their introduction to *When science and Christianity meet* (2003), David Lindberg and Ronald Numbers write that recent historians of science and religion have 'laid aside apologetic and polemical goals, choosing to understand rather than to judge'.[19]

These are very admirable historiographical principles, but they are not immune from scrutiny themselves. Historians of science are trained to raise a sceptical eyebrow at claims to be able to produce value-free knowledge. And no historian of religion will readily accept the notion that a history of religious thought might be composed that was entirely innocent of apologetic intentions. Future generations of historians will wish to historicize and question the 'impartial' and 'non-judgemental' histories of science and religion produced since the 1970s, just as the contributors to the present volume have used the tools of historical analysis to unearth the genesis of those master-narratives against which recent historians have been reacting. We should never stop asking whose interests a particular historical narrative serves and for what purposes it has been constructed. And we should not exempt our own narratives from those searching questions.

HISTORICIZING NARRATIVES AND CATEGORIES

Our histories themselves have histories, as several of the chapters in this volume illustrate. The idea that there was a 'Scientific Revolution' between 1500 and 1700 and that this marked a definitive moment of separation between science and religion was, as Margaret Osler shows, the creation of nineteenth-century positivists and twentieth-century historians, who read their own secularist aspirations and experiences back into the history of the sciences during a period when they were, in fact, pursued in a climate of diverse, serious, and vibrant theological concern. Frank Turner, who was one of the historiographical pioneers in this field thirty years ago, offers a comprehensive unpacking of the 'conflict narrative' with reference to its origins in the intellectual and cultural world of the late nineteenth century. Turner reminds us that we should not discount the existence of real conflicts between science and religion in that period as one of the reasons that such an historical narrative would emerge. But the fact that a strong public sense of a conflict between science and religion emerged when it did still itself needs to be explained. Particularly important here is an appreciation of the history of religious life and thought during the nineteenth century, and of the emergence of a new sphere of state education, over which different interest groups could tussle. Turner thus provides a definitive study of the intellectual and social milieu into which the infamous 'conflict thesis' was born.

Cantor's chapter reinforces Turner's argument about the origins of the 'conflict thesis' in the 1870s and makes the very interesting further observation that John W. Draper seemed to be predisposed to see history in almost Manichean terms as a preordained conflict between opposing forces. Shortly before composing his notorious *History of the conflict between religion and science* (1875), Draper had completed a history of the American Civil War which was organized around the central narrative of an inevitable conflict between two essentially opposed ideologies – in this case freedom *versus* slavery, rather than science *versus* religion. It makes one wonder whether individual psychology as well as social history needs to be employed in an explanation of the origins of our ideas of a conflict between science and religion.

Chapters by Harun Küçük and Salman Hameed put famous historical narratives of conflict between science and Christianity in a different light by looking at the role given to Islam within such works. Küçük points out that both Draper and Andrew Dickson White, author of *A history of the warfare of science with theology in Christendom* (1896), made polemical use of the history of Islamic science in their works. In both cases a narrative of harmony between Islam and science was used as a foil for the main narrative, according to which either Christian theology in general or Roman Catholicism in particular was to be held responsible for an outrageous antipathy to scientific progress. Hameed also notes that Draper congratulated Muslim thinkers for having originated the idea of organic evolution centuries before Darwin. Thus a narrative of conflict between science and one religious tradition can simultaneously be reinforced by a story of harmony with another.

Understanding the provenance of dominant historical narratives is an important step, but only the first step, towards a fuller historicizing of our contemporary thoughts about 'science and religion'. The next step is to examine the histories and meanings of the very terms 'science' and 'religion' themselves. If, for instance, Draper and White alleged that Islam, unlike Christianity, had historically been hospitable to scientific endeavours, then that implies that, at the very least, we need to specify which religion we have in mind when we speak of the relationship between 'religion' and science. However, as Peter Harrison demonstrates in his chapter, what is in fact required is a deeper questioning of these categories. The idea that Christianity and Islam are both members of the generic category 'religion' is itself a product of the nineteenth-century development of the sciences of religion, which Harrison and Küçük both explore. And the category of 'science', as any student of the subject knows, has certainly not had a stable meaning over the centuries. Nor can we easily exchange our 'science' for an earlier category of 'natural philosophy'. Harrison reproduces a telling quotation from John Locke who, while explaining the difference between empirical investigations and more certain knowledge, wrote that he suspected 'natural philosophy is not capable of being made a science'.[20] It is debatable when modern 'science' as we now understand it emerged, but the question of the continuity or lack of it between attempts to comprehend nature in earlier periods and the activities of scientists today has profound implications for any research into the history of 'science', including the question of its relationships with whatever we might mean by 'religion'.

What might we mean by 'religion'? One of the recurring questions below, which emerges not only in Harrison's chapter but also in those by Jan Golinski and Jonathan Topham, is whether 'religion' refers to something cognitive or to something practical; to beliefs or to practices. Harrison sympathizes with the view of Wilfred Cantwell Smith that 'religion' has come, partly through the influence of the sciences, to be taken as a term for a set of intellectual beliefs expressed as propositions.[21] What began as a reduction of Christianity to a set of beliefs was then generalized to include all non-Christian faiths in this same propositional category of 'religions'. This tended to obscure the fact that religious traditions include elements of practical piety, inward spirituality, social organization, and much else beyond the purely intellectual. It also made for easy comparisons with scientific theories, which were also expressible in propositional form. Yet this strategy usually worked to the detriment of religion.

How, then, might historians recover a proper sense of the practical as opposed to the propositional nature of religion? Jan Golinski approaches this question through the work of the anthropologist and sociologist of science Bruno Latour, whose analysis of religion as a 'performative' realm is less well known than his theories about the practices of science. Golinski explores the implications for discussions of science and religion of adopting such a non-propositional view. Topham, in summarizing the key contributions that historians of the book and of publishing have made to the field, likewise suggests that a shift in historical focus from beliefs to practices is an important recent trend. All of this amounts to a powerful case for rethinking our categories along less propositional, less cognitive lines. Histories of experimenting and writing, preaching and worshipping, publishing, and reading can offer historical insights to complement histories that have focussed on the cognitive dimensions.[22]

These recent reappraisals of the categories of 'science' and 'religion' have shared a basic philosophical outlook with what went before. The historiography of science and religion articulated by Brooke, Cantor, Lindberg, Numbers, and many others has always been nominalist rather than realist in tone. To put it another way, the new historians of science and religion from the 1970s onwards were always opposed to the reification of categories of thought. But nominalism about our categories can be pushed to uncomfortable extremes. Any category at all can be profitably historicized. The various and unexpected semantic shifts through which a category has passed may well give us good reason to pause before using it ourselves.[23] We might ask, however, whether there are special reasons for ultra-nominalism in the cases of 'science' or 'religion'. Are these terms any more problematic than, say, 'nature' or 'God'? Historical awareness about our categories is absolutely essential, but we shall sadly never be able to lay our hands on any unproblematic alternative categories which somehow transcend history. And it is for this reason that books about 'science and religion' routinely, simultaneously, and unavoidably both use and problematize those central categories.

THE POLITICS OF KNOWLEDGE

Recognizing that science and religion involve worldly practices as well as intellectual beliefs encourages us to become aware of the political dimension. If the main strategies involved in Brooke's own overturning of the conflict narrative were complexification and contextualization, for other scholars the same end has been pursued through politicization. As I have already implied, historians of science and religion have learned to ask whose interests are served by the promotion of particular scientific or religious ideas, and the same question can be asked about historical narratives themselves. In other words, the tools of social and political history can be used to look for the power struggles that motivated intellectual disputes.

The chapters below reveal that the power struggles that give motive and meaning to engagements between science and religion can be global or local in scale. Osler and Turner both identify large-scale social shifts in European history that can explain conflicts between natural knowledge and religious teachings. Osler points out that socio-political factors, including urbanization, were responsible for the decline in the influence of religion in modern Europe. This was just as important a factor as intellectual disputes about the compatibility of the new sciences with Christian teaching. In the same vein, Osler notes that the new seriousness with which historians of science have recently engaged with early modern religion and theology must also tell us something about the politics of the late twentieth and early twenty-first centuries.

Looking beyond Europe, the struggles involved are no longer always between interest groups within the borders of one society but rather involve the added dimension of encounters between the colonizers and the colonized. Sujit Sivasundaram's chapter, focussing on the impact of the British empire in Africa, Asia, and the Pacific, shows that to reject or accept European science in the nineteenth century could simultaneously be a way to resist or to be assimilated by a colonizing power (and by their religion). For example, Sivasundaram recounts the story of Nan Inta, who was converted simultaneously to Christianity and to western science by a correct astronomical prediction. Hameed's chapter reveals that colonial dynamics have persisted in the Islamic world up to the present day. Evolutionary science has been accepted by some Muslims as a mark of modernity and as an intellectual development in harmony with their faith and prefigured in the Qu'ran, while being rejected by others as an oppressive, corrupting, and illegitimate western influence. Hameed further points out that Muslim engagements with evolutionary science have varied in line with the different political contexts to be found in Islamic countries, whether secular or theocratic, monarchical or republican, democratic or elitist.

To recognize the importance of pre-existing political contexts is one way to politicize the relationship between science and religion. A more direct politicization treats science and religion as forms of power themselves. And it is in the histories of education and publishing, innocuous as such subjects might initially sound, that we find the history of the raw exercise of power in the production and reproduction of knowledge. If knowledge is power, in other words, then those who control the dissemination of knowledge are those who wield the real power. This highlights the importance of Turner's observation, mentioned above, that the story of an historical conflict between science and religion was produced by those engaged in a struggle for dominance in the newly created domain of state education in the nineteenth century. The chapters by Adam Shapiro and Bronislaw Szerszynski reinforce this point in twentieth-century contexts,

with reference to the famous 1925 Scopes trial and to more recent
developments in debates about the content of science education. These
chapters show that the conflict between evolutionists and creationists is a
struggle to control the apparatus of state education. Shapiro sheds fascinating new light on the Scopes case by unearthing evidence of the local
political skirmishes in the town of Dayton, Tennessee, that led up to
the infamous 'Monkey Trial'. Szerszynski's chapter contrasts modern
European and American educational systems and, using recent sociological
research, suggests that religious education is just as important as scientific
education in shaping popular attitudes to evolutionary science and to
creationism.

   To control the production and dissemination of the tracts, treatises,
books, and periodicals through which ideas are spread is, in addition to
deciding what should be included in school syllabuses, another way to
exercise this sort of power. Historians of publishing, who are interested in
this process of dissemination, are able to suggest answers to absolutely
fundamental questions about how people come to have ideas about
science and religion in the first place. The answer, very often, has been
through reading books and periodicals made available to them by a
trusted individual or an authoritative institution. The distribution of ideas
in books and periodicals gives a certain amount of influence to individual
authors, and the history of science and religion has, up until now, been
overwhelmingly a history of authors. But historians are now turning their
attention to publishers and readers as well as authors in order to fill out
our understanding of the processes involved.[24] The chapters by Shapiro,
Sivasundaram, and Topham all illustrate the great importance of recognizing that it is in the history of publication and reading, as well as in
literary and intellectual history, that we find the means of production of
those rather abstract-sounding 'relationships between science and religion'
with which we are concerned.

ISLAM, CHRISTIANITY, AND EVOLUTION

As is clear from the preceding comments, understanding the politics of
knowledge often entails also studying the geography of knowledge.[25] Ideas
and practices do not travel around the world in disembodied form but are
taken to particular places in particular forms by particular people. Much
of the pioneering work in the history of science and religion focussed on
the ways that ideas about Christianity and its engagement with such
sciences as astronomy, geology, and evolutionary biology had developed

in British, European, and North American contexts. More recent work has pushed back the geographical and the confessional as well as the methodological boundaries of this enterprise by asking how modern European science historically interacted with non-European peoples and their religions. The history of science looks very different when it is viewed from a Jewish, Buddhist, or Hindu perspective rather than from the point of view of Catholic or Protestant Christianity. Historians have made considerable progress in reconstructing those many and various views.[26] In the present volume, however, there is a particular comparative focus on Islamic and Christian perceptions, which itself reflects one of the main political preoccupations of the early twenty-first century.

Unsurprisingly, given the crucial importance of Islamic culture to the development of the sciences in the medieval and early modern periods, there is a strong tradition of Muslim thought according to which Islam and science are in harmony. Sivasundaram mentions nineteenth-century Muslim translators and promoters of Darwin's works who sought to use Darwin to reinforce Islamic faith by quoting Qu'ranic verses about life beginning in water. Hameed's chapter shows that this same tradition flourished in the twentieth century, in such works as Maurice Bucaille's book *The Bible, the Qu'ran, and science* (1976), and in the prevailing positive attitude towards science in the modern Islamic world, where the conflict model is generally, albeit not absolutely, absent. As we have already seen, this existence of harmony between Islam and science was used by John William Draper and Andrew Dickson White in the nineteenth century to suggest that the conflict with science was a peculiarly Christian religious problem. To some extent, then, the idea of Islam as an anti-intellectual or anti-scientific tradition is a minority view, and one imposed from outside the tradition itself. Küçük's chapter traces the idea back to the work of Ernest Renan and other European scholars of religion in the late nineteenth century. In fact both harmonious and conflictual histories of Islam and science were used by opportunistic secularists in that period to emphasize the anti-scientific animus they claimed to be so characteristic of the Christian churches in general and Roman Catholicism in particular.

As Hameed, Szerszynski, and Numbers all explain, the organized anti-Darwinian creationist movement was created by American fundamentalist Protestants during the twentieth century. To the extent that an Islamic creationist movement has now emerged in the Muslim world, that is often as much a western export as was Darwinian biology. And there is a danger, as Hameed points out, that if Islamic creationists such as Harun

Yahya, who have borrowed their ideas from American Protestant creationists, succeed in identifying evolutionary biology with atheism – an identification that is also made by scientific atheists like Richard Dawkins – then a new level of conflict between Islam and modern science may soon emerge. These chapters thus raise the important question of how to interpret the globalization of American creationism. It is undoubtedly true that creationism and, more recently, 'Intelligent Design' (ID) arose when and where they did because of a uniquely American set of religious, legal, and educational circumstances.[27] The question then is whether it is misleading, or indeed complacent, to continue to insist that creationism is a peculiarly American phenomenon. Numbers's comparison of creationism and ID with hip-hop and blue jeans is apt. These are all phenomena that have spread around the world but without losing their strong and distinctive associations with American culture and history.

Important and Brookean morals can be drawn from all this. As Brooke wrote in 1991: 'Conflicts allegedly between science and religion may turn out to be between rival scientific interests, or conversely between rival theological factions. Issues of political power, social prestige and intellectual authority have repeatedly been at stake'.[28] In the case of apparent conflicts between Islam and evolution there are several such issues at stake. In one way the conflict is a mere shadow of a western battle between fundamentalist Christians and evolutionists, which itself has been extensively historicized and deconstructed. One might also interpret tensions between Islam and evolution as consequences of historic political hostilities between colonizers and colonized. Or perhaps the most significant conflict here is between modernizers and conservatives within the Islamic world itself.

COMPLEXITY, CONFLICT, AND BEYOND

Finally, what answers do these recent developments in the historical study of science and religion suggest to the historiographical questions with which I began this introduction? Do they, for instance, amount to a recipe for yet more complexification and the final abandonment of narrative and of generalization? Emphases on particularities of place and on the experiences of individual readers can sometimes make it seem that way. Among the closing chapters of this volume mapping out historiographical ways forward, Noah Efron brings out extremely clearly how radically pluralist a Brookean historiography can become. Efron is essentially an enthusiast for such a development but realizes that an emphasis on historical contingency can be a barrier not only to historical generalization but also to interfaith discussions. If there is no single 'relationship between science and religion', if each faith tradition has encountered the sciences in very particular ways, and if neither 'science' nor 'religion' has even had a stable meaning across time, then it becomes extremely difficult for a discussion to take place about common experiences and shared concerns. Harrison's chapter makes similar points. And, as Efron puts it, this realization may well demoralize (in more ways than one) those who wish to study science and religion as a way to make sense of their own identities and to answer their own present-day concerns.

Although histories of science and religion produced in recent decades have tended to argue that complexification and contextualization militate against all master-narratives, whether of conflict or of harmony between science and religion, in reality historians' efforts have been directed almost exclusively towards the destruction of conflict narratives. One might be forgiven for thinking that there was some pro-religious apologetic intention lurking here.[29] At the very least, whatever the intentions of particular historians, the scholarly destruction of the conflict thesis is of obvious utility to those seeking to argue for the reasonableness of religious belief on the basis of its compatibility with modern science. What Harrison and Efron spell out, however, is that the true import of recent work on the history of science and religion for religious believers is much less reassuring than that.

It is also evident that there is still plenty of room for narrative and generalization in a post-Brookean historiography. Although the experiences of people of different faiths and on different continents were widely divergent, that does not prevent the historian from successfully generalizing about, for instance, the dynamics of power between colonizers and colonized, or about the centrality of education and publishing to the history of science and religion. Numbers directly addresses the question of what 'mid-scale generalizations' can now be made about science and religion, and suggests several useful answers. He notes, for example, that the gradual removal of God-talk from professional scientific publications can be dated and documented. This was clearly a post-Darwinian development, since *On the origin of species* (1859) both began and ended with references to God. Both Numbers and Cantor also point to the growing autonomy of professional science from the churches as one reason for nineteenth- and twentieth-century conflicts. Although, as Osler's chapter shows, many twentieth-century historians of science over-stated the separation of science from religion between 1500 and 1700, such a separation had certainly emerged by the twentieth century. Indeed, it was just that separation which inclined historians to impose something similar on earlier centuries.

An extremely important task, undertaken especially by Harrison and Cantor, is the attempt to find an historically respectable way to get conflict back into the story. Of course, in some respects, conflict never went away. There have been two approaches to conflict in the new historiography. One has been to accept conflict in certain circumscribed cases but to deny it as a general characterization of engagements between science and religion. The second, more popular approach has been to keep the conflict story but to recast the protagonists. One famous example of this is the suggestion that the Galileo case was a conflict between two factions within the Catholic Church about how to read the Bible, or a contest between the old and the new astronomy, rather than between the Church on the one hand and modern science on the other.[30] The various recastings of the Victorian conflict over evolution in sociological, political, and professional terms by Frank Turner, James Moore, and Adrian Desmond constitute another excellent example. What emerges in this case is a contest between scientific professionalizers and the Anglican establishment for control of the institutions of science and education.[31]

Harrison and Cantor suggest two particularly important further ways in which conflict needs to be put back into our understanding of science and religion. The first is the recognition of psychological conflict within particular individuals. Cantor starts his chapter with the example of the eighteenth-century Dublin Quaker and apothecary John Rutty, whose spiritual diary reveals how he was torn between the pursuit of science and medicine on the one hand and his spiritual life on the other. The second way that conflict needs to be reinstated, for both Harrison and Cantor, is by recalling the legitimate 'prophetic' voice of religion. It has long been a function of religion and theology to provide resistance to dominant social forces. While science and technology remain among those dominant forces, then religious resistance of some kind might be welcomed. A lack of conflict in this case, Cantor argues, could be a sign of the failure of religions to engage with the wider world with sufficient critical awareness.

Future histories of science and religion will inevitably and rightly reflect the concerns of those who produce them, which are impossible to predict. The present volume is offered as a collective reflection on the motives, methods, and meanings to be discerned in past and contemporary histories of the subject. It is intended as a combination of stock-taking and agenda-setting. The impact of John Hedley Brooke's work, and that of his colleagues in this area of scholarship, has been very considerable. It has established a new consensus about the right way to approach the history of engagements between science and religion. The contributions below sometimes endorse and sometimes challenge that consensus. They pursue still further the ambition to understand both the sciences and religions of the past on their own terms and in their own contexts. They also indicate ways to go beyond the cognitive dimension by thinking more sociologically and practically about both religion and science, and they give us tools with which to reflect critically on our own historical practices as well as on those of the nineteenth-century writers who have so frequently served as the villainous foils to more virtuous recent historiographies.

My own hope is that future studies will further extend the application of techniques from literary and cultural history to this subject. In addition to the histories of publishing and reading, which have already been developed in this area, there are histories yet to be written of the way that relationships between science and religion have been represented in literature, drama, the cinema, and the visual arts. Historians of science have explored some of the classic locations of the 'conflict narrative' in works of history, but there are many more sources to be explored before we shall understand how this resilient narrative took such a hold on our culture. Bertolt Brecht's play *The life of Galileo*, composed during the Nazi era, and the 1960 film *Inherit the wind*, which used the Scopes trial as a way to attack anti-Communist purges of the McCarthy era, both show that the idea of a conflict between a heroic scientific individual and an authoritarian religious establishment is a very compelling one, and one which can be used to many different political ends. It might be the conflict between the heroic individual and the authoritarian regime that is the most significant element of the story, but we still must wonder about the recurrence of the scientific and religious motifs. We might also ask whether there are equally powerful stories to be told, or that have already been told, in which heroic religious individuals stand up against technocratic and scientific regimes.

Theoretical trends and methodological preferences may come and go, but Brooke's suspicion of reification, his demolition of master-narratives, and his relishing of differentiation have already made their mark on the historiography of science and religion. The example his work provides of how history can be conducted as a work of intellect, imagination, sympathy, and humanity is also of enduring value. What accounts for the real historical power of Brooke's work is his constant attempt, at once as a professional duty and as a philosophical discipline, to achieve something that is ultimately impossible: to put aside his own preconceptions and concerns, and even his own intellectual categories and beliefs, in order to listen to what other people living in very different cultures from his own were really trying to say and to understand why they were saying it. The particularity that features most regularly in Brooke's own writings has been the particularity of the individual human personality. It is through a disciplined and imaginative engagement with other minds that Brooke has set about accomplishing the deceptively simple task he set himself at the outset of his classic study: not 'to tell a complete or definitive story' about science and religion but 'to assist in the creation of critical perspectives'.[32]

NOTES

I am grateful to all those who have contributed to this volume, and to the Lancaster conference from which it arose, for their help and collaboration in bringing this project to fruition. I would like especially to thank my co-editors, and not only for their perceptive and constructive comments on this introduction. Stephen Pumfrey was the driving force behind the conference in John Brooke's honour, and provided encouragement and guidance at every stage. Geoffrey Cantor, himself one of the pioneers of the new historiography of science and religion, provided the unfailing support, guidance, and graft which made the production of this book possible.

1 John Hedley Brooke, *Science and religion: Some historical perspectives* (Cambridge: Cambridge University Press, 1991). A list of all Brooke's principal publications from 1977 to 2010 is included as the first section of the Select Bibliography below.
2 See Nick Jardine, 'Whigs and stories: Herbert Butterfield and the historiography of science', *History of Science* 41 (2003), 125–40.
3 Thomas S. Kuhn, *The structure of scientific revolutions* (Chicago: University of Chicago Press, 1962). For helpful reflections of the massive impact of this work both within and beyond the history of science, see: Thomas S. Kuhn, *The road since structure: Philosophical essays, 1970–1993, with an autobiographical interview*, ed. James Conant and John Haugeland (Chicago: University of Chicago Press, 2000); Alexander Bird, *Thomas Kuhn* (Chesham: Acumen, 2000); John Preston, *Kuhn's 'The structure of scientific revolutions': A reader's guide* (London: Continuum, 2008).
4 John Brooke and Geoffrey Cantor, *Reconstructing nature: The engagement of science and religion. The 1995–6 Gifford Lectures at Glasgow* (Edinburgh: T & T Clark, 1998). Chapter 1 provides an excellent articulation of this approach.
5 Important early contributions to this tradition were Frank M. Turner, 'The Victorian conflict between science and religion: A professional dimension', *Isis* 49 (1978), 356–76; James R. Moore, *The post-Darwinian controversies: A study of the Protestant struggle to come to terms with Darwin in Great Britain and*

America, 1870–1900 (Cambridge: Cambridge University Press, 1979). Other significant milestones include two collections edited by David C. Lindberg and L. Ronald Numbers: *God and nature: Historical essays on the encounter between Christianity and science* (Berkeley, CA: University of California Press, 1986) and *When science and Christianity meet* (Chicago: University of Chicago Press, 2003). James Moore's review of Brooke's *Science and religion* in *History of Science* 30 (1992), 311–23 is also very helpful on these historiographical matters. I have discussed these issues in two places: Thomas Dixon, 'Looking beyond "The Rumpus about Moses and Monkeys": Religion and the sciences in the nineteenth century', *Nineteenth Century Studies* 17 (2003), 25–33; Dixon, *Science and religion: A very short introduction* (Oxford: Oxford University Press, 2008), ch. 1.

6 Geoffrey Cantor had himself already made important contributions to reforming the historiography of science and religion, notably in *Michael Faraday: Sandemanian and scientist* (London: Macmillan, 1991). Cantor's subsequent research has enriched historical understandings of the subject through an investigation of Jewish and Quaker engagements with the sciences; see Geoffrey Cantor, *Quakers, Jews, and science: Religious responses to modernity and the sciences in Britain, 1650–1900* (Oxford: Oxford University Press, 2005), and Cantor and M. Swetlitz (eds.), *Jewish tradition and the challenge of Darwinism* (Chicago: Chicago University Press, 2006).

7 Some of Brooke's early writings are included in John Hedley Brooke, R. Hooykaas, and Clive Lawless, *New interactions between theology and natural science* (Milton Keynes: Open University Press, 1974).

8 John Hedley Brooke, 'Joining natural philosophy to Christianity: The case of Joseph Priestley', in Brooke and Ian Maclean (eds.), *Heterodoxy in early modern science and religion* (Oxford: Oxford University Press, 2005), pp. 319–36, on p. 329.

9 John Hedley Brooke, 'Presidential address: Does the history of science have a future?', *British Journal for the History of Science* 32 (1999), 1–20, on 9.

10 John Hedley Brooke, 'Darwin and Victorian Christianity', in Gregory Radick and Jonathan Hodge (eds.), *The Cambridge companion to Darwin* (Cambridge: Cambridge University Press, 2003), pp. 192–213, on p. 199.

11 Brooke, *Science and religion*, pp. 5, 51.

12 Edward B. Davis, review of Brooke, *Science and religion* in *Isis* 83 (1992), 469–70.

13 Brooke, 'Presidential Address', p. 2.

14 Ibid., p. 3.

15 Jim Endersby, *A guinea-pig's history of biology: The plants and animals who taught us the facts of life* (London: Heinemann, 2007).

16 Georgina Ferry, review of Endersby, *Guinea-pig's history* in the *Guardian*, 2 June 2007. The lone-genius model of the historiography of science is also discussed in Brooke, 'Presidential Address', with reference to Dava Sobel's bestselling *Longitude: The true story of a lone genius who solved the greatest scientific problem of his time* (London: Fourth Estate, 1996).

17 Richard Olson, review of Brooke, *Science and religion*, in *American Historical Review* 99 (1994), 191–2, on 192.

18 Brooke and Cantor, *Reconstructing nature*, p. 68.

19 Lindberg and Numbers, *Science and Christianity*, p. 2.

20 John Locke, *Essay concerning human understanding*, IV.12.10, ed. P. Nidditch (Oxford: Clarendon Press, 1975), p. 645.

21 See Harrison's discussion below and the original thesis as developed in Wilfred Cantwell Smith, *The meaning and end of religion* (New York: Macmillan, 1963).

22 'Cognitive dimensions' is also the subtitle of one of Brooke's co-edited volumes: John Hedley Brooke, M. Osler, and J. van der Meer (eds.), *Science in theistic contexts: Cognitive dimensions. Osiris XVI* (Chicago: University of Chicago Press, 2001).

23 My own work in the history of science and philosophy has taken exactly this approach: Thomas Dixon, *From passions to emotions: The creation of a secular psychological category* (Cambridge: Cambridge University Press, 2003); *The invention of altruism: Making moral meanings in Victorian Britain* (Oxford: Oxford University Press for the British Academy, 2008).

24 Notable among many recent works in this vein are James A. Secord, *Victorian sensation: The extraordinary publication, reception, and secret authorship of* Vestiges of the natural history of creation (Chicago: University of Chicago Press, 2000); Geoffrey Cantor and Sally Shuttleworth (eds.), *Science serialized: Representations of the sciences in nineteenth-century periodicals* (Cambridge, MA: MIT Press, 2004); Aileen Fyfe, *Science and salvation: Evangelical popular science publishing in Victorian Britain* (Chicago: University of Chicago Press, 2004); Bernard Lightman, *Victorian popularizers of science: Designing nature for new audiences* (Chicago: University of Chicago Press, 2007).

25 The geography of scientific knowledge has been another growth area in recent scholarship. See, for instance, Sujit Sivasundaram, *Nature and the godly empire: Science and evangelical mission in the Pacific, 1795–1850* (Cambridge: Cambridge University Press, 2005); David N. Livingstone and Charles W. J. Withers (eds.), *Geography and revolution* (Chicago: University of Chicago Press, 2005).

26 See the Select Bibliography (under 'Particular (non-Protestant) religious traditions') at the end of this volume for suggested starting points for further reading on the history of science in particular faith traditions.

27 The definitive study is Ronald L. Numbers, *The creationists: From scientific creationism to intelligent design*, 2nd edn (Cambridge, MA: Harvard University Press, 2006); see also Edward J. Larson, *Summer for the gods: The Scopes trial and America's continuing debate over science and religion* (New York, Basic Books, 1997); Larson, *Trial and error: The American controversy over creation and evolution*, 3rd edn (Oxford: Oxford University Press, 2003); or, for a more condensed account of the emergence of creationism in modern America, see Dixon, *Science and religion*, ch. 5.

28 Brooke, *Science and religion*, p. 5.

29 I have suggested as much myself in reviews of some of the works produced in this recent tradition. See, for instance, Thomas Dixon, review of Brooke and Cantor, *Reconstructing nature*, in *Religion* 34 (2004), 161–2; Dixon, review of Lindberg and Numbers, *Science and Christianity*, in *British Journal for the History of Science* 38 (2005), 469–71.

30 David C. Lindberg, 'Galileo, the Church, and the cosmos', in Lindberg and Numbers, *Science and Christianity*, pp. 33–60; Brooke and Cantor, *Reconstructing nature*, ch. 4.

31 Turner, 'Victorian conflict'; Adrian J. Desmond, *The politics of evolution: Morphology, medicine, and reform in radical London* (Chicago: University of Chicago Press, 1989); Desmond, *Huxley: From devil's disciple to evolution's high priest* (London: Penguin, 1998); Moore, *Post-Darwinian controversies*.

32 Brooke, *Science and religion*, p. 5.

PART I

Categories

'Science' and 'religion': constructing the boundaries

Peter Harrison

Over the past decade a number of historians of science have expressed strong reservations about whether their particular subject of interest actually has much of a history. Science, as the discipline is currently understood, emerged only during the nineteenth century, they tell us. Prior to that, students of nature had thought of themselves as pursuing 'natural philosophy' or 'natural history' – disciplines with a somewhat different orientation from that of twenty-first-century science. This claim has obvious ramifications for those whose concern lies with the past relationship between science and religion, for, if true, such a relationship cannot be older than the nineteenth century. Similar historical sensitivities are evident in the sphere of religious studies, in which increasing numbers of scholars have suggested that the idea 'religion', like 'science', is a modern development. 'Religion', and the plural 'religions', it is claimed, did not begin to take on their present meanings until the seventeenth century. The notion that there are 'religions', distinguished by discrete sets of beliefs and practices and linked by a common and generic 'religion', is actually a product of the European Enlightenment. During that period, the acute need to arrive at some criterion to adjudicate between different faiths led to the construction of 'religions' as sets of propositional beliefs that could be impartially compared and judged.

In this chapter I shall explore in some detail the historical circumstances of the emergence of the dual categories 'science' and 'religion' with a view to showing their direct relevance for contemporary discussions of the science–religion relation. As we shall see, to a degree both categories distort what it is they claim to represent, and such distortions inevitably carry over into discussions of their relationship. Consideration of the historically conditioned nature of 'science' and of 'religion' brings to light a number of unspoken assumptions in some mainstream science-and-religion discussions and highlights the need for serious revision of common approaches to this issue.

HISTORY OF SCIENCE: A SUBJECT WITHOUT AN OBJECT?

Until relatively recently it was quite uncontroversial to claim a venerable history for the discipline of science. The classic histories of science, for example, customarily begin their accounts with the science of the ancient Greeks. Indeed, George Sarton's monumental *A history of science* (1927–59), a work of nine projected volumes, scarcely progressed beyond them, ending prematurely with the Hellenistic age in the third volume.[1] Most accounts, it must be said, concede a long hiatus during the middle ages in the West, but in the seventeenth century, according to the standard view, science once again found itself back on track, with the birth of 'modern' science. If the progenitors of the modern discipline – typically identified as Galileo or Newton – were of much more recent vintage, their spiritual forebears were nonetheless identified as those investigators of nature who had pioneered the scientific enterprise in antiquity.

Over the past few decades, however, many historians have expressed reservations about presumed continuities in the history of science. These reservations have been expressed in a variety of ways, but common to them all is a plea against the anachronistic assumption that the study of nature in earlier historical periods was prosecuted more or less along the same lines as those adopted by modern scientists. Margaret Osler, for example, has questioned the uncritical assumption 'that disciplinary boundaries have remained static throughout history'.[2] In a similar vein Paolo Rossi has charged historians of science with having concerned themselves with 'an imaginary object', arguing that 'science' is a quite recent invention.[3] Philosopher of science David Hull reinforces this point, observing that '[s]cience as a historical entity no more has an essence than do particular scientific theories or research programs. The sorts of activities that are part of science at any one time are extremely heterogeneous, and they change through time'.[4] Andrew Cunningham, perhaps the most vocal critic of the traditional view, bluntly asks whether, when we study science in the past, it is science in any meaningful sense.[5]

These viewpoints are supported by an impressive range of evidence, but perhaps the clearest indication of the relative novelty of the discipline can be seen in the broad connotations of the term 'science' prior to the nineteenth century. It is often assumed that science began with the ancient Greeks, but, as one of the foremost authorities on the thought of this period has pointed out, '[s]cience is a modern category, not an ancient one: there is no one term that is exactly equivalent to our "science" in Greek'.[6] David Lindberg, in his magisterial survey of the study of nature in antiquity and the middle ages, has similarly pointed out that, even if we could agree on a definition of modern science, to investigate only those aspects of classical and medieval disciplines 'insofar as those practices and beliefs resemble modern science' would give rise to a 'distorted picture'. We must therefore avoid 'looking at the past through a grid that does not exactly fit'.[7] Thus, while it is not absurd to regard Aristotle, for example, as having practised 'science', it must be remembered that the activities so described bear only a loose genealogical relationship to what we would now consider to be science. The same is true for the middle ages, when, owing largely to the influence of Aristotelian classifications, philosophers spoke of three 'speculative sciences' – metaphysics (also known as 'sacred science' or theology), mathematics, and natural philosophy.[8] Strictly, to speak of the relationship between theology and science in this period is to ignore the categories that the historical actors themselves were operating with. Again, this is not to deny that there can be fruitful historical exploration of the relationship between natural philosophy and theology during this period. But the fact that both of these disciplines were speculative sciences makes an important difference to our enquiry.

In the era that is most commonly associated with the birth of modern science similar considerations apply. Nicholas Jardine has observed that 'no Renaissance category even remotely corresponds to "the sciences" or "the natural sciences" in our senses of the terms'.[9] In the early modern period the study of nature took place within a number of disciplines, the most important of which were 'natural philosophy' and 'natural history'.[10] It was natural philosophy, for example, that Isaac Newton understood himself to be undertaking, as the title of his most famous work bears witness: *Philosophiae naturalis principia mathematica* (1687) – 'The mathematical principles of natural philosophy'. Curiously, at this time neither natural history nor experimental natural philosophy were thought exact enough to warrant the label 'science', the former because it was an historical enterprise, the latter because it was thought to lead to knowledge that was merely probable and not demonstrable.[11] John Locke, a champion of the empirical approach to knowledge, thus observed that 'natural philosophy is not capable of being made a science'.[12] Neither were natural history and natural philosophy synonyms for what we now call natural science. Rather, they entail a different understanding of knowledge of nature: they were motivated by different concerns and were integrated into other forms of knowledge and belief in a way quite alien to the modern sciences. The provinces of these enterprises were not co-extensive with that of 'science' as it was understood then or now.

Nowhere is the difference between these disciplines and modern science more apparent than in those religious elements which were integral to the practice of the early modern study of nature. Natural history and natural philosophy were frequently pursued from religious motives, they were based on religious presuppositions, and, inasmuch as they were regarded as legitimate forms of knowledge, they drew their social sanctions from religion. This was particularly so in England, where up until the mid-nineteenth century natural history was internally ordered according to the theological principle of design. The intimate connections between the study of nature and religious notions are apparent in the ubiquity of early modern images of nature as God's book. Physician Thomas Browne provides us with a typical statement of this approach: 'There are two books from whence I collect my divinity', he wrote, 'besides that written one of God, another of his servant Nature – that universal and public manuscript that lies expansed into the eyes of all'.[13] In a similar vein, Johannes Kepler described astronomers as 'priests of the most high God, with respect to the book of nature'.[14] Naturalist John Johnston also spoke of 'Nature's book, wherein we may behold the supreme power'. 'God', he continued, 'is comprehended under the title of natural history'.[15] Best known of all is the stance of seventeenth-century virtuoso Robert Boyle, who described natural philosophy as 'the first act of religion, and equally obliging in all religions'. Boyle regarded his own activities and those of his peers as 'philosophical worship of God'.[16] According to one historian, natural philosophy in the early modern period was about 'God's achievements, God's intentions, God's purposes, God's messages to man'.[17] The legitimacy, or, as its seventeenth-century practitioners would have it, the 'usefulness', of natural philosophy in the English context derived in large measure from this religious orientation.[18]

So inextricably connected were the dual concerns of God and nature that it is misleading to attempt to identify various kinds of relationship between science and religion in the seventeenth and eighteenth centuries. 'Science' and 'religion' were not independent entities which might bear some positive or negative relation to each other, and to attempt to identify such connections is to project back in time a set of concerns that are typically those of our own age. As historian Charles Webster has expressed it:

Conclusions about the independence of scientific activity in the seventeenth century are based not on the impartial and exhaustive examination of evidence, but are rather dictated by the requirements of current ideology, and describe not the relationship which actually existed, but the relationship which it is felt ought to have existed on the basis of present-day opinion about the methodology of science.[19]

The birth of the modern discipline, it is now generally agreed, took place during the nineteenth century. According to Simon Schaffer, it was the nineteenth century which witnessed 'the end of natural philosophy and the invention of modern science'.[20] Andrew Cunningham agrees that the 'invention of science' was 'an historical event of the period c1780–c1850'.[21] The term 'scientist' was coined by William Whewell in 1833, and, while it was not widely adopted until the end of the century, it is indicative of an important new alliance of once distinct disciplines. During this time, also, the first professional bodies for scientists came into existence.[22] The British Association for the Advancement of Science, for example, was established in the early 1830s. With the founding of such associations came a new status for scientific practitioners and, accompanying this status, a new set of professional commitments.[23]

The transformation of natural history into scientific 'biology' was a vital part of this process. Whereas natural history had traditionally been dominated by the clergy, the new scientific disciplines of biology and geology gradually achieved independence from clerical influence while at the same time legitimizing a new set of non-ecclesiastical authorities.[24] This was in fact the explicit mission of such figures as Thomas Huxley and his colleagues in the 'X-Club', who sought with an evangelical fervour to establish a scientific status for natural history, to rid the discipline of women, amateurs, and parsons, and to place a secular science into the centre of cultural life in Victorian England.[25] It served the political purposes of this clique to deploy a rhetoric of conflict between theology and science, a conflict that was supposedly not unique to the nineteenth century but that had supposedly characterized the ongoing relation of these two hypostasized entities. Largely as a consequence of the efforts of those who sought to promote the political fortunes of 'science', there emerged the historical thesis of an ongoing science–religion conflict – a view epitomized in the now unfashionable histories of Andrew Dickson White and John William Draper. A good sense of the general tenor of these works can be gleaned from their titles: respectively, *A history of the warfare of science with theology in Christendom* (1896) and *History of the conflict between religion and science* (1875).[26] The enduring legacy of this group, however, has been the perpetuation of the myth of a perennial warfare between science and religion.

This is not to assert that the new nineteenth-century discipline had uncontested boundaries. A number of Victorian naturalists were initially reluctant to identify their activities as something distinct from philosophy, ethics, and theology. Herbert Spencer, the evolutionist who coined the phrase 'the survival of the fittest', considered the Victorian classifications of the sciences to be artificial, particularly in the separation of science and art and science and common sense.[27] But such misgivings did not prevail. By the end of the century, there was an almost universal, if tacit, understanding that the term 'science' excluded the aesthetic, ethical, and theological. By 1922 Max Weber was thus able to speak of the scientific vocation as one which was narrowly specialist and in which no place could be found for the broader questions of value and meaning.[28] Thus, while disagreements persist into the twenty-first century about precisely which activities might be included under the rubric 'science', there is a consensus that certain things are to be excluded.

With the benefit of hindsight we can now see that over the course of the past 150 years a remarkable reversal has taken place. Whereas once the investigation of nature had derived status from its intimate connections with the more elevated disciplines of ethics and theology, increasingly during the twentieth century these latter disciplines have humbly sought associations with science in order to bask in its reflected glory – whence bioethics and science-and-religion. The nineteenth century saw the baton of authority pass from those pursuing the religious vocation to the new breed of scientist. As historian A. W. Benn observed firsthand, '[a] great part of the reverence once given to priests and to their stories of an unseen universe has been transferred to the astronomer, the geologist, the physician, and the engineer'.[29] At the same time the 'wonders of nature' increasingly came to be regarded as the 'wonders of science'. The coalescing of this new alliance of disciplines under the banner 'science' made possible for the first time a relationship between 'science' and 'religion'.

It was almost inevitable that in historical accounts of the relevant human activities various aspects of the new nineteenth-century relation would be projected back onto the past. As we have already noted, this approach is epitomized in the writings of Draper and White. Other historical developments were also to feed the myth of a perennial conflict between science and religion. The emergence of the scientific profession meshed neatly with progressivist conceptions of history, such as that of the positivist Auguste Comte, who believed that his own age was witness to humanity's transition from the 'metaphysical stage' to the higher, scientific or 'positive' level of development. Andrew Dickson White provides a classic example of this view of history, making reference to 'a conflict between two epochs in the evolution of human thought – the theological and the scientific'.[30] Moreover, with the growth in popularity of the 'great man' theory of history, there arose a tendency to identify heroic figures in the past, credit them with great achievements, and pit them against unyielding institutions and dogmatic traditions. The demise of natural philosophy and the emergence of science, writes Simon Schaffer, 'was marked by the reification of heroic discoverers and prized techniques'.[31] 'Galileo *versus* the Inquisition' is the stock example here. This mode of presenting the history of science is still today the one which most excites the popular imagination, and indeed not all scholarly historians are immune to its attractions.[32]

From this history we can arrive at some provisional conclusions about the 'science–religion' relation. Perhaps the most obvious lesson to be drawn from this analysis is that the notion that there can be a relationship between science and religion prior to the nineteenth century runs the risk of anachronism. To some degree there has been a recognition of this fact among more discerning historians. John Brooke has warned that '[t]he very enterprise of abstracting the "science" and the "theology" of earlier generations with a view to seeing how they were related can lead to artificial results'.[33] Claude Welch, too, speaks of 'the hypostatization of "science" and "religion"' which the works of Draper and White represent.[34] However, at times critics of Draper and White seem to imply that their mistake lay only in characterizing the past relationship between science and religion as negative when the true picture was that the relation was positive or 'complex'. In fact, their more fundamental error lay in the assumption that science and religion are categories that can be meaningfully applied to all periods of western history and, to a degree, to the historical development of non-western cultures.

It is not only historians who need to heed the lessons of their own discipline. To a degree, the dangers of the 'artificial results' against which Brooke warns bulk just as large for those currently engaged in relating science and religion, for to speak of some generic entity 'science' is to be committed to a vast over-simplification. The history of the term shows that 'science' is a human construction or reification. This is not necessarily to say that scientific knowledge is socially constructed: rather, it is the category 'science' – a way of identifying certain forms of knowledge and excluding others – that is constructed. These historical claims about the origin of the discipline are thus quite independent of any claims which might be made on behalf of the activities it describes. However, an inevitable consequence of the construction of the category is that science will have a disputed content and contested boundaries.[35] The persistence of questions about the unity of science, which arise out of either an awareness of the histories of the sciences or present-day analyses of the objectives and methods of the various sciences, suggests that there can be no normative science–religion relation as such, for the sciences are plural and diverse. As Fraser Watts has observed, 'there are many different sciences, and each has its own history, methods and assumptions. Each also has a different relationship to religion'.[36]

A preferable course of action might seem to be the discussion of distinct sciences in their relation to religion, but this too is not without its difficulties. Apparent affinities between science and religion are in some measure a function of where the relevant boundaries are drawn. Speaking of the kinds of discipline which have been included in the sciences, philosopher of science David Hull uses a familiar biological metaphor, pointing out that '[m]ore often than not, more variation exists within a species than between closely related species'.[37] In other words, there may be greater differences among the sciences themselves than between a particular science and some other non-science discipline (say, theology). That cosmology and quantum physics in recent times have been grist to the mill of theologians says less about some general relationship between science and religion than it does about the proximity of these sciences to the border with theology. Indeed, in no instance does Paul Feyerabend's claim that 'science is much closer to myth than a scientific philosophy is prepared to admit' seem more true than in the case of quantum cosmology.[38] To draw attention to these affinities is thus to make a point about the boundaries of the respective disciplines rather than to assert something about a genuine substantive relation between independent entities. There is a still a point worth making here, but we need to be clear about what it is.

To sum up the argument to this point, while the study of nature in the West has a long ancestry, 'science' as we currently understand it is a category that took on its characteristic form during the nineteenth century. To speak of a relationship between science and religion prior to that time requires a number of careful qualifications. Moreover, what 'science' includes and excludes is attributable to some extent to accidents of history. Thus, any relationship that 'science' has with other human institutions is going to be conditioned by the circumstances of its origins. As we are about to see, this is particularly the case when the other party to the relationship, in this instance 'religion', may itself be regarded as an intellectual construction.

'RELIGION', THEOLOGY, AND 'THE RELIGIONS'

While a number of historians of science have been conscious of the conditions that generated the modern notion 'science', few have been aware that a number of historians of religion have claimed that the modern idea 'religion' emerged only 150 years prior to this. If 'science' was invented in the nineteenth century, 'religion', it may be said, was invented during the course of the European Enlightenment, in the wake of the post-Reformation fragmentation of Christianity. Wilfred Cantwell Smith, who first drew attention to the artificial nature of the category 'religion', writes, 'The concept "religion", then, in the West has evolved. Its evolution has included a long-range development that we may term a process of reification: mentally making religion into a thing, gradually coming to conceive it as an objective systematic entity'.[39] As Smith's pioneering work demonstrated, the religious emphasis of the medieval West had been faith or piety – an inner dynamic of the heart. In early modern religious controversy, however, attention was increasingly focussed upon those external, objective aspects of the lives of the faithful, as it became an urgent matter to identify those crucial differences upon which eternal salvation was thought to depend. As a consequence, specific creeds and ritual practices became the essence of the newly ideated 'religion'. True religion now had less to do with sincerity of commitment than with whether or not the propositions to which one gave intellectual assent were true. In keeping with the developing spirit of the Enlightenment, reason came to be the ultimate arbiter of true religion, thus confirming the objective, rationalist, orientation of the new entity. Since the first appearance of this thesis, a number of historians have further developed its major implications.[40]

If the invention of science in the nineteenth century made possible for the first time a relationship between science and religion, the birth of 'religion' and 'the religions' during the Enlightenment made possible a comparative exercise of a different kind – the comparison of one 'religion' with another. Once again, reason was given a role in the 'impartial' comparison of the religions and in theory enabled adjudication of the relative merits of competing creeds and cults. The science of comparative religion thus emerged out of the objectification of early modern faiths, and the process was in due course extended from Christianity to the other three 'religions' – 'Mahometanism', 'the Jewish Religion', and the catch-all category, 'Heathenism' – each of which had been constructed, in varying degrees, as an inferior version of the original paradigm, Christianity. In each case, the faiths and ways of life of whole peoples tended to be reduced to bodies of dogma, and the chief characteristic of a religion became what it was that its adherents believed. 'Religion' thus became the conceptual grid through which knowledge of exotic peoples was filtered into the western imagination.

In the era of colonization that followed upon the voyages of discovery, more and more empirical data was gathered from distant lands, which led to the generation of particular kinds of 'heathenism'. In time, 'the Eastern religions' coalesced as inferior and incomplete versions of Christianity, with their imperfect deities, their erroneous scriptures, their fraudulent miracles, and their superstitious cults. These entities had their birth in the imaginations of western thinkers for whom distant and exotic locations came to form a backdrop onto which could be projected the parochial confessional concerns of Europe.[41] Crucially, just as the multiple forms of Christianity were presumed to be mutually exclusive, so too were these other 'religions'. The world religions, in short, were created through a projection of Christian disunity onto the world. Their fabrication in the western imagination is registered in the terms which indicate their birth: 'Boudhism' makes its first appearance in 1821, 'Hindooism' in 1829, 'Taouism' in 1829, and 'Confucianism' in 1862.[42]

Finally, if the nineteenth century witnessed the creation of the eastern religions as reified entities, it also represents a further stage in the development of 'religion'. For if this is the period during which 'science' was eventually to emerge as a discipline evacuated of religious and theological concerns, logically 'religion' was itself now understood as an enterprise that excluded the scientific. The birth of 'science' was part of the ongoing story of the ideation of 'religion'.

The consequences of these not altogether happy historical processes are these. First, there are a number of fracture points that highlight the fragility of the dual categories 'religion' and 'the religions'. Notoriously, most scholars have considerable difficulty in providing an exact definition of religion.[43] Failure to arrive at a consensus of what 'religion' really is or what counts as 'a religion' can reasonably be taken as evidence for the problematic nature of the category. Furthermore, we can also call upon categories that cut across the various traditions yet retain some integrity. 'Mysticism', for example, describes adherents of a variety of faiths, and it might be said that some Christian, Jewish, Islamic, and Buddhist mystics have more in common with each other than they do with others who subscribe to the same 'religion'.[44] The category 'fundamentalist' likewise seems to identify some core set of attitudes that, again, does not respect the neat boundaries of 'the religions'. Indeed, the term 'fundamentalist' can be applied with some justification to more extreme proponents of scientific naturalism.

Second, the philosophical problem of religious pluralism – that the world religions make competing truth claims and thus cannot all be true – is in part a creature of the category 'religion'. The conflicting truth claims of the world religions arise not out of the ways religious individuals practise their faith but out of the classification of what they are doing as practising a 'religion'. By classifying beliefs as doctrines and imposing upon them the kind of status which they might have within post-Enlightenment Christianity, conflicts are generated. The consequences of this process are most apparent in the so-called eastern religions. The common western assumption that there are three religions in China – Confucianism, Taoism, and Buddhism – forces upon the Chinese categories which they themselves would not recognize. Many Chinese combine aspects of these three traditions without any conscious confusion. This makes nonsense of the notion that Confucianism, Taoism, and Buddhism are discrete and mutually exclusive 'religions'. This confusion is to be attributed to the category. As Smith observes with respect to one of these traditions, the question of whether Confucianism is a religion is a question that the West has never been able to answer and the Chinese never able to ask.[45]

Third, and following on from the previous point, the categories are frequently rejected by those whom they purport to characterize. Christianity is not a religion, insisted neo-orthodox Protestant theologian Karl Barth. Dietrich Bonhoeffer advocated a 'religionless Christianity'.[46] To reduce Judaism to a religion 'is a betrayal of its true nature', declares Milton Steinberg. Adherents of other so-called religions are equally adamant: 'Buddhism is not a religion'; 'Islam is not merely a "religion"'; 'It is hardly possible to say whether Hinduism is a religion or not'.[47] While it must be conceded that the concepts 'religion' and 'the religions' have considerable currency in their place of origin, the West, it can be argued that this acceptance, in particular by those who identify themselves as religious, has led to an impoverishment of the religious life.

If we take the history of Christianity as an example, we can gain some impression of what was lost to the tradition in the early modern transformation from 'Christian faith' to '*the* Christian religion'. The first expression had referred to a faith which was Christ-like; the second denoted a religion – a set of beliefs – supposedly preached by Christ. The Christian life, in this new conception, was less about emulating Christ than it was about giving intellectual assent to the doctrines that he had preached. The concept of revelation underwent a parallel transformation. Whereas God was thought once to have revealed himself in Christ, now he revealed doctrines.[48] Epitomizing these changes, seventeenth-century comparative religionist Nathaniel Crouch claimed that 'Christianity is the Doctrine of Salvation, delivered to man by *Christ Jesus*'.[49] Thus the early modern confessional controversies, in the heat of which the Christian religion was forged, focussed not on the best way to lead a Christ-like life but on identifying those particular doctrines that Christ and his legitimate heirs were supposed to have promulgated. This is the view according to which Christianity is a religion, and indeed the paradigmatic religion which provided the pattern for the construction of the 'other religions'.

While many contemporary Christians conceive of themselves as sub-scribing to a 'religion' in the modern sense, and certainly this is how they are perceived by outsiders, protests have been raised against the categoriza-tion. The reservations of Barth and Bonhoeffer about 'religion' have already been noted. Raimundo Panikkar has made similar observations, evincing a nostalgia for pre-modern piety: 'Christian faith must strip itself of the "Christian religion"'.[50] Panikkar points to important distinctions between Christendom (a civilization), Christianity (a religion), and Chris-tianness (a personal religiosity): to be a Christian, he argues, does not necessarily entail subscribing to 'the Christian religion'. Hence 'to be a Christian can also be understood as confessing a personal faith, adopting a Christlike attitude inasmuch as Christ represents the central symbol of one's own life. I call this Christianness. Christianness differentiates itself from Christianity, as Christianity extricated itself from Christendom'.[51]

While we have focussed mostly upon the subtle transformations of Christian self-understanding brought about by the emergence of the con-cept 'religion', there is sufficient evidence to suspect similar distortions in the other traditions. 'Religion', like 'science', has a history, and this history has a crucial bearing on claims made about its relationship with other human activities and forms of knowledge. There is no suggestion in this historical analysis that doctrinal commitments play no legitimate role in religious life or that religious beliefs should be regarded as 'non-cognitive'. It is rather that the concept 'religion' leads to an elevation of the importance of propositional claims and that the subsequent comparison of 'religions' or of 'religion' and 'science' similarly promotes the idea that these enterprises have essences which are to be identified solely with their cognitive content.

A comprehensive analysis of what has taken place in other traditions must necessarily be the subject of other studies, but brief comment can be made on some recent work on Buddhism and science. The case of Buddhism is particularly pertinent to the argument presented in this chapter because the western construction of an ideal textual Buddhism in the Victorian period coincided with the invention of modern science.[52] Not surprisingly, perhaps, a number of influential western apologists for Buddhism were to present this newly 'discovered' religion as especially compatible with western science. In light of the controversies generated by evolutionary theory, it was claimed that Buddhism was more consonant with recent scientific developments than Christianity. Helena Blavatsky, leader of the Theosophical movement, boldly declared Buddhism to be more scientific and philosophically pure than any of the religious alternatives. The American advocate of a 'scientific Buddhism', Paul Carus, also highlighted the scientific credentials of Buddhism, claiming it to be 'a religion which recognises no other revelation except the truth that can be proved by science'.[53] These claims were matched by some Asian Buddhists themselves, most notably Anagarika Dharmapala, who aligned notions of evolution, laws of nature, and the principle of cause and effect with basic Buddhist teachings. There is a sense in which Dharmapala was invoking a kind of inverse orientalism or, to use James Ketelaar's term, a 'strategic occidentalism'. As David McMahon has suggested, each side – both western appropriators and indigenous apologists – 'constructed Buddhism in scientific rationalist terms in response to separate crises in their various cultural contexts'. In one case, this was the Victorian crisis of faith, in the other, a crisis engendered by colonialism.[54] However, even these attempts to promote a Buddhism that was uniquely consonant with modern science – and on that account enjoying advantages over Christianity – did so by imposing on Buddhism those deep structures of Protestant religion that had played so significant a role in the creation of the concept 'religion'.[55] What is interesting about the case of Buddhism is that its reconstruction into a scientific form was one that was not merely imposed from without but was appropriated as an apologetic strategy by some within. In this latter respect there is a curious similarity between 'scientific Buddhism' and 'scientific Christianity', both of which have become self-inflicted categories.

RELATING 'SCIENCE' AND 'RELIGION'

The history of the cultural construction of each category in the pairing 'science and religion' is of profound importance for any present attempt to discern putative relationships between them. While, as we have seen, a few commentators have been attuned to the reified nature of one of the terms in the relation – 'science' – most often it has been assumed that the other term in the relation is relatively unproblematic. We are now in a position to see that this is not the case. One possible response to the history of 'religion' would be to focus attention on the relation of individual religious traditions to science (or more properly to individual sciences). This would address, to some extent, the misleading view that there is a generic something – 'religion' – shared by all those traditions we label 'religions'. To a degree this option is already in play, for the vast majority of works purporting to address the relationship between science and religion actually deal with science and Christian theology. Given the nature of the category 'religion', this may seem to be a promising development. However, it may serve only to perpetuate the distortions of the more general category, for it is often assumed both that 'the Christian religion' can be unproblematically identified with Christian theology and that a consideration of Christian theology and science will throw light on the broader question of science and religion.

For example, in an influential account of the relationship between science and theology, Arthur Peacocke has claimed that the relation of Christianity to science 'has a special significance for all forms of religious experience and cultures'.[56] In his justification of this claim, Peacocke alludes to the unique history of Christianity:

The second reason why the Christian religion merits special attention as a paradigm case of a religion operating in the new cultural climate associated with the rise of science is that the Christian religion has had to take up the gauntlet thrown down by what is loosely called the 'Enlightenment'. It, almost alone among the major world religions, has been subject within its own culture to critical, historical, linguistic and literary analysis of its sacred literature and its sources; has had its beliefs exposed to sceptical philosophical critique; its attitudes to psychological examination; and its structures to sociological enquiry.[57]

It can be affirmed that 'the Christian religion' is indeed a 'paradigm case', such that an explication of its relationship to science is worthy of 'special attention'. Yet we are now in a position to see why and in what sense this is true. Christianity is the paradigmatic religion because the 'other religions' were constructed in its image. Moreover, the subjection of Christian faith to the various forms of rational enquiry described by Peacocke does not represent the history of the Christian religion in its relationship with a critical culture. Rather, this process is actually the coming into existence of 'the Christian religion' conceived as a body of propositional truths that can be subjected to the canons of rational enquiry. 'The Christian religion' is thus constituted by these interactions, rather than being one of the co-respondents in a relationship. It was precisely the Enlightenment development of the supremacy of rational authority that produced the idea of religion and its archetype, 'the Christian religion'.[58]

The problem of the relation of Christianity to science is thus a problem generated to a large degree by the categories in question. In much the same way that the objectifying and logocentric tendencies of the Enlightenment produced the 'other religions', creating at the same time the vexed question of their relation to each other, so too 'science and religion' is a relationship that has only come about because of a distorting fragmentation of sets of human activities. With the production of each category has come an unhelpful abstraction from reality. Historian Andrew Cunningham has argued the point with respect to science: 'The customary focus of our attention as historians of science has not primarily been on people in the practice of this human activity "science", but on one or other abstraction of a different kind – abstracted, that is, from the human activity which constitutes it'.[59] Not only is this observation true for the category 'religion' as well but its consequences for the activities that it is supposed to represent are even more damaging than in the case of 'science'. Unreflective use of 'religion' thus serves to perpetuate an Enlightenment ideal of 'the Christian religion' as an enterprise that is primarily intellectual and (while this consequence is less obvious) serves also to preserve a privileged position for Christianity among the world religions. Both tendencies are to a large extent unconscious and perhaps even undesired consequences of uncritical use of the categories.

Consider again Arthur Peacocke's *Theology for a scientific age.*[60] Here we find the early disclaimer that its conclusions are in no way 'meant to imply that other non-Christian religions cannot be a path to that reality which is, as I shall argue, God'.[61] Yet this statement sits oddly with a number of topics discussed in the book: 'God's interaction with the world'; 'God's communication with humanity'; 'The long search and Jesus of Nazareth'; 'Divine being and becoming human'. If contemporary science is shown to be compatible with the existence of a personal Deity who interacts with the world, who communicates with humankind, who became incarnate in the person of Christ, what are the implications for the truth claims of atheistic Buddhism, polytheistic Hinduism, and the strict monotheism of Judaism and Islam? *Pace* Peacocke, the closer the affinities established between science and Christian beliefs, the more one seems committed to Christian exclusivism – the position according to which the truth claims of Christianity are true, while those of other religions are false. Thus one of the unforeseen implications of this common approach is that if science can validate certain religious convictions, it will necessarily rule out others.

I am not assuming here that Christian exclusivism is necessarily wrong. It is not clear that there is any philosophical or moral impropriety in religious exclusivism, although some have mounted cases to this effect. However, it may be that the desire to seek rapprochement between Christianity and science will reduce the prospects of meaningful dialogue between Christianity and other faiths. The argument of a close fit between modern science and the Christian religion perpetuates the Enlightenment ideal of a rational Christianity as the religion best able to withstand the assaults of reason and natural philosophy. The appeal to reason, we should remind ourselves, was not primarily to defend Christian beliefs against the assaults of atheism or natural philosophy but to establish the truth of Christianity, or one of its confessional forms, against rival modes of religiosity. Arguably, these past victories for Christianity were achieved only at the cost of distorting both Christian faith and the religious lives of those who were unwillingly enrolled in the other 'religions'.

The dilemma faced by those who would provide a rational and dispassionate account of science and Christian belief parallels almost exactly that faced by those who, during the Enlightenment, sought to compare 'the religions' objectively, only to conclude, almost invariably, that Christianity was superior. As I have suggested, the categories in question are largely responsible for this situation, but these categories, in turn, represent conflicting commitments – on the one hand, to the truth of a single tradition, and on the other, to a set of rational, critical, procedures which will enable a disinterested comparison of the alternatives. Without the element of neutrality, the comparison is pointless. But is such neutral objectivity compatible with religious conviction? The Enlightenment argued that it was, a position that, as we have seen, resulted in the transformation of Christian faith into 'the Christian religion' – a set of doctrines which could sustain rational criticism – and, in its train, the construction of 'other religions', similarly conceived, though less able than the original to withstand the assaults of reason.

The difficulty with such a view of religion is that it effectively sidelines those personal and affective commitments that might reasonably be argued to be important to faith communities. It reduces faith to theology; it turns piety into 'a religion'. Even as these transformations were being effected, this marginalizing of piety and faith did not pass without protest. Witness the rise of Evangelicalism in the early eighteenth century and even before this Blaise Pascal's famous distinction between the God of faith, 'of Abraham, Isaac, and Jacob', and 'the God of the philosophers' – one inhabiting the realm of faith, the other of reason and 'religion'.[62] It is, I suspect, the God of the philosophers who figures in many discussions of the science–religion relation – the God who is necessary cause for the existence of the universe, who sustains the created order and its mathematical laws, who works, if necessary, within quantum uncertainties, in short the God in whom reason induces belief. This God is also the God of 'religion' and thus of 'science and religion': whether he is compatible with the God of faith remains an open question.

Ultimately, normative responses to questions of this kind cannot be provided by the historian. It is quite conceivable that the kinds of conceptual transformation sketched out in this chapter might be welcomed by some of the faithful. A scientifically oriented Christianity may well be regarded as a positive development by those whose Christian commitments are not in serious doubt. Neither can it be ignored that some advocates of a 'scientific Buddhism', for example, have impeccable Buddhist credentials – after all, the Dalai Lama has enthusiastically embraced the scientific vindication of aspects of Buddhist practice. What historians can do, however, is provide data that those with religious commitments may find helpful in evaluating certain historical transitions and their impact. It is important, at the very least, to be aware that these transitions have taken place. The subsequent question of how well these developments – specifically the emergence of the modern ideas 'science' and 'religion' – cohere with the long history of the traditions should be a question of considerable importance for those who identify themselves with those traditions.

CONCLUSION: WHAT FUTURE FOR 'SCIENCE AND RELIGION'?

In the light of all of these considerations what can be said about the future prospects of science–religion discussions? In concluding, let me make some brief and tentative proposals. First, it must be conceded that abstractions of various kinds are a necessary condition for knowledge. So too with 'science' and 'religion'. While these categories, like many others, have a tendency to take on a life of their own and to overshadow the realities they are meant to represent, they nonetheless occupy so secure a position in the present-day lexicon that it would be futile to attempt to dispense with them completely. What should by now be evident, however, is that those who rely on these terms need to deploy them with a renewed sensitivity to their limitations and to the inherent distortions to which they inevitably give rise. Religious dogmas do not comprise the totality of the religious life; neither do scientific theories embody all that there is to the scientific enterprise. It should also be clear that once the constructed nature of the categories is taken into consideration, putative relationships between science and religion may turn out to be artifacts of the categories themselves. Whether science and religion are in conflict, or are independent entities, or are in dialogue, or are essentially integrated enterprises will be determined by exactly how one draws the boundaries within the broad limits given by the constructs.[63] Indeed, the fact that at this point in history each of these stances can attract adherents is suggestive of the artificial nature of the terms in the relation.

Second, and following directly from the first point, it is important to pay attention to the political dimensions of the categories and their relations. As John Bowker has succinctly put it, the issue between science and religion is less to do with propositions than with power.[64] Viewed in this light, some well-meaning attempts to promote science–religion dialogue, or the integration of theology and science, may tacitly reinforce the cultural authority of the sciences, distort Christian and other faith traditions, and perpetuate the problematic features of the category 'religion'. Sometimes what passes for interaction between religion and science turns out to be, in reality, a disguised appeal to the prestige of the sciences, with the attendant danger of a loss of what is distinctive about religious traditions. Symptomatic of this tendency is a recent rash of studies of Christian beliefs and practices that purport to show that forgiveness is good for one's health, that church attendance increases longevity, or that petitionary prayer has been shown to be medically efficacious. Such studies are harmless enough at one level, but the common assumption, albeit unspoken, that this empirical research has significant religious implications arises out of a deep confusion. Promotion of such programmes from religious motives is indicative of the extent to which agendas of material progress and physical health have come to displace traditional religious values. Buddhism has also suffered from occasional tendencies to surrender its epistemic autonomy to scientific experts. One of the growth areas of empirical studies of Buddhism has been studies of meditative states using magnetic resonance imaging (MRI) machines. The outcomes of such studies – which report, for example, high activation of the 'pleasure centres' of the brains of meditating monks – are often presented as vindications of Buddhist teachings, as if religious practices and beliefs remain conditional until granted the imprimatur of empirical verification.[65]

A related instance of an unseemly collusion between science and religion concerns the religious and moral sanctioning of biotechnological 'advances'. Bioethics, whether in its theological or secular guise, has thus frequently (though not invariably) been a source of legitimation for contemporary medicine, contributing to the perpetuation of questionable models of scientific medicine and to the medicalization of western society in the name of scientific progress.[66] The lesson in this is the need for a critical distance to be maintained between theology and science. This is not an advocacy of the kind of independence model which sets out discrete spheres in which theology and science can operate without fear of mutual interference. Far less is it a criticism of those many individuals who seek to provide moral and religious signposts in an arena in which such guidance is arguably more necessary than ever before. The suggestion is rather that it will be impossible for theology to exercise a critical or, in religious terms, 'prophetic' role in a society unless it maintains an appropriate distance from dominant cultural forces. This is an independence of theology from science which leaves room for legitimate conflict.

Third, it should be clear that discussions of the relation of science and religion cannot be considered in isolation from the issue of religious pluralism. The common nineteenth-century assumption that all of the 'religions' share some common essence or represent various manifestations of some central truths has become increasingly difficult to sustain in our own era. Science–religion dialogue cannot be conducted on the assumption that the religion pole of the discussion is a kind of generic natural religion that is essentially neutral with regard to the more specific contents of various faiths. Assertions made about the compatibility of scientific claims with the religious dogmas of one tradition are bound to have implications for the truth claims of other traditions. Those committed to discussions of the relationship between science and religion cannot ignore this dimension. It is tempting to think that the solution to this dilemma lies in exploring the relations of each tradition to the sciences. However, the historical considerations set out in this chapter suggest that 'science and religion' is primarily a western problem, for it is here that the respective categories emerged and are most potent. Science–religion issues impinge, for example, on 'the eastern religions' only to the extent that those in the East consider themselves to be subscribing to 'a religion'. There is something to be learned from the relative indifference of those in other faith traditions to the issue of science and religion – and I refer here to those who have remained immune to the western concept 'religion' and the cultural authority of science. It might be better simply to emulate this indifference than to export a set of problems that are to a large degree creatures of the categories of western knowledge. As for the growing profile of science-related issues in such traditions as Islam and Buddhism, these would make interesting test cases for the thesis outlined in this chapter.

Fourth, the personal dimensions of both scientific and religious activities ought to be taken more seriously. There is a sense in which we need to read abstract discussions of theology and science more as personal statements than as assertions about the relationship between two independent systems of thought. Theoretical accounts of science and theology are perhaps best understood as autobiographical statements about how individuals who take religious beliefs seriously have personally come to terms with a powerful and dominating view of the natural world that they find themselves unable to ignore. To a degree, such a reading is merely an extension into the contemporary debate of the historical 'case study' approach, and, on the assumption that this is a fruitful avenue for coming to an understanding of the past, there is no reason it should not also be so for the present. This suggested reframing is not intended as a devaluing or denigration of works purporting to address substantive issues. After all, there is in the West a long tradition of religious biography and autobiography, although admittedly this practice suffered a setback with the Enlightenment invention of propositional 'religion'. Perhaps we need also to think of 'scientific' critics of religion in a similar, autobiographical, light. Historian Owen Chadwick, referring to the putative conflict between science and religion in the Victorian era, distinguished 'between science when it was against religion and the scientists when they were against religion'.[67] Such a characterization is no less appropriate now. There are still those in the early twenty-first century who, with an endearing quaintness, carry a torch for the 'warfare model' of the relationship between science and religion. There is a strong sense in which such convictions betray more about what such individuals personally conceive 'religion' and 'science' to be than they do about two supposedly conflicting approaches to the world. The power of their rhetoric, moreover, is often less to do with the coherence of their views than with their cultural authority as scientists.

Finally, and in a sense related to all of the previous points, historical analysis has a central role to play in contemporary science–religion discussions. It is history that gives insights into the power dimensions of human activities, whether they concern religious faith or the study of the natural world, and it is through historical studies that the human element which is fundamental to both scientific and religious activities can become more visible. John Brooke, among others, has already called for more case studies in the history of science, the better to capture the nuances and complexities of the variety of relations, and this seems entirely appropriate.[68] While historical considerations are often thought marginal to arguments about the contemporary status of the science–religion relation, historians can make significant contributions to the ongoing discussion by drawing attention to the historical conditions which gave rise to the categories now in play. It is history, moreover, that shows the settings in which human actors are at work and that can provide unique insights into the ways in which various aspects of their lives – including the 'scientific' and 'religious' – are related.

NOTES

1 George Sarton, *A history of science* (New York: Norton, 1970).
2 Margaret J. Osler, 'Mixing metaphors: Science and religion or natural philosophy and theology in early modern Europe', *History of Science* 36 (1998), 91–113, on 91.

3 Paolo Rossi, *The dark abyss of time: The history of the earth and the history of nations from Hooke to Vico* (Chicago: University of Chicago Press, 1984), p. vii.

4 David Hull, *Science as a process* (Chicago: University of Chicago Press, 1988), p. 25.

5 Andrew Cunningham, 'Getting the game right: Some plain words on the identity and invention of science', *Studies in the History and Philosophy of Science* 19 (1988), 365–89, on 365.

6 G. E. R. Lloyd, *Early Greek science* (New York: Norton, 1970), p. iv.

7 David C. Lindberg, *The beginnings of western science* (Chicago: University of Chicago Press, 1992), pp. 2ff.

8 See, e.g., Boethius, *De trinitate* II; Thomas Aquinas, *Expositio supra librum Boethii de Trinitate* (translated as *The division and methods of the sciences*, trans. Armand Maurer, 4th edn (Toronto, 1986)), Q.5 A.1. Compare Aristotle, *Metaphysics*, 1025b–1026a; Plato, *Republic*, 509a–511d. For the medieval and Renaissance understanding of 'natural philosophy', see William Wallace, 'Traditional natural philosophy', in Charles Schmitt and Quentin Skinner (eds.), *The Cambridge history of Renaissance philosophy* (Cambridge: Cambridge University Press, 1988), pp. 201–35.

9 Nicholas Jardine, 'Epistemology of the sciences', in Schmitt and Skinner, *Cambridge history of Renaissance philosophy*, p. 685. See also Nicholas Jardine, 'Demonstration, dialectic, and rhetoric in Galileo's *Dialogue*', in Donald R. Kelley and Richard H. Popkin (eds.), *The shapes of knowledge from the Renaissance to the Enlightenment* (Dordrecht: Kluwer, 1991), pp. 101–21; Pierre Wagner (ed.), *Les philosophes et la science* (Paris: Gallimard, 2002), intro.

10 Cunningham, 'Getting the game right', 384. See also Andrew Cunningham, 'How the *Principia* got its name: Or, taking natural philosophy seriously', *History of Science* 28 (1991), 377–92; Christoph Lüthy, 'What to do with seventeenth-century natural philosophy? A taxonomic problem', *Perspectives on Science* 8 (2000), 164–95.

11 See, e.g., Bacon, *Advancement of learning*, I.i.3 and II.xvii.7, in *The works of Francis Bacon*, ed. James Spedding, Robert Ellis, and Douglas Heath, 14 vols. (London: Longman, 1857–74), vol. III, pp. 267, 405; John Sergeant, *The method to science* (London, 1696), sig. d1r. See also Ernan McMullin, 'Conceptions of science in the scientific revolution', in David C. Lindberg and Robert Westman (eds.), *Reappraisals of the scientific revolution* (Cambridge: Cambridge University Press, 1990), pp. 27–92.

12 John Locke, *An essay concerning human understanding*, ed. A. C. Fraser, 2 vols. (New York: Dover, 1959), IV.xii.10 (vol. II, p. 349). See also Locke, *Essay*, IV. iii.26 and IV.iii.29; Locke, *Some thoughts concerning education*, ed. John W. Yolton and Jean S. Yolton (Oxford: Clarendon Press, 1989), p. 244.

13 Thomas Browne, *Religio medici*, 1.16, in *Religio medici hydriotaphia, and The garden of Cyrus*, ed. Robin Robbins (Oxford: Clarendon Press, 1982), pp. 16ff.

14 Johannes Kepler, *Gesammelte Werke* (Munich: C. H. Beck, 1937–45), vol. VIII, p. 193. On this metaphor and how early modern naturalists differ

from modern scientists, see Peter Harrison, '"Priests of the most high God, with respect to the book of nature": The vocational identity of the early modern naturalist', in Angus Menuge (ed.), *Reading God's world* (St Louis: Concordia, 2005), pp. 55–80.

15 John Johnston, *Wonderful things of nature* (London, 1657), sig a3v.

16 Robert Boyle, *Some considerations touching the usefulness of experimental natural philosophy*, in *The Works of the Honorable Robert Boyle*, ed. Thomas Birch, 6 vols. (Hildesheim: Georg Olms, 1966), vol. II, pp. 62ff.

17 Cunningham, 'Getting the game right', 384. On the essentially religious nature of the discipline, see also Peter Harrison, *The Bible, Protestantism, and the rise of natural science* (Cambridge: Cambridge University Press, 1998), pp. 169–76; John Hedley Brooke, *Science and religion: Some historical perspectives* (Cambridge: Cambridge University Press, 1991), pp. 192–225; Osler, 'Mixing metaphors'; Andrew Cunningham and Perry Williams, 'De-centring the big picture: The origins of modern science and the modern origins of science', *British Journal for the History of Science* 26 (1993), 387–483.

18 See, e.g., Boyle, *Usefulness of natural philosophy*; Thomas Sprat, *The history of the Royal-Society of London* (London: J. Martyn, 1667), pt. III; Joseph Glanvill, *The usefulness of real philosophy to religion*, in *Essays on several important subjects in philosophy and religion* (London, 1676). There is room for debate over the extent to which natural history and natural philosophy were *intrinsically* religious. These activities might have been 'about God', but they were not just about God. For recent discussions of Cunningham's view, see Peter Dear, 'Religion, science, and natural philosophy: Thoughts on Cunningham's thesis', *Studies in History and Philosophy of Science* 32A (2001), 377–86; Andrew Cunningham, 'A response to Peter Dear's "Religion, science, and natural philosophy"', *Studies in History and Philosophy of Science* 32A (2001), 387–91; Peter Harrison, 'Physico-theology and the mixed sciences: Theology and early modern natural philosophy', in Peter Anstey and John Schuster (eds.), *The science of nature in the seventeenth century* (Dordrecht: Springer, 2005), pp. 165–83.

19 Charles Webster, *The great instauration: Science, medicine, and reform, 1626–1660* (London: Duckworth, 1975), p. 494. For similar observations about other historical periods, see Wolfgang van den Daele, 'The social construction of science: Institutionalisation and definition of positive science in the latter half of the seventeenth century', in E. Mendelsohn, P. Wengart, and R. Whitley (eds.), *The social production of scientific knowledge* (Dordrecht: Reidel, 1977), p. 39; Robert M. Young, *Darwin's metaphor* (Cambridge: Cambridge University Press, 1985), p. 167; Amos Funkenstein, *Theology and the scientific imagination* (Princeton, NJ: Princeton University Press, 1986), p. 3.

20 Simon Schaffer, 'Scientific discoveries and the end of natural philosophy', *Social Studies of Science* 16 (1986), 387–420, on 413.

21 Cunningham, 'Getting the game right', 385.

22 Sydney Ross, '"Scientist": the story of a word', *Annals of Science* 18 (1962), 65–86. Compare *Dictionnaire historique de la langue française* (Paris: Dictionnaire Le Robert, 1992), s.v. 'scientifique'; Wagner, *Les philosophes et la science*, esp.

intro. and ch. 6; Helmut Holzhey, 'Der Philosoph im 17. Jahrhundert', in Jean-Pierre Schobinger (ed.), *Grundriss der Geschichte der Philosophie. Reihe 17. Jahrhundert* (Basle: Schwabe, 1993), vol. I, pp. 3–30, esp. pp. 13ff.

23 Frank Turner, 'The Victorian conflict between science and religion: A professional dimension', *Isis* 49 (1978), 356–76; Brooke, *Science and religion*, pp. 5, 50.

24 Turner, 'Victorian conflict'; Brooke, *Science and religion*, pp. 5, 50; Patrick Armstrong, *The English parson-naturalist: A companionship between science and religion* (Leominster, Herefordshire: Gracewing, 2000); David Livingstone, 'Science and religion: Toward a new cartography', *Christian Scholar's Review* 26 (1997), 270–92.

25 Ruth Barton, '"An influential set of chaps": The X-Club and Royal Society politics, 1864–85', *British Journal for the History of Science* 23 (1990), 53–81; T. W. Heyck, *The transformation of intellectual life in Victorian England* (London: Croom Helm, 1982).

26 A. D. White, *A history of the warfare of science with theology in Christendom*, 2 vols. (New York: Appleton, 1896); John Draper, *History of the conflict between religion and science* (London: King, 1875).

27 Herbert Spencer, 'The genesis of science', *British Quarterly Review* 20 (1854), 108–62, esp. 152–9; Richard Yeo, *Defining science: William Whewell, natural knowledge, and public debate in early Victorian Britain* (Cambridge: Cambridge University Press, 1993), pp. 49ff.

28 Max Weber, 'Science as a vocation', in Peter Lassman and Irving Velody (eds.), *Max Weber's* Science as a vocation (London: Unwin, 1989). This work highlights the impact of Weber's conception of 'the scientist'. See also William A. Durbin, 'What shall we make of Henry Margenau? A religion and science pioneer of the twentieth century', *Zygon* 34 (1999), 167–93.

29 A. W. Benn, *A history of English rationalism in the nineteenth century*, 2 vols. (London: Longmans, Green, & Todd, 1906), vol. I, p. 198.

30 White, *History of the warfare*, vol. I, p. ix.

31 Schaffer, 'Scientific discoveries and the end of natural philosophy', 413.

32 See, e.g., John Brooke, 'Does the history of science have a future?' *British Journal for the History of Science* 32 (1999), 1–20.

33 John Brooke, 'Science and theology in the Enlightenment', in W. Mark Richardson and Wesley J. Wildman (eds.), *Religion and science: History, method and dialogue* (London: Routledge, 1996), p. 23; cf. Brooke, *Science and religion*, pp. 6–11. See also David Wilson, 'On the importance of eliminating *science* and *religion* from the history of science and religion: The cases of Oliver Lodge, J. H. Jeans and A. S. Eddington', in Jiste van der Meer (ed.), *Facets of faith and science* (New York: University Press of America, 1996), pp. 27–47.

34 Claude Welch, 'Dispelling some myths about the split between theology and science in the nineteenth century', in Richardson and Wildman, *Religion and science*, pp. 29–40, esp. p. 29.

35 Peter Galison and David Stump (eds.), *The disunity of science* (Stanford, CA: Stanford University Press, 1996); R. G. A. Dolby, *Uncertain knowledge* (Cambridge: Cambridge University Press, 1996), pt. II; Joseph Margolis, *Science*

without unity (Oxford: Blackwell, 1987); S. Jasonoff, 'Contested boundaries in policy-relevant science', *Social Studies of Science* 17 (1987), 195–230; Charles Taylor, *Defining science: A rhetoric of demarcation* (Madison: University of Wisconsin Press, 1996). For a vigorous argument against the notion that there is methodological uniformity in science, see Paul Feyerabend, *Against method: Outline of an anarchistic theory of knowledge* (London: Verso, 1975).

36 Fraser Watts, 'Are science and religion in conflict?', *Zygon* 32 (1997), 125–39.

37 Hull, *Science as a process*, pp. 512ff.

38 Feyerabend, *Against method*, p. 295.

39 Wilfred Cantwell Smith, *The meaning and end of religion* (London: SPCK, 1978), p. 51.

40 See, e.g., Michel Despland, *La religion en occident: Évolution des idées et du vécu* (Montreal: Fides, 1979); Ernst Feil, *Religio: Die Geschichte eines neuzeitlichen Grundbegriffs vom Frühchristentum bis zur Reformation* (Göttingen: Vandenhoeck and Ruprecht, 1986); Feil, 'From the classical religio to the modern religion: Elements of a transformation between 1550 and 1650', in Michel Despland and Gérard Vallée (eds.), *Religion in history: The word, the idea, the reality* (Waterloo, Ontario: Wilfrid Laurier University, 1992), pp. 31–43; Peter Harrison, *'Religion' and the religions in the English Enlightenment* (Cambridge: Cambridge University Press, 1990); John Bossy, 'Some elementary forms of Durkheim', *Past and Present* 95 (1982), 3–18. See also Russell McCutcheon, 'The category "religion" in recent publications: A critical survey', *Numen* 42 (1995), 285–301; Nicholas Lash, *The beginning and end of 'religion'* (Cambridge: Cambridge University Press, 1996).

41 As Edward Said writes of the process of 'orientalism':

> The imaginative examination of things Oriental was based more or less exclusively upon a sovereign Western consciousness out of whose unchallenged centrality an Oriental world emerged, first according to general ideas about who or what was an Oriental, then according to a detailed logic governed not simply by empirical reality but by a battery of desires, repressions, investments, and projections.

Said, *Orientalism* (London: Routledge and Kegan Paul, 1978), p. 8. See also Talal Asad, *Genealogies of religion: Discipline and reasons of power in Christianity and Islam* (Baltimore, MD: Johns Hopkins University Press, 1996); Richard King, *Orientalism and religion: Postcolonial theory, India, and 'The mystic East'* (London: Routledge, 1999).

42 Smith, *Meaning and end of religion*, p. 61. For more detailed accounts of the inventions of these traditions, see Philip C. Almond, *The British discovery of Buddhism* (Cambridge: Cambridge University Press, 1988); P. J. Marshall (ed.), *The British discovery of Hinduism in the eighteenth century* (Cambridge: Cambridge University Press, 1970); Tomoko Masuzawa, *The invention of world religions* (Chicago: University of Chicago Press, 2005).

43 See, e.g., Thomas Lawson and Robert McCauley, *Rethinking religion* (Cambridge: Cambridge University Press, 1990); J. Samuel Preuss, *Explaining religion: Criticism and theory from Bodin to Freud* (New Haven, CT: Yale

University Press, 1987); Stewart Guthrie, 'Religion: What is it?', *Journal of the Scientific Study of Religion* 35 (1996), 412–20; Guthrie, 'Buddhism and the definition of religion', *Journal for the Scientific Study of Religion* 32 (1993), 1–17; Brian K. Smith, 'Exorcising the transcendent: Strategies for defining Hinduism and Buddhism', *History of Religions* 27 (1987), 32–55.

44 On the history of the category 'mysticism', see Leigh Eric Schmidt, 'The making of modern "mysticism"', *Journal of the American Academy of Religion* 71 (2003), 273–302.

45 Smith, *Meaning and end of religion*, p. 69.

46 Karl Barth, *Church dogmatics*, 4 vols. (Edinburgh: T & T Clark, 1936–69), vol. I/2, p. 288; Dietrich Bonhoeffer, *Letters and papers from prison* (New York: Macmillan, 1962), pp. 161–9, 194–200, 226.

47 Examples cited by Smith, *Meaning and end of religion*, pp. 125ff.

48 On these transformations, see Harrison, *'Religion' and the religions*, pp. 19–28.

49 Nathaniel Crouch, *The strange and prodigious religions, customs, and manners of sundry nations* (London, 1683), pp. 27ff.

50 Raimundo Panikkar, *The Trinity and the religious experience of man* (Maryknoll, NY: Orbis, 1973), pp. 2–3.

51 Raimundo Panikkar, 'The Jordan, the Tiber, and the Ganges', in John Hick and Paul F. Knitter (eds.), *The myth of Christian uniqueness* (London: SCM Press, 1988), pp. 104–5.

52 On the discovery, or construction, of modern Buddhism, see Almond, *British discovery of Buddhism*, esp. pp. 24–8. I am indebted in this paragraph both to Almond's book and to David L. McMahon, 'Modernity and the early discourse of scientific Buddhism', *Journal of the American Academy of Religion* 72 (2004), 897–933.

53 Paul Carus, *Buddhism and its Christian critics* (Chicago: Open Court, 1897), p. 114, quoted in McMahon, 'Discourse of scientific Buddhism', 917. See also Almond, *British discovery of Buddhism*, pp. 84–93.

54 James Ketelaar, '"Strategic occidentalism": Meiji Buddhists at the World's Parliament of Religions', *Buddhist Christian Studies* 11 (1991), 37–56; McMahon, 'Discourse of scientific Buddhism', 908, 924ff.

55 Stephen Prothero, *The white Buddhist: The Asian odyssey of Henry Steel Olcott* (Bloomington, IN: Indiana University Press, 1996), pp. 7–9; MacMahon, 'Discourse of scientific Buddhism', 924ff. See also Don Lopez Jr., *A modern Buddhist bible: Essential readings from East and West* (Boston, MA: Beacon, 2002), intro.

56 Arthur Peacocke, *Theology for a scientific age*, enlarged edn (London: SCM Press, 1993), p. 3.

57 Ibid., pp. 4ff.

58 Variations on this move are not uncommon in the science-and-religion literature. John Polkinghorne opens the discussion in *Belief in God in an age of science* (New Haven, CT: Yale University Press, 1998) by stating that different religious communities have different answers to the question of what it means to believe in God. Thus at the outset polytheistic and atheistic

religions seem to be excluded. The chapter 'Science and religion compared', with its discussion of Christology, inexorably moves to a discussion of 'science and [Christian] theology' (pp. 45–7). Philip Clayton states that the God–world relation 'is a question shared by numerous religious traditions, each of which turns to a different set of scriptures for its answer', again implying the paradigmatic nature of monotheistic 'religions of the book'; Philip Clayton, *God and contemporary science* (Grand Rapids, MI: Eerdmans, 1997). Admittedly, elsewhere Clayton seems more sensitive to the difficulties generated by religious pluralism (see, e.g., pp. x, 58, 66 n. 12, 155), but these difficulties are, in effect, put aside. Keith Ward is also attuned to the problem of religious pluralism, but his sympathetic treatment of 'other religions' is not really integrated into his account of the relation of Christianity to science. See Ward, *God, faith, and the new millennium: Christian belief in an age of science* (Oxford: Oneworld, 1997), pp. 10ff., 152–71.

59 Cunningham, 'Getting the game right', 372.

60 I return to Peacocke's work not because I consider it to be especially vulnerable to criticism. On the contrary, I believe it to be one of the best examples of the genre. Nonetheless, it is the presuppositions of that genre that I wish to investigate.

61 Peacocke, *Theology for a scientific age*, p. 3.

62 Blaise Pascal, 'The Memorial', in his *Pensées* (Ringwood, NJ: Penguin, 1976), p. 309. Søren Kierkegaard alluded to a similar quandary faced by the advocate of an objective and rational religion:

> The inquiring subject must be in one or the other of two situations. *Either* he is in faith convinced of the truth of Christianity, and in faith assured of his own relationship to it; in which case he cannot be infinitely interested in all the rest, since faith itself is the infinite interest in Christianity, and since every other interest may readily come to constitute a temptation. *Or* the inquirer is, on the other hand, not in an attitude of faith, but objectively in an attitude of contemplation, and hence not infinitely interested in the determination of the question.

> Søren Kierkegaard, *Concluding unscientific postscript*, trans. David Swenson and Walter Lowrie (Princeton, NJ: Princeton University Press, 1968), p. 23.

63 I have relied here on Ian Barbour's familiar typology for categorizing science–religion relations: conflict, independence, dialogue, and integration. *Religion and science: Historical and contemporary issues* (San Francisco: HarperSanFrancisco, 1997), ch. 4.

64 John Bowker, 'Science and religion: Contest or confirmation?', in Fraser Watts (ed.), *Science meets faith* (London: SPCK, 1998).

65 See, e.g., Richard Davidson and Anne Harrington (eds.), *Visions of compassion: Western scientists and Tibetan Buddhists examine human nature* (Oxford: Oxford University Press, 2001); Cary Barbour, 'The science of meditation', *Psychology Today* 34 (May 2001), 54–60; Daniel Goleman, 'Taming destructive emotions', *Tricycle: The Buddhist Review* 47 (2003), 75–8; McMahon, 'Discourse of scientific Buddhism', 927ff.

66 Stanley Hauerwas, 'Styles of religious reflection in medical ethics', in Allen
   Verhey (ed.), *Religion and medical ethics: Looking back, looking forward*
   (Grand Rapids, MI: Eerdmans, 1996).

67 Owen Chadwick, *The Victorian church*, 2 vols. (Oxford: Oxford University
   Press, 1970), vol. II, p. 3.

68 Brooke, 'Religious belief and the natural sciences: Mapping the historical
   landscape', in van der Meer, *Facets of faith and science*, vol. I; Durbin, 'What
   shall we make of Henry Margenau?'; Geoffrey Cantor, *Michael Faraday:
   Sandemanian and scientist* (London: Macmillan, 1991); Brooke and Cantor,
   Reconstructing nature: The engagement of science and religion (Edinburgh:
   T & T Clark, 1998), pp. 247–81. Cf. Michael Shortland and Richard Yeo
   (eds.), *Telling lives in science: Essays on scientific biography* (Cambridge:
   Cambridge University Press, 1996).

CHAPTER 3

Science and religion in postmodern perspective: the case of Bruno Latour

Jan Golinski

> Theology, unfortunately, has been for a long time in the same dire state where epistemology and aesthetics were before the onslaught of constructivism.
>
> Bruno Latour[1]

Bruno Latour is well known as an anthropologist and sociologist of science and technology. His books include *Science in action* (1987), *We have never been modern* (1993), *The pasteurization of France* (1988), and *Pandora's hope* (1999). He has done fieldwork in a molecular biology laboratory, organized museum exhibits, and written essays that also venture into philosophy, politics, and art history. His work is highly original, hard to summarize, and harder still to classify within current academic categories. He is often described as a leading 'postmodern' thinker, and he does indeed have things in common with others to whom that label has been applied, although it is not one he is happy to accept. Latour claims that what is usually thought of as modernity has never really prevailed, so it is not possible to move beyond it into a postmodern phase. In his view, the characteristically modern attempt to segregate the natural realm from the human one has never entirely succeeded. Hybrid entities have continuously been fabricated, despite all efforts to demarcate the two domains. To recognize this is to adopt what he calls an 'amodern' or 'non-modern' perspective.[2] Latour also accepts the label of 'constructivist' to describe his approach to science studies, which is to say that he is interested in studying the practices by which scientific facts are made, rather than considering how knowledge relates to the world in the mode of classical epistemology.[3] He does not, however, call himself a '*social* constructivist', because he does not try to explain the construction of scientific knowledge by resort to a traditional social ontology. Latour's world is one in which human and non-human 'actants' are ascribed equivalent agency. In this respect he can also be called a 'post-humanist'.[4]

In his remarkably wide-ranging body of work Latour has often mentioned his personal commitment to Catholicism. His papers also include some extended analyses of religious iconology, and he has addressed the relations between science and religion in a couple of articles in English. In a book not yet translated from French, *Jubiler – ou les tourments de la parole religieuse* (2002), he is quite explicit about the form of religious devotion he thinks appropriate to the present time.[5] In declaring himself so forthrightly, he is not just studying religion from the outside, as in the discipline of religious studies. Rather, his metaphysical assertions constitute an implicit theology, albeit of a rather peculiar kind that does not stipulate the existence of God as such. He does, however, address general issues of ontology, specifically how 'existence' has normally been conceived and demonstrated, and in this way his outlook has implications for fundamental theological questions. Instead of endorsing a particular set of beliefs, he argues that religion should not be understood as a matter of belief at all. Thus Latour is not neutral on the basic questions that concern religious people, but nor does he offer conventional answers. My aim in this chapter is to try to understand what Latour means by a religion without belief. While I cannot say how it might be received by people of religious faith, I want to explore some of its implications for those who are studying the relations between religion and science.

There does not seem to have been much commentary on this aspect of Latour's work.[6] Several people have told me they think the topic is worth addressing, but nobody, at least in the field of science studies, seems to have been willing to take it on. The subject of his religion seems to be surrounded by embarrassment in the English-speaking world, where Latour's work on science and technology has been followed most keenly but given an entirely secular interpretation. His passing remarks about praying or attending church on Sundays could almost have been calculated to evoke Anglo-Saxon suspicions of continental Catholicism. Such suspicions would probably only be strengthened if *Jubiler* were to be translated. In offhand remarks some of Latour's colleagues have expressed the suspicion that his Catholicism constitutes a hidden agenda for his work in science studies. I think, in fact, that this gets things the wrong way round. Rather, I shall argue that his work on religion comprises an attempt – perhaps an over-ambitious one – to extend his perspective on scientific practice. The suspicions are understandable, however, because Latour has breached conventional decorum by publicly mentioning his own religious devotion – normally treated as a private matter – and by appropriating religious imagery and genres to advance his claims.

The tendency in response has been to relegate the subject to the realm of personal gossip, making the topic impossible to discuss except in an impolite *ad hominem* way.

Latour is clearly aware of this reaction; sometimes he seems to be provoking it. He discusses at some length the embarrassment surrounding religious discourse in contemporary academia, the way religion can be analysed only historically or in the idiom of one of the social sciences. Even in private, he points out, the conventions of public discourse exert an inhibiting effect: 'I have been raised a Catholic; and ... I cannot even speak to my children of what I am doing at Church on Sunday'.[7] He responds to these difficulties by adopting a typically provocative stance, situating himself within religious discourse rather than outside it. In order to see what he has to offer, we have to set aside any embarrassment provoked by his avowals of personal devotion and decline the temptation to dismiss them or explain them away by biographical speculation or gossip. We need to consider what Latour has to say on its own terms, if we are to determine its possible value to scholars studying the relations between religion and science.

RELIGION WITHOUT BELIEF

According to Latour himself, a major obstacle to discussing religion in any public context is that the talk immediately gets deflected into questions about *belief*: 'What exactly do you believe?' 'Do you believe in God, or not?' 'Surely you don't believe in the virgin birth?' and so on. We can talk about religion more easily, he suggests, if we give up the notion that it is to be defined by beliefs. One problem with such a belief-centred definition is that it assimilates religion to a scientific or factual model, in which it is taken to be primarily concerned with making claims about reality. This, he asserts, is to misunderstand the purpose of religious language and imagery, to identify it inappropriately with a different 'regime of enunciation', namely that of science. In other words, the problem with traditional religious notions is not that they constitute false beliefs but that the model of belief to which they are held is shaped by the epistemic practices of the sciences, whose authority Latour wants to call into question.[8]

This is where Latour's understanding of the construction of scientific knowledge becomes relevant. Science, he claims, operates by assembling networks of instruments, models, and images in order to bring under scrutiny what is too distant, too rare, too large, or too small to be contemplated directly. Its success depends upon the alignment of representations with one another, the building of what he calls 'chains of reference', and the transmission along those chains of 'immutable mobiles' that convey information about the world. He describes how representations of various kinds, including photographs, diagrams, specimens, statistical data, and the 'inscriptions' of instruments, are mobilized serially so that they can be *read through* to give access to a putative reality beyond. Science is the practice of collecting and aligning such representations so that they become transparent, at least for a while, and allow reference to be made to the natural world that is supposed to lie behind them. In fact, according to Latour, 'information' is just that which is transmitted unaltered by these layers of mediations, and 'external reality' and 'nature' are artifacts of the practices by which they are aligned. Scientific practices produce knowledge by manipulating and layering representations, but knowledge remains an attribute of these networks – it is not possible to compare it directly with an unmediated reality.[9]

Latour's analysis is couched in terms of semiotics; he shows how knowledge emerges from certain signifying practices. But it also has fairly clear metaphysical implications, because the description of these semiotic practices implies a certain ontology. Latour identifies the construction of knowledge about things with the construction of the entities that become known. His case studies of scientists' work in laboratories show them making facts at the same time that they fabricate the things they claim to know. He uses the term 'technoscience' to drive home the point that scientific knowledge is intimately bound up with the making and distributing of manufactured entities.[10] Furthermore the actors involved in making knowledge are themselves constructed as part of the same process. As 'actants', the human subjects of knowledge are placed on the same level as the non-human and inanimate entities they manipulate. This has been a source of considerable unease with Latour's perspective, among both scientists themselves and other scholars in the field of science studies. He is clearly issuing a challenge to realism, whether it is the realism of scientists who believe in the objects they study or that of the sociologists who reify human agency when they try to explain scientists' beliefs by referring to the choices the scientists make in pursuit of their interests. While other science studies scholars have deliberately refrained from commitment to such metaphysical claims, Latour has no hesitation in overstepping these bounds.[11]

Religion is characterized by contrast with this image of science. According to Latour, it is misunderstood if it is taken to operate in the same way science does. It does not share the aim of aligning representations so that information is transmitted effectively. It is not directed at conveying an image of some distant reality, such as a 'supernatural' or 'spiritual' realm. The notion that religious imagery and language represent a hidden reality behind that experienced by science is a double mistake: mistaken in its assumption that science grasps reality directly, and mistaken in ascribing the same aim to religion. Thus, to quote Latour, '*belief is a caricature of religion exactly as knowledge is a caricature of science*'.[12] Or, again, 'no one, absolutely no one, ever believed in anything according to the manner imagined by science'.[13]

The slogans are typically provocative, but the general point may strike a chord with anyone who has attended to current debates about religion and science. Those who are familiar with contemporary polemics might well be inclined to agree that they are often tainted by the assumption that religion can be identified with – or reduced to – a system of factual knowledge on the model of the sciences. Polemical atheists often make this identification of religion with 'wrong' science, with a belief in outdated cosmologies, spontaneous acts of divine creation, miracles, and so forth. Thus Richard Dawkins declares that the publication of Darwin's *On the origin of species* (1859) made it possible to be an intellectually satisfied atheist, which had not been possible before. Or Christopher Hitchens announces that religion is 'a babyish attempt to meet our inescapable demand for knowledge', a demand that can now be more adequately met by the sciences.[14] If religion is weighed in the same scales as science, it does seem particularly vulnerable to knock-down refutation.[15] Apparently at the other extreme from the atheists, there are biblical fundamentalists, who are often said to reject science but in fact claim that religion provides an alternative source of the same sort of factual knowledge – that the scriptures are a guide to geology, for example. Their attempt to place religion on an equal footing with science requires them to invent their own system of purportedly 'scientific' knowledge, so-called 'creation science', which is not taken seriously by the scientific community at large.[16]

Latour suggests that both of these extreme positions share the fault of regarding religion as a matter of belief and measuring that belief against the standard of scientific facts. But his critique goes further than this, taking us on to the territory on which some have tried to reconcile science and religion. He calls into question any attempt to forge such a reconciliation on the grounds of factual knowledge, any claim that science and religion provide similar or convergent knowledge of the world. Such claims have been made, for example, by physicists who discern some underlying rationality behind the values of the fundamental constants, or by the 'Intelligent Design' (ID) movement contemplating the history of life on earth.[17] According to Latour, such attempts at reconciliation are weakened by having accepted at face value the epistemic claims of science and by having assumed that religion is in the same business of providing factual knowledge of the world. Both assumptions, he insists, are mistaken.

But if religion is not a system of factual knowledge or beliefs, what is it? The alternative, according to Latour, is to appreciate religious discourse in what he calls its 'performative' aspect, that is to say, how it transforms both enunciator and audience by being produced in a specific context. He uses the analogy of love-talk. When people say they love one another, they do not employ language as a means of reference but rather for what linguists call its 'phatic' function, as a way of connecting people or making them present to one another. It is the saying of 'I love you' at a particular time and place that is transformative; its function cannot be discharged by conveying the same information in another way, for example by handing over a written message or playing a tape-recording. The primary social meaning of this kind of discourse does not lie in the information it communicates. Rather, what is at stake in such an utterance, as Latour puts it, is 'transformation of messengers instead of the transport of information'.[18] Latour's argument is that this is also the case with religious language and imagery – with prayer, liturgical language, the scriptures, and religious art. Devotional images, for example, in their rich materiality and stylistic originality, direct viewers' attention to the means by which they 're-present' their meaning. They do not transparently represent an anterior reality. They do not communicate information. Rather, they operate performatively by making something present in the act of enunciation; and what they make present is what Latour calls 'the divine'.[19]

This 'divine' is not defined by Latour; he refuses to hypostatize it as the original reality lying behind religious language and imagery. That would be to treat such imagery as a chain of reference – as a series of representations – like the telescopes and photographs that enable scientists to posit the existence of a distant galaxy. It would be to seek 'the daguerreotype of God', succumbing to a type of idolatry or fetishism of images. Religion doesn't work like that. Latour prefers to quote St John the Evangelist on the divine as 'the Word' – which he interprets not as an entity situated at the origin of a lengthy series of representations but as the meaning made present by each signifying act. It reveals itself in the misalignments or gaps between representational layers, the ways in which they fail to transmit images of the realm beyond. 'God is another mediation', as Latour puts it.[20]

Elsewhere he contemplates abandoning belief in God altogether in order to renew the religious message for a secular age.[21]

In some respects, nonetheless, Latour works hard to present his account as a development of the Catholic theological tradition. He suggests that the immanence of meaning in religious language and imagery can be understood in terms of the doctrine of incarnation. The Word is incarnate in material things, not a spiritual entity hidden behind them. To quote Latour: 'Religion is not about transcendence, a Spirit from above, but all about immanence to which is added the renewal, the rendering present again of this immanence. (I am not inventing anything, this is called "incarnation" in Christian dogma.)'[22] He reads the story of Pentecost as signifying how the Christian message must be continuously deformed and 're-presented' anew, to speak to every people in their own language. Failure to realize this – by theological conservatives in the Vatican, for example, or by Protestant scriptural fundamentalists – is a source of stagnation in Christianity.[23] Latour rejects the fundamentalism that tries to strip away all the layers of religious discourse to disclose some ultimate truth. There is no original message to be uncovered behind the accretions of religious imagery, no spirit or essence to be believed in independently of a constantly renewed tradition. To think that there is would be to mistake religious enunciations for the output of instruments, to try to interpret devotional language as if it were the prose of a scientific report.

THE MEANING OF RELIGIOUS ART

These broader claims to theological legitimacy are spelled out in *Jubiler*. In his English-language publications, on the other hand, Latour has mostly expounded his theology through analysing religious art. Discussing particular sculptures and paintings, he explains how they thwart viewers' expectations that they should point beyond themselves to a transcendent or spiritual realm. Instead, by failing as representational images, they repeatedly draw attention to their own status as mediators, as 'broken images' or 'faithless messengers'. The claim is substantiated by reference to paintings of angels in scenes of the Annunciation or Resurrection, by Fra Angelico, Piero della Francesca, and other Renaissance artists. It is a mistake, Latour insists, to analyse such iconic images in terms of what they represent, whether it be a scene from the scriptures or some point of doctrine. Rather, they are to be understood as having a performative function, refusing to be aligned with other representations: 'Avoiding information transfer is what all these visual cultures have in common'.[24] All Christian imagery enacts this kind of refusal of transparency, according to Latour, subverting the regime of representation that would allow a transcendent reality to be communicated effectively.

Just as it is hard to imagine Vatican theologians embracing Latour's version of Catholicism, so it is hard to envision art historians accepting such readings, at least when applied quite generally to all Christian art from all periods, media, and styles. The degree to which a particular visual image serves a referential purpose is usually thought to vary according to the style and subject of the work, not to mention the artist's aims and the context in which it was produced. Art historians stipulate these factors with considerable sophistication and tend to see them all as relevant when assessing the representational function of an image. Latour treats all such factors as additional mediations that do not affect the basic dichotomy in which he is interested: that between a regime of enunciation in which information is transmitted and one in which meaning is made by the mediations themselves.[25] For him, to read works of art for what they reveal about the style of the period or the mind of the artist would be to submit to the scientific regime of enunciation. In the case of religious images, at least, it would be to miss their meaning entirely.

A critical problem with this approach, however, is that it is far too general in its application. Latour is unable to distinguish between the different ways in which works of art strike a balance between referential and performative meaning. Consider, for example, Piero della Francesca's fifteenth-century painting now known as 'The Flagellation of Christ'. The work has a rigorously calculated scheme of linear perspective, allowing for the placing of the figures in three-dimensional space to be determined quite precisely. Scholars have even been able to reconstruct the ground plan, showing the spatial locations of the figures and buildings. In the interpretations of art historians, the referential function of the picture is related to Piero's training and expertise in mathematics, his purpose in painting the picture, the context in which it was to be displayed, and so on.[26] Mechanisms of pictorial reference, in other words, depend on a whole set of conventions that are, to some degree, tied to specific historical contexts. One can grasp this by reflecting that the costumes and architectural elements in Piero's painting are typical of the Renaissance rather than of the biblical era the work depicts. Historical authenticity in these respects was not so important in Piero's time as it would subsequently become. Later artists would make use of new pictorial conventions to enhance the referential function of their works, just as Renaissance artists used the conventions of their own time, including linear perspective.

Art historians are surely right to insist that some discrimination of styles and genres is necessary to specify how art fulfils – or fails to fulfil – its referential function. Otherwise, couldn't Latour's account apply just as well to art not normally recognized as religious, or indeed to practices not normally thought of as art at all? Much twentieth-century art firmly thwarts representational expectations. So, is abstract art the most religious of all? (Some have suggested as much in connection with an artist like Mark Rothko.) What about other kinds of challenge to the representational tradition, such as those of the surrealists? When Marcel Duchamp exhibited a urinal as a piece of sculpture, was that a religious act? (Some people have thought it did look a bit like the Madonna.) Or what about when people engage in political demonstrations, or wave banners to support their teams at sporting events? These are acts that are unquestionably performative in the way they make meaning. Is all of this, also, religion? It seems that a serious problem with Latour's analysis is its inability to differentiate between true religious art and a more general domain of aesthetic expression.

Latour does seem to realize that he needs to address issues of aesthetics and to distinguish aesthetic appreciation from what he wants to claim is the authentically religious meaning of certain works of art. He rejects the suggestion that he is proposing to reduce religious imagery to its purely aesthetic function, asserting that such a reduction would be as unsatisfactory as attempts to rationalize religion or to explain it in symbolic terms. Art, he writes, offers neither salvation nor conversion; it is too mysterious, enigmatic, and spiritual.[27] But it remains the case that the focus on art does lead Latour to tend to conflate religious experience with artistic appreciation. Non-believers, at least, will find it difficult to distinguish between the quality of the 'presence' supposedly enacted by artifacts, rituals, and music in a religious context and a purely aesthetic appreciation of those creative forms. Many non-believers will say that they do appreciate religious art, literature, and music for their purely aesthetic qualities, and it is hard to see how Latour could convince them that they are missing something.

There is another problem besetting Latour's analysis, concerning his use of the category of 'religion'. He repeatedly talks about religion as a single entity, as if what he says applies to all religious orientations, although he draws examples only from his own Catholic tradition. He evokes the etymological origins of *religio* as a 'tying together' of entities, which he understands as the construction of networks of signs and images. He shows no awareness of the recent scholarship that has shown how 'religion' and 'science' emerged as comprehensive categories in the course of the last few centuries. Peter Harrison, for example, has described how the two concepts came to embrace a wide range of intellectual and social phenomena, and were defined in ways that increasingly set them in opposition to one another, between the seventeenth and nineteenth centuries.[28] Latour also overlooks recent work on the subtleties of the interactions between the two domains, represented for example in this volume, much of which has tended to deconstruct the global concepts and their categorical opposition.

At the same time that he casually talks about religion as a single entity, Latour is scornful of attempts by the social or human sciences to comprehend it within their intellectual schemes. He rejects the notion of encompassing religion as a whole within the scientific regime of enunciation.[29] On the other hand, to define it (as he does) in terms of semiotics looks like another way of subjecting it to the human sciences by reducing it to an expression of representational practices.[30] Having dismissed the claims of the sciences to understand religion, isn't Latour offering a replacement cast from the same mould? Discussing religion as a certain kind of human phenomenon, even if not in conventional sociological or historical terms, could be said to be placing oneself broadly within the tradition of the modern human sciences, which have repeatedly characterized religion as a universal category of human culture. Latour shares this perspective, seeing religion as a human phenomenon to the extent that he even professes himself comfortable with the idea that humans fabricate their own deities. After all, for him – in religion as in science – something 'constructed' is at the same time completely real. Those who pioneered the study of religion as an aspect of human culture thus deserve credit for realizing that gods are human creations, according to Latour. He even suggests that Voltaire, Feuerbach, Nietzsche, Marx, and Freud should be canonized as fathers of the Church![31]

Not all religious believers will welcome such a provocation. Those who hold certain theological doctrines as central to their faith will see Latour's analysis as another version of the human sciences' attempt to explain religion – and thereby to explain it away. Such an attempt is often seen as patronizing of believers, as well as of their beliefs. Latour is aware that this might be some people's reaction. He compares the human scientists' study of religion with sociologists' studies of science. In each case, the studies proceed by bracketing out of consideration the question of the ontological status of the entities that each group believes in. Scholars engaged in religious studies do not debate the reality of the Holy Spirit, any more than those in science studies feel they have to decide whether the entities the scientists talk about – such as genes, atoms, and electrons – really exist. This kind of agnosticism drew howls of protest in the course of the 'science wars' of the 1990s. It seemed outrageous to some leading scientists that sociologists of science professed an indifference to the truth or otherwise of scientific beliefs. Latour's own work was prominent among those that provoked such a reaction.[32] Now he is courting a similar response from religious believers. Indeed, he seems to be going beyond the degree of professional agnosticism characteristic of religious studies when he specifically discounts the referential function of religious language.[33] Some people of faith may be happy to go along with this, willing to give up a seemingly hopeless competition with science to establish the factual reality of the entities they invoke. Many, however, will want to insist on the ontological reality of the things they believe in and will not be happy to have their religion reduced to the manipulation of signs that lack any reference to the real world.

HISTORICAL IMPLICATIONS

By this point, some of the limitations of Latour's analysis of religion should be apparent. First, he depends on personal responses and a rather cursory understanding of art history to advance his interpretations of religious art. Thus he ignores issues of style, genre, audience, and so on that art historians have established are crucial to interpreting the meanings – whether referential or performative – of artistic works. As a result he does not satisfactorily discriminate between religious and aesthetic responses to art, music, and ritual. Second, he advances an interpretation of religion that proposes to account for it in terms of the human sciences, broadly defined, though without rigorous methodological preparation. Thus he generalizes about the nature of religion and about the functions of religious language. Such language surely *is* often taken as referential, even if attempts to back up the reference by layering representational images on top of one another are not normally taken very far.[34] Religious believers can justifiably be offended by Latour's attack on the notion that they actually believe anything, although they might accept that their beliefs are not subject to scientific verification and that reference to reality is not the only function of religious language. The metaphysical implications of Latour's semiotic analysis get him into trouble here, as they did with the scientists whose beliefs he also called into question by reducing them to an incidental product of semiotic practices.

A third, perhaps more fundamental, weakness in Latour's account of religion is its lack of responsiveness to history. As we have seen, understanding the meanings of religious art requires an analysis of the artistic conventions prevailing in a particular context. Similarly, charting the relations between religion and other domains of social or cultural experience, such as art and science, is a task for historical analysis. We need some account of the complex historical changes, unfolding over several centuries, that are often summed up as the process of 'secularization'.[35] Latour does have an account of secularization, albeit a highly schematic one. His description of the 'modern era' emphasizes that it was founded on a fundamental segregation of facts from values and nature from society. For Latour, this dichotomy, which he calls the 'modern constitution', amounts to a kind of fall from grace, a wound at the heart of modern culture that needs to be healed. He acknowledges the influence of Alfred North Whitehead, who wrote of the 'bifurcation of nature' created by the emergence of modern science and philosophy.[36] Becoming 'non-modern' or 'amodern' requires us to reject this modern constitution, to reconcile facts and values, and to recognize the interpenetration of nature and society. In relation to religion, it means redressing the feature that Latour calls 'the crossed-out God', whereby the divinity is removed from any direct activity in either nature or society but remains available as a 'spiritual' entity in individuals' private experience.[37] It also means abandoning the iconoclasm that reads religious images as inadequate scientific representations and overcoming the simplification that portrays religion as a system of naïve beliefs.[38]

As a general model, this may have its virtues, but a subtle grasp of historical periodization is not one of them. Latour surely overstates his case when he asserts that religion has only been construed as a system of beliefs since science established its epistemological primacy – to the degree that it did – in the seventeenth century (or since the sixteenth-century Reformation, as he sometimes suggests).[39] Did Christians of prior centuries really not consider their religion as a set of doctrines? What were all those theological disputations and heresy trials about, if not? More probably, the conception of religion as primarily a matter of belief emerged in the course of doctrinal disputes over many centuries, against Jews and Muslims, against those judged 'heretics', and between Catholics and Protestants.[40] Latour proposes that the conception of religion as a matter of belief was a product of the conflict between science and religion.[41] But this probably ascribes too much influence to what we would recognize as scientific modes of knowledge in the early modern period, when such knowledge was actually a good deal more contested and insecure than has often been supposed. It was surely possible for early modern thinkers to conceive of religion in terms of a commitment to certain doctrinal beliefs without invoking the sciences as a model of factual knowledge.

On the other hand, the notion that science provided an epistemic model that influenced conceptions of religion has more plausibility in the nineteenth century, when the cultural authority accorded to science had increased considerably. Latour's perspective highlights episodes in that period when religious thought did attempt to appropriate the methods of science to try to create factual knowledge of its own. Religious ideas, such as the survival of human life after death, were reinterpreted in the nineteenth century as aspects of a 'spiritual' realm supposedly lying beyond the natural world. And this realm was thought to be knowable through the kind of epistemic practices already being used in the natural sciences. Thus investigators used new technologies, including the electric telegraph and photography, to secure evidence of this supernatural domain.[42] They claimed that the telegraph delivered messages from the spirit world and that photographs could show its inhabitants. They explored experimental phenomena, such as the 'sensitive flame', which appeared to manifest spiritual entities.[43] The use of these methods was testimony to the prestige of science, which stood high enough that its methods were conceded a monopoly on the means of producing factual knowledge. In such cases it was assumed that religion can exploit the practices of science to reveal a world beyond scientific experience, that representations could be mobilized to yield a reference in the realm of the supernatural.

The use of such practices in connection with religious beliefs continues into our own times, although it perhaps holds a more marginal place in scientific and religious institutions than it once enjoyed. Experimental methods are still sometimes used to investigate purported miracles, as when carbon-dating techniques were applied to the Turin Shroud.[44] Instances like this can be taken to show the dominance of what Latour calls the 'fetishism' that privileges scientific practice as a mode of knowledge-production in the modern era. In studying this kind of overlap between scientific and religious domains, historians might derive some benefit from Latour's perspective. He has shown how scientific practice constructs representations of hidden and distant entities by aligning signs and images. By these means it discloses an invisible world beyond immediate perception. Insofar as it does so, science shares metaphysical preoccupations with religion. But the common features of science and religion are not only to be understood on the grounds of metaphysics: no less crucial are the concrete practices that enable that metaphysics to be constructed. It is these that Latour's analysis highlights: the instances where religious language *is* intended to be referential (and not just reverential), where it does aspire to an epistemic function. Doing so, it mobilizes epistemic practices that are common to science, a tribute to the authority of scientific modes of constructing knowledge in modern culture.

To suggest such an application of Latour's ideas about science and religion is to read him selectively and perhaps rather perversely. Rather than following his assertions as to what distinguishes science from religion, I propose we use his insights into science to discern what religion has – at certain times and places – shared with science. For Latour this is exactly the wrong way to understand or practise religion, which should not attempt to mimic the epistemic practices of the sciences. But, historically, it seems to me necessary to recognize that that is often what it has done, and indeed that Latour may have something to contribute in terms of showing us how. My suggestion, therefore, is that Latour's perspective on science has an application to religion, but one that is more complementary than contrasting and narrower in its historical range than he himself claims. Latour displays the social connections of scientific knowledge but sometimes seems to regard religion as personal and private. I am proposing that his most important insights concern those features religion shares with science, when it assumes the function of producing knowledge and hence becomes implicated in networks of representations, instruments, and artifacts, as science is.[45] I therefore suggest we should look beyond Latour's comments on his personal religious sentiments and should not be deflected by the obvious deficiencies of his analysis of religious art. The connections he points out between scientific and religious techniques of making knowledge may be more historically specific than he acknowledges, but they are nonetheless important features of the modern era. Latour's insights may not illuminate 'religion' as such, even assuming such a thing can be identified in general, but they do offer some useful pointers to the intersection of scientific and religious practices.

There may well be other features of value in Latour's discussion of religion. I have approached his writings on the subject as an historian, seeking to place them within the traditions of the human sciences and to consider their value to historians of science and religion. I have not adopted the stance of a theologian or a believer, and I may have been wrong in anticipating a generally negative response from those quarters.[46] I do think that Latour's analysis deserves more than embarrassed neglect from secular-minded readers, even if it is hard to envision any of them being won over to the kind of religious devotion he upholds. It is in fact rather difficult to assess who might be persuaded by Latour's writings on religion, although his ideas certainly have the appeal of startling originality. His mode of argument is suggestive and ironic rather than rigorous or exhaustive, and he frequently uses the rhetorical tactic of emphasizing how weak his case is, how it is assailed from all sides by apparently fatal objections. This willingness to make himself seem vulnerable is one of Latour's most appealing features, if sometimes also a frustrating one. A certain line of development of French philosophy, from Montaigne to Foucault, has explored the potential of self-exposure as a means of intellectual exploration. Latour could be placed in that tradition as well. His writings on religion are exercises in self-development that take some significant personal risks, inviting us as readers to find ourselves as the author has found himself in the writing. For taking these risks, for making the transgressive gesture of introducing personal religious feelings into the hostile environment of secular academic discourse, Bruno Latour deserves our thanks.

NOTES

1   Bruno Latour, 'How to be iconophilic in art, science, and religion?', in Caroline A. Jones and Peter Galison (eds.), *Picturing science producing art* (New York: Routledge, 1998), pp. 418–40, on p. 433.

2   See esp.: Bruno Latour, 'Postmodern? No, simply amodern! Steps towards an anthropology of science', *Studies in History and Philosophy of Science* 21 (1990), 145–71; Latour, *We have never been modern*, trans. Catherine Porter (Cambridge, MA: Harvard University Press, 1993). It is worth noting, nonetheless, that Latour's approach shares some features with those of other writers usually classified as postmodern, including: an opposition to dualistic systems of metaphysics, a focus on the single ontological level of images and representations, a challenge to the epistemic claims of science, a willingness to remove the human subject from the centre of epistemological concerns, and perhaps also the deployment of a playful and ironic style of writing.

3   On this point, see Bruno Latour, 'Nature at the cross-road: The bifurcation of nature and its end', and 'What is the style of matters of concern?': Lectures given in Amsterdam for the Spinoza Chair in Philosophy, University of Amsterdam, April and May 2005, available at: www.bruno-latour.fr/articles/ article/97-STYLE-MATTERS-CONCERN.pdf

4 Those who follow Latour and Michel Callon in this 'Actor network theory' give a semiotic account of scientific and technological practice that portrays humans and non-humans in equivalent roles. On the other hand, many sociologists and most historians have been unwilling to reduce entities with quite distinct powers of agency to the same ontological level. For a discussion of this, see John H. Zammito, *A nice derangement of epistemes: Post-positivism in the study of science from Quine to Latour* (Chicago: University of Chicago Press, 2004), pp. 183–202.

5 The most pertinent articles are Latour, 'How to be iconophilic'; Latour, '"Thou shalt not take the Lord's name in vain": Being a sort of sermon on the hesitations of religious speech', *Res: Anthropology and Aesthetics* 39 (Spring 2001), 215–35 (available at: www.bruno-latour.fr/articles/article/079.html); Latour, '"Thou shall not freeze-frame", or, how not to misunderstand the science and religion debate', in James D. Proctor (ed.), *Science, religion, and the human experience* (New York: Oxford University Press, 2005), pp. 27–48. In addition, see esp.: Latour, *Jubiler – ou les tourments de la parole religieuse* (Paris: Le Seuil, 2002), a book with an unusual and slightly forbidding form: 207 pages of continuous text, beginning on the front cover and continuing onto the back, with no chapter or section breaks. A literal translation of the title would be: 'To rejoice: or the torments of religious speech'. Or perhaps: 'To celebrate the jubilee . . .', which captures the allusion to the fact that the year 2000 was designated a Jubilee Year by the Catholic Church.

6 Exceptions are two articles that appropriate Latour for the authors' own postmodern theological purposes: Robert Matthew Geraci, 'Signaling static: Artistic, religious, and scientific truths in a relational ontology', *Zygon* 40 (2005), 953–74; Simon Oliver, 'The Eucharist before nature and culture', *Modern Theology* 15 (1999), 331–53. A valuable commentary is also provided by an article I discovered only after writing this chapter: Martin Holbraad, 'Response to Bruno Latour's "Thou shall not freeze-frame"', *Mana: Estudos de antropologia social* 10 (2004), 349–76.

7 Latour, 'Thou shall not freeze-frame', 27. See also Latour, *Jubiler*, pp. 1–17. Compare a rather startling aside in another article, where he mentions his praying in the same breath as his battle against colon cancer: Latour, 'Why has critique run out of steam? From matters of fact to matters of concern', *Critical Inquiry* 30 (2004), 225–48, on 243.

8 There are clear parallels between Latour's rejection of the notion that religion is to be characterized in terms of beliefs and the 'non-realism' developed in other varieties of postmodern theology. I cannot pursue these parallels here, but readers who wish to do so will find useful points of departure in the following collections: Andrew Moore and Michael Scott (eds.), *Realism and religion: Philosophical and theological perspectives* (Aldershot: Ashgate, 2007); Gavin Hyman (ed.), *New directions in philosophical theology: Essays in honour of Don Cupitt* (Aldershot: Ashgate, 2004); Graham Ward (ed.), *The Blackwell companion to postmodern theology* (Oxford: Blackwell, 2001).

9 There is more to Latour's analysis of the construction of scientific knowledge, but these are the essential features as regards the comparison with religion. For a fuller picture, see esp.: Bruno Latour, *Science in action: How to follow scientists and engineers through society* (Cambridge, MA: Harvard University Press, 1987).

10 Bruno Latour and Steve Woolgar, *Laboratory life: The construction of scientific facts*, 2nd edn (Princeton, NJ: Princeton University Press, 1986); Latour, *Science in action*, pp. 174–5.

11 See esp. H. M. Collins and Steven Yearley, 'Epistemological chicken', in Andrew Pickering (ed.), *Science as practice and culture* (Chicago: University of Chicago Press, 1992), pp. 301–26; Simon Schaffer, 'The eighteenth Brumaire of Bruno Latour', *Studies in History and Philosophy of Science* 22 (1991), 174–92; (for a summary of the debate) Jan Golinski, *Making natural knowledge: Constructivism and the history of science* (Cambridge: Cambridge University Press, 1998), pp. 27–46.

12 Latour, 'Thou shall not freeze-frame', 45 (italics in original).

13 Latour, 'How to be iconophilic', 433.

14 Richard Dawkins, *The blind watchmaker* (London: Penguin Books, 1988), pp. 5–6; Christopher Hitchens, *God is not great: How religion poisons everything* (New York: Twelve, 2007), p. 64.

15 Hence, perhaps, the Archbishop of Westminster's reported remark that believers are mistaken to regard God as 'a fact in the world'. See the BBC News report of a lecture by Cardinal Cormac Murphy-O'Connor, 9 May 2008, at: news.bbc.co.uk/2/hi/uk_news/7390941.stm

16 See esp. Ronald L. Numbers, *The creationists: From scientific creationism to intelligent design*, expanded edn (Cambridge, MA: Harvard University Press, 2006).

17 On Intelligent Design, see Numbers, *Creationists*, pp. 373–98; Robert T. Pennock (ed.), *Intelligent design creationism and its critics: Philosophical, theological, and scientific perspectives* (Cambridge, MA: MIT Press, 2001).

18 Latour, 'Thou shall not freeze-frame', 31. See also Latour, *Jubiler*, pp. 30–1, 58–9, 84–8.

19 Latour, 'How to be iconophilic', 432.

20 Ibid., 434.

21 Latour, 'Thou shalt not take the Lord's name'. See also Latour, *Jubiler*, pp. 7–9.

22 Latour, 'Thou shalt not take the Lord's name'.

23 Latour, *Jubiler*, pp. 143–66.

24 Latour, 'How to be iconophilic', 432. Compare the discussions of art in Latour, 'Thou shall not freeze-frame', 39–44; Latour, 'Thou shalt not take the Lord's name'.

25 Latour, 'How to be iconophilic', 423, 437.

26 J. V. Field, 'Mathematics and the craft of painting: Piero della Francesca and perspective', in J. V. Field and Frank A. J. L. James (eds.), *Renaissance and revolution: Humanists, scholars, craftsmen and natural philosophers in early modern Europe* (Cambridge: Cambridge University Press, 1993), pp. 73–95.

27 Latour, *Jubiler*, pp. 123–5.

28 Peter Harrison, *'Religion' and the religions in the English Enlightenment* (Cambridge: Cambridge University Press, 1990); see also Harrison's chapter in the present volume.

29 Latour, 'Thou shall not freeze-frame', 28.

30 On the interpretive tradition in the human sciences, see Roger Smith, *Being human: Historical knowledge and the creation of human nature* (Manchester: Manchester University Press, 2007), pp. 122–72.

31 Latour, *Jubiler*, pp. 166–72.

32 On the scandal surrounding Latour's work among scientists, see Zammito, *Nice derangement*, pp. 183–95, 251–70; Barbara Herrnstein Smith, *Scandalous knowledge: Science, truth and the human* (Durham, NC: Duke University Press, 2006), pp. 1–17; Alan Sokal and Jean Bricmont, *Fashionable nonsense: Postmodern intellectuals' abuse of science* (New York: Picador USA, 1998), pp. 124–33. Latour attempted to placate some of this outrage, and to diagnose its cause, in Latour, *Pandora's hope: Essays on the reality of science studies* (Cambridge, MA: Harvard University Press, 1999).

33 While this stance is shared by some theologians and philosophers of religion, it contravenes the neutrality normally adopted in the discipline of religious studies. On the latter, see Robert A. Segal, 'The contribution of the social sciences to the study of religion: Correcting misconstruals', paper delivered at conference on 'Science and Religion: Historical and Contemporary Perspectives', University of Lancaster, 23–26 July 2007.

34 My thanks to the late Peter Lipton for pressing this point in the discussion following my initial presentation of this paper. See also Lipton, 'Science and religion: The immersion solution', in Moore and Scott, *Realism and religion*, pp. 31–46.

35 Of course, as John Brooke and others have pointed out, one can easily be misled by assuming that secularization has been a uniform or universal trend over recent centuries. The history is inevitably much more complex than that, although, as Charles Taylor has recently shown, the complexity of its history does not imply that the notion of secularization is without validity as a general framework, simply that it challenges us to characterize it in sufficient detail. See: John Hedley Brooke, *Science and religion: Some historical perspectives* (Cambridge: Cambridge University Press, 1991); Charles Taylor, *A secular age* (Cambridge, MA: Harvard University Press, 2007).

36 Latour, 'Thou shalt not take the Lord's name'.

37 Latour, *We have never been modern*, pp. 32–5.

38 Bruno Latour, 'A few steps toward an anthropology of the iconoclastic gesture', *Science in Context* 10 (1997), 63–83, on 81. See also: Latour, *We have never been modern*; Oliver, 'The Eucharist', for a sympathetic reading of Latour on the 'modern constitution'.

39 Latour, *We have never been modern*, pp. 13–20; Latour, 'Thou shalt not take the Lord's name'.

40 See Harrison, *'Religion' and the religions*, which traces the history of the identification of religion with factual or propositional knowledge in English

Protestant thought during the Reformation, the Scientific Revolution, and the subsequent Enlightenment; see also Harrison's chapter in the present volume.

41 Latour, *Jubiler*, p. 35.

42 On spiritualism, see: Janet Oppenheim, *The other world: Spiritualism and psychical research in England, 1850–1914* (Cambridge: Cambridge University Press, 1985); Deborah Blum, *Ghost hunters: William James and the search for scientific proof of life after death* (New York: Penguin Press, 2006). On the telegraph, see Richard J. Noakes, 'Telegraphy is an occult art: Cromwell Fleetwood Varley and the diffusion of electricity to the other world', *British Journal for the History of Science* 32 (1999), 421–59. On spirit photography, see Jennifer Tucker, *Nature exposed: Photography as eyewitness in Victorian science* (Baltimore, MD: Johns Hopkins University Press, 2005), pp. 65–125.

43 Richard Noakes, 'The "bridge which is between physical and psychical research": William Fletcher Barrett, sensitive flames, and spiritualism', *History of Science* 42 (2004), 419–64.

44 For a discussion of these studies, see H. E. Gove, 'Dating the Turin Shroud – An assessment', *Radiocarbon* 32 (1990), 87–92.

45 My thanks to Thomas Dixon for suggesting this way of putting it.

46 Compare, for example, the favourable responses by Oliver, 'The Eucharist'; Geraci, 'Signaling static'.

PART II

Narratives

CHAPTER 4

Religion and the changing historiography of the Scientific Revolution

Margaret J. Osler

The notion of the 'Scientific Revolution', spanning roughly the period from 1500 to 1700, has served as the linch-pin for historians of science from at least the late nineteenth century, although it did not acquire that name until the 1930s.[1] Encompassing the time between Copernicus and Newton, it has traditionally served as the *terminus ad quem* for the ancient and medieval developments that preceded it and the *terminus a quo* for all that followed.[2] According to traditional accounts, this period witnessed the birth of modern science and its attendant methods and institutions.[3] Not itself an explanatory concept, the Scientific Revolution has become the focus for questions that guide historians of science, questions about what it was, what exactly happened, why it happened, and why it happened when and where it did.[4] The past century has witnessed many changes in the historiography of the Scientific Revolution. Yet, as this chapter will demonstrate, there has been a close interrelation between conceptions of the Scientific Revolution and assumptions about the relationship between science and religion. Focussing on the way the Scientific Revolution was defined in the late nineteenth and throughout the twentieth centuries, a period when science and religion were generally portrayed as separate, analysis of the formation of that view and its ultimate demise will highlight the close relationship between changes in the historiography of the Scientific Revolution, on the one hand, and ideas about the relationship between science and religion, on the other.

The history of science, although not at that time a recognized academic discipline, assumed its modern form during the eighteenth and nineteenth centuries, a period that witnessed the growth of many other historical disciplines. For example, in the *Encyclopédie, ou dictionnaire raisonné des sciences, des arts et des métiers, par une société de gens de lettres* (1751–80) Denis Diderot (1713–84) and Jean le Rond d'Alembert (1717–83) gave several historical accounts of the sciences and the methodology on which they were founded. They praised thinkers of the seventeenth

century – Francis Bacon (1561–1626), René Descartes (1596–1650), Isaac
Newton (1642–1727), and John Locke (1632–1704) – for casting off
scholasticism, 'the blind admiration for antiquity', and 'the abuse which
a few powerful theologians dared to make of the submission of peoples',
traditions and practices that the encyclopaedists regarded as obstacles to
the development of the sciences.[5] Diderot and d'Alembert admired the
achievements of science and its method of enquiry while scorning what
they considered the irrationality and authoritarian attitude of religion.

THE LONG SHADOW OF POSITIVISM

Two lines of thought deeply influenced the way historians of science
understood the relationship between science and religion during the
nineteenth century: the positivism of Auguste Comte (1798–1857) and
Ernst Mach (1838–1916), on the one hand, and, in North America, the
controversies surrounding the establishment of the teaching of science
within secular universities, on the other.

In his *Cours de philosophie positive* (1830–42), Comte articulated several
principles, each of which directly influenced the way subsequent historians
understood the relationship between science and religion.[6] He maintained
that only claims based on direct observation can be considered legitimate
knowledge. He propounded an historical 'law' according to which both
humanity in general and the developing individual pass through three
stages: (1) a theological stage, in which events are explained by divine actions;
(2) a metaphysical stage, in which events are explained by the influence of
forces and essences; and (3) a positive or scientific stage, in which knowledge
is based on observation and empirical evidence. In addition to this vision of
historical development, Comte proposed an epistemological 'law', which
classified the sciences in a hierarchy determined by their sequence of arriving
at the positive state and their increasing complexity. Comte regarded mathematics as the fundamental science because it was the simplest, dealing with
the most abstract concepts, and was the first to to achieve positive status. In
order of complexity astronomy, physics, chemistry, biology, and sociology
followed in the hierarchy he described.[7] He envisaged that in time each of
these more concrete sciences would be reduced to mathematically expressed
laws. Accordingly Comte initiated an historiography that saw developments
in the mathematical and physical sciences as the model for the history of all
the other sciences. Yet religion had to be eschewed before positive science
could progress.

Because metaphysics – claims about ultimate reality – could not be proven empirically and because such claims were traditionally associated with religion, positivist thinkers attempted to expunge all metaphysics from the realm of positive knowledge. Further elaborating positivism as a philosophy of science, Ernst Mach, whose rejection of metaphysics in *Die Mechanik in ihrer Entwicklung historisch-critisch dargestellt* (1883) located the origin of modern science in Galileo Galilei's (1564–1642) transition from his adhering to Aristotelian mechanics to his framing of a concept of inertial motion, reinforced Comte's emphasis on the mathematical sciences. Like Comte, Mach thought that there had been steady progress in science from the darkness of the middle ages to the Enlightenment of the eighteenth century. He blamed religion for the slow progress of science in earlier periods:

It stands to reason that in a stage of civilization in which religion is almost the sole education, and the only theory of the world, people would naturally look at things from a theological point of view, and that they would believe that this view was possessed of competency in all fields of research. If we transport ourselves back to the time when people played the organ with their fists, when they had to have the multiplication table visibly before them to calculate, when they did so much with their hands that people now-a-days do with their heads, we shall not demand of such a time that it should *critically* put to the test its own views and theories.[8]

Although Mach rejected Comte's notion that all the sciences could be reduced to mathematics and physics,[9] he envisioned the Scientific Revolution as the period when science became largely independent of theology – a process that was completed by the end of the eighteenth century:

During the entire sixteenth and seventeenth centuries, down to the close of the eighteenth, the prevailing inclination of inquirers was, to find in all physical laws some particular disposition of the Creator. But a gradual transformation of these views must strike the attentive observer. Whereas with Descartes and Leibniz physics and theology were still greatly intermingled, in the subsequent period a distinct endeavour is noticeable, not indeed wholly to discard theology, yet to separate it from the purely physical questions. Theological disquisitions were put at the beginning or relegated to the end of physical treatises. Theological speculations were restricted, as much as possible, to the question of creation, that, from this point onward, the way might be cleared for physics.

Towards the close of the eighteenth century a remarkable change took place – a change which was apparently an abrupt departure from the current trend of thought, but in reality was the logical outcome of the development indicated. After an attempt in a youthful work to found mechanics on Euler's principle of least action, Lagrange, in a subsequent treatment of the subject, declared his intention of utterly disregarding theological and metaphysical speculations, as in their nature precarious and foreign to science . . . All subsequent scientists of eminence accepted

Lagrange's view, and the present attitude of physics to theology was thus substantially determined.

The idea that theology and physics are two distinct branches of knowledge, thus took, from its first germination in Copernicus till its final promulgation by Lagrange, almost two centuries to attain clearness in the minds of investigators.[10]

Mach argued that despite Newton's avowed religiosity, he maintained a clear demarcation between religion and science, as did both Galileo and Christiaan Huygens (1625–95). Mach insisted that although these great minds of the seventeenth century made huge strides, 'rationalism does not seem to have gained a broad theatre of action till the literature of the eighteenth century'.[11] Regardless of the precise chronological details, Mach understood the history of science to involve a steady separation of science from metaphysics and religion. Mach's outline of the history of science and its increasing disengagement from religion and theology profoundly influenced the formation of the history of science as an academic discipline in the twentieth century.[12]

The other major influence on the historiography of science and religion came from American defenders of secular education in the sciences. Although arguments about secular education occurred in many countries, its American defenders exerted a formative influence on attitudes about the relationship between science and religion. Their defensive strategies reinforced the anti-metaphysical and anti-religious approach of positivism. John William Draper (1811–82), an English chemist and physiologist who moved to the United States as a young man, argued that human history consisted of a battle between advocates of constant supernatural intervention in the world and those who regarded both the natural and human worlds as governed by one universal law. In his *History of the conflict between religion and science* (1875), Draper's target was the Roman Catholic Church, which had recently published a 'Syllabus of Errors', according to which public institutions teaching literature and science should conform to the authority of the Church. In another proclamation, deemed offensive by Draper, the Church had declared the Pope's infallibility in matters of faith and morals.[13]

Similarly, educational issues propelled Andrew Dickson White (1832–1918), the founding president of Cornell University, to write *A history of the warfare of science with theology in Christendom* (1896) as a corrective to Draper, emphasizing that the problem lay with theology rather than religion *per se*. Deeply troubled by the opposition he faced from various clergymen as he set out to establish a secular university, White used the metaphor of warfare to characterize the relationship between science and theology.[14] Surveying the history of every field of science to provide evidence for his thesis that religion is necessarily hostile to and impairs the development of science, White cited Galileo Galilei's conflict with the Roman Catholic Church during the first third of the seventeenth century as a prime example of the warfare that religion waged on science.[15] White's use of the warfare metaphor dominated discussions of the relationship between science and religion until the 1980s, when historians of science began to articulate a more nuanced understanding of the relationship.

The attitudes of the positivists and White deeply influenced the field of the history of science as it developed in the early twentieth century. George Sarton (1884–1956), founder and first editor of the flagship journal *Isis* (1912) and founder of the institutional history of science in North America, shared the outlook of the positivists. His vision of the history of science as the new humanism grew directly out of his commitment to Comtean positivism.[16] He stated that 'Auguste Comte must be considered as the founder of the history of science, or at least as the first who had a clear and precise, if not a complete, apprehension of it'.[17] In line with his endorsement of Comtean positivism – evident in many of his attitudes – Sarton accepted the idea that a gradual and increasing separation from religion marked the progress of science. 'The progress of science is absolutely dependent upon its emancipation from non-scientific issues, whatever they be, and in particular, upon its laicization'.[18]

Science and religion have never ceased to influence one another, even in our own time and in the countries where science has reached a high degree of perfection and independence. But of course the younger science was, and the farther we go back through the ages, the more numerous these interactions are.[19]

Although he acknowledged that sometimes the interaction between science and religion has been positive ('I know many cases where the priests themselves have been the transmitters of knowledge from one generation to the following'),[20] he stated that most of the interactions 'have often had an aggressive character'.[21] Sarton explicitly referred to Andrew Dickson White's warfare metaphor and accepted White's claim that the real warfare has been between science and theology.

Influenced by these traditions and focussing on the period from 1500 to 1700 that became known as the Scientific Revolution, historians of science in the twentieth century tended to see what they considered a progressive separation of science from religion. According to this interpretation, the study of nature and its parts was embedded in a theological matrix during the middle ages. The Renaissance witnessed an increased emphasis on the human capacity to understand and control the natural world. Developments during the sixteenth and seventeenth centuries, starting with Copernicus and culminating in the work of Isaac Newton, resulted in the growing separation of science and religion and thus led to the view of knowledge that has increasingly characterized western culture from the Enlightenment to the present day.

An historiography based on the idea of the Scientific Revolution was central to this interpretation. Starting in the 1920s, a number of historians – including Edwin Arthur Burtt, Alexandre Koyré, Herbert Butterfield, and Richard S. Westfall – saw the Scientific Revolution as the central episode in the history of science. Earlier attempts to explain the world were judged by the extent to which they led to the Scientific Revolution, and subsequent developments were understood as following from these early modern developments. The Scientific Revolution became so important that it became common to question why other cultures did not have one.[22] Most of these historians of science have agreed that the Scientific Revolution was a dramatic break with earlier ways of thinking and that it resulted in a profound change in the concept of nature. Accordingly the medieval philosophers, who drew on both Aristotle and the Bible, were portrayed as having understood the cosmos to be finite, hierarchical, and qualitatively differentiated. The natural world was considered to be the stage for human probation and redemption. Theology was the queen of the sciences. God created the world and designed its parts with care. His providence applied both to the universe as a whole and to human beings in particular. In contrast, the universe after Newton was thought to be infinite, uniform, and isomorphic, fully understandable in mathematical terms. In the words of Richard S. Westfall, 'the idea of the Scientific Revolution has been our central organizing idea ... Scientists of today can read and recognize works done after 1687. It takes a historian to comprehend those written before 1543'.[23] Some historians claimed that the Scientific Revolution witnessed the elimination of finality, miracles, spirit, and providence from the natural world. Projecting twentieth-century metaphysical presuppositions onto the ostensibly revolutionary thought of early modern natural philosophers, E. A. Burtt declared in 1924:

Medieval philosophy, attempting to solve the ultimate *why* of events instead of their immediate *how*, and thus stressing the principle of final causality (for the answer to such a question could only be given in terms of purpose or use), had its appropriate conception of God. Here was the teleological hierarchy of the Aristotelian forms, all heading up in God or Pure Form, with man intermediate in reality and importance between him and the material world. The final *why* of events in the latter could be explained mainly in terms of their use to man; the final *why* of human activities in terms of the ultimate quest for union with God. Now [in the seventeenth century], with the superstructure from man up banished from the primary realm, which for Galileo is identified with material atoms in their mathematical relations, the *how* of events being the sole object of exact study, there had appeared no place for final causality whatsoever. The real world is simply a succession of atomic motions in mathematical continuity. Under these circumstances causality could only be intelligibly lodged in the motions of the atoms themselves, everything that happens being regarded as the effect solely of mathematical changes in these material elements.[24]

This process of separation was said to continue through the Enlightenment and to culminate in Darwin's *Descent of man* (1871), which reduced human nature to that of the animals.

Although Burtt was not a positivist, he shared the encyclopaedists' and the positivists' account of the growing autonomy of science during the early modern period, but, instead of celebrating these developments, he lamented the loss that they represented and viewed them as laying the foundation for the rise of materialism and positivism in the early twentieth century. For Burtt, in contrast to the positivists, it was a change in metaphysical foundations that led to the rise of modern science, a change that he thought led to a distorted and one-sided philosophy of the human mind – a materialist interpretation of mind that neglected to account for 'a universe organized into a living and sensitive unity'.[25] He held Newton partially responsible for this development because he thought that Newton had reduced the deity to one of a number of metaphysical entities comprising the world:

Newton thus apparently takes for granted a postulate of extreme importance; he assumes, with so many others who bring an aesthetic interest into science, that the incomparable order, beauty, and harmony which characterizes the celestial realm in the large, is to be eternally preserved. It will not be preserved by space, time, mass, and ether alone; its preservation requires the continued exertion of that divine will which freely chose this order and harmony as the ends of his first creative toil. From the Protoplast of the whole, God has now descended to become a category among other categories; the facts of continued order, system, and uniformity as observed in the world, are inexplicable apart from him.[26]

Burtt based his interpretation of Newton's theology on Newton's published, 'scientific' works, thus overlooking Newton's passionate concern with theological issues, such as his rejection of the doctrine of the Trinity and his interest in the fulfilment of the biblical prophecies, interests that later scholars have found both vexing and revealing.[27] Despite the fact that, contrary to the positivists' rejection of metaphysics, Burtt saw a change in metaphysics as the driving force behind the Scientific Revolution and his concern about the apparently negative consequences of these developments, he shared the positivists' conviction that the period we call the Scientific Revolution witnessed the separation of science from religion and theology.

The historians responsible for formulating and promoting the historiography centred on the Scientific Revolution tended to divorce the important developments in science from religion and theology. Alexandre Koyré, probably the individual whose work most influenced thinking about the Scientific Revolution, described the revolution in terms of two fundamental conceptual changes: the dissolution of the cosmos and the mathematization of nature, both of which he ascribed to a rejection of Aristotelianism and an adoption of Platonism. Following Mach, he located this change in Galileo's shift from impetus physics to one based on an inertial concept of motion.[28] Despite his philosophical idealism, Koyré agreed with the positivists' hierarchical categorization of the sciences, giving priority to developments in mathematical physics. For Koyré, these changes were matters of abstract philosophy and physics but were unrelated to theology or religion, topics which had no place in his seminal work:

The infinite Universe of the New Cosmology, infinite in Duration as well as in Extension, in which eternal matter in accordance with eternal and necessary laws moves endlessly and aimlessly in eternal space, inherited all the ontological attributes of Divinity. Yet only those – all the others the departed God took away with him.[29]

Like the positivists and Koyré, Herbert Butterfield emphasized the centrality of astronomy and physics to the Scientific Revolution. Although he was not so hostile to religion as his predecessors – indeed, he was a practising Christian – he saw a decline of religion in the second half of the seventeenth century as an important part of a more general cultural change, of which the rise of science was an important aspect:

What was in question was a colossal secularisation of thought in every possible realm of ideas at the same time, after the extraordinarily religious character of much of the thinking of the seventeenth century . . . This came at the appropriate moment for combination with the work of the scientific revolution at the close of the seventeenth century; yet it would appear that it was not itself entirely the result of the scientific achievements – a certain decline of Christianity appears to have been taking place for independent reasons.[30]

Butterfield pointed to increasing urbanization that chipped away at the power of priests and princes, travel literature that questioned the universality and centrality of Christianity, and the rise of Deism as factors that worked along with advances in the sciences and led to a general decline of religion in the period.[31]

Westfall – loyal heir to the historiography of the Scientific Revolution as articulated by Burtt, Koyré, and Butterfield – reiterated these themes, and, in an odd way, his works exemplified them. In his book on the Scientific Revolution he made virtually no mention of religion or theology and focussed on the physical sciences and the mechanical philosophy, within the terms of which he attempted to incorporate all of the other sciences.[32] In his first book, *Science and religion in seventeenth-century England* (1958), he examined the struggles of the virtuosi (the term used by early members of the Royal Society to refer to adherents of the new experimental philosophy) with 'the new science' and the mechanical philosophy, both of which seemed to challenge traditional religious ideas such as miracles and providence. While fully attentive to the fact that the virtuosi were generally believers and wrote extensively on religious and theological themes, he interpreted much of their writing as a defence against what they perceived as an imminent threat to their religion, a threat coming from the new philosophy and new science. Indeed, the book concluded with an image of Newton fighting to stave off the inevitable secularization of his culture:

That picture of Newton in his old age writing and revising his statement on religion is the symbol of the insecurity that goaded the virtuosi as they sought a foundation for certainty. But certainty there was not to be. Following the birth of modern science the age of unshaken faith was lost to western man.[33]

While, in Westfall's view, the 'new science' threatened the foundations of religion, the same process made possible the emergence of modern science:

At least one ... dimension of the Scientific Revolution demands notice – a new relation between science and Christianity ... From the point of view of science, it does not seem excessive to speak of its liberation. Centuries before, as European civilization had taken form out of the chaos of the dark ages, Christianity had fostered, molded, and hence dominated every cultural and intellectual activity. By the end of the seventeenth century, science had asserted its autonomy.[34]

CHALLENGING POSITIVIST ASSUMPTIONS

Although Burtt, Koyré, Butterfield, and Westfall were not the only historians developing the concept of the Scientific Revolution in the middle decades of the twentieth century, they influenced the thinking of a generation of scholars, to whom they brought some unexamined assumptions formulated by the nineteenth-century positivists, namely the hierarchy of the sciences and the use of the mathematical sciences as models for changes in all other aspects of the study of nature. These assumptions have faced

major challenges since the 1970s. A new generation of scholars has challenged the viability of the historiography of the Scientific Revolution and
the concomitant claim that this period witnessed a separation between
science and religion.

Examples of these challenges abound, and I shall mention only a few. One
example is the debates surrounding Copernican astronomy that often reflected
theological positions and hinged on the relative weight given to theological,
philosophical, or astronomical claims.[35] For example, the Lutheran intellectuals around Wittenberg tended to use Copernican methods without
accepting his major cosmological views.[36] Indeed, Lutheran theology, especially Lutheran ideas about providence, may have been one of Kepler's
primary motives for seeking order in the cosmos.[37]

A second challenge arises from the many seventeenth-century natural
philosophers who rejected Aristotelianism, instead adopting some version
of the mechanical philosophy in order to explain natural phenomena in
terms of matter and motion. The particular theories of matter that they
adopted and their ideas about the epistemological status of knowledge
about the world reflected their theological presuppositions.[38]

Close examination of early modern texts refutes the claim of Burtt and
earlier historians of science that the adoption of the mechanical philosophy involved the rejection of teleological explanations, and, more generally, paved the way for materialism, Deism, and atheism. For example,
Pierre Gassendi (1592–1655) asserted that there is in fact a role for final
causes in physics – contrary to Francis Bacon and René Descartes, who
had ruled them out – and Robert Boyle (1627–91) published an entire
treatise on the role of final causes in natural philosophy.[39] Isaac Newton
(1642–1727) explicitly endorsed the appeal to final causes and argued that
natural philosophy, properly pursued, leads to knowledge of the Creator.
Thus in the fourth edition of his *Opticks* (1730) he wrote:

Whereas the main Business of Natural Philosophy is to argue from Phaenomena
without feigning Hypotheses, and to deduce Causes from Effects, till we come to
the very first Cause, which certainly is not mechanical; and not only to unfold the
Mechanism of the World, but chiefly to resolve these and such like Questions.
What is there in places almost empty of Matter, and whence is it that the Sun and
Planets gravitate towards one another, without dense Matter between them?
Whence is it that Nature does nothing in vain; and whence arises all that Order
and Beauty which we see in the World? ... How came the Bodies of Animals to
be contrived with so much Art and for what ends were their several Parts? Was
the eye conceived without Skill in Opticks, and the Ear without Knowledge of
Sounds? How do the Motions of the Body follow from the Will, and whence is
the Instinct in Animals? ... And these things being rightly dispatch'd, does it not

appear from Phaenomena that there is a Being incorporeal, living, intelligent, omnipresent, who in infinite Space, as it were in his Sensory, sees the things themselves intimately, and thoroughly perceives them, and comprehends them wholly by their immediate presence to himself ... And though every true Step made in this Philosophy brings us not immediately to the Knowledge of the first Cause, yet it brings us nearer to it.[40]

Here Newton explicitly invoked teleological explanations of natural phenomena that he thought provided a strong argument for the existence of God. For Newton, science and religion were intimately related.

Most importantly the entire enterprise of studying the natural world was embedded in a theological framework that emphasized divine creation, design, and providence.[41] These themes are prominent in the writings of almost all the major seventeenth-century natural philosophers. They believed that the study of the created world provided knowledge of the wisdom and intelligence of the Creator, and they used the argument from design to establish God's providential relationship to his creation.[42] Arguments for the immateriality and immortality of the human soul were evoked not only to prevent the mechanical philosophers from falling into materialism but also to define the limits of mechanism in early modern natural philosophy.[43] Newton, whose physics the traditional historians regarded as the climax of the Scientific Revolution, shared these concerns, and, contrary to Mach's assertions, he clearly believed that theology was an intrinsic part of natural philosophy. '[T]o treat of God from phenomena is certainly a part of "natural" philosophy', he wrote in the third edition of the *Principia* (1726).[44]

Recognizing the continuing interaction between the sciences and theology in early modern natural philosophy has been a consequence of a sea-change in the historiography both of the Scientific Revolution and of the relationship between science and religion in the early modern period.[45] Many historians have contributed to this shifting tide. P. M. Rattansi and J. E. McGuire were among the first scholars to recognize that Newton's intellectual agenda was markedly different from our own. Their seminal paper 'Newton and the "Pipes of Pan"' (1966)[46] was one of the first scholarly studies of the 'other' Isaac Newton. They concluded their study of Newton's deep concern with the *prisca theologia*[47] by remarking that:

It is certainly difficult for us in the twentieth century to conceive of one whose scientific achievements were so great, pursuing with equal interest and energy such other studies, especially when his efforts in those fields produced so little of enduring value. It is even more difficult for us to imagine the mechanics and cosmology of the *Principia* being influenced by Newton's theological views and his belief in a pristine knowledge. Sir Isaac Newton, however, was not a 'scientist' but a Philosopher of Nature. In the intellectual environment of his century, it was a legitimate task to use a wide variety of material to reconstruct the unified wisdom of Creation.[48]

By highlighting the importance of the *prisca* tradition for Newton, Rattansi and McGuire situated him within the broader context of Renaissance humanism and its appeal to ancient sources rather than reading backwards in a search for the origins of modern science. The importance of theology to Newton's project has been reinforced by B. J. T. Dobbs and Stephen D. Snobelen, whose work respectively emphasizes the importance of alchemy and religious heterodoxy for understanding the theological dimensions of Newton's project.[49] Likewise Peter Harrison has argued for the importance of Protestant approaches to biblical interpretation to the seventeenth-century development of empirical methods in the sciences.[50] In contrast to the positivist accounts of earlier historians,[51] Jan W. Wojcik demonstrated that Boyle's theology influenced his ideas on method and natural philosophy more generally.[52] These examples are but a small sample of the scholars who have taken the early modern preoccupation with religion and theology seriously and have demonstrated that the modern separation between science and religion did not occur during the period of the Scientific Revolution.

SHIFTING TIDES

Why did this sea-change occur? A full answer would be very complicated, but some speculative suggestions can be made. During the middle decades of the twentieth century the historiography of the Scientific Revolution flourished in the same environment that witnessed the growth of big science and massive government funding. However, the optimism that fuelled those developments faced serious challenges starting in the 1960s. Fear of nuclear holocaust, the growing awareness of environmental degradation, and, today, the spectre of global warming have all eroded the optimism of the post-war period about the benevolent role of science. The revival of an interest in occult practices, such as astrology and New Age spirituality, perhaps created an environment in which historians of science became more open to considering a broader range of influences on the development of the sciences. Exposure to social history and feminism led to the consideration of various social groups – not just the stars of science – and their impact on the development of the sciences. And the astonishing growth of fundamentalist religion, not only in Christianity but also in Islam and Judaism, undermined the unqualified assertions that science is overcoming faith and superstition or that science is bringing unmitigated progress to the world. In the context of these broad cultural changes, historians of science have come to recognize that the relationships between science and religion are complex, and that, although the early modern period witnessed the birth of Newton's law of universal gravitation, it did not simultaneously witness the separation of science from religion.

The narrative of the Scientific Revolution inspired by the positivists' claim that the separation of science from religion was an important, progressive step towards modernity and the warfare metaphor popularized by Draper and White have not been replaced by a new master-narrative. Complexity rather than simplicity is the result of recent scholarship. To quote John Brooke, historians of science have learned 'that religious beliefs have penetrated scientific discussions on many levels [and] to reduce the relationship of science and religion to conflict is therefore inadequate'.[53] The complexity of the relationship between these two powerful intellectual forces in early modern Europe undermines the story of their early separation and accordingly profoundly modifies one important component of the historiography of the Scientific Revolution.

NOTES

I am grateful to Lawrence M. Principe and Martin S. Staum for helpful suggestions on an earlier draft of this chapter. Suggestions from Geoffrey Cantor and Thomas Dixon have improved the chapter considerably.

1　H. Floris Cohen, *The scientific revolution: A historiographical inquiry* (Chicago: University of Chicago Press, 1994), p. 21.

2　See, e.g., Edward Grant, *The foundations of modern science in the middle ages: Their religious, institutional, and intellectual contexts* (Cambridge: Cambridge University Press, 1996); Edwin Arthur Burtt, *The metaphysical foundations of modern physical science*, rev. edn (London: Routledge & Kegan Paul, 1932; first published 1924).

3　Consider, for example, the following old standards: Herbert Butterfield, *The origins of modern science, 1300–1800*, rev. edn (New York: Free Press, 1957; first published 1949); A. Rupert Hall, *The revolution in science, 1500–1750* (New York: Longman, 1983; first published 1954); Richard S. Westfall, *The construction of modern science: Mechanisms and mechanics* (New York: John Wiley, 1971).

4　Floris Cohen organizes his *Scientific revolution* around this set of questions. See also Toby E. Huff, *The rise of early modern science: Islam, China, and the west* (Cambridge: Cambridge University Press, 1993).

5　Jean le Rond d'Alembert, *Preliminary discourse to the* Encyclopedia *of Diderot*, trans. Richard N. Schwab and Walter E. Rex (Indianapolis: Bobbs-Merrill, 1963), p. 71.

6　See John Brooke and Geoffrey Cantor, *Reconstructing nature: the engagement of science and religion* (Edinburgh: T & T Clark, 1998), pp. 47–57.

7　Angèle Kremer-Marietti, 'Comte, Isidore-Auguste-Marie-François-Xavier (1798–1857)', in Edward Craig (ed.), *Routledge encyclopedia of philosophy,* 10 vols. (Routledge: London and New York, 1998), vol. II, p. 496. See Auguste Comte, *Cours de philosophie positive,* 6 vols. (Paris: Bachelier, Everat, 1830–42), vol. I, pp. 47–95.

8　Ernst Mach, *The science of mechanics: A critical and historical account of its development,* trans. Thomas J. McCormack, 6th edn (La Salle, IL: Open Court, 1960), p. 553.

9　Ibid., p. 596.

10　Ibid., pp. 551–3.

11　Ibid., pp. 553–4.

12　'The fact that science has been used as a resource both by Christians and their critics may call into question another common assumption – that modern science has been largely responsible for the secularization of society ... Critics point out that it may be an unquestioned survival from nineteenth-century positivism when a sense of liberation through science was at its height ... The place of science in secularization may also require reevaluation in the light of religious resurgence in polities where science-based technologies are not conspicuous by their absence.' John Hedley Brooke, *Science and religion: Some historical perspectives* (Cambridge: Cambridge University Press, 1991), p. 11.

13　John William Draper, *History of the conflict between religion and science* (New York: Appleton, 1875), ch. 12. See: Brooke, *Science and religion,* pp. 34–5.

14　Andrew Dickson White, *A history of the warfare of science with theology in Christendom,* 2 vols. (New York: Appleton & Co., 1896; reprinted New York: Dover, 1960), vol. I, pp. vi–vii.

15　White, *History of the warfare,* vol. I, chs. 3–5.

16　'The main characteristic of the New Humanism ... [is] the combination of youthful energy and curiosity with reverence for the past. It implies a continuous struggle on two opposite fronts, against iconoclastic technicians and crude materialists on the one side and against blind and futile idealists, the chickenhearted humanists of the old school on the other ... The New Humanism is a double renaissance: a scientific renaissance for men of letters, and a literary one for men of science.' George Sarton, 'The new humanism', in Sarton, *The history of science and the new humanism* (Cambridge, MA: Harvard University Press, 1937; first published 1931), pp. 158–9.

17　George Sarton, 'The history of science', in Sarton, *The life of science: essays in the history of civilization* (New York: Henry Schuman, 1948), p. 30.

18　George Sarton, *Introduction to the history of science,* 3 vols. (Baltimore, MD: Williams and Wilkins, 1927), vol. I, p. 28. See also Tore Frängsmyr, 'Science or history: George Sarton and the positivist tradition in the history of science', *Lychnos* 12 (1973–4, published in 1975), 104–44.

19　Sarton, 'History of science', p. 36.

20　Ibid., p. 38.

21 Ibid.

22 See, for example, Nathan Sivin, 'Why the scientific revolution did not take place in China – or didn't it?', *Chinese Science* 5 (1982), 45–66; Cohen, *The scientific revolution*, ch. 6; Huff, *Rise of early modern science*.

23 Newton's *Principia* (*The mathematical principles of natural philosophy*) was published in 1687. Copernicus's *De revolutionibus orbium coelestium* (*On the revolutions of the heavenly spheres*) was published in 1543. Richard S. Westfall, 'The scientific revolution reasserted', in Margaret J. Osler (ed.), *Rethinking the scientific revolution* (Cambridge: Cambridge University Press, 2000), pp. 55 and 44.

24 Burtt, *Metaphysical foundations*, pp. 98–9.

25 Ibid., p. 324.

26 Ibid., pp. 296–7.

27 Ibid., p. 338.

28 Alexandre Koyré, *Études galiléennes*, 3 vols. (Paris: Hermann, 1939). Translated as *Galileo studies*, trans. John Mepham (Atlantic Highlands, NJ: Humanities Press, 1978). Koyré referred to Mach at least twelve times in his *Études galiléennes*. Koyré promulgated his ideas in the English-speaking world in two very influential articles: 'Galileo and the scientific revolution of the seventeenth century', *Philosophical Review* 52 (1943), 333–48 and 'Galileo and Plato', *Journal of the History of Ideas* 4 (1943), 400–28. Both of these articles have been reprinted in Koyré, *Metaphysics and measurement: Essays in the scientific revolution* (London: Chapman and Hall, 1968), pp. 1–15, 16–43.

29 Alexandre Koyré, *From the closed world to the infinite universe* (Baltimore, MD: Johns Hopkins University Press, 1957), p. 276.

30 Butterfield, *Origins of modern science*, p. 194.

31 Ibid., pp. 195–7.

32 Westfall, *Construction of modern science*.

33 Richard S. Westfall, *Science and religion in seventeenth-century England* (New Haven, CT: Yale University Press, 1958), p. 220.

34 Westfall, 'Scientific revolution reasserted', pp. 49–50.

35 Kenneth J. Howell, *God's two books: Copernican cosmology and biblical interpretation in early modern science* (Notre Dame, IN: University of Notre Dame Press, 2002).

36 Robert S. Westman, 'The Melancthon Circle, Rheticus, and the Wittenberg interpretation of the Copernican theory', *Isis* 66 (1975), 165–93.

37 Peter Barker and Bernard R. Goldstein, 'Theological foundations of Kepler's astronomy', *Osiris* 16 (2001), 88–113.

38 Margaret J. Osler, *Divine will and the mechanical philosophy: Gassendi and Descartes on contingency and necessity in the created world* (Cambridge: Cambridge University Press, 1994).

39 Robert Boyle, *A disquisition about the final causes of natural things: Wherein it is inquir'd, whether, and (if at all) with what cautions, a naturalist should admit them?* (1688), in Michael Hunter and Edward B. Davis (eds.), *The works of Robert Boyle*, 14 vols. (London: Pickering and Chatto, 2000), vol. XI, pp. 80–151.

40 Isaac Newton, *Opticks; or a treatise on the reflections, refractions, inflections, and colours of light* (New York: Dover, 1952), pp. 369–70. See also Betty Jo Teeter Dobbs, *The Janus faces of genius: The role of alchemy in Newton's thought* (Cambridge: Cambridge University Press, 1991); James E. Force and Richard H. Popkin, *Essays on the context, nature, and influence of Isaac Newton's theology* (Dordrecht: Kluwer Academic, 1990); Stephen D. Snobelen, '"God of Gods and Lord of Lords": The theology of Isaac Newton's General Scholium to the *Principia*', *Osiris* 16 (2001), 169–208.

41 Andrew Cunningham, 'Getting the game right: Some plain words on the identity and invention of science', *Studies in History and Philosophy of Science* 19 (1988), 365–89.

42 See: Westfall, *Science and religion*; Jan W. Wojcik, *Robert Boyle and the limits of reason* (Cambridge: Cambridge University Press, 1997).

43 Osler, *Divine will and the mechanical philosophy*, pp. 59–77; Alan Gabbey, 'Henry More and the limits of mechanism', in Sarah Hutton (ed.), *Henry More (1614–1687): Tercentenary studies* (Dordrecht: Kluwer Academic, 1990), pp. 19–36.

44 Isaac Newton, *The principia: Mathematical principles of natural philosophy*, trans. I. Bernard Cohen and Anne Whitman (Berkeley, CA: University of California Press, 1999), pp. 942–3.

45 Margaret J. Osler, 'Mixing metaphors: Science and religion or natural philosophy and theology in early modern Europe', *History of Science* 36 (1998) 91–113.

46 P. M. Rattansi and J. E. McGuire, 'Newton and the "Pipes of Pan"', *Notes and Records of the Royal Society of London* 21 (1966), 108–43. For more recent affirmations of this understanding of Newton, see Andrew Cunningham, 'How the *Principia* got its name: Or, taking natural philosophy seriously', *History of Science* 29 (1991), 377–92.

47 The phrase '*prisca theologia*' refers to the ancient, pristine theology. Many early modern thinkers believed that an ancient theological tradition existed, flowing directly from the divine mind and known by a sequence of ancient prophets and philosophers, including the legendary Hermes Trismegistus, Zoroaster, and Plato. See Frances A. Yates, *Giordano Bruno and the Hermetic tradition* (Chicago: University of Chicago Press, 1964), pp. 14–18.

48 Ibid., p. 138.

49 See Betty Jo Teeter Dobbs, *The foundations of Newton's alchemy: Or, 'The hunting of the greene lyon'* (Cambridge: Cambridge University Press, 1975) and *The Janus faces of genius*; Snobelen, 'God of Gods and Lord of Lords'; Rob Iliffe, *Newton: A very short introduction* (Oxford: Oxford University Press, 2007).

50 Peter Harrison, *The Bible, Protestantism, and the rise of natural science* (Cambridge: Cambridge University Press, 1998).

51 Most notably Marie Boas Hall, *Robert Boyle on natural philosophy: An essay with selections from his writings* (Bloomington, IN: Indiana University Press, 1966).

52 Wocjik, *Robert Boyle and the limits of reason*.

53 Brooke, *Science and religion*, p. 50.

CHAPTER 5

The late Victorian conflict of science and religion as an event in nineteenth-century intellectual and cultural history

Frank M. Turner

Between 1750 and 1870 – from the publication of the *Encyclopédie* to the early work of Nietzsche and of Darwin's *Descent of man* – the relationship of science and religion in the western world passed from fruitful co-operation and modest tensions to harsh public conflict, a situation that many observers have since come incorrectly to assume to be a permanent fact of modern cultural life. To understand that Victorian clash and why historians and others should not draw excessively pessimistic conclusions from it, one must analyse the earlier nineteenth-century relations of science and religion so as to present the late-century controversy as an event to be explained rather than as an inevitable occurrence arising from necessary, existential hostilities.

Many years ago Gordon Allport observed, 'A narrowly conceived science can never do business with a narrowly conceived religion'.[1] Such narrow conceptions had not prevailed in 1750, but as a result of transformations within scientific and religious communities and changes in the structure of publication, education, and wider cultural discourse a narrowing of focus had come into being by the middle of the nineteenth century and with that narrowing the conflict of science and religion. In this respect Thomas Henry Huxley wrote more presciently than he may have realized when he once claimed:

The antagonism between science and religion about which we hear so much, appears to me to be purely factitious – fabricated, on the one hand, by short-sighted religious people who confound a certain branch of science, theology, with religion; and, on the other, by equally short-sighted scientific people who forget that science takes for its province only that which is susceptible of clear intellectual comprehension.[2]

What Huxley did not recognize was the historically conditioned circumstance that led to the antagonism he described and to which he had so fervently contributed.

SCIENCES AND RELIGIONS

The relationship of science and religion, as numerous historians have argued, has not always been and is not one of essential conflict or warfare, no matter how much late nineteenth-century authors such as Huxley, Andrew Dixon White, John William Draper, and John Tyndall may have contended. As James Moore long ago demonstrated, the metaphor of warfare served polemical rather than analytical purposes.[3] Yet however much the conflict may be qualified and contextualized, there is no question that between approximately the mid-1840s and the mid-1890s conflict did occur and involved writers of considerable ability and professional standing on both sides. Instances of fierce controversy erupted over Chambers's *Vestiges of the natural history of creation*, Darwin's theory of evolution by natural selection, Spencer's cosmic evolution, Tyndall's materialism, various anthropologists' theories of human pre-history and religion, and the relationship of scripture to all of these topics. And then, as Peter Bowler has argued, the conflict substantially subsided for several decades, only to erupt again on somewhat different grounds towards the middle of the twentieth century.[4]

As part of the reason for rejecting the idea of a necessary or existential conflict, we must recognize that during the century under consideration there existed no single entity constituting either 'science' or 'religion'.[5] Even among its practitioners the term 'science' or the pursuit of 'natural knowledge' differed in structure, self-understanding, self-definition, philosophy, and institutionalization from decade to decade, from country to country, between distinct regions within countries, among individuals in the same region, and among practitioners in different religious communities. Modes of idealism, *naturphilosophie*, natural religion, theism, and ethical progressionism informed the work and personal values of numerous natural philosophers. These metaphysical, theological, and moral factors were not extrinsic to their pursuit of natural knowledge but part and parcel of it and for many scientists, particularly Scottish physicists, remained so certainly to the end of the nineteenth century, if not well beyond. Moreover a man of science who was thoroughly naturalistic in his own area of research might embrace a broad theism or ethical idealism for his understanding of the scientific enterprise as a whole. By the middle of the nineteenth century, however, within the various scientific communities there arose networks of individuals who sought to define science within a narrower professional and naturalistic framework. This drive led to conflict within scientific communities themselves as well as between some scientists and religious figures over the character, goals, and cultural authority of natural knowledge.

Likewise, in ways too rarely recognized by historians of science, the social, institutional, devotional, and theological phenomena subsumed under the term 'religion' proved to be equally pluralistic, complicated, and arguably even more rapidly changing. Across early nineteenth-century European religious life manifestations of liberal, rational, or moderate religion associated with the eighteenth century gave way to Evangelical Protestantism increasingly attached to bibliolatry, to a revived Roman Catholicism asserting new theological and ecclesiastical authority, and to emerging Anglo-Catholicism that in one way or another emphasized a dogmatic revealed, sacramental religion. All of the European churches, as well as religious sects and lay organizations that had not existed in 1750, believed they must re-Christianize their nations and cultures. As a result much hostility arose between and among Christian groups, as well as between them and the secular culture, as various Christians accused each other of being less than sufficiently Christian. Sincerely religious individuals who had either embraced or moderately accommodated themselves to the rational strains of Enlightenment thought suddenly found themselves accused of lack of religious seriousness. Thus, by 1860, European churches were engaging with their cultures, asserting their authority, and championing the Bible much more intensely than their forebears had a century earlier.

It was the changing configurations between and among those increasingly complex communities of natural knowledge and of faith as they embraced new and expanding venues for publication and exchange of ideas that determined at any given moment what we call the relationship of science and religion. And because of these complexities surrounding both science and religion, every generalization invites significant qualification.

FROM TENSION TO CONFLICT

At any given period of modern European thought Christian writers have seen themselves confronting a dangerous or corrosive 'other', sometimes within the broad Christian world but often outside it. That 'other' might be understood to attack Christianity directly or to lead to religious unorthodoxy. For most of the century under consideration, however, the 'other' perceived as dangerous to Christianity was not science but rather materialism or atheism (neither ever well-defined), sceptical rationalism, theological heterodoxy, ecclesiastical irregularity, or outright attacks by the secular state. For some Christians by about 1860, however, the threatening 'other' would *become* science. But that situation was novel, and much of the harshness of the furore arose because of that novelty, which seemed to many people to constitute a change in the rules of the culture.

Similarly, writers pursuing the creation and dispersion of natural knowledge have also frequently seen themselves endangered by a dangerous 'other', but it has not always been religion. Isaac Newton, to be sure, feared theological opponents, but they were theologians who might discover his unorthodox views on the Trinity, not theologians who might attack his views of natural knowledge. Voltaire certainly saw theological and religious opponents surrounding him, but he saw them as attacking his views on the Bible, toleration, or ecclesiastical authority, not his (and Madame du Chatelet's) book on Newton's physics. David Hume encountered numerous clerical opponents for his philosophic critique of miracles, not for the impact of his philosophy on science. Both Roman Catholics and Protestants attacked Rousseau for the theological speculations of *Émile*, not for what he had to say about natural knowledge. Immanuel Kant encountered royal censorship towards the end of his life for his views on religion within the limits of reason but not for anything he had said about science. Antoine Lavoisier was executed and Joseph Priestley attacked by a mob not for their views on oxygen but for their politics. Moreover in German universities from the third quarter of the eighteenth century to the second quarter of the nineteenth the science that was most likely to lead to difficulty with religious authorities was not physical science or natural knowledge but philology.

For complicated reasons the years of the French Revolution with its assault on Christianity raised an apprehension that scientific thought or culture might endanger religion and the social status quo. The conservative reaction to the French Revolution commencing with Edmund Burke, using polemical categories developed earlier by French Roman Catholics, blamed the excesses of the revolutionary government on the Enlightenment and on a materialistic atheism supposedly spawned by the Enlightenment and in Britain by Non-conformist religion, especially Unitarianism.[6] Continental writers of both Roman Catholic and Protestant persuasion, drawing on and developing Burke's thought, as well as pre-revolutionary critiques of the Enlightenment, similarly presented atheism and materialism as the sources of the violence, anti-clericalism, and immorality of the revolution. It became quite easy for British commentators to confuse and conflate the few radical materialistic voices in the continental Enlightenment with the much more moderate English Enlightenment, which was associated with the general pursuit of natural knowledge in a theistic context.[7] Such became even more the case in the wake of Napoleon's support of science and technology. Science could thus seem to be socially, politically, and religiously dangerous, especially when it displayed connection or sympathy with French culture.

For over half a century across Europe men of science as well as other progressive intellectuals worked within the conservative ideological climate that had originated in the 1790s and that continued to be reinforced by energized religious forces. John Stuart Mill made this point privately to Auguste Comte in early 1841. After confessing to 'concessions [in my writings] I felt forced to make to the prevailing attitudes of my country', Mill went on to explain:

You are doubtless aware that here an author who should openly admit to antireligious or even antichristian opinions, would compromise not only his social position, which I feel myself capable of sacrificing to a sufficiently high objective, but also, and this would be more serious, his chance of being read. I am already assuming great risks when, from the start, I carefully put aside the religious perspective and abstained from rhetorical eulogies of the wisdom of Providence, customarily made even by unbelievers among the philosophers of my country.[8]

Darwin's notebooks from the late 1830s demonstrate that he similarly feared the social ramifications of having his thought associated with transmutation and materialism, as did his long suppression of his evolutionary views.[9] As late as 1865 Joseph Dalton Hooker, then head of Kew Gardens, wrote to Darwin:

It is all very well for [Alfred] Wallace to wonder at scientific men being afraid of saying what they think – he has all 'the freedom of motion in vacuo' in one sense. Had he as many kind and good relations as I have, who would be grieved and pained to hear me say what I think, and had he children who would be placed in predicaments most detrimental to children's minds by such avowals on my part, he would not wonder so much.[10]

Conservative social, political, and religious forces had created a climate of opinion in early and mid-Victorian Britain and elsewhere in Europe whereby the price of challenge or conflict might include among other things potential loss of employment, loss of influence, or social ostracism.

As a consequence of these conservative polemics and the intellectual confusions they fostered, ill-defined philosophical materialism and atheism constituted a kind of limiting boundary that respectable British thinkers of scientific outlook avoided approaching or transgressing. They sharply criticized the radicalism associated with both the Unitarianism and materialistic metaphysics of Joseph Priestley and the anatomy pursued on the fringes of the London medical community displaying sympathy for materialistic anatomy and transformation of species associated with French science. As Arnold Thackeray, Jack Morrell, Adrian Desmond, and others have contended, by the 1830s British establishment scientists did all in their power to forestall any association of their endeavours with political radicalism or unorthodox metaphysics which might appear to endanger the status quo. As John Brooke and Geoffrey Cantor have observed, one reason the scientists were 'decidedly overburdened in having to maintain the fabric of design ... was the need to avert suspicion'.[11] Natural religion functioned as a broad ideological umbrella beneath which anyone pursuing natural knowledge might dwell and appear politically benign. Moreover the organizational structures of the British Association for the Advancement of Science kept establishment science as far from political and social matters as possible, while at the same time demonstrating considerable utility for science in the provincial cities where they met. Both deeply conservative and moderately liberal scientists saw plenty of natural knowledge to be explored without moving into politically dangerous territory. In that respect, they both consciously and unconsciously acted as self-censors.

The intellectual stance internalized by conservative Anglican and Nonconformist scientists, as well as by conservative clerical figures throughout the transatlantic world, might be described as 'If this, then that'. That is to say, they directly or indirectly claimed that *if* ideas bearing the whiff of French materialism, transformationism, or religious heterodoxy were embraced, published, or advocated, *then* atheism, immorality, anti-clericalism, and social disruption might (or must) follow. This stance led to various accommodations between spokesmen for religion and science, who were often the same people. The eruption of the classic mid-century era of conflict between science and religion occurred when numerous writers within the intellectual elite or aspiring to enter that elite rejected the 'If this, then that' stance. How did this come to pass?

In various intellectual settings across Europe from the 1840s to the 1860s there occurred a rejection of religious and philosophical outlooks used to defend the social status quo for a half-century or more. These rejections arose from radical critiques of existing political and social structures on the one hand, and from a new confidence in those very structures, on the other. Paradoxically there existed both more criticism and more confidence.

Robert Devigne, in his recent analysis of the thought of John Stuart Mill, has contributed an important new framework for interpreting the turn from tension to conflict in the relations of mid-nineteenth-century science and religion. Devigne quite convincingly contends that advanced mid-Victorian authors in a number of fields sought to reform what they had come to regard as unsatisfactory compromises achieved by writers associated with the late Enlightenment.[12] That is to say, mid-Victorian writers, among whom one can include figures so diverse as Darwin, Wallace, Spencer, J. S. Mill, Marx, and the German materialists, sought to reform, radicalize, or naturalize the generally moderate, theistic, thought of the Enlightenment. As a result, much of the scientifically, politically, or economically radical thought of the mid-century actually to a greater or lesser degree embraced the very naturalistic, materialistic, and even atheistic attitudes that the conservative critics of the 1790s had incorrectly associated with the eighteenth-century Enlightenment. The earlier polemical caricature came to describe reality in the third quarter of the next century. Within this interpretive framework conflict between science and religion involved both a rejection of biblical literalism and ecclesiastical authority and a simultaneous rejection of earlier moderate Enlightenment accommodation. The much-examined and familiar rejection of the former has often obscured the rejection of the latter.

Within the scientific community the Darwinian rejection of William Paley's natural theology illustrates this mid-nineteenth-century discontent with moderate Enlightenment. Anything but a biblical literalist, Paley had pursued a powerful strain of moderately rational Enlightenment natural religion underpinning conservative politics and morality. But as John Gascoigne has shown, towards the close of the eighteenth century a different religiosity, championed by opponents of the French Revolution and political reform, emerged in Cambridge emphasizing revealed and sacramental religion in place of the Enlightenment religious sensibilities embodied in Paley's thought. Gascoigne notes that the mid-nineteenth-century critique of Paley by Darwin and others actually involved a rejection of Enlightenment religion rather than of those new strains of religion emphasizing revealed scripture or clerical authority.

The struggle between religion and science that occurred in the wake of the publication of Darwin's *On the origin of species* thus actually involved a generally unrecognized two-fold conflict: first, the rejection of Paleyan natural theology, and second, a clash with a largely post-Paleyan biblical literalism. The former represented an effort to reform or radicalize the Enlightenment heritage, while the latter involved conflict with newer post-Enlightenment contemporary religious forces. The critique of Paley originated within the scientific community and represented a re-orientation of its intellectual framework. The struggle with bibliolatry originated

primarily from outside that community and represented an effort to
maintain its intellectual independence against novel religious forces, which
will be considered later in this chapter.

THE DISRUPTION OF THEODICIES

Perhaps the most important and still least-noticed aspect of British natural
theology from the late seventeenth century onwards was its providing both a
theological and a social theodicy.[13] From John Ray to the authors of the
Bridgewater treatises natural theologians combined intricate theological expli-
cations of nature with arguments supporting the contemporary British social
and political status quo. Consequently people may have accepted natural
theology because of its arguments regarding nature and God or because they
believed in the social structures for which those arguments provided an
ideology. They therefore might abandon natural theology because they
changed their views of nature or because they wished to challenge the social
status quo or because they believed the social status quo no longer needed
such ideological support.

   Paley's individual arguments regarding design and utility in nature are too
often cited in isolation rather than as part of the larger and longer intellectual
effort to sustain faith in British social institutions. Moreover it should be
recognized that Paley's mode of analysing and justifying pain and evil in
nature constituted an important building block for wider European efforts to
construct theodicies. In particular his work informed Hegel's analysis of evil
in history. The German philosopher, having familiarized himself with British
natural theology, did for history what Paley had done for nature. The two
theodicies closely paralleled each other. In his *Lectures on the philosophy of
history* (delivered during the 1820s and first published in 1837) Hegel wrote:

The aim of human cognition is to understand that the intentions of eternal wisdom
are accomplished not only in the natural world, but also in the realm of the [spirit]
which is actively present in the world. From this point of view, our investigation can
be seen as a theodicy ... It should enable us to comprehend all the ills of the world,
including the existence of evil, so that the thinking spirit may be reconciled with the
negative aspects of existence; and it is in world history that we encounter the sum
total of concrete evil ... In order to justify the course of history, we must try to
understand the role of evil in the light of the absolute sovereignty of reason.[14]

Elsewhere in the same lectures Hegel declared:

The aim of philosophy is to recognize the content and reality of the divine idea,
and to defend reality against its detractors ... Philosophy, therefore, is not really

a means of consolation. It is more than that, for it transfigures reality with all its apparent injustices and reconciles it with the reality; it shows that it is based upon the Idea itself, and that reason is fulfilled in it.[15]

These passages may be read as a profound commentary on and transformation of Paley's natural theology.

Both Paley and Hegel in the most fulsomely disarming ways admitted the appearance and reality of suffering, violence, and by implication evil in the world, yet both portray that suffering and violence as achieving higher ends.[16] In his determination 'to defend reality against its detractors' Hegel closely approached Paley's remarkable declaration after his utilitarian justifications of numerous examples of suffering in nature: 'It is a happy world after all. The air, the earth, the water, teem with delighted existence'.[17] In anticipation of Hegel's appeal to 'the intentions of eternal wisdom' Paley had stated, 'In a religious view . . . privation, disappointment, and satiety, are not without the most salutary tendencies'.[18] Numerous similar arguments filled the *Bridgewater treatises* and other works of natural theology. The individual arguments for design in nature supplied the building blocks to the larger, more important conclusion of the ultimate rationality of nature. Hegel then applied the same kind of argumentation to history.

Substantial intellectual, moral, and religious cracks in the theodicies that held both religion and science within conventional social and intellectual bounds had long been recognized. As early as the third quarter of the eighteenth century Voltaire and Hume had dissected the idea of theodicy, but with little immediate impact because each was regarded as an infidel whose arguments could be set aside. However, religiously engaged writers also recognized significant challenges. Clerical authors explicitly understood that the whole system of ultimate divine justice beyond a visibly unjust world functioned only on the assumption of the immortality of the soul. If defenders of natural theology were left to contemplate only this earthly life, the system failed. Malthus in his *Essay on the principle of population* had realized that the world he had portrayed with reproduction in population outstripping food production envisioned a world gone awry. Only by presenting human life on earth as a schoolhouse preparatory for the next world could he make sense of the creation. Many years later Thomas Chalmers forthrightly confessed in his *Bridgewater treatise*:

If there be no future state, the great moral question between heaven and earth, broken off at the middle, is frittered into a degrading mockery. There is a violence done to the continuity of things. The moral constitution of man is stript of its significancy and the Author of that constitution is stript of His wisdom and authority and honour. That consistent march which we behold in all the cycles, and progressive movements of the natural economy, is, in the moral economy, brought to sudden arrest and disruption – if death annihilate the man, instead of only transforming him. And it is only the doctrine of his immortality by which all can be adjusted and harmonized.[19]

In his fascinating species notebooks Charles Lyell made similar comments regarding a future state and a naturalistic view of humankind.[20]

Other Christian writers further recognized that the vision of natural knowledge supporting natural theology might be fairly easily naturalized. Thomas Rennell of Cambridge, foreshadowing Susan Faye Cannon's argument of Darwin's having essentially naturalized natural theology, declared:

In all his researches into the phaenomena of the world, and the laws by which they are regulated, the philosopher directs his attention so exclusively to what he terms *Nature*, and the operations of *Nature*, that he at last begins to attribute to this delusive term, an actual existence, and to ascribe to a word only and a shadow, what he ought to ascribe to the being and to the agency of God. The word Nature is, certainly, a very convenient term for expressing the uniform action of the first almighty cause, according to certain laws, which in his wisdom he has enacted – but when by frequent repetition, we lose sight of the real meaning of the term, or by associating it with the phaenomena around us, we begin to give it an actual existence, then it is that we are encouraging the growth of a Sceptical principle in the mind. By substituting in our speculations, *Nature* for God, we keep out of sight the Creator and the Governor of the universe, till we finally doubt the reality of his Providence and of his power.[21]

Rennell and others of his generation saw such a naturalization of the theistic framework of natural theology as arising from infidel science infected by French thought and the rejection of Newton's conviction that natural knowledge inherently supported both revealed and natural religion. Nonetheless Rennell clearly understood how easily the naturalistic transformation in the conceptual framework might occur.

Consequently long before conflict erupted, scientists and clergymen, who were often one and the same person, understood that the peace and mutual accommodation between science and religion achieved through natural theology were very fragile, and that was why both worked so hard to preserve it in the face of the challenges arising initially from materialistic French psychology in the medical community, then from Chambers's *Vestiges of the natural history of creation* in the popular sphere, and finally from Darwin within the context of elite respectable natural knowledge. In the first half of the century among the British and European intellectual elites it was in few people's interest to let tensions move into conflict. Those few writers who were willing to entertain or instigate conflict could be, and were, pressed to the margins.

Between about 1840 and 1870 across Europe these theodicies imploded as a younger generation of scientists and other scientifically engaged intellectuals abandoned them. Core problems inherent in these theodicies came home to roost as writers found good reasons to liberate their thought from those frameworks. They might wish such liberation in order to permit their scientific reasoning to advance in directions previously forestalled by natural theology or in rejection of the social realities sustained by the ideology of natural theology. In other words discontent or even disgust with either the scientific or the social implications of natural theology, or in some instances both, could lead to its rejection. The classical age of conflict between science and religion erupted as writers either rejected such theodicies or recast them so as to be fulfilled on earth with little or no reference to the traditional divine rather than in eternity.[22]

Just as the third quarter of the century saw nations willing to reject the post-Congress of Vienna balance-of-power arrangements, ambitious young men of science in Britain and radical social thinkers in Germany, some of whom were scientists, breached the peace so long sustained by fragile theodicies. There is a direct parallel in the undermining of socially conservative natural theology in Britain during the 1840s and 1850s and the contemporary assault by radical German materialistic thinkers on conservative Hegelian idealism. Indeed, there exists a remarkable similarity in chronology between Darwin's privately working his way out of the Paleyan framework of natural knowledge in his transmutation notebooks of the late 1830s and Marx's working his way out of Hegelianism in the 1840s, including the fact that neither writer published his work at the time. Moreover, in both Germany and Britain, young reformers of differing degrees of social radicalism saw either a materialistic or deeply naturalistic science as a vehicle for advancing themselves personally and their professional and social agendas. Marx differentiated his socialism from that of more conventional radicals by claiming to have a scientific basis for it. Darwin, Huxley, and the voices of advanced English science from the late 1850s onwards contended that their science was more scientific by virtue of its being more thoroughly naturalistic. None of these younger thinkers feared for or regretted the world of thought they would lose.

As Robert Young, Adrian Desmond, James Secord, John van Wyhe, and Mark Francis, and long before them R. K. Webb in his biography of Harriet Martineau, have demonstrated, the cultural interstices of the British medical profession and the religiously and politically multitudinous British provincial public sphere of publishing and lecturing were filled with people eager to challenge genteel establishment science and to entertain materialism, transformationism, and religious heterodoxy. Such people found ethical norms in what their more devout contemporaries regarded as materialism and heterodox religion, and felt no need for the theodicies of natural religion. Anti-Corn Law League and Chartist activity and flamboyant practitioners of phrenology and mesmerism flourished in the provinces without the world falling apart, as so many in the London–Oxbridge scientific circuit feared. As leaders of the British Association the latter might exclude voices of political and social radicalism from their peripatetic meetings in provincial cities, but those voices already commanded the streets and lecture halls of the very cities they annually visited.

The most important texts manifesting these radical impulses were, of course, George Combe's *Constitution of man* (1828) and Robert Chambers's *Vestiges of the natural history of creation* (1844), both of which disrupted first the Evangelical order of Scotland and then the Anglican order of England. They challenged the morality of the churches, the elitism of the major scientific societies, and the idea that any elite could control the discourse of natural knowledge. Moreover, they associated ethics and moral development with what amounted to a materialistic metaphysics. Each proved able to reach vast popular audiences in British cities populated by unchurched, anti-clerical workers whose forebears had long ago delighted in Tom Paine. For these provincial urban readers naturalistic ideas did not undermine religious orthodoxy, because they had not embraced such orthodoxy or because they associated it with a much-detested clerical and aristocratic privilege. They were the same people who took pleasure in visiting the dinosaur models at the Crystal Palace while experiencing no religious dissonance, because they had never entertained serious biblical literalism in the first place.[23]

The vast debate over *Vestiges of the natural history of creation* demonstrated that radical scientific and metaphysical ideas could permeate British society without public order or morality collapsing. Charles Lyell, having earlier recorded in his species notebooks the retreat of younger scientists in the 1850s from a strong anti-transformationist position, observed in 1856 that 'The popularity of the *Vestiges* arises from any theory being preferred to … a series of miracles, a perpetual intervention of the First Cause as constant as is the dying out of species & as it has been from the beginning – so far as we can see back into the past'.[24] Ambitious young men of science discovered that by defining science in a thoroughly naturalistic manner they could advance themselves socially and professionally against older clerical scientists and scientists beholden to the clerical elites. As Martin Fichman has so well summarized the situation regarding the young spokesmen for scientific naturalism:

> as advocates of a specific idea of science professionalization they were committed to constructing a definition of value-neutral and hence 'objective' science ... The scientific naturalists recognized the professional gains to be had by proclaiming the ideological neutrality of science. Huxley and his camp could claim that they spoke as objective experts, not political or ideological partisans. This strategy involved erecting an epistemological divide between science and politics, ethics, religion, and other cultural forces. It also encouraged a distinction between elite and popular science ... Such a strategy was brilliant but disingenuous. The scientific naturalists invoked an 'ideologically pure' science that concealed their own varied sociopolitical agenda behind the banner of rigorous professionalism.[25]

Their efforts paralleled the much more socially and politically radical group of scientific intellectuals associated contemporaneously with German materialism about whom Frederick Gregory has written with such insight.[26] In this respect Bernard Lightman was very much on target when urging, 'Scientific naturalism was the English version of the cult of science in vogue throughout Europe during the second half of the nineteenth century'.[27] And the champions of that vogue were at one in rejecting the theodicies of both natural religion and history so long employed to support the social and religious status quo.

NEW DIRECTIONS IN RELIGIOUS THOUGHT

Too often neglected in the master-narrative of the eruption of a mid-century conflict between science and religion is the role played by religious forces as novel as the new ideas and organization of natural knowledge. Aggression and new thinking did not erupt only from the side of uppity young scientists. By about 1850 the contours of religious thought had undergone as much reconfiguration as science. Some of these changes very much narrowed contemporary understandings of religious orthodoxy, thus breeding new conflict. Others, however, actually opened the way to rethinking religion so that it might be seen as much less dependent on natural theology as a bulwark for its authority. Still other writers allowed scientists to question traditional orthodoxy without abandoning a sense of spirituality in themselves or the universe. Finally, a few religious authors sought to embrace advanced scientific thought for the sake of religion itself.

Bibliolatry in direct opposition to scientific knowledge is largely a product of the nineteenth century and beyond. At the close of the eighteenth century and well into the nineteenth a devoutly earnest Evangelical such as Thomas Scott could write an extensive, widely read biblical commentary without seeking to draw significant conclusions about science or history from that reading. He may or may not have thought that the Bible conveyed scientific and historical truth, but he did not need to insist upon it. Rather, his commentaries illuminated biblical narrative and drew conclusions pointing to pious living.[28]

During the 1820s, however, in Scotland and Ireland the forerunners of modern fundamentalism emerged, placing far more emphasis on a literal reading of scripture and exploration of the prophecies.[29] These groups also founded new religious journals, including the *Record*, which despite its increasingly narrow purview became the major weekly paper of the Church of England. Contemporaries within and without the English Church were aware of the new narrowing of biblical commentary that also touched Non-conformist communities as well. Thus in the late 1840s the Unitarian Harriet Martineau, who was well read in both eighteenth- and nineteenth-century biblical commentary, noted:

We may know that there was far more freedom of religious imagination, reasoned argument, and, I may say, knowledge among our Protestant divines a century ago than there is now. This corruption of bibliolatry has so increased upon, our faithless and irreverent timidity has so grown upon us, even in that time, that it would be an act of great courage in divines of our day to publish what divines of a century ago were honored for publishing.[30]

Consequently advanced modern biblical criticism in Britain in the form of *Essays and reviews* (1860), published almost simultaneously with *On the origin of species*, confronted more aggressive and narrow-minded Protestants than would have been the case a half-century before. A similar situation occurred in Germany. Furthermore, as Jon Roberts has demonstrated in the United States, both scientists and theologians became narrower and more uncompromising in their attitudes in the quarter-century after the publication of Darwin's *Origin*, resulting in much sharper conflict over science years after the book appeared than immediately upon its appearance.[31]

On the other side of the equation, vigorous conservative efforts to make a literal reading of the Bible mesh with new scientific knowledge could ironically pave the way for possible acceptance of radically advanced ideas. For example, conservative scriptural geologists, such as William Buckland and Hugh Miller, accepted the actual presence of extinct and then new species at different points in geological stratification as compatible with the Genesis account of creation over seven days culminating in man. Charles Lyell privately predicted that such accommodations unwittingly provided the groundwork for the acceptance of the idea of transmutation of species.[32] Charles Goodwin, writing publicly in *Essays and reviews*, agreed, commenting:

Both these theories [of Miller and Buckland] divest the Mosaic narrative of real accordance with fact; both assume that appearances only, not facts, are described, and that in riddles, which would never have been suspected to be such, had we not arrived at the truth from other sources. It would be difficult for controversial-ists to cede more completely the point in dispute, or to admit more explicitly that the Mosaic narrative does not represent correctly the history of the universe up to the time of man.[33]

For both Lyell and Goodwin it was only a few steps from this meshing of geological change with progressive changes in creation to understanding God as working through natural laws rather than through miracles. The same compromises would eventually lead to a reverent dismissal of Ussher's chronology among theologians, but that development lay in the future.[34]

Roman Catholicism also underwent major intellectual transformations in the third quarter of the century – changes that precipitated outright conflict with scientists across Europe. Pope Pius IX in 1864 issued the Syllabus of Errors as well as other previous and subsequent documents that put the Roman Catholic Church as never before in direct opposition not only to liberal politics but also to much science. In the papal letter entitled *Tuas libenter* (21 December 1863), Pope Pius stated:

While Catholics may cultivate these sciences safely, explain them, and render them useful and certain, on the other hand they cannot do so if their natural intellect, in investigating natural truth, does not supremely venerate the infallible intellect of God as revealed in Christianity.[35]

Portions of the Syllabus directly limited free scientific or general intellec-tual inquiry. In 1870 the First Vatican Council declared:

Even though faith is above reason, there can never be any real disagreement between faith and reason ... all faithful Christians are forbidden to defend as legitimate conclusions of science those opinions which are known to be contrary to the doctrines of faith, particularly if they have been condemned by the church; and furthermore they are absolutely bound to hold them as errors ... faith delivers reason from errors and protects it.[36]

Later in the century Pope Leo XIII announced, 'It is absolutely wrong and forbidden ... to admit that the sacred writer has erred'.[37] These actions on the part of the Roman authorities constituted another major new factor in the theological climate of opinion fostering the classical age of conflict between science and religion.

Ironically the voice of dogmatic religion also undermined confidence both in scripture and in the early Victorian theodicies. The Tractarian Movement leader, John Henry Newman, in *Lectures on scripture proof of the doctrines of the church* (*Tract 85*) of 1838, cast doubt on the historical authority for the Bible and argued that the authority of the Church rather than that of the letter of the Bible should direct the faith of Christians. Newman pointed to the human origins of the biblical texts and discrepancies among them. Years later Huxley contended that Newman had provided arguments as strong as those of any agnostic to undermine the authority of scripture.[38]

In 1841, in *Letters on the Tamworth reading room*, published as letters to *The Times*, Newman directly attacked the religious validity of natural theology by rejecting the Baconian two-book view of divine revelation. Newman had long believed (and preached) that the conclusions of natural theologians flowed from their observations of nature only because of the presuppositions they brought to that observation.[39] In his essays of early 1841 Newman urged:

The truth is, that the system of Nature is just as much connected with religion, where minds are not religious, as a watch or a steam-carriage. The material world, indeed, is infinitely more wonderful than any human contrivance; but wonder is not religion, or we should be worshipping our railroads. What the physical creation presents to us in itself is a piece of machinery, and where men speak of a Divine Intelligence as its author, this God of theirs is not the Living and True, unless the spring is the god of a watch, or steam the creator of the engine.[40]

Newman was demanding a different understanding of the divine from that implied by the natural theologians. He could surrender their theodicy because their God was simply too small.

During the 1840s and later Newman's one-time Tractarian followers in the Church of England moved steadily away from seeing natural religion as a source of religious knowledge. As early as 1846 Richard Church, later Dean of St Paul's, wrote in the *Guardian*, 'Keep in view the great principle that nature is not the real basis of religion, and we can safely afford full and free scope to science'.[41] As time passed, other Oxford High Churchmen came to argue that nature and sense experience in general revealed virtually no certainties about religious truth. The most important of these was Henry Longueville Mansel, whose 1858 Bampton Lectures on *The limits of religious thought* may be seen as providing the philosophical basis for agnosticism.

In 1864 in his *Apologia pro vita sua* Newman himself returned to these issues. There he wrote that when he looked 'into the world of men' he saw a sight that filled him 'with unspeakable distress'. He mused that if he looked into a mirror and did not see his face, he should have 'the sort of feeling' that actually came upon him when he looked 'into this living busy world' and saw 'no reflexion of its Creator'. While refusing to deny 'the real force of the arguments in proof of a God, drawn from the general facts of human society and the course of history', he nonetheless confessed that those arguments 'do not warm me or enlighten me; they do not take away the winter of my desolation or make the buds unfold and the leaves grow within me, and my moral being rejoice'. For Newman 'the sight of the world' was 'nothing else than the prophet's scroll, full of "lamentations and mourning, and woe"'.[42] He thus refused the comfort supposed offered by the great contemporary theodicies of either nature or history.

At the other end of the religious spectrum the impact upon contemporary religious life of Romantic views of religion stemming largely from German philosophy and Friedrich Schleiermacher's theology of feeling provided a new context for men of science and others attracted to the authority of science to question with good conscience older, traditional modes of religious life. Throughout Europe and America the idea spread that religion should be spiritual or based on feelings or subjective longings for the divine rather than being realized through dogmatic theological or formal ecclesiastical settings. In Britain Thomas Carlyle represented the major cultural conduit of these ideas, although they appeared in numerous poets as well. Manifesting this outlook in 1860, Thomas Henry Huxley privately stated, '*Sartor Resartus* led me to know that a deep sense of religion was compatible with the entire absence of theology'.[43] This new, fervent spiritual impulse informed by Carlyle's natural supernaturalism allowed men and women to believe they could be genuinely religious while dwelling outside established or organized religious institutions.[44] Idealism in numerous mediated forms also permitted some men of science to have an almost mystical view of matter. Such ideas liberated them morally and spiritually to attack with clear conscience the ecclesiastical establishment and the theodicies associated with natural religion.

Finally, voices of liberal biblical interpretation looked to advances in the physical sciences to aid them in their efforts to transform the reading of scripture and to challenge ecclesiastical authorities on that subject. In *Essays and reviews* Baden Powell declared, 'And if to later times records written in the characters of a long past epoch are left to be deciphered by the advancing light of learning and science, the spirit of faith discovers continually increasing attestation of the Divine authority of the truths they include'.[45] J. B. Colenso, Bishop of Natal and one of the most controversial biblical critics of the 1860s and 1870s, repeatedly pointed to new scientific knowledge as a mode of new divine revelation. According to Colenso, science itself along with scripture is the gift of God: 'God's precious gift, light coming from the father of Lights, and specially coming in greater splendour in this very age in which we live, and given to us by His Grace in order that, by means of it, we may see more clearly than before His Glory and His Goodness'.[46] He asked how ecclesiastical authorities could expect their communicants to accept outmoded readings of scripture that ran counter to the new scientific knowledge.

In effect, Colenso, probably never having read the book, implicitly agreed with Newman's contention in his *Idea of a university* that natural philosophers 'look out for the day when they shall have put down Religion, not by shutting its schools, but by emptying them; not by disputing its tenets, but by the superior worth and persuasiveness of their own'.[47] Colenso believed theology and religious teaching must instead decide to ride the crest of the wave of new natural knowledge rather than resist it. Colenso attracted few followers and many harsh critics, but there did arise during the late century and early twentieth century religious writers who asserted that a new theology compatible with the new science must confront bibliolatry. Such confidence on the part of advanced theologians fostered conflict, as more traditionally minded religionists attempted to defend older opinions that stood in contradiction to the emerging ideas of science.

INTO THE PUBLIC SPHERE: PROSPERITY, EDUCATION, AND PUBLISHING

Changes external to the scientific and religious communities permitted the emerging conflict between them to reach wider audiences and thus to constitute a wider intellectual and cultural event. Between 1750 and 1870 the sphere of public discourse and the instruments for the publication and dispersion of scientific and religious ideas underwent unprecedented expansion. More journals commenting on subjects of the day, more scientific publications, more religious papers and magazines, and more Bibles became available throughout the transatlantic world, the last the result of the various new Bible societies.[48] This relentless expansion of publication meant that by mid-century across the transatlantic world there were more places for people of differing points of view to present their ideas to a wide variety of audiences. The learned periodicals came to constitute a world of self-referential exchange and debate, especially in Great Britain. Furthermore, enterprising editors eager to attract readers encouraged debates in their journals between spokesmen for religion and science.[49]

The expansion of education during the second half of the nineteenth century represented another major change in the European public sphere. The growth of government expenditures for education fostered new conflict because there were finally significant educational resources and institutions for the different religious denominations and their opponents to fight over. There was actual new turf available for conquest by the forces of either religion or naturalistic science, and part of the eruption of conflict related to that expansion of contested turf. The denominations, of course, fought among themselves, but they also fought against secular forces, with the voices of science normally associated with secularization. Across Europe public scientists, such as Huxley and John Tyndall, vigorously opposed the influence of Roman Catholicism in the field of education.

Finally, all of these debates occurred within an atmosphere of new social and political confidence. Anglican and other commentators might still bemoan the moral and social dangers arising from materialism and the collapse of natural religion and biblical authority, but few people in the prosperous 1850s and politically confident 1860s really believed that it would happen, Matthew Arnold's jeremiads to the contrary.[50] The old theodicies no longer seemed necessary as a new, more secure material world dubbed by Huxley 'a new Nature begotten by science upon fact' emerged.[51] It was now safe enough to press scientific naturalism and for spokesmen of science and religion to engage in open conflict. As James Secord has argued:

> The *Origin* was important in resolving a crisis, not in creating one. It offered the opportunity to reduce the tensions between those who advocated specialist ideas of research, and those who looked to developmental cosmology as the underpinning of a new kind of society. These distinctive visions could now be debated under the broad banner of 'Darwinism'.[52]

The relative orderliness of the debate manifested itself in the 1860s by supporters and critics of Darwinian science occupying the presidency of the British Association in alternate years and later in the civil evenings enjoyed in philosophical debate among the members of the Metaphysical Society.

CONCLUDING THOUGHTS

Intellectual history is not only the narrative of changing ideas. It is also the record of events that occur in intellectual life as a result of the engagement and organization of human beings with ideas and with the values they associate with them. Between 1750 and 1870 the ideas and organization

informing the life of both scientific and religious endeavours in the transatlantic world underwent dynamic internal transformations within a no less
rapidly changing climate of political and social revolution. During much of
this period the scientific and religious communities, which often overlapped
each other, sought and achieved accommodations to new ideas in science,
most often in the English-speaking world through the embrace of natural
theology and the social theodicy it provided.

Commencing in the 1840s, however, a younger generation of scientists
became restless with the existing boundaries of thought and action.
Because of their own research and professional ambitions they began to
challenge the status quo of the organization and ideas of science. These
challenges occurred most notably in the realms of geology and biology.
The younger generation of scientists were willing to risk previously avoided
accusations of materialism and transformationism. They found ready allies
in the popular scientific culture of the provincial cities. The publication of
Chambers's *Vestiges of the natural history of creation* opened what became a
far broader challenge to existing modes of genteel accommodation between
the forces of science and religion, and precipitated the public conflict and
controversy that reached its peak in the three decades following the publication of Darwin's *Origin*.

The dynamic world of mid-Victorian science stood paralleled by a no
less dynamic religious world. Contemporary with the emergence of a new,
more fully naturalistic science, there had arisen through the influence of
radical Evangelicalism a new championing of a narrower and more literal
Protestant reading of the Bible. For its own internal reasons, the Roman
Catholic Church in the third quarter of the century undertook a direct
challenge to modern culture, including the emerging culture of science.
Both Protestant and Roman Catholic proponents of dogmatic religion
stood prepared to abandon loyalty to natural religion just as scientists did
the same. Just as the emerging generation of scientists sought to pursue
new professional independence in thought and organization, various
religious groups and theologians sought to establish their own intellectual
and institutional independence, which might or might not involve any
close relationship with natural knowledge.

Consequently, within both the mid-century scientific and religious
communities, various groups saw more to be gained by abandoning the
accommodations of the previous century and setting out on their own,
novel, self-determining directions, with conflict resulting. Had these new
departures occurred in 1800, they would have taken place within a world
of relatively few readers and few journals and quite limited opportunities

for education. Taking place as they did at the mid-century, there were scores of new publications and hundreds of thousands of new readers, and an emerging new educational infrastructure. Thus the late Victorian conflict between science and religion became an event in the life and thought of the expanding literate sectors of transatlantic intellectual life.

NOTES

1 Gordon Allport, *The individual and his religion: A psychological interpretation* (New York: Macmillan, 1950), p. vi.

2 T. H. Huxley, *Science and the Hebrew tradition* (New York: D. Appleton & Co., 1898), pp. 160–1.

3 James Moore, *The post-Darwinian controversies: A study of the Protestant struggle to come to terms with Darwin in Great Britain and America, 1870–1900* (Cambridge: Cambridge University Press, 1979), pp. 19–100.

4 Peter J. Bowler, *Reconciling science and religion: The debate in early-twentieth-century Britain* (Chicago: University of Chicago Press, 2001).

5 Bernard Lightman suggested this important point by adding plurals to the title of his article on 'Victorian sciences and religions: Discordant harmonies', *Osiris* 16 (2001), 343–66. See also: David Wilson, 'Victorian science and religion', *History of Science* 15 (1977), 52–67; Geoffrey Cantor, *Quakers, Jews, and science: Religious responses to modernity and the sciences in Britain, 1650–1900* (Oxford: Oxford University Press, 2005); Crosbie Smith, *Science of energy: A cultural history of energy physics in Victorian Britain* (London: Athlone, 1998).

6 Darrin McMahon, *Enemies of the enlightenment: The French counter-enlightenment and the making of modernity* (New York: Oxford University Press, 2001), pp. 28–42.

7 On the divergence of the continental and British Enlightenments, see Jonathan I. Israel, *Radical enlightenment: Philosophy and the making of modernity, 1650–1750* (Oxford: Oxford University Press, 2001) and *Enlightenment contested: Philosophy, modernity, and the emancipation of man 1670–1752* (New York: Oxford University Press, 2006); Roy Porter, *The creation of the modern world: The untold story of the British Enlightenment* (New York: W. W. Norton, 2001).

8 Mill to Comte, 18 December 1841, *Correspondence of John Stuart Mill and Auguste Comte* (New Brunswick, NJ: Transaction Publishers, 1995), p. 42. On this subject, see also Joseph Hamburger, *John Stuart Mill on liberty and control* (Princeton, NJ: Princeton University Press, 1999).

9 Frank M. Turner, *Contesting cultural authority: Essays in Victorian intellectual life* (Cambridge: Cambridge University Press, 1993), pp. 56–61.

10 J. D. Hooker to C. Darwin, 6 October 1865, in Leonard Huxley, *Life and letters of Joseph Dalton Hooker*, 2 vols. (London: John Murray, 1918), vol. II, p. 54.

11 John Brooke and Geoffrey Cantor, *Reconstructing nature: The engagement of science and religion* (New York: Oxford University Press, 1998), pp. 155–6.

12 Robert Devigne, *Reforming liberalism: J. S. Mill's use of ancient, religious, liberal, and romantic moralities* (New Haven, CT: Yale University Press, 2006).

13 Turner, *Contesting cultural authority*, pp. 101–30.

14 Georg Wilhelm Friedrich Hegel, *Lectures on the philosophy of history*, trans. H. B. Nisbet (Cambridge: Cambridge University Press, 1992), pp. 42–3.

15 Ibid., p. 67.

16 On the problem of evil during this period, see Susan Neiman, *Evil in modern thought: An alternative history of philosophy* (Princeton, NJ: Princeton University Press, 2002).

17 William Paley, *Natural theology* (Houston, TX: St Thomas Press, 1972), p. 314.

18 Ibid., p. 392. One also encounters theodicy arising from natural religion in Malthus, who, while having pointed to 'the unhappy persons who, in the great lottery of life, have drawn a blank', for his part justified reality against its detractors by considering life in this world as a preparation or schoolhouse for the next. Thomas Malthus, *An essay on the principle of population* (London: J. Johnson, 1798), p. 72.

19 Thomas Chalmers, *On the power, wisdom, and goodness of God as manifested in the adaptation of external nature to the moral and intellectual constitution of man*, new edn (Philadelphia: Lee and Blanchard, 1836), pp. 194–5.

20 Leonard G. Wilson (ed.), *Sir Charles Lyell's scientific journals on the species question* (New Haven, CT: Yale University Press, 1970), pp. 86, 121, 205.

21 Thomas Rennell, *Remarks on skepticism, especially as it is connected with the subjects of organization and life being an answer to the views of M. Bichat, Sir T. C. Morgan, and Mr. Lawrence, upon these points* (London: Thomas and George Underwood, 1819), pp. 46–7. See also Walter F. [Susan Fay] Cannon, 'The bases of Darwin's achievement: a revaluation', *Victorian Studies* 5 (1961), 109–34.

22 Mark Francis, *Herbert Spencer and the invention of modern life* (Stocksfield: Acumen, 2007), pp. 189–225; Jim Moore, 'Herbert Spencer's henchmen: The evolution of Protestant liberals in late nineteenth-century America', in John Durant (ed.), *Darwinism and divinity: Essays on evolution and religious belief* (Oxford: Blackwell, 1985), pp. 76–100.

23 Nancy Rose Marshall, '"A dim world, where monsters dwell": The spatial time of the Sydenham Crystal Palace Dinosaur Park', *Victorian Studies* 49 (2007), 286–301.

24 Wilson, *Charles Lyell's scientific journals*, pp. 56–7, 84.

25 Martin Fichman, *An elusive Victorian: The evolution of Alfred Russel Wallace* (Chicago: University of Chicago Press, 2004), p. 2.

26 Frederick Gregory, *Scientific materialism in nineteenth-century Germany* (Dordrecht: Reidel, 1977).

27 Lightman, 'Victorian sciences and religions', 346.

28 Thomas Scott, *The Holy Bible, containing the old and new testaments, with original notes, practical observations, and copious marginal references*, originally published in 1788, with numerous subsequent editions.

29 Ernest R. Sandeen, *The roots of fundamentalism: British and American fundamentalism, 1800–1930* (Chicago: University of Chicago Press, 1970); W. H. Oliver,

Prophets and millennialists: The use of biblical prophecy in England from the 1790s to the 1840s (Auckland: Auckland University Press and Oxford University Press, 1978).

30 Harriet Martineau, *Eastern life: Past and present* (Philadelphia: Lea and Blanchard, 1848), p. 384.

31 John Rogerson, *Old Testament criticism in nineteenth-century England and Germany* (Philadelphia: Fortress Press, 1985), pp. 79–90; Jon H. Roberts, *Darwinism and the divine in America: Protestant intellectuals and organic evolution, 1859–1900* (Madison: University of Wisconsin Press, 1988). See also David N. Livingstone, *Darwin's forgotten defenders: The encounter between evangelical theology and evolutionary thought* (Grand Rapids, MI: Eerdmans, 1987).

32 Wilson, *Charles Lyell's scientific journals*, pp. 59–60, 87–9. In 1856 Lyell also wrote, 'Hugh Miller is more of an advocate for the evolution of Man out of preexisting inferior grades than I have been' (p. 88).

33 Charles Wycliffe Goodwin, 'Mosaic cosmogony', in Victor Shea and William Whitla (eds.), *Essays and reviews: The 1860 text and its reading* (Charlottesville: University Press of Virginia, 2000), p. 368.

34 Ronald L. Numbers, *Science and Christianity in pulpit and pew* (New York: Oxford University Press, 2007), pp. 113–28.

35 As quoted in Dan O'Leary, *Roman Catholicism and modern science: A history* (New York: Continuum, 2006), p. 49.

36 As quoted in ibid., pp. 55–6.

37 As quoted in Harvey Hill, *The politics of modernism: Alfred Loisy and the scientific study of religion* (Washington, DC: Catholic University of America Press, 2002), p. 59.

38 Bernard Lightman, *The origins of agnosticism: Victorian unbelief and the limits of knowledge* (Baltimore, MD: Johns Hopkins University Press, 1987), pp. 114–15. As a Roman Catholic, Newman published a revised Tract 85 in *Discussions and arguments on various subjects* (1872) under the title 'Holy Scripture in its Relation to the Catholic Creed'.

39 Frank M. Turner, 'John Henry Newman and the challenge of a culture of science', *The European Legacy* 1 (1996), 1694–1704.

40 *Letters and diaries of John Henry Newman*, 32 vols. (New York: Oxford University Press, 2000), vol. VIII, pp. 559–60.

41 Richard Church, *Guardian*, 18 March 1846, pp. 141–2, as quoted in James Secord, *Victorian sensation: The extraordinary publication, reception, and secret authorship of* Vestiges of the natural history of creation (Chicago: University of Chicago Press, 2000), p. 258.

42 John Henry Newman, *Apologia pro vita sua and six sermons*, ed. Frank M. Turner (New Haven, CT: Yale University Press, 2008), pp. 322–3.

43 T. H. Huxley to Charles Kingsley, 23 September 1860, Leonard Huxley, *Life and letters of Thomas Henry Huxley*, 2 vols. (New York: D. Appleton & Co., 1900), vol. I, p. 237.

44 Turner, *Contesting cultural authority*, pp. 131–50.

45 Baden Powell, 'On the study of the evidences of Christianity', in Shea and Witla, *Essays and reviews*, p. 261.

46 John William Colenso, *The Pentateuch and book of Joshua critically examined*, pt. IV, 2nd edn rev. (London: Longmans, Green, and Co., 1864), p. 303.

47 John Henry Newman, *The idea of a university defined and illustrated, new edition* (London: Longmans, Green, and Co., 1893), p. 403.

48 Leslie Howsam, *Cheap bibles: Nineteenth-century publishing and the British and Foreign Bible Society* (Cambridge: Cambridge University Press, 1991); Aileen Fyfe, *Science and salvation: Evangelical popular science publishing in Victorian Britain* (Chicago: University of Chicago Press, 2004).

49 Alan Willard Brown, *The metaphysical society: Victorian minds in crisis, 1869–1880* (New York: Columbia University Press, 1947); Bernard Lightman, *Victorian popularizers of science: Designing nature for new audiences* (Chicago: University of Chicago Press, 2007).

50 Frank M. Turner, 'The letters of Matthew Arnold', *Victorians Institute Journal* 35 (2007), 251–80.

51 T. H. Huxley, *Collected essays*, 9 vols. (New York: D. Appleton & Co., 1894–8), vol. I, p. 51.

52 Secord, *Victorian sensation*, p. 514.

CHAPTER 6

Islam, Christianity, and the conflict thesis

B. Harun Küçük

The infamous late nineteenth-century 'conflict thesis' focussed primarily on alleged antagonisms between Christianity and science. However, it was the broad and comparative perspective on religion taken by these nineteenth-century accounts that differentiated them from earlier, exclusively anti-Christian polemics. The purpose of the present chapter is to highlight the important role played by ideas about Islam in the articulation of ambitious theses claiming to expose the essential relationship between science, on the one hand, and a generalized category of 'religion', on the other.

Historical studies of Islam, Christianity, philosophy, and science came together in the nineteenth century in a way that was made possible by the fashioning of 'science and religion' as a coherent field of enquiry. A close look at nineteenth-century accounts of the conflict between science and religion shows that Islam and Christianity were often interlinked, and that the narrative accounts of one often complemented the other. Modern historiographies of Christianity and Islam, and their relationships with science, have been closely intertwined.

There were two main – and contradictory – versions of the history of Islamic science as it featured in the narratives of conflict: first, as an intellectually progressive religion that was a true friend of science; and second, as the most backward and anti-scientific religion. In both cases Islam served to accentuate claims about Christianity. Earlier histories of science and religion often adopted the first of these positions, praising Islam for its progressiveness. This was the consequence of the rising scholarly interest in European medieval thought. Studies in this vein investigated the relationship between science and religion in the middle ages, and tended to focus on Arab thinkers whose works had become canonical in the development of European thought. Such works portrayed Arabic thought as a progressive tradition and Islam as a religion more in harmony with science than was Christianity. Islam featured here as a telling exception, as a religion that was completely separate from Christianity and in harmony with science.

In the second version of the history of Islam and science, however, Islam was used as the basis of a transhistorical understanding of all religion. In this latter capacity the study of Islam was used not only to level criticisms against the medieval church but also to lead to conclusions about the very nature of religion, and of Christianity, that were as valid in the middle ages as they were in nineteenth-century Europe. Many scholars maintained that Islam represented the purest form of Semitic monotheism and that it boasted the additional advantage of being historically accessible due to its relatively late emergence. Consequently the study of Islam became an integral part of the philological, historical, and anthropological criticism of monotheistic faith, especially in Protestant faculties of theology. The resulting critique of monotheistic backwardness and superstition was extensively deployed in attacks against the Catholicism of nineteenth-century Europe. The historical study of Islam, therefore, was seen as playing a key role in transforming understandings of the conflict between science and Christianity.

One of the main actors who rendered Islam useful both as a discursive tool in the study of medieval philosophy and as a means to define religion was Ernest Renan. His landmark thesis of the conflict between Islam and science was one of various uses made of Islam in broader science-and-religion debates that targeted Christianity. Renan's eloquent synthesis seemed to have sealed the fate of the history of Islamic science and effectively sequestered its study from both western historiography of science and from the history of the relationship between science and religion. The close reading of Renan's *L'Islamisme et la science* undertaken below helps to explain why we no longer treat Islam as an integral part of scholarship on the history of science and religion.[1]

While the uses of Islam for European ends do not capture the totality of interest in nineteenth-century scholarship on Islam, the uses of Islam have without doubt determined the boundaries of its study. In the closing pages of this chapter I shall address how the conception of Islamic science developed in the science-and-religion debates of the nineteenth century decisively shaped the subsequent concerns of historians of Islamic science and philosophy.[2]

ISLAM'S CONTRIBUTION TO MEDIEVAL SCIENCE
AND PHILOSOPHY

Islam played an important role in the formation of well-known conflict narratives produced in the nineteenth century. Both John William Draper and Andrew Dickson White used the early and rudimentary histories of

Islamic science and philosophy to accentuate their attack on Christianity. Draper devoted a whole section to Islam and dubbed it 'the First Southern Reformation', placing Islam at variance with Catholicism from the outset. White had a good sprinkling of anecdotal treatments of Islam to draw on, but no extended narrative account.[3] In the accounts of both authors Islam appeared as a religion that could, quite unlike Christianity, co-exist with science. This picture of Islam functioned as an ornamental addition to the central story of a conflict between science and Christianity in the middle ages.

What made Islam appear so friendly to science was the context in which it was treated. Since the development of European thought owed more to translations from Arabic in the twelfth century than it did to European thought prior to those translations, Islam's advantage over (Catholic) Christianity required no explanation, only embellishment. Islam appeared very progressive in comparison with medieval Europe. Islam had also effectively created both European scholasticism and Aristotelianism. It was in Islam's role as a source of medieval European thought that it began to attract significant attention from historians in the nineteenth century. And not coincidentally, questions asked of Islam closely mirrored the expectations from Islam as a discursive tool by which to define some of the essential properties of medieval philosophy, and especially the role of the Catholic Church. There was a measure of anti-Catholic sentiment in nearly all nineteenth-century celebrations of Islam.

A short but important episode in the early phases of scholarship on the history of Islamic philosophy illustrates this point. The first academic monograph[4] on the history of Arabic philosophy was written in 1842 by the philologist Franz August Schmölders, who was something of an exception to this typical interest in Arabic philosophy.[5] In this work, *Essai sur les écoles philosophiques chez les Arabes et notemment sur la doctrine d'Algazzali*, Schmölders articulated a contempt for Arabic philosophy that would gain currency only after his death.[6] There was no such thing as Arabic philosophy in the sense that there is Greek or German philosophy, Schmölders claimed. In his account most Arabic thinkers were not original but remained within well-defined philosophical camps. These are claims that most historians of Islamic science and philosophy are still familiar with, even today.

While Schmölders's depiction of Arabic philosophy could have been palatable as a scholarly verdict about the nature of Arabic thought to his contemporary audience, it was in fact received with disappointment. What Schmölders had omitted from this work was any explanation of the significance of the Islamic contribution to the development of philosophy in medieval Europe. Furthermore he had argued that the best characterization of Arabic philosophy was by reference to theological positions specific to Islam. Schmölders's version of Arabic philosophies as varieties of theology presented a self-contained tradition and completely overlooked what Europe could borrow from the internal and culturally specific products of Arabic thought.

The first to voice his disappointment was Heinrich Ritter, easily the most influential historian of philosophy of his generation.[7] Ritter wrote a forty-two-page review of Schmölders's *Essai* in which he harshly criticized Schmölders for his failure to address the relevance of Arabic philosophy to 'our progress', by which he meant the development of Arabic Aristotelianism that later became the centrepiece of progressive European thought in the middle ages. From an historiographical standpoint, Ritter also expected to see a tighter integration of religious sentiment with classical rationalism in Arabic philosophy, an expectation guided by what he knew of European philosophy. It was not without reason that the title of his short essay on Arabic philosophy was so blunt in framing the problem: *On our knowledge of Arabic philosophy.* We knew practically nothing that could help us properly place Arabic thought on the timeline of human progress.

Ritter's early critique of Schmölders's *Essai* contained a vision of Arabic philosophy, as well as an agenda for future research. Ritter believed that the most genuinely 'Arabic' part of Arabic philosophy was the thought of the *mutakallimin*, or the rational theologians, who had achieved a perfect synthesis of faith and philosophy, above and beyond the articulation of specific theological positions. This identification of Arabic philosophy later featured prominently in Ritter's *Geschichte der Philosophie*, where he included Arabic philosophy under the general rubric of Christian philosophy precisely because he accepted that the synthesis of faith and reason that began in Arabic thought culminated in Christian Europe in subsequent centuries. Besides their historically unique function as those first to achieve such a synthesis, the Arabs were the torchbearers of Greek philosophy through the middle ages. They were also the ones who carried into Europe secular Aristotelian thought, which would lay the groundwork for modern philosophy. These two important elements in the history of Arabic thought, Ritter argued, both stood in need of empirical investigation.

Ritter was soon joined by two other scholars, Ernest Renan and Salomon Munk. Renan was a promising young scholar from Paris who later became the most important scholar of Islamic philosophy, while Munk, already a well-established historian of Jewish thought, had criticized Schmölders for the absence of Arabic Aristotelianism in his account and had supplemented Ritter's critique with philological corrections to the *Essai.*[8] Munk and

Renan were both primarily interested in the secular Arabic philosophy that was persecuted by religious authorities and in Arab-influenced Jewish and Latin thought, which was also eventually persecuted in Europe.[9]

Schmölders's ultimately unsatisfying *Essai* was to be completely supplanted by another that did respond to the pressing questions that scholars addressed regarding the history of Arabic science and philosophy. The new work that would address Ritter's questions and would eventually launch the history of Arabic science into its new career was Ernest Renan's 1852 dissertation, *Averroès et l'averroïsme*. This work was essentially an examination of the influence of Averroës' philosophy on the development of secular thought in Europe from the middle ages to the sixteenth-century Aristotelian school of Padua.[10] One could hardly do better than Renan in connecting some of the most secular ideas inherited from Arabic philosophy with the progress of European thought. Renan also discussed Averroës in a way most conducive to thinking about the relationship between science and religion in Europe.

Although Renan was generally impervious to the Arabic context of Averroës' philosophy, he achieved what Schmölders did not. He had shown that Averroism, broadly defined as 'negation of the supernatural, of miracles, angels, demons, divine intervention; and explaining religion and moral beliefs by means of imposture',[11] had exerted a lasting impact on the European intellect. Renan's dissertation was significant not only because it was the point of origin for the systematic study of Arabic philosophy and one of the first studies of medieval philosophy but also because it was an original historical formulation of the relationship between science and religion. Renan had crafted his narrative of the career of Averroism as one of conflict between Christian theologians and genuine philosophers.

Both Draper and White made ample reference to Renan. According to many other authors Renan had shown the admirable performance of Arabic philosophy in stark comparison to the darkness that lulled contemporary Europe, for which Christianity was responsible. The general understanding of Renan's work as a celebration of Arabic philosophy and an attack on Catholicism reflects the layers of irony that surround the reception of this work and exposes the fact that the primary interest of the readers was to understand science and religion in the European context.

First and foremost, Renan did not really write a history of Arabic philosophy. His dissertation focussed on Averroës' philosophy, and only a minute portion of the entire work addressed Averroës, Arabic thought, or the relationship between Islam and philosophy. Regardless, Renan made a few remarks on the general features of all Arabic philosophy, which were also generally overlooked. His preface to the first edition set the tone of his work as a contribution to the history of Arabic and European medieval philosophy:

Philosophy among the Semites lacks fecundity and has never been anything other than something purely external, a foreign loan, or an imitation of the Greeks. It is necessary to say as much about medieval philosophy. The Middle Ages, so profound, so original, so poetic in its outburst of religious enthusiasm, is, as regards intellectual culture, nothing other than a long period of trial and error in the effort to return to the great schools of sublime thought, i.e. to antiquity.[12]

Second, although most works devoted to the history of Arabic philosophy and science expressed a negative opinion of Arabic science, these works ironically became the source of much positive commentary on Arabic science and philosophy at the expense of medieval Christianity. Among such positive responses were those of Draper and White, but we could multiply our examples, even to include Bertrand Russell's *History of western philosophy*.[13] Islam helped to highlight the conflict between Christianity and science by offering a strong contrast with Christianity. The disparity between the nineteenth-century historiography of Arabic science and philosophy and its uses is nowhere clearer than on this issue.

Schmölders, whose failure to satisfy his readership is even more remarkable when we see that he was the only scholar with a persistent interest in Arabic philosophy itself, was the exception who explained the rule in the study of Arabic philosophy in the nineteenth century. While Ritter and Renan both occupied prized chairs in Göttingen and the Collège de France respectively, Schmölders spent the rest of his career isolated in Breslau, on the fringes of the German academe of his day. With Schmölders's marginalization, no other author before Ignaz Goldziher would object to the dependence of the readings of the history of Arabic philosophy on the European preoccupation with 'science and religion' and progress.[14]

ISLAM, BIBLICAL SCHOLARSHIP AND CONFLICT

This engagement with Arabic science and philosophy as the source of medieval European thought was one of the meagre and superficial contributions of the study of Islam to the European understanding of the relationship between science and religion. It was Islam's role as the archetype of religion and as the purest form of Semitic monotheism that contributed most to the conceptualization of science and religion, in both direct and indirect ways.[15] The study of Islam helped articulate what many thought was the real conflict.

What we see in the nineteenth century, especially in continental Europe, is a convergence of Islamic studies and theology, and the formulation of a much broader and deeper crisis within European culture that encompassed more than just science and religion.[16] As such, the study of Islam was in the same league and worked towards the same ends as biblical higher criticism, histories of ancient Israel, and histories of early Christianity. That is, it worked towards the historical, philological, and anthropological criticism of monotheistic faith in general and Christianity in particular.[17] The leverage provided by the study of Islam was more pronounced than other veins of enquiry, because Islam was the only living example of genuine Semitic monotheism.

Semitic monotheism as a rigorous and scientific concept was the product of a philological movement that culminated in the acceptance of the science of religion as a legitimate and important academic discipline.[18] The study of all three Semitic monotheisms first took place within faculties of theology, particularly in German Protestant universities, especially Göttingen, in the context of the rise of oriental philology. Oriental philology had been a staple subject of European learning at least since the Renaissance. However, the beginnings of biblical higher criticism in Tübingen charged philology with a different task: to understand the origins of Christianity. Soon enough Göttingen followed this example and started producing a comprehensive philological criticism of the Old Testament under the aegis of Heinrich Ewald. In 1838 Ewald demanded that oriental studies, which included the philological treatment of religious texts, be 'fully separated' from 'all that is theological'.[19] The movement soon spread to much of Europe, and students of philology started leaving theology departments of which they had been members. Their enquiry, they argued, was scientific and had nothing to do with theology. As a consequence of these bold moves philology was beginning to bring science into the study of religion. At no point were oriental philologists so relevant to European faith as at this time, when philological research was systematically used against established programmes of study in faculties of theology. And at no point were they as destructive to theology as when they turned into the 'sciences of religion' in the 1870s. The establishment of chairs of science of religion in universities across Europe shows the emergence of this new academic subject: 1868 in France and 1876 in the Netherlands.[20]

Oriental philology's power came from its ability to offer new sources for understanding religion. Philology was a scientific and self-sufficient discipline, unlike theology, and it drew its understanding of religion not from philosophizing on the gospels but from historicizing the sources.

It was no longer the Church fathers but the histories of ancient Israel that were the preferred sources. The true historical record of Christianity was no longer St Jerome's Latin Vulgate but a collection of Aramaic manuscripts from the era. Consequently Christianity was no longer seen as a Roman or European religion but as a cultural product of the Hebrews of Israel, where Christianity had first emerged.[21]

A survey of scholars of the history of Islam will show that they were key actors in this reconceptualization of genuine Christianity, and this fact only deepens the co-dependence of the study of Islam and Christianity, mediated through the Semitic connection. Important figures in the nineteenth-century study of Islam such as Julius Wellhausen, Ernest Renan, Abraham Kuenen, and Theodor Nöldeke also contributed greatly to the rise of the science of religion as an academic discipline and to the formulation of the idea of Semitic monotheism.

Semitic monotheism found its sharpest expression when it was placed side by side with the theory of Indo-European, Indo-Germanic, or Indo-Aryan races. Most authors trace the introduction of the latter concept to Herder, one of the key figures in the creation of German nationalism, but the idea put on scientific garb only after Franz Bopp, an important philologist, decisively showed the family resemblances between Indian, Persian, and ancient European languages.[22] Bopp's linguistic theory was also supplemented by other comparative studies of mythology, philosophy, religion, and culture.

Indo-European races were viewed as inherently polytheistic, artistic, democratic, and, most importantly, scientific. The evidentiary basis for this claim was quite wide, ranging from a Herderian understanding of the original German *volk* to Schlegel's studies of Indian myths, and from Greek philosophy to the emergence of modern science.[23] Nineteenth-century conceptions of Semitic monotheism, closely paralleling the study of the Indo-European races, also had many layers, including a thorough-going racial framework. Many scholars of Semitic monotheisms argued for the existence of a distinct Semitic race. This argument was based on the shared grammatical structure of Aramaic, Hebrew, and Arabic, on similarities in legends and myths, and on the origins of all religions in the Middle East. The Semites, it was argued, displayed certain common anthropological characteristics and were the original monotheistic people. The Semites also had no identifiable polytheistic faith in their history, had produced no myths, and tended towards despotic rule. Semites, thus defined, were the photographic negative of Indo-Europeans.

The nearly contemporary articulation of the two racial theories seemed to explain much of European history and addressed many problems in nineteenth-century Europe. European culture was seen as the combination of the cultural products of the Semites and the Indo-Aryans. Semites gave Europe religion, and the Indo-Aryans gave it science and democracy. These ideas called for a re-orientation of European identity. Formerly, European identity had two sources: the Athens of Greek philosophy and the Jerusalem of Christian faith. According to these new ideas about the sources of European culture, ancient India appeared to be a better source for understanding Europe than did ancient Israel. At this juncture the science-and-religion question became one of the many facets of a more fundamental and many-layered tension between two races, the cultural products of which had mixed to produce contemporary European culture. The idea that original Christianity, like Judaism and Islam, was just another example of Semitic monotheism, and hence alien to the original European peoples, greatly eroded the Christian element in European identity.[24]

Christianity now seemed closer to Islam and Judaism and further from Europe than it ever had. Islam reflected the purest form of Semitic monotheism for several reasons. First and foremost, it was the product of a Semitic race, the Arabs, and found its expression in a Semitic language, Arabic. Judaism and Christianity were similar to Islam in that they were born to another Semitic race, the Hebrews, and were expressed in Semitic languages, Hebrew and Aramaic. However, both Judaism and Christianity had complex engagements first with the Roman empire, then with the European peoples. This had enriched their traditions but also clouded their true nature. Islam, on the other hand, had proven resistant, first to Hellenization by Greek thought, then to Europeanization in the nineteenth century. Since Islam had resisted external influence better than Judaism and Christianity, it was the best example of Semitic monotheism to study.[25]

Furthermore the comparative study of the Semitic races offered a direction for future reform. Islam epitomized many of the outdated social and moral precepts of Christianity, particularly Catholic Christianity.[26] Considering that science, democracy, and many other prized institutions of contemporary Europe were now traceable to the racial properties of Indo-European races, living by the laws of an alien, Semitic, culture appeared less and less attractive to most intellectuals. It was at this juncture that Islam became the explicit articulation of Europe's implicit problems with the Christian religion. Islam, having remained alien to Indo-European peoples, stood in stark opposition to all the cultural products of Indo-Europeans and was also a summary of everything religious that stood in opposition to science.

The conflict between science and religion was a particularly touchy subject, since science had risen to an unprecedented prominence within

Europe. It was Ernest Renan who expressed the implications of the original tension in European identity most clearly:

The intolerance of the Semitic people is a necessary consequence of their monotheism. The Indo-European nations before their conversion to Semitic, that is to Jewish, Christian or Mussulman ideas, having never accepted their religion as absolute truth, but as a sort of family or caste inheritance, of necessity remained strangers to intolerance and to proselytism; it is only among these people therefore that we find liberty of thought, the spirit of investigation and of individual research.[27]

That Islam had once been a friend of science seemed more like an isolated fact than a statement about the nature of Islam, especially when juxtaposed against the long-lasting paucity of Arabic science. Indeed, studying the exceptional intellectual successes of the Islamic middle ages as a passing moment of scientific efflorescence stuck between periods of ignorance and dogmatism characterized the next period in the historiography of Islamic science. Precedent alone could not explain how and why Islam came to be understood as a religion inimical to science; some of the most negative opinions about Islam were already evident at least thirty years before the 1870s, when they again became popular. The cause was the development of a theoretical framework for the treatment of all Semitic religions that could use Islamic science to illustrate the very nature of the relationship between science and religion. Once again Renan most effectively expressed the new direction in the study of the relationship between Islam and science:

There are monotheistic as there are polytheistic races; and this difference is due to an original diversity in their way of looking at nature. In the Arabian or Semitic conception, nature is not alive. The desert is monotheistic. Sublime in its uniform immensity, it revealed the very first day the idea of the infinite, but not that thought of fruitful activity which a nature incessantly creative has inspired in the Indo-European mind. This is why Arabia has always been the bulwark of monotheism. Nature plays no part in the Semitic religions; they are all of the head, all metaphysical and psychological. The extreme simplicity of the Semitic mind – without compass, without diversity, without plastic arts, without philosophy, without mythology, without political life, without progress – has no cause but this: in monotheism there is no variety.[28]

These theories successfully turned the nineteenth-century conflicts within European culture between science and religion, between absolutism and democracy, and between liberty and servitude, into irreducible states of affairs. The stakes appeared much higher and the conflict appeared much more difficult to resolve. Moreover the varieties of conflict between science and religion no longer appeared to be different in kind but in degree.

RENAN'S 'L'ISLAMISME ET LA SCIENCE' AS AN HISTORIOGRAPHICAL LANDMARK

It was this broader context that informed the most powerful nineteenth-century expression of the idea of an historic conflict between science and Islam. Renan's *L'Islamisme et la science* is the classic account of the conflict thesis in the Islamic context. Historians of Arabic science and philosophy cite this short lecture in nearly all historiographical accounts, in much the same way that historians studying the relationship between science and Christianity cite Draper and White. Since there have been no close readings of this seminal text, it is useful to attempt a brief summary that will show that Renan's real target was monotheism in general, not just Islam.

L'Islamisme et la science opens with the claim that Renan will be treating a 'subject of utmost subtlety', and that he intends to dispel the misunderstandings in history that are engendered by 'the want of precision in the use of those words that designate nations and races'.[29] The particular lack of precision that Renan wished to dispel was the 'equivocation contained within these words: Arabic science, Arabic philosophy, Arabic art, Muslim science and Muslim civilisation'. Renan went on to speak of the political and intellectual poverty of Islam. He assumed that he shared with anyone who had been to the Middle East the experience of the 'strikingly narrow mind of a true believer', 'the iron circlet that covers his head', and the Muslim's inability to 'understand anything or come up with any novel idea'.[30] In turn Renan extended the charge to Catholicism and claimed that the fact that Galileo was a Catholic was a psychological stumbling block to his scientific research.[31]

However, Islam was unique in that it imbued the believer with the 'indignant folly' of thinking that the truth of his religion alone was absolute. The Muslim therefore had no regard for the merit of another, 'for education, science, and for all that constitutes the European mind'. Renan particularly noted Islam's inability or unwillingness to become European. This claim carried far more gravity than might at first appear. Renan himself had already given more than a hint about how to interpret this statement in 1862: 'The future, gentlemen, is therefore for Europe and Europe alone. Europe will conquer the world and pour out her religion, which is law, liberty and human rights'.[32] The reference was unmistakably to the relationship between the Semitic races and the Indo-Aryans.

Harking back to his famous work on Averroës, Renan noted that all peoples who had come under the rule of Islam, regardless of their race or nationality, had become a homogeneous whole characterized solely by

Islam.[33] The Persians were the only exception to this, because they were 'Shiites more than they were Muslims'. While a supple mind would be needed to show how one can be a Shiite without being a Muslim first, this issue was not addressed by Renan: the point he was trying to make had to do with the fact that Persians, unlike Arabs, were Indo-European.[34] Persians were pantheistic, creative, and scientific like all other Indo-Europeans, while the Semites lacked all of these features and possessed an exclusive predilection and genius for monotheism.[35]

To supplement further the essential racial tension, Renan also offered a short historical exegesis. According to Renan, the early period of Islam was a 'thousand leagues away from all that can be called rationalism or science'.[36] In the year 750, when 'the Persians got the upper hand and helped the Abbasids overcome the Umayyads' and the centre of Islam 'found itself moved to the region between Euphrates and Tigris', there were many 'signs of the most brilliant civilisation known to the East, that of the Sassanids'. This Sassanid revival was the most outstanding characteristic of the reign of the Abbasids. According to Renan, the Persians had proven extremely resilient against Islam and had retained their national cult of 'Persism', as he called it. This was also the time when Greek influence was slowly making itself felt through Harran, which had 'a considerable contingent of learned men who were entirely foreign to revealed religion'. The resultant mixture was characterized not by the Arabs but by Indo-Europeans. In this period, Renan maintained, the caliphs themselves were hardly Muslims and had no interest in becoming any more pious than was necessary to keep their appearance as 'the popes' of Islam.[37]

Renan later outlined his peculiar interpretation of the translations of philosophical works from Greek to Arabic. He recognized the role of Syrian Christians in undertaking these translations. Renan claimed that these translations gave rise to a new type of intellectual in Muslim lands, the *feylesuf*s (philosophers), who were invariably called *zindiq*s (unbelievers) by their co-religionists. The word *feylesuf* was of Greek origin and connoted someone foreign to Islam.

According to Renan, even these figures represented Greco-Sassanid philosophy written in the Arabic language. Then, 'while Averroës, the last Arab philosopher, was dying in Morocco, sad and lonely, our West was in full vigilance'.[38] After 1200 'the theological reaction swept philosophy out completely. Philosophy was then abolished in the Muslim lands'. He proceeded to argue that, early in the thirteenth century, an Arabicized Aristotelian philosophy made its 'triumphant entry to the University of Paris', and the West shrugged off its 'four or five hundred years of inferiority'. 'From shortly after 1275, two distinct movements appear: First, the Muslim lands are spoiled in a state of sorry intellectual decadence; second, Western Europe starts up in this great avenue of scientific research for truth – an immense curve the amplitude of which cannot be measured'.[39]

Whatever happened before the thirteenth century was due to the fact that Islam was 'eaten away with sects, and tempered by a kind of Protestantism (called *mutazilism*), [that was] far less organized, and far less fanatical' than it was afterwards, in the hands of Berber and Tartar races, that were 'heavy-handed, brutal and lacking in intellect'.[40] Renan's final verdict on Arabic and Islamic science was damning:

Islam is the union of the spiritual and the temporal, it is the reign of a dogma, it is a chain heavier than mankind has ever carried. In the first half of the Middle Ages, I repeat, Islam supported philosophy, for it had not the power to stop it. It had not the power because it was without cohesion and ill equipped for terror.[41]

The confounding of the spiritual and the temporal, and the tension between science and religion were subjects his European audience could easily relate to, based on their own problems. One of Renan's concluding remarks drove the point home in case there was any confusion about the lessons for Christians to learn from this short lecture on Islam: 'Mistakenly attributing to Arabia the entirety of Arab philosophy and science is the same as attribut-ing all Christian Latin literature, all the Scholastics, the Renaissance in its entirety, the science of the sixteenth and seventeenth centuries to the city of Rome, because it was written in Latin'.[42] The attitudes of Islam and Christianity towards science were remarkably similar.

THE AFTERMATH OF 1883

Although Renan's account of the conflict between Islam and science was articulated on the basis of a broad racial dynamics that was intended to be as valid for Christianity as for Islam, most scholars continue to read Renan's work as an attack on Islam alone. Quite a few scholars, the most famous among whom would be Eilhard Wiedemann and Heinrich Suter, did much of the groundwork for the history of Arabic astronomy, alchemy, and the mechanical arts but remained within Renan's frame-work. Another good example where Renan's opinions have been repro-duced almost verbatim is T. J. de Boer's famous 1903 book on the *History of philosophy in Islam*.[43] These writers perceived themselves as working within a scientific and philosophical tradition that was truly alien to and persecuted by Islam. The absorption of Renan's essentially racial account of the development of Islamic science into the very organization of the field has been key to the subsequent isolation of the history of Islamic science from adjacent fields of enquiry.

The irony of the recalcitrance of Renan's ideas is quite evident when we look at those scholars who were otherwise seeking to improve their fields. Eilhard Wiedemann, a well-known historian of Arabic alchemy and mechanical arts, voiced his discomfort about the European ignorance of Arabic science in an inaugural lecture in 1890, while remarking upon the felicitous establishment of a seminar for Oriental languages in Berlin under Eduard Sachau. In the same year a similar discomfort was voiced by Heinrich Suter, the distinguished historian of Arabic astronomy. While the work of both scholars boded well for the future of empirical enquiries into the history of Arabic science, their general narrative of the history of science was not very different from that of Renan. For while the idea that all Semitic religions were opposed to science faded from the scholarship on Arabic science, the thesis that only Arabs and Islam were necessarily inimical to science assumed a prominent role among expert researchers.

Suter quoted and agreed with Renan on many significant points. He, too, considered the most important characteristic of the Arabs to be their Semitism, that is, their exclusive intellectual focus on matters of religion, and he found the origins of Arabic science in the Greeks and the Indo-Europeans.[44] Both Suter and Wiedemann associated the flowering of Arabic science with a weak Islamic government which, upon gaining strength, dispensed with intellectual enquiry. Both Wiedemann and Suter found that Islam and scientific enquiry never went together, and that most of the philosophers or scientists of the so-called Arabic golden age followed wholesale either the Qu'ran or Aristotelian rationalism. They also wrote that the Arabs lacked and were unable to understand the independent scientific spirit of Greek genius. This new version of the conflict narrative, formulated by a second generation of scholars working on Arabic science, retold the story in a way that was specific to the Arabs, and to their supposed lack both of creative thought and of scientific imagination.[45]

Remaining within the Islamic context, most scholars of Islam interpreted Renan's narrative as solely applicable to Islam. A key step in the separation of the history of Islamic science from the broader history of science came when Catholic apologetics rose to prominence in the early twentieth century. Pierre Duhem's *Système du monde* was a particularly influential example of this genre, deliberately separating the history of Islamic science from the broader science-and-religion question. In the section treating Maimonides and Averröes, Duhem claimed that '[t]he supple intelligence of the Jew, able to turn down contrary opinions, to weigh advantages and inconveniences, knows how to remain in suspense between two risky choices, while the simple Arab, disdainful of subtle distinctions and indecisive attitudes, gives himself entirely to the party he has once embraced'. As Jamil Ragep noted recently, while Duhem did not adopt Renan's thesis of the conflict between science and Semitic religion (or science and Catholicism) wholesale, the anti-Arabic element persisted in his work, along with the added charge against Arabic thinkers of scientific realism – an undesirable attitude towards science that Duhem associated with a lack of scientific imagination.[46]

It was not until the 1950s that the study of Islamic science and philosophy became fashionable again, as multicultural sensibilities developed in reaction to the Second World War.[47] Renan once again came to prominence but now as an author to react against. Most work after 1950 was motivated by the desire to redistribute the credit of scientific achievement in order to include Islamic science. Most of these works accepted that there was such a thing as Islamic science. This has resulted in a quite different type of study that highlighted the originality of Islamic science. Of course, the question of originality has led to a very strong internalist tradition in the historiography of Islamic science, concerned mainly with unearthing the specific scientific and technical achievements of Muslim scholars. However, this type of work has proven very easy to confuse with an apology for Islamic science, since it was a reaction against a wholesale attack on the nature of Islam. However, such an apology would be hard to sustain. Most Islamic countries today are not at the forefront of scientific research, and many of them continue to be sites of struggle between democracy and religion. Hence, without properly historicizing the enterprise of science and Islam, it will be impossible to address Renan's *L'Islamisme* in a satisfactory fashion.

Furthermore, despite the efforts of many scholars, the typically European interest in Islamic science – an interest that favours those parts of Islamic science that made it into the European canon – still exerts a strong influence on the organization of research. An inordinate amount of scholarship on Islamic science is still focussed on the middle ages, a fact that cannot simply be explained by reference to the comparative richness of that period. The organization of research continues to exclude both the subsequent history of Islamic science, and also the social and cultural factors surrounding science and philosophy in traditionally Muslim settings. These previously excluded factors will be the keys to a proper revision of the understanding of science and religion in the Islamic context, which is, in turn, important for a fuller appreciation of the relationship between science and religion.

Writing in 2007, George Saliba, a prominent historian of Arabic astronomy, articulated how the combination of ignorance and Renanian disdain had exerted an extremely adverse influence on the study of Arabic science. Speaking of the classical narrative, which Renan defended in 1883, Saliba wrote: 'These surrounding civilisations [especially the Greeks and the Persians] are usually endowed with considerable antiquity, with high degrees of scientific production, and with a degree of intellectual activity that could not have existed in the Islamic desert civilisation'.[48] Saliba's testimony shows that the thesis of a conflict between science and Islam continues to haunt the historiography of Islamic science with exceptional force, despite the fact that it was a by-product of much earlier anti-Christian polemics. Historians of Islamic science have recently offered serious revisions to the classical narrative,[49] but finding a new place for Islam in the history of science will very much depend on the reception of their work in adjacent fields, among which historians of science and religion form perhaps the most important and numerous group. That Islam occupies a significant position in the present volume suggests that a major corrective to our understanding of the relationship between science and Islam is finally underway.

NOTES

I would like to thank Thomas Dixon, Geoffrey Cantor, and Robert S. Westman for their invaluable contributions to the preparation and revision of this chapter.

1 Ernest Renan, *L'Islamisme et la science: Conférence faite à la Sorbonne le 29 Mars 1883* (Paris: Édition Calmann Lévy, 1883). The 2003 publication of the same lecture changes the title to *L'Islam et la science*. The explanation offered is quite terse: Islamism does not mean what it used to mean then. A similar change in meaning could be found in *Christianisme*/Christianity. See Ernest Renan, *L'Islam et la science: Avec la réponse d'Afghani* (Montpellier: Archange Minotaure, [2003]), p. 1.

2 For a succinct expression of this problem, see D. Gutas, 'The study of Arabic philosophy in the twentieth century: An essay on the historiography of Arabic philosophy', *British Journal of Middle Eastern Studies* 29 (2002), 5–25. Other important historiographical articles include: A. I. Sabra, 'The appropriation and subsequent naturalisation of Greek science in medieval Islam', *History of Science* 25 (1987), 223–43; H. Daiber, 'Science and technology versus Islam: A controversy from Renan and Afghani to Nasr and Needham and its historical background', *Annals of Japan Association for Middle East Studies* 8 (1993), 169–80; F. J. Ragep, 'Duhem, the Arabs and the history of cosmology', *Revue de Synthèse* 83 (1990), 201–14. George Saliba's *Islamic science and the*

making of the European Renaissance (Cambridge, MA: MIT Press, 2007) also brings a new and critical perspective to both the significance and the cultural context of Islamic science.

3 J. W. Draper, *History of the conflict between religion and science* (New York: Appleton, 1874), pp. xiv, xvi, 102–19; A. D. White, *A history of the warfare of science with theology in Christendom*, 2 vols. (New York: Appleton, 1896), vol. I, ch. 5; vol. II, chs. 16–20. However, White's use of Islam is much less casual than that of Draper because of his involvement with the rise of the science of religion, which I shall discuss below.

4 The absence of Jakob Brucker's *Historia critica philosophiae* (1742–4) here is intentional, since his view of Arabic philosophy, and the internal divisions thereof, is highly confusing and ultimately unreliable. See on this point Kurt Flascher, 'Jakob Brucker und die Philosophie des Mittelalters', in Wilhelm Schmidt-Biggemann and Theo Stammen (eds.), *Jacob Brucker (1696–1770): Philosoph und Historiker der europäischen Aufklärung* (Berlin: Akademie Verlag, 1998), pp. 187–97.

5 For a brief biography, see *Allgemeine deutsche Biographie*, Bd. XXXII, pp. 58–9; see also Udo Wörffel, 'August Franz Schmölders (1809–1880), Orientalist an der Universität Breslau', *Jahrbuch der Schlesischen Friedrich-Wilhelms-Universität zu Breslau*, Bd. XLII/XLIII/XLIV (2001–3) for the entry on Schmölders in the faculty album at Breslau, where his *Essai* is mentioned, along with how he showed 'some weakness with respect to philology'. None of Schmölders's critics judged his knowledge of the Arabic language unfavourably. However, that seems to be the implication of the epitaph. The most prominent apology offered in his name for his lack of success in his field is the time in which he lived – a time when oriental studies were not fully developed.

6 August Franz Schmölders, *Essai sur les écoles philosophiques chez les Arabes et notemment sur la doctrine d'Algazzali* (Paris: Didot, 1842).

7 Heinrich Ritter, *Über unsere Kenntniss der arabischen Philosophie und besonders über die Philosophie der orthodoxen arabischen Dogmatiker* (Göttingen: Dieterich, 1844), p. 4: 'But the points about which we mainly seek his advice, since they [the Arabs] have had a very powerful impact on the progress of our sciences [Entwicklung unserer Wissenschaften], are very much ignored'.

8 Hans Daiber, 'The reception of Islamic philosophy in Oxford in the 17th century: The Pococks' (father and son) contribution to the understanding of Islamic philosophy in Europe', in Charles E. Butterworth and Blake A. Kessel (eds.), *The introduction of Arabic philosophy into Europe* (Leiden: Brill, 1994), pp. 73–4.

9 Salomon Munk, *Mélanges de philosophie juive et arabe* (Paris: A. Franck, 1859), pp. 334–8 and Renan, *Averroès et l'averroïsme* (Paris: Levy, 1866 [1852]). Schmölders, unlike most scholars who were interested in the history of Arabic philosophy as a means to understanding the relationship between science and religion in the middle ages, was neither Protestant, nor Jewish, nor an atheist: he was Catholic and consorted with the Catholic elite in Germany. This in part explains why his account of Arabic philosophy could not easily be turned

into polemics against Christianity, nor address the all-important 'science-and-religion' question.

10 Johann Fück, *Die Arabischen Studien in Europa: Bis in den Anfang des 20. Jahrhunderts* (Leipzig: Harrassowitz, 1955), p. 201.

11 Renan, *Averroès*, p. 432.

12 Ibid., p. viii.

13 Bertrand Russell, *A history of western philosophy* (New York: Simon and Schuster, 1972 [1945]), p. 427: 'Between ancient and modern European civilization, the dark ages intervened. The Mohammedans and the Byzantines, while lacking the intellectual energy required for innovation, preserved the apparatus of civilization – education, books, and learned leisure. Both stimulated the West when it emerged from barbarism – the Mohammedans chiefly in the thirteenth century, the Byzantines chiefly in the fifteenth'.

14 Ignaz Goldziher, 'The attitude of orthodox Islam toward the ancient sciences', in Merlin R. Swartz (ed. and trans.), *Studies on Islam* (Oxford: Oxford University Press, 1981), pp. 185–215. This is a translation of 'Stellung der alten islamischen Orthodoxie zu den antiken Wissenschaften', *Abhandlungen der Königl. Preuss. Akademie der wissenschaften* Jahrgang 1915, pp. 4–46. See also L. I. Conrad, 'Ignaz Goldziher on Ernest Renan: From orientalist philology to the study of Islam', in Martin Kramer (ed.), *The Jewish discovery of Islam: Studies in honor of Bernard Lewis* (Tel Aviv: Tel Aviv University Press, 1999), pp. 137–80.

15 Tomoko Masuzawa, *The invention of world religions or, how European universalism was preserved in the language of pluralism* (Chicago: University of Chicago Press, 2005), pp. 196–7.

16 Suzanne Marchand, 'German orientalism and the decline of the West', *Proceedings of the American Philosophical Society* 145 (2001), 465–73.

17 Sabine Mangold, *Eine 'weltbürgerliche Wissenschaft': Die deutsche Orientalistik im 19. Jahrhundert* (Stuttgart: F. Steiner, 2004).

18 Robert Wistrich, 'Radical antisemitism in France and Germany (1840–1880)', *Modern Judaism* 15 (1995), 109–35.

19 Mangold, *Eine 'weltbürgerliche Wissenschaft'*, p. 53.

20 Arie L. Molendijk, 'Transforming theology: The institutionalisation of the science of religion in the Netherlands', in Arie L. Molendijk and Peter Pels (eds.), *Religion in the making: The emergence of the sciences of religion* (Leiden: Brill, 1998), pp. 70–1.

21 Renan's *Life of Jesus*, trans. Charles E. Wilbour (New York: Carleton, 1864) and Abraham Kuenen's Hibbert Lectures from 1882, published as *National religions and universal religions* (London: Williams & Norgate, 1883), are good depictions of Christianity as a cultural product of the Hebrews.

22 Franz Bopp, *Vergleichende Grammatik des Sanskrit, Zend, Griechischen, Lateinischen, Lituanischen, Gotischen und Deutschen*, 4 vols. (Berlin: F. Dümmler, 1833–42); see also *A comparative grammar of the Sanskrit, Zend, Greek, Latin, Lithuanian, Gothic, German, and Slavonic languages*, trans. E. B. Eastwick (Hildesheim: Georg Olms, 1985).

23 S. Arvidsson, *Aryan idols: Indo-European mythology as ideology and science* (Chicago: University of Chicago Press, 2006).

24 See Marchand, 'German orientalism'.

25 Masuzawa, *Invention of world religions*, p. 196.

26 See Maurice Olender, *The languages of Paradise: Aryans and Semites, a match made in heaven*, trans. Arthur Goldhammer (Cambridge, MA: Harvard University Press, 1992), pp. 51–81, 93–104; Tuska Benes, 'Comparative linguistics as ethnology: In search of Indo-Germans in central Asia, 1770–1830', *Comparative Studies of South Asia, Africa and the Middle East* 24 (2004), 117–32, 119.

27 Ernest Renan, 'The history of the people of Israel', in Renan, *Studies of religious history and criticism*, trans. O. B. Frothingham (New York: Carleton, 1864), p. 117.

28 Ibid., p. 103.

29 Renan, *L'Islamisme*, p. 1.

30 Ibid., p. 2.

31 Ibid., p. 19.

32 Ernest Renan, *De la part des peuples sémitiques dans l'histoire de la civilisation: Discours d'ouverture du cours de langues hébraïque, chaldaïque et syriaque, au Collège de France* (Paris: M. Lévy Freres, 1862), p. 28.

33 Renan, *L'Islamisme*, p. 3.

34 See Renan, *Histoire générale et comparé des langues sémitiques*, 2nd edn (Paris: M. Lévy Frères, 1858).

35 Ibid., p. 3.

36 Renan *L'Islamisme*, p. 5.

37 Ibid., pp. 6–7.

38 Ibid., p. 12.

39 Ibid., pp. 13–14.

40 Ibid., p. 16.

41 Ibid., p. 17.

42 Ibid., p. 15.

43 T. J. de Boer, *History of philosophy in Islam*, trans. E. R. Jones (Dover, 1967 [1903]).

44 Heinrich Suter, *Die Araber als Vermittler in deren Übergang vom Orient in den Occident* (Aarau: Saurländer, 1897 [1894]).

45 Eilhard Wiedemann, *Über die Wissenschaften bei den Arabern* (Hamburg: Perthes, 1890).

46 Pierre Duhem, *Le système du monde*, 5 vols. (Paris: A. Hermann, 1914–[1954]), vol. II, p. 140; Ragep, 'Duhem'.

47 Most scholars today will note especially the roles played by Franz Rosenthal and Otto Neugebauer in the resuscitation of the field.

48 Saliba, *Islamic science*, pp. 1–2.

49 George Saliba, Dimitri Gutas, and Jamil Ragep have obviously made significant contributions to the revision of the classical narrative and its underpinnings. The current young generation of historians of Arabic science and philosophy, among

whom I have had the pleasure of knowing the work of Anna Akasoy, Kevin van Bladel, Khaled El-Rouayheb, and Avner Ben-Zaken, continues to expand the boundaries of the field. See, e.g., Khaled El-Rouayheb, 'Sunni Islamic scholars on the status of logic, 1500–1800', *Islamic Law and Society* 11 (2004), 213–32; Avner Ben-Zaken, 'Heavens of the sky and the heavens of the heart: The Ottoman cultural context for the introduction of post-Copernican astronomy', *British Journal for the History of Science* 37 (2004), 1–28.

PART III

Evolution and creationism

CHAPTER 7

Evolution and creationism in the Islamic world

Salman Hameed

In the Muslim world Islam and modern science are often seen as compatible. It is common for people to cite verses in the Qur'an or the achievements of medieval Muslim philosophers to support this view. Furthermore, there is widespread recognition that science (usually in its applied form) is essential for progress. In fact the dominant narrative in the Muslim world sees Islam as a rational religion in harmony with modern science. At the same time many Muslims see the theory of biological evolution as a challenge to the Islamic account of creation. Thus, when a well-established scientific idea, such as biological evolution, clashes with the religious beliefs of many Muslims, we find complex reactions, ranging from selectively rejecting the relevant science to ignoring the troublesome idea, without harming the outwardly harmonious framework.

It is quite possible, nonetheless, that the Muslim world will become the focal point of evolution–creation controversies in the coming years. Low educational standards in combination with widespread misinformation about evolutionary ideas make many countries in the Muslim world fertile ground for anti-evolutionary movements. In addition there already exists a growing and highly influential Islamic creationist movement, which made headlines in Europe in 2007 when French public schools received an unsolicited gift of an 850-page colour *Atlas of creation*, produced by a Muslim creationist from Turkey known by the name of Harun Yahya.[1]

Biological evolution, however, is still a relatively new concept for the majority of Muslims, and a serious debate over its compatibility with religion has not yet taken place. The circumstances for the debate are, in many ways, significantly different from the engagement between evolution and creation in the West. For example, all of modern science, including evolution, is an import for Muslims, often seen through the complicated lens of modernity and the interaction with European colonial powers. The situation is further complicated by the fact that many Muslim countries are investing in biomedical fields that make use of evolutionary theory.

Similarly we find support for stem-cell research in several Muslim countries concurrently with widespread opposition to biological evolution. This is indeed a contemporary arena where John Hedley Brooke's emphasis on complexity is especially appropriate.[2] I present here an analysis of this complex interaction of science and religion in the Islamic world by focussing on responses to the issue of biological evolution.

On the surface, debates about evolution and creation in the Muslim world look similar to those taking place in the West. This is particularly true for the details of scientific objections to evolution, which have often been borrowed straight from American creationists. They also appear similar because, as Taner Edis puts it, 'after all, there are a limited number of ostensibly scientific creationist arguments possible'.[3] While the 'science' behind Islamic creationism is similar to that in the West, the cultural and social dimensions that shape the reception of evolutionary theory are markedly different and may provide an insight into the interaction of science and religion in the Muslim world.

THE NARRATIVE OF CREATION STORIES IN THE QUR'AN

The Qur'an plays a central role in defining beliefs and lifestyle in the Muslim world. It is considered an arbiter on all issues, big and small. The centrality of the text can be gauged from the commonly held belief among Muslims that the Qur'an is *the* miracle given to Muhammad.[4] Thus it is crucial to examine the narrative of creation in the Qur'an and how it affects the debate over biological origins.

Unlike the creation story in Genesis, the Qur'an does not narrate specific details of the creation of either the universe or human beings.[5] The verses that address creation are spread out at different locations in the Qur'an and are often presented in the context of other subjects. The Qur'anic account, like its biblical counterpart, includes a six-day account of creation (often interpreted as periods in modern translations). A typical example would be 7:54:

Surely your Lord is Allah, Who created the heavens and the earth in six periods of time, and He is firm in power; He throws the veil of night over the day, which it pursues incessantly; and (He created) the sun and the moon and the stars, made subservient by His command; surely His is the creation and the command; blessed is Allah, the Lord of the worlds.[6]

The length of each period, however, is not clearly specified in the Qur'an. At one place, the period is defined as 'in a day the measure of which is a thousand years of what you count' (32:5) and in another location as 'a day the measure of which is fifty thousand years' (70:4). The resulting ambiguity has two important consequences for the debate over biological origins. First, it leaves open the possibility of a very old earth. Indeed, young-earth creationism is wholly absent from the Muslim world, and a universe billions of years old is commonly accepted. Second, since the length of days is not explicitly specified in the Qur'an, this ambiguity makes room for the acceptance of a scientific account to fill in the information. The Big Bang cosmology presents an example of such a synthesis. It is quite common for pious, educated Muslims to support the Big Bang theory by pointing to 2:117, especially the end of the verse, which reads: 'The Originator of the heavens and the earth! When He decrees a thing, He says to it only: "Be!" And it is'. Thus, for many, this is an account of the beginning of the universe with later details borrowed from the scientific Big Bang theory.[7]

The account of biological creation in the Qur'an also lacks specific details. There are some verses that refer to the origin of life from water (24:45, 'And Allah has created from water every living creature'), while others talk about the creation of man from clay (55:14, 'He created man from dry clay like earthern vessels'). But additional details are absent. Many defenders of evolution in the Islamic world take advantage of this ambiguity and use these verses to justify evolution within an Islamic context, as long as the special status of humans is protected. The uniqueness of human beings centres on the issue of the 'ensoulment' of humans and, in fact, presents the most formidable challenge to the acceptance of evolution in the Muslim world:

Who made good everything that He has created, and He began the creation of man from dust.

Then He made his progeny of an extract, of water held in light estimation.

Then He made him complete and breathed into him of His spirit, and made for you the ears and the eyes and the hearts; little is it that you give thanks. (32:7–9)

However, it is not clear how this will affect the evolution debate. Just like the creation story of the universe, the account of biological creation in the Qur'an is spread out over a number of different verses and is often presented in the context of another subject. Thus, while opponents of evolution point to a general creation story in the Qur'an, no specific verses have, as yet, been consistently identified as being against evolution. Hence, in the context of debates about evolution, the Qur'an does not end up playing such a central role for Muslims as the Bible has done for fundamentalist Christians.

THE CONTEXT OF EVOLUTION AND MODERN SCIENCE
IN THE MUSLIM WORLD

The context of the Muslim encounter with modern science is perhaps the most important factor that shapes the current dialogue over evolution. The concept of evolution, as indeed most of modern science, is an imported idea for Muslims and is mostly employed for practical applications. Thus cultural and social debates about evolution in the Muslim world have significantly different concerns from the ones taking place in nineteenth- and twentieth-century Europe.

Most of the Muslim world encountered modern science through colonial interactions or through military conflicts with European powers during the last few centuries. The reception of science in the Muslim world has, therefore, been closely tied to political responses to the challenge of European powers. These responses range from a complete rejection of all foreign influences, including modern science, to the wholesale adoption of western ideals and values.[8] Most modern-day Muslims adopt a position somewhere in the middle – they generally accept technology and science without reservation and hold the view that science is essential for progress and economic independence. At the same time they are wary of cultural influences from the West. Thus they are able to separate religion and culture from work based on the applications of modern science – from software development and medical innovations to geology and nuclear science.

Evolutionary theory, however, provides a unique challenge. On the one hand, it is the cornerstone of modern biology and is thus essential for scientific development. On the other, evolutionary theory is often singled out as responsible for the spread of secularism and atheism in western societies, and Muslims therefore view it as a cultural threat. Indeed, most of the objections to evolution in the Muslim world have been tied to political and social concerns rather than to scientific critiques. It is thus likely that the acceptance or rejection of evolutionary theory by Muslims will depend on whether it is perceived as a successful scientific idea or as a corrosive western cultural influence.

No one can better illustrate this entanglement than Jamal al-Din al-Afghani (1839–97), a highly influential nineteenth-century Muslim intellectual. He is one of several Muslim reformers who responded to the challenge posed by European expansion and the colonization of Muslim territories. Not only did he embody this tension but in many ways his views about science have come to dominate much of the Muslim world.

Afghani was also the first prominent Muslim scholar to reject Darwin's theory of evolution.[9]

Afghani's political ideology was directed against western imperialism, but he understood the importance of modern science and the role it played in the ascendancy of European powers. At one point he wrote, '[t]here was, is, and will be no ruler in the world but science'.[10] In fact he attributed the decline of Islamic civilization to the neglect of science and philosophy by Muslims and wanted them to pursue modern science. Thus, while he rejected western imperialism and all things associated with it, he sought to present modern science as independent of the West, to make sure that science and reason did not appear opposed to Islamic truths. He presented Islam as a rational religion and the religion closest in spirit to science. In this way he articulated the dominant narrative of harmony between Islam and science in the modern Muslim world that is so popular even today:

The father and mother of science is proof, and proof is neither Aristotle nor Galileo. The truth is where there is proof and those who forbid science and knowledge in the belief that they are safeguarding the Islamic religion are really the enemies of that religion. The Islamic religion is the closest of religions to science and knowledge, and there is no incompatibility between science and knowledge and the foundation of the Islamic faith.[11]

However, Afghani did not go into any detail about what to do in those instances where science conflicted with Islam. Yet in 1881 he launched a scathing attack against Darwin and his evolutionary theory in 'The truth about the *Neicheri* sect and an explanation of the *Neicheris*', which was later given the short title, *The refutation of the materialists*.[12] The focus of this book was neither Darwin nor evolution. Its main purpose was to counter the political stance of some of his contemporaries who had favoured materialism. In particular he was responding to Syed Ahmad Khan (1817–98), a prominent Muslim reformer in British India, who had an opposing vision of how to respond to the colonial powers and had written in support of Darwin's theory of evolution.

Like Afghani, Khan promoted the need for Muslims to adopt modern science. However, after seeing the aftermath of the failed Indian uprising against the British in 1857, he favoured complete westernization and wanted to reform Islam accordingly. Khan believed that all Islamic principles and beliefs, including the Qur'an, must be interpreted in accordance with reason and nature. He accepted Darwin's theory of evolution and wrote a controversial commentary on the Qur'an that explained away miracles using scientific explanations and presented the Qura'nic creation story of Adam and Eve in the light of Darwin's theory of evolution.[13]

Afghani took exception to this approach, because he believed that Khan was causing divisions between Muslims at a time when anti-western sentiment was gaining ground. In *Refutation* Afghani painted Khan and his followers as irreligious materialists. It is in this context that he attacked Darwin and his theory of evolution. However, it is not clear if he had even read *On the origin of species* before writing *Refutation*, given his bizarre definition of evolution:

One group of materialists decided that the germs of all species, especially animals, are identical, that there is no difference between them and that the species also have no essential distinction. Therefore, they said, those germs transferred from one species to another and changed from one form to another through the demands of time and place, according to need and moved by external forces.[14]

The point of *Refutation*, however, was not scientific accuracy (indeed, much of his criticism is based on popular misconceptions of evolution at the time) but rather to generate pan-Islamic solidarity against the West. He was angry with Khan and, according to Afghani's friend and associate, Mohammad Abduh, he wrote *Refutation* while he was in a passionate state of anger against these advocates of complete westernization.[15] But in the process he also became the first prominent Muslim intellectual to reject evolutionary theory.

Only a few years after writing *Refutation* Afghani accepted evolution and natural selection (although not human evolution). It is not clear why he changed his mind, but although he now accepted evolution, he called Darwin a mere collector of specimens and attributed the idea of evolution to Muslim thinkers of the middle ages. This strategy of appropriation reduced the perception of cultural threat and resolved the dilemma of appearing to borrow science from the West; instead, it now became an act of repossession by Muslims. While this response has not been limited to evolution, defenders of evolutionary theory in the Muslim world often use it to justify their reasoning. In fact, according to Adel Ziadat, author of *Western science in the Arab world: The impact of Darwinism 1860–1930*, the Muslim world's response to Darwin's theory of evolution is quite unique, as almost all Arab thinkers have referred to their ancestors' contributions to the subject.[16]

Thus Muslim debates over creation and evolution have some important differences from those in the United States and Europe. In particular the debate over evolution does not centre on any particular verse in the Qur'an, as the creation story is spread throughout the text and offers few specific details. Furthermore the concept of evolution, as indeed most of modern science, is an imported idea for Muslims, and its reception is shaped by the Muslim encounter with European powers over the last two centuries.

THE LACK OF AN 'OFFICIAL' ISLAMIC POSITION ON EVOLUTION

Just as there is no monolithic Islam, there is no unified Islamic position on evolution. This is all the more to be expected in the absence of a clear position expressed by the Qur'an. In addition the contemporary Muslim world represents a broad spectrum of culture and politics, ranging from secular Turkey and the post-Soviet central Asian republics, like Kazakhstan and Azerbaijan, to the conservative monarchy of Saudi Arabia and the Shia theocratic democracy of Iran. The range of responses to evolution is shaped by these political variations. This diversity of opinion is to be expected, since Islam lacks a centralized and hierarchical system for enforcing orthodoxy.[17] Thus it is no surprise that Islamic scholars and popular writers hold a wide range of opinions on evolution.

As with the creationist fundamentalists in America, there are many who reject evolution completely. Adnan Oktar, who goes by the pen-name of Harun Yahya, is perhaps the most prominent present-day creationist in the Islamic world. Over 200 books, including the *Atlas of creation*, have been released in his name, and some bookstores in the Muslim world even devote a special section to his output.[18] His organization, based in Turkey, has produced slick anti-evolution documentaries and hundreds of pamphlets and books, and has made them available for download, free of cost, from his website.[19] He came into prominence in the late 1990s through his book *Evolution deceit: The collapse of Darwinism and its ideological background*. From the perspective of scientific or philosophical arguments, he does not break any significant new ground but recycles standard creationist narratives borrowed heavily from the creationists in the United States and, more recently, from Intelligent Design (ID) advocates.

While much of his strategy mimics American creationists, he has made modifications suitable for his Muslim audience. As mentioned earlier, the idea of an ancient earth is not controversial among Muslims, and, as a result, Harun Yahya is comfortable in presenting biological creationism in a universe billions of years old. In fact he presents himself as the defender of science by embracing the 'good' science of the Big Bang theory that provides direct evidence for the Creator *versus* the 'bad' science of evolution. For him, evolution is outdated science 'that may have been successful in the late 1800s and 1900s' but that the science of the modern era has shown to be false.[20]

Yahya's main arguments are closer to natural theology and are motivated by Quranic verses that speak of signs of Allah's creation in nature:

And He has made subservient for you the night and the day and the sun and the moon, and the stars are made subservient by His commandment; most surely there are signs in this for a people who ponder; And what He has created in the earth of varied hues most surely there is a sign in this for a people who are mindful. (6:12–13)

His books make this connection explicit with such titles as *The miracle of the honey bee, The miracle of the creation of DNA, Allah's artistry in color*, and *Signs of God: Design in nature*.[21]

While criticism of evolution is the central theme in all of his work, following Afghani, Yahya's attacks have a broad social and cultural range. He warns of the influence of western culture on Muslims and writes about the dangers of communism, romanticism, and atheism, and lately also about the end of time and his belief in the coming Messiah. However, he believes that evolution is the root problem, and thus, regardless of the topic, he includes at least one chapter against evolution in all of his books, one of which opens with the following disclaimer:

The reason why a special chapter is assigned to the collapse of the theory of evolution is that this theory constitutes the basis of all anti-spiritual philosophies. Since Darwinism rejects the fact of creation, and therefore the existence of Allah, during the last 140 years it has caused many people to abandon their faith or fall into doubt. Therefore, showing that this theory is a deception is a very important duty, which is strongly related to the religion. It is imperative that this important service be rendered to everyone. Some of our readers may find the chance to read only one of our books. Therefore, we think it appropriate to spare a chapter for a summary of this subject.[22]

It is difficult to gauge the overall impact of Yahya's organization. His books have been widely translated and are easily available in bookstores all over the Muslim world and even in Muslim diasporas in Europe and America. Similarly his documentaries are shown regularly on television. However, it is not clear if his populist religious rhetoric resonates with educated and professional, middle-class Muslims.

Europe has certainly taken notice of his work. In December 2007 the Council of Europe Parliamentary Assembly's Committee on Culture, Science, and Education released a report on 'the dangers of creationism in education' and dedicated considerable space to Harun Yahya and his brand of creationism. Indeed, some Muslim medical students in England sparked controversy in 2006 when they distributed creationist leaflets backing the works of Harun Yahya during an Islam Awareness Week at King's College, London.[23] A similar incident took place in the Netherlands when some Muslim students cited Yahya's work in their essays on evolution.[24] There are many others in the Islamic world who reject evolution using similar creationist arguments. However, no one has been so successful as Harun Yahya, who has perfected his message for the age of mass media and the internet. Today he is clearly the leading representative of Islamic creationism.

Surprisingly some prominent Islamic scholars teaching in western institutions also reject evolution. For example, Seyyed Hossein Nasr, a professor of Islamic studies at George Washington University and one of the leading scholars of Islam, does not consider evolutionary theory to be more than an ideology. He believes that 'The theory of evolution is the peg of the tent of modernism. If it were to fall down, the whole tent would fall on top of the head of modernism. And therefore it is kept as an ideology and not as a scientific theory which has been proven'.[25] He claims that the criticisms that have been brought against the theory of evolution 'are at once metaphysical and cosmological, religious, logical, mathematical, physical and biological, including the domain of paleontology'.[26] While written in a more sophisticated language than Harun Yahya's, his scientific objections often cite the work of creationists such as the Institute for Creation Research (ICR) and the advocates of ID. Furthermore he is severely critical of any Islamic version of theistic evolution – the idea that God works through the process of natural selection – because 'it ties the Hands of God through a process we believe we know, but we really do not know'.[27]

A similar view is found in the works of Muzaffar Iqbal, a biochemist in Canada and editor of *Islam & Science: Journal of Islamic Perspectives on Science*. In an editorial he wrote that the logical implication of evolution is 'nothing but the destruction of the sanctity of species'. Rejecting evolution, he concludes, 'Not only does each species preserve its characteristics, but it also receives Divine command ... and acts accordingly, the Qur'an tells us. The ant and the honeybee have always been the ant and the honeybee and will always remain so'.[28] Thus, while opposition to evolution in North America is mostly limited to those outside the academic community, Islamic creationism has powerful advocates within it, and in some sense they provide a level of respectability not enjoyed by Christian creationists in the West.[29]

With the rising popularity of the ID movement in the United States it was only a matter of time before it made inroads into the Islamic world.

The chief popularizer of ID in the Muslim world is the Turkish journalist, and former disciple of Harun Yahya, Mustafa Akyol. He sees evolution as an enemy of both Islam and Christianity and believes that ID can be a 'bridge' between Islam and the West.[30] He has close ties with the Discovery Institute, the chief proponent of ID in the United States, and, in 2006, he was even called to testify on its behalf at the Kansas School Board hearing on the teaching of ID in science classrooms. The Discovery Institute reciprocated in early 2007, when two of its fellows, Paul Nelson and David Berlinski, spoke at a conference in Istanbul organized by Akyol and billed as the first ID conference in Turkey (and perhaps the Muslim world).

Yet, to date, ID appears to have gained little support within the Muslim world. On the surface it would appear that the Muslim world is primed for such a concept. After all, the Qur'an contains several verses that urge believers to look for signs of God in nature.[31] Indeed, Muslim creationists have eagerly co-opted some of the examples provided by the ID movement. But we have not witnessed a wholesale acceptance of ID. Perhaps it is because in the most widely known American publications the evidence of the Designer is identified in relatively obscure realms, such as the studies of the flagellum of some prokaryotic and eukaryotic bacteria.[32] For most Muslims such ideas are far removed from the Quranic evidence for a Creator – in plain sight and obvious to those 'who reflect' (30:21). Or perhaps it is because of the reluctance of the American ID movement to identify God clearly as the designer.[33] While this hesitancy among American proponents of ID results from their strategy of circumventing the constitutional requirement of the separation of church and state, this is perplexing to most Muslims. For them the Designer has to be Allah. Indeed, Akyol's former mentor, Harun Yahya, has also denounced ID, saying, 'some people are trying to turn others away from belief in Allah by imposing His superior attributes onto such abstract concepts as "intelligent design" and "intelligent power". This is virtually the same as adopting an idol by the name of Intelligent Design'.[34]

There are also many scholars in the Muslim world who accept various interpretations of evolution. Often this acceptance is justified in the context of the Qur'an. For example Qur'anic verse 24:45 is cited to support guided or theistic evolution: 'And Allah has created from water every living creature: so of them is that which walks upon its belly, and of them is that which walks upon two feet, and of them is that which walks upon four; Allah creates what He pleases; surely Allah has power over all things'. However, to preserve their uniqueness, humans are usually excluded from this argument. Some Muslims, though, have come up with creative ways to reconcile Islam with evidence for early hominid species. For example Maurice Bucaille, famous in the Islamic world for his 1976 book, *The Bible, the Qur'an and science*, accepts animal evolution up to early hominid species and then posits a separate hominid evolution leading to modern humans.[35] Nonetheless he still rejects natural selection as the mechanism for evolution and posits a more active role for God in the modification of species.

Similarly, as we have already seen with Afghani, some scholars find a justification for accepting evolution by attributing the origins of evolutionary ideas to Muslim philosophers of the middle ages. For example, writing in the early twentieth century, the South Asian philosopher and poet, Mohammad Iqbal, while reluctantly accepting evolution, credited the ninth-century philosopher al-Jahiz with the idea of evolution and Ibn Maskwaih in the eleventh century with being the 'first Muslim thinker to give a clear and in many respects a thoroughly modern theory of the origin of man'.[36] Indeed, a few medieval Muslim philosophers did elaborate theories of common descent known at the time, but none postulated any process similar to natural selection. Interestingly, this idea of the Muslim origin of evolution also captured the attention of Darwin's contemporary, John William Draper. He called it the Mohammedan theory of evolution of man from lower forms and considered it, in some ways, more advanced than even Darwin's theory. Portraying past Muslim achievements in a positive light and contrasting them with Christianity's, Draper wrote in his 1875 *History of the conflict between religion and science*: 'Thus our modern doctrines of evolution and development were taught in their schools. In fact, they carried them much farther than we are disposed to do, extending them even to inorganic or mineral things'. He attributed these ideas to Al-Khazini in the twelfth century.[37] While Draper has been responsible for popularizing the conflict thesis in the West, paradoxically his book is frequently quoted on websites that support compatibility between evolution and Islam.[38]

It should be noted that there are also many Muslim scholars, and scientists in particular, who accept evolution in ways that are similar to religious scientists in the West. Some follow theistic or guided evolution such as that proposed by the Catholic Church, while others prefer a separation of science and religion, with explanations of the natural world sought by science and moral issues attributed to the domain of religion.[39]

Thus at present there appears to be no consensus among scholars, nor is there any 'official' Islamic position on evolution. How, then, does the general Muslim population view evolution?

MUSLIM PUBLIC OPINION ON EVOLUTION

We do not know much about general views on science in Muslim countries, let alone about the specific question of evolution. Nevertheless a few
recent studies enable us to paint a broad picture of the Muslim world. In
2006 Miller, Scott, and Okamoto published a study of public acceptance of
evolution in Japan, the United States, and thirty-two European countries,
including Turkey, the only Muslim country in the sample.[40]

The study focussed on America, where only 40 per cent of adults agreed
with the statement 'Human beings, as we know them, developed from
earlier species of animals', whereas the acceptance of evolution was over
80 per cent in Iceland, Denmark, Sweden, and France. The only country
in the sample where a smaller proportion of adults than in the United
States was likely to believe in evolution was Turkey, with an acceptance
level around 25 per cent. The result is all the more striking as Turkey is
one of the most educated and secular of Muslim countries.

But we get a broader picture of opinions about evolution from a recent
sociological study by Riaz Hassan, who analysed religious patterns in
six Muslim countries: Indonesia, Pakistan, Egypt, Malaysia, Turkey, and
Kazakhstan.[41] Interestingly, the question on evolution was included as an
example of an idea that challenges a 'fundamental religious belief widely
held by Muslims'. The respondents were asked the following question: 'Do
you agree or disagree with Darwin's theory of evolution?'

Figure 1 shows that in the samples only 16 per cent of Indonesians,
14 per cent of Pakistanis, 8 per cent of Egyptians, 11 per cent of Malaysians,
and 22 per cent of Turks agree that Darwin's theory is *probably* or *most
certainly* true. Despite the lack of consensus on an 'official' Islamic
position regarding evolution, the vast majority of adult Muslims do not
accept the theory of biological evolution. The former Soviet republic of
Kazakhstan, already showing significant differences in religious patterns
from other countries in the study, had the highest proportion accepting
evolutionary theory. In fact only 28 per cent of Kazakhs rejected evolution, a much lower percentage than that of the adult American population
(where approximately 40 per cent reject the theory outright).[42]

It should be noted that the question regarding evolution is too open-
ended and relies heavily on the definition of evolution as understood by
individual respondents. This is especially a problem when many, perhaps
most, in the Muslim world confuse evolution (and Darwinism) with
atheism and consider it inherently opposed to religion. In fact this is
why the evolution question was included in the first place in Hassan's

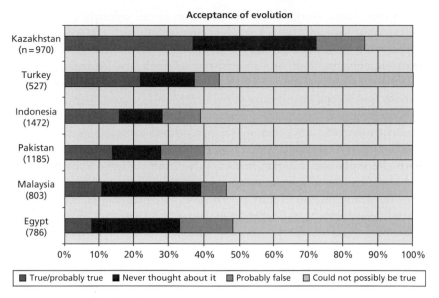

Figure I. Acceptance of evolution in six Muslim countries. The data is taken from a study of religious patterns in Muslim countries by Riaz Hassan and is presented here in graph form. The number of participants for each country is given in parentheses.

study of religious patterns in the Muslim world. However, we do get some measure of confidence in these results when we compare the responses from Turkey in the two surveys, Turkey being the one country that both surveys cover. Indeed, we find that the numbers are comparable to within a few percentage points.

It is also instructive to note that a high proportion of respondents, particularly in Egypt, Malaysia, and Kazakhstan, claim never to have thought about evolution and that, in almost all six countries, the percentage that offered this response is either comparable to or greater than the percentage that accepted evolution. Nevertheless a vast majority of respondents in the Muslim world think that the theory of evolution 'could not possibly be true'. So, while there is no 'official' position on evolution among scholars, public opinion is coalescing solidly against the theory.

A COMPLEX INTERACTION OF SCIENCE AND RELIGION

While the survey results may point to widespread rejection of evolutionary theory, the reality is more complicated. Medical colleges are thriving. Biomedical and biotechnology departments are sprouting up at universities across the Islamic world. Even embryonic stem-cell research, a religiously controversial issue in America, is advancing well in such countries as Iran, Egypt, and Malaysia. In fact Iran's supreme leader, Ayatollah Ali Khamenei, has publicly supported human embryo research and recently issued a *fatwa* that Iran's goal should be to become the 'leader of science' in the Middle East in the next twenty years.[43]

Furthermore evolutionary biology is included in the high-school curricula of many Muslim countries. In fact science foundations in fourteen Muslim countries, including Pakistan, Iran, Turkey, Indonesia, and Egypt, recently signed a statement by the InterAcademy Panel (IAP), a global network of science academies, in support of the teaching of evolution, including human evolution.[44] Indeed, the practical aspects of these attitudes vary widely and depend on the political and cultural climate of individual countries. In Turkey, for example, Islamic creationism made inroads into its traditionally secular school system in the 1980s, when an Islamist party came into power.

In general, however, biology (as is true for all other subjects) is taught in a highly religious environment where the separation of state and religion often does not exist. In Pakistan, for example, the goal of the national biology curriculum for grades nine to twelve (equivalent to GCSEs and A-levels in the British system of education) is to 'enable the students to appreciate that Allah ... is the Creator and Sustainer of the universe', and textbooks include the relevant Quranic verses on the origin and creation of life.[45] For example the chapter on reproduction in a twelfth-grade (equivalent to British A-level) biology textbook starts off with the Quranic verse, 'Then fashioned We the drop a clot, then fashioned We the clot a little lump, then fashioned We the little lump bones, then clothed the bones with flesh, and then produced it as another creation. So blessed be Allah, the best Creator of all!' (23:14).[46] Apart from this epigraph there are no religious references, and the remaining text of the chapter is similar to textbooks in any secular western country. Biology textbooks in Pakistan also contain a chapter on evolution and evolutionary theory, which is presented as a fact of science. Nevertheless the epigraph for the evolution chapter in the same textbook is the Quranic verse, 'And He is Who had produced you from a single being' (6:98). And again there are no religious references to creation or origins in the remaining chapter or in the suggested questions at the end of the book.

Although evolutionary theory is presented as a fact, human evolution is conspicuously missing from these textbooks. Instead the emphasis is on the practical aspects of biology, such as health, the environment, and biotechnology. Science teachers fill the gap in information about human evolution and often present creation stories that are a mixture of science and religion. In 2007 Anila Asghar, from Johns Hopkins University, and Brian Alters, from McGill University, interviewed eighteen science teachers in Pakistani schools located in Karachi and Lahore and found that all favoured using religious explanations of the creation of life. However, most of them presented both scientific and religious perspectives when teaching biological evolution. Most of these science teachers either accepted or at least held possible the evolution of living organisms. Yet at the same time they rejected human evolution, because they believed that 'human beings did not evolve from monkeys'. Not surprisingly their biology lessons often include a disclaimer about evolution, particularly human evolution, stating that the 'Islamic perspective on creation disconfirms evolution'. Yet they do not reject the study of evolution, because they believe that 'it is science and [students] should study it for knowledge'. Significantly, all teachers, irrespective of their views regarding evolution, agreed that there is no contradiction between Islam and science.[47]

These contradictory attitudes were also reflected in a recent study of twenty-five Muslim university students from Turkey and Morocco who are studying various subjects in Holland.[48] The study suggests widespread misconceptions about evolutionary theory and about Darwin. While most accepted microevolution, almost all rejected macroevolution and connected the idea to atheistic aspirations and to the impossibility of chance and mutations leading to complex species. At the same time, fragments of evolutionary theory were accepted and sometimes creatively reinterpreted. For example, a female student found evolutionary significance in Islamic women wearing headscarves and claimed that headscarves provided a necessary protection against unwanted sexual attention from men, whose habits and minds have been shaped by evolutionary processes. Another student considered evolution to be a necessary step for science to pass through before it could reach the ultimate truth of the Quranic account of creation. Thus, instead of outright rejection, many students found creative ways to embrace elements of evolutionary theory. As with the science teachers in Pakistan, none of these students in Holland expressed anti-science attitudes or foresaw any significant tension between Islam and science. Indeed, it is hard to draw firm conclusions from these limited studies, but we can nonetheless see a broad outline of Muslim reactions to the theory of evolution.

So, although biology is taught in a highly religious environment, evolutionary theory does not face serious objections, as long as human evolution is excluded. Furthermore science is mostly seen in a positive light, and the conflict model of science and religion (in this case, Islam) is largely absent. Following Afghani, the defining narrative in the Muslim world sees Islam as a rational religion in harmony with modern science. Thus, when the scientific idea of human evolution challenges this harmony, the reactions vary from selectively rejecting or reinterpreting the relevant science to ignoring the idea altogether.

But the boundary of what is deemed acceptable science changes over time. In the Muslim world the discussion of evolution has so far been taking place among the educated elites, which constitute a small, but highly influential, minority. Furthermore engagement with science at a research level is minimal, and a serious dialogue about the philosophical implications of evolution for Islam has yet to take place. However, for the majority, science is synonymous with technology. There are countless mobile phones, computers, and iPods. At the same time there are government-sanctioned prayers for rain in many Muslim countries, and belief in miracles is quite common. Even in Malaysia, perhaps the most technologically advanced Muslim country, whose computer exports rival those of many industrialized countries and who had an astronaut visit the International Space Station, 95 per cent of the population believe in miracles.[49]

The stage is set for the evolution–creationism encounter in the Islamic world. Rising levels of education and increasing access to the internet are bringing the topic of human evolution to the forefront. If creationists like Harun Yahya and evolutionary biologists like Richard Dawkins are successful in associating evolutionary theory with atheism, a mass rejection of evolution is likely to follow. On the other hand, the increasing association of evolutionary science with practical applications, from medical sciences to biological computing, might make complete rejection of the theory less likely.

CONCLUSION

In his *Science and religion: Some historical perspectives*, John Hedley Brooke laid out the diversity and complexity of historical interactions between science and religion, and cautioned against drawing broad general theses, as serious scholarship in the history of science has not been kind to many such ideas. The diverse reaction of Muslims to evolutionary theory provides yet another example of complexity. Some have rejected the theory because of its naturalistic assumptions; others accept it because they find verses in the Qur'an that support evolutionary ideas; some reject it because of its association with the West; others justify its acceptance by attributing its origins to medieval Muslim philosophers.

Nevertheless we can identify three key elements that characterize contemporary debate over evolution in the Muslim world. First, the creation story in the Qur'an does not lay out specific details, reducing the role of textual opposition to evolution. At the same time, a universe billions of years old is generally accepted, and young-earth creationism is wholly missing from the Muslim world.

Second, there is widespread recognition that science is essential for progress, and, more importantly, there is a strong perception that there is no tension between Islam and science. The roots of this perception can be traced to nineteenth-century Muslim reformers who were responding to the threat of western colonial powers. They acknowledged the role of science and the resultant technology behind the rise of the western powers, and considered science essential for the Muslim revival and self-reliance. Reformers like Afghani and Syed Ahmad presented Islam as a rational religion and the one closest in spirit to science, and they highlighted – and often exaggerated – the role of medieval Muslim scholars in the development of modern science. In a time of decline these associations not only made the borrowing of science easier but also made the case for the uniqueness of Islam and its role in history.

Finally, the concept of evolution, as indeed most of modern science, is an imported idea for Muslims, adopted primarily for its practical applications. Thus the cultural and social debates in the Muslim world about evolution are significantly different from those that took place in nineteenth-century Europe. Afghani, for example, advocated the adoption of modern science, while at the same time warning of the cultural influences of the West. His rejection of evolution was driven more by his political stance against those Muslim reformers who stood for the wholesale westernization of Muslim societies and for the acceptance of evolution. Afghani targeted evolution because he blamed the theory for the spread of secularism, nihilism, and communism, and identified it as a threat to Islam. These arguments against evolution are not unique to Islam, but they played a role in debates over the revival of Islam and the shape of the Muslim response to the western powers. Today Muslim creationists like Harun Yahya and Islamic scholars like Seyyed Hossein Nasr, in their own different ways, are drawing upon this tradition to argue for the overthrow of evolution and for the rescue of modern civilization from materialism by a resurgent Islam. Nevertheless in their scientific arguments they borrow extensively from Christian creationists and ID advocates in America.

NOTES

1 Martin Enserink, 'In Europe's mailbag: A glossy attack on evolution', *Science* 315 (2007), 925.

2 John Hedley Brooke, *Science and religion: Some historical perspectives* (Cambridge: Cambridge University Press, 1991), p. 5.

3 Taner Edis, *An illusion of harmony: Science and religion in Islam* (New York: Prometheus Books, 2007), p. 122.

4 Seyyed Hossein Nasr, *The heart of Islam: Enduring values for humanity* (San Francisco: HarperSanFrancisco, 2004), p. 23. The comparison stems from the Muslim belief that the Word of God, a term applied to Christ as *logos* in Christianity, in Islam refers to the Qur'an (as communicated by Muhammad).

5 There are two creation stories in Genesis: *Genesis 1* provides the linear account of a six-day creation, with the creation of man on the sixth day, whereas *Genesis 2* provides an account of the creation of the first man and woman in Eden.

6 All Quranic verses are from the translation of the Qur'an by M. H. Shakir. Online text is available from http://quod.lib.umich.edu/k/koran/

7 Pope Pius XII also endorsed the Big Bang theory in a speech before the Pontifical Academy of Sciences in 1951. Modern science, the Pope stated, 'has confirmed the contingency of the universe and also the well-founded deduction as to the epoch when the cosmos came forth from the hands of the Creator'. 'The proofs for the existence of God in the light of modern natural science', Address to the Pontifical Academy of Science, 22 November 1951 (www.ewtn.com/library/PAPALDOC/P12EXIST.HTM).

8 A. A. Ziadat, *Western science in the Arab world: The impact of Darwinism, 1860–1930* (New York: St Martin's Press, 1986), p. 84.

9 Ibid., p. 85.

10 N. R. Keddie, *An Islamic response to imperialism: Political and religious writings of Sayyid Jamal ad-Din 'al-Afghani'* (Berkeley, CA: University of California Press, 1983), p. 102. I have used Keddie's translation for all of Afghani's referenced works.

11 Ibid., p. 62.

12 Ibid., p. 130.

13 P. A. Hoodbhoy, *Muslims and science: Religious orthodoxy and the struggle for rationality* (Lahore: Vanguard Books, 1991), p. 66.

14 Keddie, *Islamic response*, p. 135.

15 N. A. Bezirgan, 'The Islamic world', in T. Glick (ed.), *The comparative reception of Darwinism* (Austin: University of Texas Press, 1972), pp. 375–87, on p. 384.

16 Ziadat, *Western science in the Arab world*, p. 126.

17 This statement more accurately defines Sunni Islam, which represents 80–85 per cent of the total Muslim population. Shia Islam, as it is practised in Iran, has a more hierarchical structure, the Supreme Ayatollah providing guidance on religious affairs.

18 Since over 200 books have appeared under the name of Harun Yahya in the span of a few years, some critics suspect that more than one author is responsible for this output.

19 See www.harunyahya.com

20 H. Yahya, *Nightmare of disbelief* (New Delhi: Goodword Books, 2002), p. 2.

21 All of these books are available online at www.harunyahya.com

22 Yahya, *Nightmare of disbelief*, p. 2.

23 'Academics fight rise of creationism at universities', *Guardian*, 21 February 2006: www.guardian.co.uk/world/2006/feb/21/religion.highereducation (accessed 24 September 2008).

24 Danielle Koning, 'Anti-evolutionism among Muslim students', *International Institute for the Study of Islam in the Modern World Review* 18 (2006), 48.

25 Seyyed Hossein Nasr, 'On the questions of biological origins', *Islam & Science* 4 (2006), 181–97.

26 Seyyed Hossein Nasr, *Knowledge and the sacred* (Albany, NY: State University of New York Press, 1989), p. 235.

27 Nasr, 'On the questions', 181–97.

28 Muzaffar Iqbal, 'On the sanctity of species', *Islam & Science* 4 (2006), 89–92.

29 There are some exceptions, especially in relation to ID advocates. For example Michael J. Behe, the author of *Darwin's black box: The biochemical challenge to evolution* (New York: Free Press, 1996), is Professor of Biochemistry at Lehigh University.

30 'Under God or Under Darwin: Intelligent Design could be a bridge between civilizations', *National Review Online*, 2 December 2005: www.nationalreview.com

31 There are many verses in the Qur'an that end with 'most surely there are signs in this for a people who reflect' – for example *The Romans* 30:21.

32 Behe, *Darwin's black box*, p. 70.

33 Partly this is because of court cases in America that prohibit the teaching of religion in school classrooms. ID proponents argue that ID theory is not based on religion.

34 'The "Intelligent Design" distraction', accessed from www.harunyahya.com (accessed 16 June 2008).

35 M. Bucaille, *What is the origin of man?* (Lahore: Al-Falah Islamic Books, 1989), p. 204.

36 M. Iqbal, *The reconstruction of religious thought in Islam* (Lahore: Ashraf Press, 1930), p. 121.

37 J. W. Draper, *History of the conflict between religion and science* (Electronic text center, University of Virginia Library: http://etext.lib.virginia.edu/toc/modeng/public/DraHist.html), p. 118.

38 For example the entry on 'Evolution and the Qur'an' on the *Talk Origins* website refers to Draper and his statement about the Mohammedan theory of

evolution being more advanced than Darwin's theory: www.talkorigins.org/origins/postmonth/nov96.html. See also B. Harun Küçük's chapter in the present volume.

39 John Paul II, 'Message to the Pontifical Academy of Sciences', *Quarterly Review of Biology* 72, 4 (1997), 381–3. Stephen Jay Gould coined the phrase 'Non-Overlapping Magisteria' (NOMA) to describe this separation of science and religion, *Rocks of ages: Science and religion in the fullness of life* (New York: Ballantine Press, 1999), p. 5.

40 Jon D. Miller, Eugenie C. Scott, and Shinji Okamoto, 'Public acceptance of evolution', *Science* 313 (2006), 765–6.

41 Riaz Hassan, 'On being religious: Patterns of religious commitment in Muslim societies', *The Muslim World* 97 (2007), 437–76. See also Salman Hameed, 'Bracing for Islamic creationism', *Science* 322 (2008), 1637–8.

42 Miller *et al.*, 'Public acceptance'.

43 John Bohannon, 'Picking a path among the fatwas', *Science* 313 (2006), 292–3.

44 IAP statement (2006) on the teaching of evolution: www.interacademies.net

45 Anila Asghar and Brian Alters, 'Science is in our brains and religion in our blood: Muslim teachers' and scientists' conceptions of biological evolution and evolution education', *Proceedings, National Association for Research in Science Teaching (NARST) Conference* (2007), New Orleans, 15–18 April 2007.

46 Punjab Textbook Board (2007), Biology 12 (Lahore: Bunyad Literacy Council, 2007), p. 87.

47 Asghar and Alters, 'Science is in our brains'.

48 Koning, 'Anti-evolutionism among Muslim students'.

49 Hassan, 'On being religious', 446.

CHAPTER 8

Understanding creationism and evolution in America and Europe

Bronislaw Szerszynski

There are few scientific texts that have rivalled Charles Darwin's *On the origin of species* (1859) for the impact they have had on the way that people understand nature and their place in it.[1] In the context of an enduring belief in the biblical account of the 'special creation' of species by God, Darwin's claim that all species were related through common descent was heterodox enough, yet not entirely novel. Darwin's grandfather, Erasmus, had been an early proponent of evolutionary thought, and the anonymous publication of the *Vestiges of the natural history of creation* (1844) by the journalist and publisher Robert Chambers had caused much controversy with its speculative history of cosmological 'transmutation', in which all living things had developed from earlier, simpler forms.[2] But what was new and arguably more significant in Darwin's work was the idea that the emergence of new and often more complex species could be explained by 'natural selection': by the way that environmental pressure will favour the reproduction of those individuals that possess certain characteristics, a process that over a long period of time can radically alter the characteristics of an interbreeding population.[3] The influence of Darwin's book was clearly also enhanced by his accessible and engaging prose, and the way that it combined detailed evidence from an extraordinary range of domains with an inductive style of scientific reasoning that went well beyond a strict Baconian method; instead he deployed metaphor to grasp the similarities between the dissimilar and then sought to persuade the reader of the reality of that metaphor.[4] Darwin used such literary techniques to show how the simple idea of natural selection might account not only for the diversity of organic forms but also for the 'infinitely complex and close-fitting ... mutual relations of all organic beings to each other and to their physical conditions of life'.[5]

   Such was the pregnancy of Darwin's ideas that, as they circulated in wider society, they were seized upon as legitimating an extraordinary range of socio-political ideologies, from Marxism to eugenics and ideas of racial supremacy. Scientifically, however, Darwinism suffered something of a decline in the early twentieth century, as laboratory-based biology eclipsed the field sciences and a revival of Gregor Mendel's work on heredity in particular provided a competing account of the emergence of new organisms through genetic mutation. But since the 1940s, when Mendelian genetics was combined with the idea of natural selection to produce what became known as 'the modern synthesis' or neo-Darwinism, and particularly since the birth of the 'environmental age' and the increasing concern for biodiversity loss, Darwin's ideas have come to be seen as a hugely important part of our understanding of living things. In 2009, as many scientific institutions around the world celebrated the 200th anniversary of his birth and the 150th anniversary of the publication of *On the origin of species*, Darwin's reputation as one of the most significant empirical and theoretical scientists in western history seemed secure.

But for the champions of Darwin there is a cloud on the horizon, a growing sense of threat from an enemy who regards Darwin's ideas not just as unproven but as contrary to biblical truth and to morality. This enemy is creationism, seen as an organized movement opposed to evolutionary thought and, by extension, sound scientific reasoning – and this at the very time when the science of biology seems more important than ever. With the invention of rDNA technology in 1973 and the reading of the human genome in 2003, biological science attained an extraordinary symbolic significance as the potential basis for technological innovation, capital accumulation, medical advance, and environmental protection. In such a context, and with echoes of Samuel P. Huntington's post-Cold War warning of a 'clash of civilizations',[6] Darwin and his theory of evolution have come to symbolize a cluster of cultural values that are seen as under threat – not just those values that one might recognize from Darwin's biography, those of Enlightenment reason and anti-dogmatism, but also the very project of mastering nature for the wellbeing of humankind. And now, as the historian Ronald Numbers and others argue, modern creationism is spreading beyond its origins in American Evangelical Christianity and is 'going global'; in such circumstances those critics of creationism in Europe and elsewhere who have assured themselves that it is a specifically American phenomenon might now seem a little complacent.[7]

Darwin's work was certainly seen by his contemporaries as a challenge to revealed religion; concern over its seeming anti-Christian implications was one reason for Darwin's tardiness in publishing his work. For, when thought through in Darwin's thoroughgoing way, natural selection seemed to offer a purely naturalistic explanation for the apparent presence of design in nature, and even for the emergence of human beings, and thus seemed to dispense with any need for a supervening spiritual agency. However, as John Hedley Brooke insists – and as found in other areas of scientific thought – the case of evolution cannot be reduced to simplistic images of a war between science and religion.[8] From the beginning, reactions to Darwin's ideas among the religious were complex and varied, ranging from outright rejection to enthusiastic acceptance – even prompting new, heterodox evolutionary religious worldviews. Today, too, there is a broad range of positions among the public. But the polarized public contest between the advocates of naturalistic evolution and those of 'scientific creationism' tends to mask the diversity and complexity of contemporary belief, and makes it difficult to form a more measured assessment of the impact that the Mosaic doctrine of creation has had on the intellectual development of humankind.[9]

How should we understand the religious objections to Darwin's ideas? My main focus in this chapter will be on understanding creationist beliefs – not just in the form of public polemics and campaigns but in terms of the private beliefs that opinion polls attempt to access. I argue that we need to situate these statements of belief against the different religious landscapes of Europe and America, because of the significantly different roles that religion plays in these societies. I then briefly look at education – not just as a key battleground in the struggle over evolutionary theory but also in terms of the role that it ought to play in facilitating a more sophisticated public debate about science and religion. I conclude by arguing that we should ask what the popularity of creationist ideas tells us about the adequacy of the alternative cultural resources which are available to people in making sense of their lives. But first I shall briefly review the state of knowledge about organized creationism, about the distribution of creationist beliefs among the public, and about why people come to adopt creationist ideas.

STUDYING CREATIONISM

The majority of writing on creationism consists of argumentative and often highly polemical literature produced by creationists and their critics.[10] However, as far as is possible I want to set this literature aside and focus instead on studies of creationists and their beliefs.

Broadly speaking, such studies can be divided into three types. The first consists of mainly historical studies of the individuals and organizations that have been actively promoting creationist ideas over the last hundred years. Notable here are the works of the historian Ronald Numbers and the philosopher Michael Ruse.[11] I shall draw on these accounts in order to give a very brief sketch of the main developments over this period but shall also show just how much creationist ideas have themselves evolved over the last century. For example, in the early twentieth century many creationists accepted the idea that the earth was very old. In 1921 the American politician and Presbyterian lay preacher William Jennings Bryan (1860–1925) launched a nationwide campaign against Darwinism, insisting that the character of the natural world could be explained only by God's miraculous intervention. Yet Bryan was not a strict biblical literalist, since he subscribed to a day-age creationism in which each 'day' of Genesis was to be interpreted as a geological epoch.[12] Other creationists at this time advocated a 'gap' or 'ruin and restoration' creationism, arguing that the universe was created aeons ago, fell into decay owing to Satan's rebellion, and was restored by God in 4004 BC through the six-day 'Edenic' creation of humans and the animal species we know today.

However, there were other creationists in the early twentieth century, such as George McCready Price (1870–1963), who insisted on a literal reading of Genesis, and thus a young earth. Recognizing that the key battleground was the geological record, he argued that the Genesis flood, rather than evolution, could explain the distribution of fossils in rock strata. His *New geology* (1923) initially had little influence outside Price's Seventh-Day Adventist Church.[13] But in the 1960s John C. Whitcomb and Henry M. Morris revived Price's ideas in *The Genesis Flood*, which helped to launch a 'creation science' movement that would use a more 'scientific' form of argumentation to promote flood geology and the idea of a young earth.[14] The work of Whitcomb and Morris allowed modern creationism to move beyond America, shaping the orientation of the Creation Science Association in Australia and the Creation Literature Society in New Zealand, and helping the home-grown creationism of British Evangelicalism expand out from its narrow base.[15]

But the 1990s saw a significant new development in the rise of the theory of Intelligent Design (ID). Unlike 'traditional' creationism, with its emphasis on the incompatibility between Darwin's account of the evolution of life and biblical truth, ID presents itself as an evidence-based refutation of naturalistic evolution, a scientific argument for supernatural intervention in the natural world. The proponents of ID argue that Darwinian natural selection can account at most for microevolution between morphologically similar organisms but not for the macroevolution that would have been necessary to produce the novel biological forms that emerge in higher taxa.

A key event in the development of ID was the publication in 1989 of the high-school biology textbook *Of pandas and people*.[16] Subsequently Phillip E. Johnson's *Darwin on trial* (1991) criticized the 'methodological naturalism' of science, arguing instead that supernatural intervention could not be ruled out *a priori*, and Michael Behe's *Darwin's black box* (1996) was the first creationist work to be published by a mainstream publisher. Here Behe argued that the 'irreducible complexity' of organic structures like the bacterial flagellum could not be explained by naturalistic evolution.[17] In 1996 ID also found its institutional base when Stephen Meyer established the Center for Science and Culture in Seattle with funding from the Discovery Institute. The Center is now infamous for a leaked memo which described the 'wedge strategy', by which they sought to split the 'tree' of materialistic science. The memo described the thin end of the wedge as *Darwin on trial* and the thick end as ID, which 'promises to reverse the stifling dominance of the materialist worldview, and to replace it with a science consonant with Christian and theistic convictions'. However, although a well-funded campaign to 'Teach the Controversy' in schools has enjoyed some temporary victories, attempts to get ID recognized as a credible scientific research programme have not been so successful.

Outside America there have been some Islamic manifestations of creationism, such as the *Atlas of creation* by 'Harun Yahya', actually the Turkish creationist Adnan Oktar, which accepts the extreme age of the earth but denies that species have evolved.[18] But the spread of young-earth creationism has generally been confined to societies with strong Protestant traditions. In Europe organized creationism is most established in the United Kingdom. The world's oldest creationist organization, the Creation Science Movement, was founded there as the Evolution Protest Movement in 1932; in 2000 it opened the Genesis Expo museum in Portsmouth in order to present the 'scientific evidence' against evolution to a wider public. At about the same time Answers in Genesis (AiG), the populist Kentucky-based organization led by Ken Ham, established its 'mission' to the United Kingdom. Two years later an AiG creationist conference, with Ham as a speaker, alerted the press to the fact that creationism was being taught at a state-funded secondary school, Emmanuel College in Gateshead.[19]

The second kind of literature on creationism consists of quantitative studies, most common in America but also carried out elsewhere, which try to determine the distribution in different national populations of ideas about the origin and development of life, and of human beings in particular. Such studies need to be read with caution, for a number of reasons. It is difficult to compare polls with different wording – for example those that ask about the evolution of life in general, or specifically of human beings, and those that use different wording to express the theistic evolution option.[20] Quantitative studies are also limited in their capacity to capture the nuances of often complex beliefs and positions. Nevertheless an examination of these studies can be instructive.

In such studies respondents are generally asked to choose which of three statements comes closest to their views on the origin and development of humans and/or other forms of life. Roughly speaking the statements are chosen to distinguish between belief in young-earth creationism, theistic evolution,[21] and naturalistic evolution, and where I present findings below I shall do so in that order so as to aid comparison. In America, for example, the polling organization Gallup regularly asks respondents to choose between the following three statements: 'God created human beings pretty much in their present form at one time within the last 10,000 years or so', 'Human beings have developed over millions of years from less advanced forms of life, but God guided this process', and 'Human beings have developed over millions of years from less advanced forms of life, but God had no part in this process'. Gallup has found fairly consistent results over the last quarter-century, indicating the high incidence of creationist beliefs among Americans: for example, in 2008 44 per cent of those polled chose the 'creationist' statement, 36 per cent the 'theistic evolution' statement, and only 14 per cent supported evolution by natural selection.[22]

Quantitative studies in Europe have generally found far greater acceptance of evolution than in America. A team led by Jon D. Miller at Michigan State University compared surveys carried out in European countries in 2002 and 2005 with contemporary data from America.[23] In the 2005 Eurobarometer survey of 32 countries, for example, members of the public were asked to answer 'True', 'False', or 'Don't know' to a list of statements, including 'Human beings, as we know them today, developed from earlier species of animals'.[24] In this survey public acceptance of evolution averaged 70 per cent across the EU, ranging from over 80 per cent in Iceland, Denmark, Sweden, and France to 50 per cent or less in Bulgaria, Lithuania, Latvia, and Cyprus. This compares with 40 per cent in America, only Turkey scoring lower among the countries studied.

However, the Eurobarometer question did not distinguish between theistic and naturalistic evolution, which means that the 70 per cent of the European population who seem to accept evolution would include those who embrace both of these positions. Other polls enable us to draw tentative conclusions about the relative preponderance of these different beliefs about evolution. In a 2002 survey the Swiss market research institute IHA-GfK asked German-speaking adults in Austria, Switzerland, and Germany how they thought the universe, the earth, and life developed. Of those interviewed 20 per cent chose 'through creation by God within the last 10,000 years', 21 per cent 'through a process of evolution and development guided by God', and 40 per cent 'through evolution as according to Darwin, without the intervention of God'.[25]

Overall it appears from poll data that, while in America the ratio of young-earth creationists to theistic evolutionists to naturalistic evolutionists is approximately 45:35:15, in Europe it is probably more like 20:20:45.[26] However, a difficulty in comparing opinion poll data arises from the fact that the options offered to respondents vary. In two British polls carried out in 2006, for example, it was 'Intelligent Design' in particular, rather than a more general belief in theistic evolution, that was offered as the intermediate position between creationism and naturalistic evolution. An Ipsos MORI poll carried out for the BBC *Horizon* programme found that 22 per cent chose creationism, 17 per cent ID, and 48 per cent naturalistic evolution.[27] Opinionpanel Research's survey of more than 1,000 students found that 12 per cent preferred creationism, 19 per cent ID, and 56 per cent naturalistic evolution.[28]

But an important third kind of scholarship involves attempts to understand *why* people believe in evolution or creationism. Some of this work has used quantitative methods. For example, using data from America and nine European countries Miller *et al.* deployed statistical analysis to try to explain why so many Americans are creationists.[29] They used their data to generate a structural equation model that predicted attitudes towards evolution in which the key determinants were found to be religious beliefs and practices associated with fundamentalist or Evangelical Christianity, pro-life attitudes, and a conservative political ideology.

Studies like this are suggestive but can only take us so far in understanding how creationist and evolutionary beliefs fit into a patterned way of making sense of the world; for this, large-scale quantitative studies need to be complemented by qualitative approaches that can attend to individual sense-making processes. A sociological analysis by Raymond Eve and Francis Harrold has contributed to such a task by situating creationism within the context of a struggle between two competing worldviews, 'cultural traditionalism' and 'cultural modernism', each promoted by its own social movement.[30] E. Margaret Evans, by contrast, takes a cognitive psychological approach, based on Piaget's idea of child development. By studying what children of different ages say when they are asked where they imagined the first animal or human came from, she concludes that both naturalistic and artifactual conceptions of the origins of things are inferences that arise intuitively in the human mind. In a sequence that seems to recapitulate the historical development of aetiological reasoning in western civilization, children first tend to understand living things as arising naturally through spontaneous generation, then imagine they are created by an intelligent agency – whether human or divine – before possibly progressing to an evolutionary naturalist explanation (albeit generally a Lamarckian one).[31] In her analysis creationist beliefs represent a stage on the way towards a more sophisticated naturalistic understanding of the origination of living things. However, this final stage can be arrested when evolutionary beliefs are 'deselected' by fundamentalist parents.

There is clearly a need for more work of this kind. But there is also a need for research that tries to combine these three very different kinds of study, and in such a way that might help us to place the holding and expression of creationist beliefs in socio-historical context. In the next section I want to make a modest contribution towards this task by situating the contemporary struggles over evolutionism and creationism against the different roles of religion in different societies.

THE EUROPEAN RELIGIOUS LANDSCAPE

It has become a commonplace in the literature on creationism to say that the main reasons creationism is less common in Europe than in America are, first, that European society is more secular, and, second, that the religious life of the continent is dominated by churches that have broadly accepted the truth of Darwinian evolution – Catholicism in southern Europe and the Lutheran churches in the north – and that generally do not tend towards Evangelical Christianity. While this is all true, there is nevertheless much more that can be said about the broad religious differences between America and Europe and how these might affect creationism.

The role that religion plays on either side of the Atlantic is not just lesser or greater but also different. In the past, sociologists of religion have tended to assume that, as societies develop over time, religion will naturally shrink and disappear. Modern societies, they have argued, are characterized by high levels of structural differentiation, in that they consist of more-or-less clearly separate realms – politics, the economy, the family, law, art, science, and so on – each of which performs a different societal function, and each of which tends to operate and evolve through its own internal mechanisms of co-ordination, without the need for any overarching myths or cosmologies to regulate them. Secularization theorists have thus assumed that, as societies modernize in this way, religion will become both unnecessary for societal co-ordination and unsuitable for individual belief systems. Against such assumptions America, with its lively marketplace in religious and spiritual beliefs and practices, and high levels of church attendance and professed religious beliefs, was seen as an exceptional case in the context of a more general, inevitable process of secularization.[32] However, other scholars, such as David Martin and Peter Berger, have recently argued that it is in fact *Europe*, with its low levels of religious practice, that is the exceptional case, and that European scholars had developed their theories of inevitable secularization by generalizing inappropriately from a distinctively European experience of religious decline.[33]

Either way, it has become recognized that secularization is not a single, unified, and linear process but one that proceeds in ways that are contextually specific. And in Europe one of the key determining factors in the recent collapse in religious practice and belief has been the close relationship between nation states and particular churches, dating back to the Augsburg Peace Treaty of 1555, where the maxim *cuius regio, eius religio* ('whose rule, his religion') was used to determine the religious life of territories on the basis of the religious affiliation of their rulers. The resulting pattern today is of course complex and varies between countries that still have state churches, such as England, Denmark, Sweden, Finland, and Greece, and those countries with a long tradition of strong separation, such as France and the Netherlands.[34] But, as José Casanova argues, the decline of religion has been highest in those countries that have retained a national church, rather than moving to the pluralist, more market-like American model, since in those countries religion is too closely tied to the central institutions of society and is felt as too alienating and inappropriate for modern subjectivities.[35]

However, as Grace Davie points out, this argument works best for southern countries such as Spain, where the clergy's resistance to economic, cultural, and political modernization has given rise to militant anti-clericalism among the population. In northern Europe, by contrast, where Protestant denominations historically carried out their *own* processes of de-clericalization as part of the Reformation, and where religious institutions have themselves often been agents and carriers of Enlightenment ideas, these countries' populations are largely secularized but are not nevertheless particularly hostile to religion.[36] Instead, in such societies the national churches, rather than being embattled denominational enclaves, play a significant role within the voluntary sector and also perform an important symbolic role, marking and legitimating key moments in the lives of individuals and the nation.[37]

This is highly relevant for understanding creationism, since it means that the predominant role of religion is different on either side of the Atlantic. This is not just about the fact that the strict exclusion of religion from public institutions and public life which has bred such resentment among certain religious groups in America does not apply in most European countries; it goes much deeper, into the role that religion is playing in society. Attending to the broadly contrasting nature of religion in America and Europe can thus not only help explain the differential *distribution* of creationist beliefs but also provide insight into their differential societal *meanings*. Organized religion in Europe, although in some ways weak, is nevertheless woven significantly into the lives of its constituent nations through binding symbols and rituals. By contrast America's religious history was shaped by the experience of pilgrimage and revolution, and was characterized by the rejection of old churches and their hierarchies. The first half of the nineteenth century saw a huge growth of Methodism and Baptism; the turn to the individual, biblical literalism, and a sacralized work ethic fitted a country being built from the bottom up by individuals and families.[38] Relatedly, in nineteenth-century America the influence of Scottish 'common-sense' realism gave rise to a particular view of scripture as a collection of propositions with self-evident meanings – a cognitive style that is evident among adherents of scientific creationism, and that shapes the understanding of what counts as valid scientific reasoning in arguments for ID.[39] Further developments in the early twentieth century, whereby rural conservative Protestant congregations became separated from the influence of more moderate urban Protestantism, resulting by mid-century in the former establishing their own educational establishments, media, and publishing houses, also helped to set the scene for the development of modern creationism.[40]

What about Catholic countries like Italy, Austria, and Poland? It is true that Catholicism has produced its own high-profile proponents of ID such as Michael Behe and Dean Kenyon. Furthermore, in 1996 Cardinal Schönborn of Vienna reacted to Pope John Paul II's endorsement of Darwinian evolution by publicly disputing the idea that humans are simply a product of 'chance and error'[41] – and certainly the Roman Catholic Church seems more likely than many other Christian denominations to feel it is called to resist secular, liberal society. However, Catholicism, with its emphasis on tradition, its sacramentalism, and its theology in which the relationship between God and the creation is one of both transcendence and immanence, has generally not been fertile ground for American-style creationism with its biblical literalism and emphasis on divine transcendence.

EDUCATION, SCIENCE, AND RELIGION

Let me turn now to the question of the relationship between education, science, and religion. One reason for this focus is that, in both Europe and America, the creationist controversy has centred on the struggle over the goal and content of high-school education.[42] In America such an emphasis dates back to the famous 1925 Scopes trial in Dayton, Tennessee, in which a high-school teacher was convicted for teaching evolution in violation of a recently passed law (see Shapiro, this volume). The highest-profile recent case was Kitzmiller *et al. v.* Dover Area School District in 2005, in which parents of pupils in Dover, York County, Pennsylvania successfully sued the Dover School Board for adding to their biology curriculum a requirement that students be 'made aware of the gaps/problems in Darwin's theory and of other theories of evolution including, but not limited to, intelligent design'.

Such controversies have been less frequent in Europe but are not unknown. In the United Kingdom, for example, there has been concern since 2003 about the teaching of creationism alongside evolution at the three state-funded comprehensive schools run by the Emmanuel Schools Foundation. In March 2005 the Minister of Education for the Netherlands, the Catholic Maria van der Hoeven, expressed her sympathy with ID on her weblog. In September 2006 a UK organization affiliated with the Discovery Institute called Truth in Science, led by Andrew McIntosh, Professor of Thermodynamics at Leeds University, sent teaching materials including DVDs explaining ID to all UK secondary schools and received positive responses from 59 of them (which admittedly represents only 1.4 per cent of all schools targeted).[43] And in October 2006, the conservative League of Polish Families (LPR), a junior coalition partner in the Polish government, started a campaign, endorsed by Deputy Education Minister Mirosław Orzechowski, to prevent Polish schools from teaching Darwinian evolution.[44]

The polls are helpful here too. In a 2008 poll of American science teachers, 16 per cent said that they were young-earth creationists – a much lower proportion than in the general public but still surprisingly high. Among the same sample of science teachers 25 per cent said they devoted at least one or two classroom hours to creationism or ID; of those, 49 per cent said that they taught them as a valid, scientific alternative to Darwinian evolution, whereas 32 per cent said that they 'emphasize that almost all scientists reject these as valid accounts'.[45] But in Britain too there is significant support for the discussion or even the teaching in schools of non-Darwinian beliefs about the origin and development of life. The Ipsos MORI poll mentioned above also asked the British public which idea or ideas they thought should be taught in school science classes: 44 per cent said creationism should be included, 41 per cent ID, and 69 per cent naturalistic evolution. In 2008 Ipsos MORI carried out a new poll of primary and secondary school teachers in England and Wales: 37 per cent of teachers, and fully 29 per cent of science teachers, at least 'tended to agree' that creationism should be taught in science classes 'alongside the theory of evolution and the Big Bang theory'.[46] Such findings have raised fears, echoing those in America, of a catastrophic collapse in the quality of science education if such views become influential.

However, in the area of education as in that of religion there are important contextual differences between America and Europe. First, Europe is characterized by greater levels of state control over educational systems than is the case in America, a tendency that was strengthened after the Second World War, when compulsory education came to be seen as an important instrument for promoting social cohesion and pro-social attitudes among European citizenry.[47] In the United Kingdom, for example, all 'maintained' schools are obliged to follow a state-endorsed National Curriculum.[48] Such a context, in which diversity of opinion is contained within a broadly social-democratic framework of shared beliefs and values, makes it far harder to promote unorthodox ideas in schools, whatever views teachers or parents may hold individually.

Second, in the United Kingdom at least, attempts to introduce discussion of creationism into science lessons, while superficially similar to those in the United States, display a rather different pattern. For example, although in the 2008 Ipsos MORI poll 37 per cent of teachers in England and Wales said that they tended to agree that creationism should be 'taught' in science classes, far more (65 per cent) thought that it should be 'discussed'. Indeed, the poll found that, although science teachers were far less likely than those in other specialities to say that creationism should be 'taught', they were *more* in favour of it being 'discussed'. Such opinions can be seen as wholly consistent with the government guidance provided in the United Kingdom's National Curriculum that pupils ought to understand how scientific ideas change over time, are shaped by social context, and can be the object of social contestation.

As we have seen, there have been attempts to teach creationism and ID in UK science classes as alternative scientific theories. However, UK controversies about creationism and science teaching have largely involved proposals merely to have creationism discussed, in order to help pupils develop a deeper understanding of the relationship between science and the wider culture. For example Oxford Cambridge and RSA Examinations (OCR), one of the three main UK examination boards, attracted much high-profile criticism in 2006, even though it was only recommending that teachers include limited discussion of the history of creationism in GCSE biology classes so that pupils would better understand the social and historical context in which the theory of evolution emerged and developed.[49] A similar controversy arose in 2008 when Michael Reiss, then Director of Education at the Royal Society, argued in public that it might be appropriate for science teachers to discuss creationism as an alternative worldview, if it is raised in science classes, as part of a general commitment to open debate and in order to help pupils understand the scientific position.[50] It is a measure of the emotional charge surrounding this issue that, despite the apparent reasonableness of such initiatives, vociferous protests from eminent scientists forced OCR to revise its guidance to teachers in the first case, and Professor Reiss to resign his post at the Royal Society in the second. If American-style fundamentalist creationism can often feel oddly inappropriate in European contexts, then so too can the strident tone of many of our public defenders of naturalistic evolution.

But such episodes also reveal that what we should be asking about educational systems in the context of the creationist controversy is not just to what extent they are becoming a battleground between different cultural forces but also how well they are equipping populations to think critically about science and religion. Jon D. Miller has conducted statistical research in America and Europe into 'civic scientific literacy', which he defines as 'the level of understanding of science and technology needed to function as citizens in a modern industrial society'. He reports that 28 per cent of American adults but only 14 per cent of European Union adults qualified as scientifically literate according to his criteria, in that they scored a minimum of 70 on his Index of Civic Scientific Literacy – 'a level of understanding sufficient to understand science and technology stories in the *New York Times* Science Times section'.[51]

But how should scientific literacy be conceived? Recent public debates about the state of science education in the United Kingdom have been organized around the distinction, echoed in Professor Miller's work, between two different ideas of its function: educating scientists, on the one hand, and creating a scientifically literate population, on the other. For some, secondary-school science education has been too much directed towards the second role, compromising its ability to deliver the first. And an important political-economic context for such concerns is the rise of global economic competition and the dominant strategy in the West to deal with it, which is to shift as rapidly as possible to a knowledge-based economy, a strategy that depends on rapid and continuous scientific and technological innovation in order to maintain economic advantage over the rising economies of the developing world. In such a context science education for the next generation of scientists and engineers – and possible threats to it from religious groups – becomes an urgent policy priority.

But others argue that scientists, and citizens in general, need not only to know about scientific facts, concepts, theories, and methods but also to understand the *social* aspects of science, for example: how the scientific enterprise depends on a particular form of social organization and social conventions; how the social relationship between science and wider society changes over time, with different rights and responsibilities placed on the scientist; and how public controversies about scientific and technological developments need to be understood in a sociologically and politically informed way.[52] Such ideas are only patchily finding their way into science education. If science education were to incorporate 'science-in-society' issues in a more thorough-going way, scientific innovation would be likely to proceed in a more socially robust manner.[53] Indeed, recent surveys of the public understanding of science suggest that mature scientific cultures are characterized by high knowledgeability but low scientism – that is, by an adequate understanding of science and technology and their impact on society but also by a scepticism towards mythicized accounts of science's capacity to provide absolute truth and to solve all practical problems.[54] An expanded scientific education would not only help produce such a mature scientific culture but would also help citizens to develop a more sophisticated understanding of phenomena like creationism as examples of the long and complex interactions between science and religion.

It is, however, not just scientific literacy but also *religious* literacy that is important here and has to be thought about in the right way. In stark contrast to America, religious education has been a standard element of most European school curricula at least since the Second World War. Davie describes religious education as having two goals, broadly parallel to the two goals of science education as distinguished above. The first is confessional, involving the transmission of the teaching of a particular religion or denomination to the next generation; the second is that of stimulating a reflexive understanding of religion and its place in history and contemporary society. In practice these two goals are sometimes hard to separate, and the level to which the second goal is pursued effectively depends very much on the individual teacher.[55] But France has started to recognize the problems that have been caused by not educating French children about religion, as French citizens generally have a poor under-standing of religion, which leaves them ill-equipped to understand a modern world in which religion plays an important role. By analogy the strength of American creationism is not simply a product of the build-up of resentment among religious communities that their own teachings and values are not represented in the education of the young; it is also a product of the lack of religious literacy in this second sense among the American population. So religious education is arguably as important as scientific education in creating the conditions for the public to under-stand and critically assess the significance of creationist ideas.

UNDERSTANDING CREATIONISM

I argued above that there is a lack of the sort of in-depth study of the cultural meaning of creationism that is required if we really want to understand what role such beliefs play in people's lives. Nevertheless the studies that have been done give us some clues; for example even the polls that merely examine the degree of certainty with which beliefs are advanced in this domain are themselves revealing. Apparently, outside the twin camps of Evangelical Christians on the one hand and practising scientists on the defensive on the other, few of those interviewed profess anything like certainty about their beliefs in this area. In the Pew poll it was those choosing young-earth creationism as closest to their own view that were more likely to say they were 'very certain' about their beliefs (63 per cent), then those choosing theistic evolution (39 per cent), leaving only 28 per cent of those choosing natural selection as 'very certain'. A Gallup poll of 2005 found similar uncertainty when they asked whether respondents thought creationism, evolution, and ID were definitely or probably true, or definitely or probably false.[56] Those who said that creationism was true, and those who said that evolution was false (probably largely the same people), were the only respond-ents where at least half described their assessment as 'definite', rather than merely 'probable'. Miller *et al.* similarly found that believers in creationism are more likely to express certainty in their belief than are believers in evolution.[57]

This is perhaps unsurprising, since the meaning of calling something a 'true belief' is quite different in the 'language game' of science from what it is in that of hard, biblical religion. But, interestingly, Miller *et al.* found that the American public are becoming less, rather than more, certain in this area: both firm belief in and outright rejection of evolution have declined over the last two decades. 'Over the past 20 years, the percentage of U.S. adults accepting the idea of evolution has declined from 45% to 40% and the percentage of adults overtly rejecting evolution declined from 48% to 39%. The percentage of adults who were not sure about evolution increased from 7% in 1985 to 21% in 2005'.[58] One way to interpret such results is to suggest that, quite independently of the public dramas provided by the clash of the certain few in this area, western societies are increasingly characterized by an open and undogmatic curiosity about how best to understand the origin and nature of life. Of course such an interpretation would have to be substantiated through sensitive qualitative research. Such research could explore the extent to which 'belief in evolution' has different meanings for different people. It would also consider the extent to which people's willingness to consider creationist accounts of origins might result from a lack of adequate alternative public vocabularies to describe the human condition that would resonate with their experience of being a living, sentient being, inhabiting a meaningful world with other such beings, capable of reason and science, and of feeling the infinite force of the moral command.

In a recent research project on the transformation of contemporary religion one significant finding was that the kinds of religion and spirituality that are growing in the developed world tend to be those that are concerned more with the here and now than with the afterlife, and with nurturing the unique, individual, lived life rather than simply promoting life in a particular prescribed social role. Paul Heelas *et al.* argued that because of this 'turn to life', organized religions with their highly normalized models of human conduct are shrinking at the expense of a growing alternative spirituality. But this research also noted that, within organized Christianity, the sectors that are experiencing growth – Evangelical and charismatic Christianity – are exactly those which have found their own ways not just to offer standardized codes of moral behaviour but also to resource individuals within the context of their own distinctive life narratives.[59] It should thus not surprise us that the cultural resources offered by these forms of Christianity can seem more attractive to many than those offered by contemporary science.

Despite the popularity of popular science publications, the public status of science and technology today has arguably less to do with its power to provide grand narratives with which individuals can orient themselves in the world and more to do with its power to meet pragmatic needs. In terms of science's power to act as a kind of 'civil religion' for modern society,[60] it seems to do so more effectively when it addresses what the anthropologist Roy Rappaport calls the *indexical* dimension of religion, focussing on present needs and situations, rather than the *canonical* dimension, concerned with abstract, impersonal ideas of cosmic order and purpose.[61] For some the fact that science tells us that the universe has no purpose and that it proceeds through a combination of blind, impersonal chance and blind, impersonal necessity is a great liberation, leaving human beings free to invent or discover their own purposes within a universe that does not force one upon them. But to others this meaninglessness can feel like an appalling burden, or even manifestly untrue. By contrast, the language of being a 'child of God', of the prototypical human not just being physically fashioned by God but only becoming human, more than mere clay, when God breathes His spirit into him or her, can be for many an image that is rich and pregnant with meaning.[62]

However, because of the highly polarized nature of the debate over creationism, the thoughtful pursuit of such lines of thought tends to be seen as a dangerous self-indulgence. Michael Ruse argues that the twin poles of evolutionism and creationism can be understood as reactions to the intellectual and social change of the nineteenth and early twentieth centuries.[63] Under conditions of rapid modernization, mainstream revealed religion no longer fitted societal needs, resulting in two competing cultural responses: on the one hand, a secularized post-millennial belief in reason and progress; on the other, a turn to emotion and faith as an historically specific form of religion. In the cultural struggle between these two worldviews evolutionary theory became what science studies scholars call a 'boundary object' – in this case a site of contest rather than one of agreement. The progressivists used evolution as a new salvation narrative which underscored progress and human achievement, the fundamentalists as a symbol for a godless, immoral culture. For creationists argue not only that evolution by natural causes is implausible, they also argue that belief in evolution makes human beings immoral, by making them think of themselves as mere animals and the universe as a meaningless accident.

But it is striking that there are parallels here with concerns expressed in the context of European Enlightenment thought about the moral and political implications of thinking of and treating human beings as merely biological beings. In the writing of European philosophers like Hannah Arendt, Jürgen Habermas, and Giorgio Agamben such concerns are particularly prompted by a paradigmatic event – not the gay marriage and abortion castigated by Evangelical Christians in America but the destruction of the Jews in the Nazi Holocaust.[64] For such thinkers, grasping the historical and philosophical significance of that fact has involved thinking about the way that the victims of the Holocaust had their distinctively human identity stripped away layer by layer – their legal identity as citizens, their religious identity, their personal identity, and finally any sense of human dignity – until they were merely biological phenomena, waiting to be snuffed out. Although all three writers have drawn upon Christian and Jewish thought, the general thrust of their critique of biological reductionism has been a particular high-Enlightenment model of the human as a non-empirical phenomenon, drawing particularly on the German idealist tradition of philosophy.

Thus, although American creationists see atheistic humanism as associated with the reduction of the human to mere biology, in the European context a very different humanism, grounded less in the natural sciences and more in the humanities and social sciences, has helped provide not just a vocabulary for thinking about what Arendt calls 'the human condition' but also its own critique of biological reductionism that has nothing to do with either biblical literalism or religious enthusiasm. Instead of interpreting the creationist controversy simply as an issue about science – about defending scientific progress from the forces of unreason – perhaps we should use it as an occasion for reflecting about the importance of the development of such rich vocabularies for the full flourishing of what it is to be human. In this reframing of the struggle over evolution the line of demarcation would then not simply divide the humanists from the religious but instead divide both humanists and theists into those who would seek to defend narrowly conceived certainties and those who are genuinely open to a shared exploration into the mysteries of the human condition.

NOTES

I would like to thank John Hedley Brooke, Geoffrey Cantor, Thomas Dixon, Willem B. Drees, Steve Fuller, Robin Grove-White, Antje Jackelén, Ulrich Kutschera, Neil Lewis, Neil Messer, Jon D. Miller, Michael Reiss, Taede Smedes, and Linda Woodhead for conversations that I found very helpful in the writing of this chapter, earlier versions of which were presented at the annual conference of the American Association for the Advancement of Science, San Francisco, 15–19 February 2007, and the conference *Science and religion: Historical and contemporary perspectives*, Lancaster University, 23–26 July 2007.

1 Charles Darwin, *On the origin of species by means of natural selection, or the preservation of favoured races in the struggle for life* (London: John Murray, 1859).
2 [Robert Chambers], *Vestiges of the natural history of creation* (London: John Churchill, 1844).
3 Of course, this idea had also been arrived at independently by Alfred Russel Wallace.

4 Gillian Beer, *Darwin's plots: Evolutionary narrative in Darwin, George Eliot, and nineteenth-century fiction*, 2nd edn (Cambridge: Cambridge University Press, 2000).

5 Darwin, *On the origin of species*, p. 80.

6 Samuel P. Huntington, *The clash of civilizations and the remaking of world order* (New York: Simon and Schuster, 1996).

7 Ronald L. Numbers, *The creationists: From scientific creationism to intelligent design*, expanded edn (Cambridge, MA: Harvard University Press, 2006). See also Numbers's chapter in the present volume.

8 John Hedley Brooke, *Science and religion: Some historical perspectives* (Cambridge: Cambridge University Press, 1991), pp. 275–320.

9 See, for example, Daniel O'Connor and Francis Oakley (eds.), *Creation: The impact of an idea* (New York: Charles Scribner's Sons, 1969).

10 For a useful collection of this material in respect of the recent creationist variant of ID, see Robert T. Pennock (ed.), *Intelligent design creationism and its critics: Philosophical, theological and scientific perspectives* (Cambridge, MA: MIT Press, 2001).

11 Michael Ruse, *The evolution–creation struggle* (Cambridge, MA: Harvard University Press, 2005); Numbers, *Creationists*. See also some of the essays in Simon Coleman and Leslie Carlin (eds.), *The cultures of creationism: Anti-evolutionism in English-speaking countries* (Aldershot: Ashgate, 2004).

12 Numbers, *Creationists*, pp. 57–8.

13 George McCready Price, *The new geology: A textbook for colleges, normal schools, and training schools, and for the general reader* (Mountain View, CA: Pacific Press Publishing Association, 1923).

14 John C. Whitcomb and Henry M. Morris, *The Genesis Flood: The biblical record and its scientific implications* (Phillipsburg, NJ: P&R Publishing, 1961).

15 Numbers, *Creationists*, pp. 357, 365–6.

16 Percival Davis and Dean H. Kenyon, *Of pandas and people: The central question of biological origins* (Richardson, TX: Foundation for Thought & Ethics, 1989).

17 Phillip E. Johnson, *Darwin on trial* (Washington, DC: Regnery Gateway, 1991); Michael J. Behe, *Darwin's black box: The biochemical challenge to evolution* (New York: Free Press, 1996).

18 Harun Yahya, *Atlas of creation* (Istanbul: Global Publishing, 2006). See also Hameed's chapter in the present volume and Willem B. Drees, 'Academic freedom and the symbolic significance of evolution', in Drees and Pieter S. Koningsveld (eds.), *The study of religion and the training of Muslim clergy in Europe: Academic and religious freedom in the 21st century* (Leiden: Leiden University Press, 2008), pp. 59–90, esp. pp. 77–80.

19 Numbers, *Creationists*, pp. 405–8. In the United Kingdom the majority of schools are 'state schools', funded by the government and providing education free of charge (the rest are fee-paying 'independent' schools, some of which are confusingly known as 'public' schools). Most state schools are 'maintained schools', which means that they are under the control of local government;

a few of these maintained schools are 'faith schools', which have formal links to a religious organization and are permitted to practise religious selection and to promote a religious ethos. The remaining state-funded secondary schools – 'City Technology Colleges', such as Emmanuel College, and 'academies', which are set up in disadvantaged areas – are independently managed but funded directly by central government, with some private or charitable sponsorship.

20 For example, in contrast to the Gallup polls reported in the next paragraph, the 2005 US survey by the Pew Research Center for the People and the Press and the Pew Forum on Religion and Public Life deliberately used wording that allowed many religious respondents to choose 'evolution by natural processes' as representing their view of the origin of living things without feeling that this committed them to atheism or deism (http://people-press.org/commentary/?analysisid=118). Some 26 per cent of respondents chose this option, compared with the 16 per cent who chose the corresponding option in the Gallup polls.

21 I shall call this middle position 'theistic evolution', even though the term has its problems – see Antje Jackelén, 'A critical view of "theistic evolution"', *Theology and Science* 5 (2007), 151–65.

22 www.gallup.com/poll/21814/Evolution-Creationism-Intelligent-Design.aspx

23 Jon D. Miller, Eugenie C. Scott, and Shinji Okamoto, 'Public acceptance of evolution', *Science* 313 (2006), 765–6.

24 EU, *Europeans, science and technology. Eurobarometer 224* (Brussels: European Commission, 2005), p. 40.

25 Rolf Höneisen, 'Gott hat die Hand im Spiel', *factum* 3 (2002), 24–7, my translations.

26 If one were to choose Pew's method over Gallup's the American figures would be 45:20:25 – see n. 20. It is also interesting to note that in Europe the proportion of 'don't knows' (which would take the sums up to 100) is higher than in America.

27 http://news.bbc.co.uk/1/hi/sci/tech/4648598.stm; www.ipsos-mori.com/content/bbc-survey-on-the-origins-of-life.ashx

28 www.opinionpanel.co.uk/clientUpload/pdf/CreationandEvolution(Tables).pdf

29 Miller *et al.*, 'Public acceptance'; supporting online materials for Miller *et al.*, 'Public acceptance' (www.sciencemag.org/cgi/data/313/5788/765/DC1/1).

30 Raymond A. Eve and Francis B. Harrold, *The creationist movement in modern America* (Boston, MA: Twayne, 1991).

31 E. Margaret Evans, 'Beyond Scopes: Why creationism is here to stay', in Karl Sven Rosengren, Carl N. Johnson, and Paul L. Harris (eds.), *Imagining the impossible: Magical, scientific, and religious thinking in children* (Cambridge: Cambridge University Press, 2000), pp. 305–33. Evans points out that even modern students studying biology and medicine at a higher level tend, like the nineteenth-century French biologist Jean-Baptiste Lamarck, to believe that biological change is a response to organisms' wants and needs, and that such acquired characteristics are passed on to offspring (p. 314).

32 For example, Steve Bruce, *God is dead: Secularization in the West* (Oxford: Blackwell, 2002).

33 Grace Davie, *Religion in modern Europe: A memory mutates* (Oxford: Oxford University Press, 2000), p. 26.

34 Reinhard Henkel and Hans Knippenberg, 'Secularisation and the rise of religious pluralism: Main features of the changing religious landscape of Europe', in Knippenberg (ed.), *The changing religious landscape of Europe* (Amsterdam: Het Spinhuis, 2005), pp. 1–13.

35 José Casanova, *Public religions in the modern world* (Chicago: University of Chicago Press, 1994).

36 David Martin, *On secularization: Towards a revised general theory* (Aldershot: Ashgate, 2005), p. 20.

37 Davie, *Religion in modern Europe.*

38 Ruse, *Evolution–creation struggle*, p. 148.

39 Taede A. Smedes, 'Social and ideological roots of "science and religion": A social-historical exploration of a recent phenomenon', *Theology and Science* 5 (2007), 185–201.

40 Simon Coleman and Leslie Carlin, 'Introduction: The cultures of creationism: Shifting boundaries of belief, knowledge and nationhood', in Coleman and Carlin (eds.), *The cultures of creationism: Anti-evolutionism in English-speaking countries* (Aldershot: Ashgate, 2004), pp. 1–28, esp. p. 10.

41 Numbers, *Creationists*, pp. 395–6.

42 Kevin Lambert, 'Fuller's folly, Kuhnian paradigms, and intelligent design', *Social Studies of Science* 36 (2006), 835–42, esp. 839.

43 See www.truthinscience.org.uk/site/, and news coverage at http://education.guardian.co.uk/schools/story/0,,1957858,00.html

44 Almut Graebsch, 'Polish scientists fight creationism', *Nature* 443 (2006), 890–1.

45 Michael B. Berkman *et al.*, 'Evolution and creationism in America's classrooms: A national portrait', *PLoS Biology* 6 (2008), 920–4.

46 www.ipsos-mori.com/content/teachers-dismiss-calls-for-creationism-to-be-taught.ashx

47 Francis Harrold *et al.*, 'Creationism, American-style: Ideology, tactics and rhetoric in a social movement', in Coleman and Carlin (eds.), *Cultures of creationism*, pp. 67–84, esp. p. 68.

48 City Technology Colleges follow a curriculum similar to the National Curriculum but with more emphasis on technological skills. Academies and independent schools are not required to follow it at all; however, many do so to a large extent.

49 http://news.bbc.co.uk/1/hi/education/4793198.stm

50 Michael J. Reiss, 'Should science educators deal with the science/religion issue?' *Studies in Science Education* 44 (2008), 157–86.

51 Jon D. Miller, 'The public understanding of science in Europe and the United States', paper presented to *The Annual Conference of the American Association for the Advancement of Science*, San Francisco, 15–19 February 2007, p. 6.

52 Robert K. Merton, 'The normative structure of science', *The sociology of science* (Chicago: University of Chicago Press, 1973), pp. 267–78; Michael Gibbons

et al., *The new production of knowledge: The dynamics of science and research in contemporary societies* (London: Sage, 1994).

53 James Wilsdon *et al.*, *The public value of science: Or how to ensure that science really matters* (London: Demos, 2005).

54 Martin W. Bauer, 'Paradigm change for science communication: Commercial science needs a critical public', in Donghong Cheng *et al.* (eds.), *Communicating science in social contexts: New models, new practices* (Berlin: Springer, 2008), pp. 7–25, esp. pp. 19–22.

55 Davie, *Religion in modern Europe*, pp. 82–97.

56 www.gallup.com/poll/18748/Most-Americans-Tentative-About-OriginofLife-Explanations.aspx

57 Supporting online materials for Miller *et al.*, 'Public acceptance', table S2.

58 Ibid., p. 765.

59 Paul Heelas *et al.*, *The spiritual revolution: Why religion is giving way to spirituality* (Oxford: Blackwell, 2004).

60 Robert N. Bellah, 'Civil religion in America', *Daedalus* 96 (1967), 1–21.

61 Roy A. Rappaport, 'Veracity, verity and *verum* in liturgy', *Studia Liturgica* 23 (1993), 35–50.

62 Richard Lewontin, 'The wars over evolution', *New York Review of Books* 52 (16) (2005), 51–4, esp. 53.

63 Ruse, *Evolution–creation struggle*.

64 Hannah Arendt, *The origins of totalitarianism* (New York: Harcourt Brace & Co., 1951); Giorgio Agamben, *Homo sacer: Sovereign power and bare life*, tr. Heller-Roazen (Stanford: Stanford University Press, 1998); Jürgen Habermas, *The future of human nature* (Cambridge: Polity, 2003).

PART IV

The politics of publishing

CHAPTER 9

A global history of science and religion

Sujit Sivasundaram

The period between the rise and the fall of the British empire – that is, from the late eighteenth to the mid-twentieth centuries – witnessed an intense encounter between religious cultures and scientific ideas across the globe. Colonialism brought with it the movement of peoples and the imposition of new political structures worldwide. Many religious believers sought to redefine their faith in line with new scientific thinking. Given the violence of the imperial experience, it is tempting to imagine that different sciences and religions came into conflict during this period. Yet it is the argument of this chapter that this is a misguided view. The formal and informal British empire saw different intellectual traditions borrow ideas and forms of organization from each other. Different communities repositioned their histories and futures by drawing on both science and religion. There was an interrogation of beliefs about nature and life in the face of fresh ideas imported from other parts of the globe, and this interrogation often led to the synthesis, collaboration, and renewal of both the sciences and religion. Thus this story cannot be reduced to either a model of conflict or of complementarity.

This chapter presents a global history of science and religion for territories that came under British control or influence; it takes 'global' as a label of historical methodology indicating the analysis of broad patterns and connections across space, rather than a comprehensive history of all regions. A discussion of how sciences and religions were linked with the global history of the British empire should be symmetric in recovering the perspective of both colonizers and colonized. To that end this chapter will begin by considering how Christian missionaries were implicated in the globalization of science. Missionaries were pivotal agents in the translation of existing indigenous science and in teaching western science. They were at the forefront of the intellectual encounters of the British empire. Because missionaries defined their vocation to include the study of God's creation, they wrote popular texts and scientific articles, often based on information gathered in the field. By contributing to the emergence of new disciplines and by defining new ways of classifying peoples and territories, Christian missionaries helped give birth to the modern scientific understanding of the world. Yet this recovers just one side of the encounter between sciences and religions in the context of colonialism.

A global history must also include the rich traditions of knowledge which were already flourishing in the world outside Europe prior to that continent's colonial expansion. It should also attribute active agency to indigenous peoples in narrating the reception of western science and religion. For Buddhist and Hindu intellectuals, Islamic reformers, Pacific islanders or African peoples, whose views will be covered in this chapter, the engagement with new scientific thinking provided a language for redefining identity. Although science contributed to secular ideologies of nationalism, and was at times resisted by religious movements that sought to return to ancient scriptures, non-western elites also frequently sought to prove the scientific heritage of their own religions and utilized the new science to project a new religious vision of their societies. For non-western peoples, as much as for colonizers, there was a lot to be gained by combining the insights of sciences and religions.

In presenting the argument that the meeting of different sciences and religions took many different and unexpected forms, and resulted in intellectual exchange and redefinition, it is possible to recast the history of science and religion in significant ways. Until very recently the grand narrative of the history of science and religion has been dominated by a western and especially a Protestant bias. This chapter shows how the story might be told in a more representative fashion. It therefore offers a way of redrawing the 'big picture'.

Inevitably this chapter relies heavily on the findings of many scholars who have contributed to the emerging global history of science and religion. While drawing on the work of others it seeks to synthesize accounts that take a national, geographic, or regional framework by showing how a larger perspective can be drawn out of many specific case studies. The argument also challenges scholars who work on the history of science and religion in either Europe or America and invites them to consider a global canvas. By considering the interaction between the sciences and religions in the non-western world it is possible to gain new insight into the placement of these intellectual traditions in the West, for colonialism forged global connections, allowing knowledge to cross oceans and continents.

In the first section I address the uses of science by Christian missionaries and then, in the second, I examine how members of several non-western peoples used the intellectual resources of different sciences and religions to come to terms with colonialism.

MISSIONARIES AND THE GLOBALIZATION OF SCIENCE

One way to understand how missionaries practised science is to regard missionaries as authors. Consider, for instance, *Missionary enterprises* (1837) by the South Pacific missionary John Williams, which is thought to have sold 40,000 copies in its first three years. Williams's book spanned ethnography, history, natural history, and geography. His information on corals was used by Charles Darwin in his discussion of *Coral reefs* (1842). Williams was significant not just as one among many sources for a celebrated man of science. His own book, which contained a chapter on corals, was a contribution to science in its own right.[1] Another South Pacific missionary, William Wyatt Gill, published numerous articles on natural history from 1872 to 1882 in the periodical *Leisure Hour*, published by the Religious Tract Society. These articles took as their subjects: the poisonous white-shelled sea crab; the deadly South Pacific octopus; the megapode bird, which builds mounds 10 ft high and 60 ft in circumference; the painful centipede; the man-eating alligator; the sacred Pua tree; the easily cultivable papaw tree; and the lemon hibiscus tree.[2] As with Williams's narrative, Gill's commentary on natural history often merged with a discussion of the perversity of indigenous customs and provided an implicit legitimation of missionary presence.

British South Pacific missionaries contributed over 200 articles to scientific journals between 1869 and 1900.[3] One example is George Brown, the Wesleyan Methodist missionary, who, according to one of his colleagues, 'cared more about his name being given to a new snake, bird or insect than he did for all the souls of New Britain people put together'.[4] Brown started to submit specimens to the Zoological Society in 1877, and his collections and observations were cited in papers read before the Zoological Society. Another South Pacific missionary, S. J. Whitmee, always kept a container attached to the front of his saddle when he entered new territories, in order to collect natural history specimens. He employed a Danish assistant as a collector of specimens and published papers under his own name in the *Proceedings of the Zoological Society* from 1875.[5]

Attention to the different stages in knowledge-making – from the collection of information, to patronage, editing, publication, and reception – is important in making sense of the different results of missionary attempts to practise science. The science in popular narratives such as

Williams's *Missionary enterprises* and in later nineteenth-century periodical articles written by missionaries fits into what Anna Johnston calls
'mutual imbrication', which she sees as characteristic of the genre of
missionary texts.[6] By this term Johnston indicates how missionaries were
forced to invent new ways of dealing with the unfamiliar, and how they
attempted to challenge and complexify tidy metropolitan categories. For
Johnston, the ambivalent relationship with imperial discourse and the
internal tensions within missionary texts mean that they may be seen as
constituting a distinctive genre. By extrapolation a case can be made that,
in writing science, missionaries hoped not only to contribute to science
but also to expand and redefine what counted as science in the metropolis.
These texts served as challenges from the periphery, in a period when
science was adopting its modern form.

As recent scholarship demonstrates, analysing missionary writing leads
very quickly to the study of the self-conception of the missionary author.
Gareth Griffiths, for instance, has shown how the output from missionary
presses in the period of high imperialism at the end of the nineteenth
century allowed evangelicals to adopt the secular tropes of hunting,
soldiering, and exploration.[7] Griffiths argues that the depiction of the
missionary hero shifted from the mid-nineteenth century, when it was tied
to humane paternalism, to the late nineteenth century, when it became
more interventionist and even violent. By the early twentieth century the
genre of missionary exploration had taken another turn by becoming
fictionalized. For the historian of science, studying the trajectory of the
missionary hero is important because it sheds light on the connections
between science and vocation. Perhaps the most important missionary hero
of the nineteenth century, David Livingstone, exemplifies the linking of
science and religion in the shifting idea of what it meant to be a missionary.
In order to capture Livingstone's ambiguous and yet successful conception
of vocation Felix Driver has called him 'a missionary of science'.[8]

Livingstone decided to become a missionary because it enabled him to
combine an interest in science with a religious vocation.[9] In Africa he
justified his enthusiasm for exploration by arguing that it helped expand
the reach of Christianity. Livingstone's great transcontinental journey
was made possible through the assistance of Sir Roderick Murchison,
President of the Royal Geographical Society, which awarded Livingstone
a sum of money for reaching Lake Ngami from Kolobeng. This money
enabled Livingstone to purchase scientific instruments that were necessary
for his epic journey. On the 1858 expedition, on which he embarked after
achieving fame, Livingstone conformed to the usual pattern of British

scientific exploration: he took with him an artist (Thomas Baines), a geologist (Richard Thornton), and a botanist (John Kirk).

Livingstone oversaw the collection of natural history specimens and African artifacts. Analysing the role of material culture will no doubt prove another fruitful avenue for historians of science and religion to expand their analysis to territories outside Europe and America. Objects played a vital role in the missionary project. As Nicholas Thomas has shown, the meanings that became attached to them changed according to the context of acquisition, transportation, and display.[10] For instance the so-called father of Protestant missionaries, the Baptist William Carey, established the most impressive private botanical garden in Asia at the start of the nineteenth century.[11] Carey's extensive correspondence network stretched from South Africa to America, via the Pacific. He gathered specimens in Serampore in north India and hoped to make his own garden and that of the East India Company centres for the study of botany. The natural history specimens that Carey collected helped him to conceptualize his relationship to 'heathen' territories. He saw natural history as a fitting intellectual enterprise for the missionary because it exercised the mind, and his study of nature enabled him to maintain the project of self-improvement he had begun before arriving in India.

By the end of the nineteenth century the missionary interest in objects was displayed on a grander canvas with such exhibitions as the Church Missionary Society's 'Africa and the East' (1909) and the London Missionary Society's 'Orient in London' (1908). Both were held in the Royal Agricultural Hall in Islington and then travelled to Manchester, Liverpool, and Birmingham, and, in a reduced form, to smaller towns.[12] Men and women from the colonies were themselves objects of curiosity, as visitors to the exhibitions watched their craftsmanship, including weaving, dyeing, carving, forging iron, and leatherwork. By studying collecting practices, historians can appreciate the contradictions inherent in the missionary engagement of science. Curiously for religious believers who set their hope on the afterlife, objects in this world became important as a means of coming to terms with the present and ensuring that the value of their work was recognizable both to themselves and others.

A. C. Haddon, Reader in Ethnology at the University of Cambridge, was personally involved in the 'Orient in London' exhibition, having been asked to assist with the display of comparative religions. In his introductory essay to the handbook to the Hall of Religions at this exhibition he provided a scholarly introduction to such terms as 'totem', 'fetish', 'ancestor cult', 'animism', and 'supernaturalism'.[13] Missionaries' engagement with the science of anthropology has recently received attention and reveals how missionaries contributed to the emergence of a classification of disciplines, and how they reacted to the widening gap between the expert and the amateur.[14] According to Patrick Harries, by the end of the nineteenth century missionaries were keen to present their credentials as scholarly anthropologists. Likewise anthropology as a discipline depended heavily on the tribal commentaries written by field missionaries.[15] Seeing that their commentaries were greatly valued, missionaries saw indigenous cultures differently by shifting their emphasis from the demonic character of local rites to an appreciation of their value. From this perspective they could make interventions in anthropological theory. For example Lorimer Fison, a Methodist missionary in Fiji, was in contact with Max Müller and Lewis Morgan in the 1860s and extended Morgan's evolutionary scheme by using it to classify kinship terminology. Likewise Robert Codrington, an Anglican missionary to Melanesia, questioned Edward Tylor's notions of animism by describing 'mana', a concept of supernatural power that he uncovered through a deep attention to translation.

However, by the second decade of the twentieth century, with the rise of functionalist anthropology and a growing distance from the older evolutionary framework, missionaries lost their status within the discipline. By the 1930s the missionary was no longer a participant in making anthropology but rather a subject for study. Missionaries' placement in the changing definition of what constituted anthropology suggests that historians should pay more attention to how missionaries defined and were subsequently excluded from emerging scientific disciplines.

The story of how missionaries engaged with the formation and changing fortunes of science has gained a considerable hold in recent years because of dramatic shifts in the general account of how missionaries fit into such major movements as the Enlightenment, the Industrial Revolution, and Darwinism. First, in relation to the Enlightenment, a recent volume of essays edited by Brian Stanley challenges the traditional view that missionaries should be viewed as counter-Enlightenment Romantic voices.[16] It urges that the modern Protestant missionary movement reworked some long-held ideas within evangelicalism in the context of the Enlightenment. These ideas included a belief in the value of reason, the power of technology to civilize other cultures, and an insistence that the Christian message was addressed to individuals. British missionaries were directly influenced by the Scottish Enlightenment and also by a continental rational and Pietist tradition. Second, with respect to industrialization, it has now been established that the upbringing of many British missionaries in urban centres, and their artisanal occupations prior to being called to be missionaries, meant that they were quick to take on manual tasks while working as missionaries, and that they paid particular attention to the material productions of the people to whom they preached. They were very keen to 'improve' themselves.[17] While in their stations many missionaries utilized skills in agriculture and printing, and their contribution to medicine has been well documented. From an interest in practical skills it was a short step to science, and indeed a case can be made that missionaries' science was often more practical than theoretical.

There have also been important shifts in how historians view the reception of Darwin's work outside Europe and America. Darwin has now been cast as an enthusiastic supporter of missions. His firsthand experience of missionary work persuaded him of its value so greatly that his first publication, with Robert Fitzroy, was a defence of missions. Throughout his life he gave money to a missionary society, and he regularly received a missionary journal.[18] Following on from Darwin himself, Ronald Numbers and John Stenhouse's edited collection of essays shows that Darwinian ideas were enthusiastically embraced by overseas Protestants, among others.[19] Marwa Elshakry's work on the reception of Darwinism in the late Ottoman empire will take this argument further.[20] William Habens, a young Congregational minister in New Zealand, provides an example of a positive response to evolution: in 1872 he claimed that 'natural evolution was even a more wonderful thing than the creation itself'.[21] These realignments in our view of the way missionaries and religious believers in the British empire responded to crucial moments in the history of science necessitate a reassessment of how we see missionaries. They need to be understood as figures who were moulded by and who successfully navigated the currents of intellectual change, rather than unthinking fanatics.

One aspect of missionaries' scientific leanings that has attracted sustained and sophisticated discussion is medicine. The call for missionaries to engage with the task of curing the sick had a biblical precedent in the life of Jesus, and curing diseases became a metaphor for curing souls. The number of medical missionaries worldwide ballooned through the long nineteenth century. Although there were only 40 in 1849, by 1925 Protestant missions from Europe and America had 1,157 doctors and 1,007 nurses in overseas clinics and hospitals.[22] In East Africa, as Megan Vaughan urges, for most Africans before the Second World War any prolonged contact with medicine came through missionaries, and this brought with it the associated Christian moral framework. Central to this framework is what Vaughan terms 'new subjectivities': medical missionaries individualized Africans and made them patients, and this discourse led easily to social control. The union of science and religion was thus vital to the changes that medical mission brought to East Africa.[23]

Missionaries also played as vital a role as teachers. The content of mission education changed dramatically across the continents, and esoteric science was given pride of place in territories deemed 'civilized', such as India or China. Elsewhere missionaries slowly adopted what became known as 'adapted' education, an education said to be appropriate to the assumed ability and temperament of colonized peoples. In Africa this meant an education aimed at turning students into agricultural workers, mechanics, and tradesmen.[24]

One illustration of the missionaries' use of science in education comes from the recent work of David Wright on China. The Society for the Diffusion of Useful Knowledge in China, founded in 1834 by one of the early missionaries to China, aimed to publish 'such books as may enlighten the minds of the Chinese, and communicate to them the arts and sciences of the West'. According to Wright, this Society took a strictly Paleyite line.[25] By the last decades of the nineteenth century scientific education had blossomed into a vast constellation of missionary schools where sciences ranging from astronomy to chemistry and botany were taught and where texts written by the likes of John Tyndall, John Herschel, and John Lindley were translated into Chinese.[26] Calvin Mateer, who taught at Dengzhou College in Shandong, wrote in 1877: 'The Chinese look upon the wonders which modern science has wrought as akin to the miraculous, and well they might, for so indeed they are. I argue hence that Protestant missionaries are not only authorized to open schools for the teaching of science but that providence calls them to do so'.[27]

Before leaving missionary science it is worth pausing to ask an important question. Does the manner in which missionaries engaged with science differ greatly from the way Christians in Britain engaged with science? Is this global story merely the European narrative that we know so well writ large? In line with the argument by historical geographer David N. Livingstone that spatiality is central to understanding how missionaries generated knowledge, we can appreciate that the results of missionary science differed significantly across the globe, and that missionary science could have a sense of authority because of its location and missionaries' firsthand experience.[28]

Working with an emphasis on spatiality means that the British history of science and religion needs to be recast in a global context, for missionary knowledge came back home and fed into both popular and elite debates, inasmuch as scientific theories articulated in Britain were carried by missionaries and reconstituted in the periphery. The question of whether the history of missionary science runs in parallel with the British history of science and religion is not the best question to ask. It is time for us to reconfigure the discipline so that we think of nation, geography, and scientific community in new ways, placing traditional sites for the history of science and religion in a global network and recognizing missionaries as vital agents in the global history of science and religion.

NON-WESTERN REDEFINITIONS OF SCIENCE AND RELIGION

So far this chapter has focussed on the British side of the engagement between science, religion, and the world outside Europe and America. Yet the globalization that resulted from empire led to multiple traditions of science and religion coming into contact in the course of the nineteenth and early twentieth centuries. The global history of science and religion did not enable only Christian missionaries to make new knowledge: a vast number of other peoples need to be brought into this narrative. Their stories are only just beginning to be written. Hindu, Buddhist, and Islamic thinkers, among others, often provided interpretive frameworks for embedding the newly arrived western science. Even as different sciences and religions encountered each other there was also a hardening-up of what counted as science and religion, and a reconceptualization of sciences and religions.

Two regions that have recently attracted attention in relation to these questions are South and South East Asia. Richard Fox Young's work has made a pioneering contribution by studying the intellectual debates between indigenous *pandits*, or scholars, and Christian orientalists about science and religion in nineteenth-century South Asia.[29] Young's work reveals how important the Paleyite tradition of evidential theology was to this debate. An informative example is provided by the work of John Muir (1810–82), a complex evangelical who was influenced by the Scottish school of Common Sense philosophy and held various appointments in the north-western provinces of the East India Company's territories between 1830 and 1853.[30] Muir also spent a year (1844–5) reorganizing the teaching at Benares Sanskrit College, which had first been established at the end of the eighteenth century in order to propagandize the Company's patronage of indigenous traditions of scholarship.[31] At the College Muir sought to direct students away from what he saw as unfounded Hindu dogma to verifiable science. Muir's book *Matapariksa*, which first took shape in 1839, was intended to be a Sanskrit Paley: 'A Sanskrit Treatise on the Evidences of

Christianity, with a refutation of Hinduism'.[32] The *Matapariksa* contained 379 verses and consisted of a dialogue between a teacher and a student. Throughout, Muir attributed the structure of the physical world to 'the maker'. He also included Paley's argument against the thesis that the world was a dream-like illusion, and he used Paley's explanation of miracles.

What is most interesting about Muir's work is not its form but the response to it by many *pandits*. One interesting example is provided by Somanatha Vyasa (1807–90) of Sajapur, a town near Gwalior, who published at least thirty-six works and who cast himself in the lineage of an ancient astronomical tradition which encompassed such astronomers as Bhaskara.[33] In responding to Muir's work he wrote that Britons were undeniably clever and skilled mechanics, and knew how to apply science to technology. They built steamships for the Ganges and flying machines, which Young suggests could be a reference to hot-air balloons. They were wise in their administration and well versed in economics. Yet they looked for differences where there was congruence. Their minds were clouded by the dogma that creation occurred in the recent chronological past, compared with the Hindu view of eons and cycles of the eternal dharma.[34] In his *Matapariksa* Somanatha hoped that his readers would understand the unity and compatibility of Hindusim, Christianity, and indeed all other religions. Young urges that while Somanatha's reponse to Muir might be seen as an attempt to encompass Christianity within Hinduism, Subaji Bapu sought to do the same for the sciences.

Subaji Bapu was a *pandit* who served another Christian orientalist, Lancelot Wilkinson. Wilkinson, who is sometimes cast as a patron saint of Sanskrit astronomy, spent most of his days in central India. Subaji was of South Indian origin, and we are only able to gain access to his life through his patron: he disappeared after Wilkinson's early death. Wilkinson hoped to weaken the attachment of people to the cosmographic traditions associated with the *Puranas*, the ancient Hindu texts, and so to popular Hinduism, by spreading Copernican philosophy. Wilkinson discussed Copernican astronomy at length with Subaji and believed that he had succeeded in converting him to both Copernicanism and Christianity. He wrote of the long process that brought this about:

The arguments by which I had for the previous eight years of our connection in vain endeavoured to impress on Subaji Bapu a conviction of the truth of the real size and shape of the earth and other important physical facts, now carried to his mind the clearest conviction when shewn to be precisely the same as those of their own astronomical authors … He was lost in admiration when he came fully to comprehend all the facts resulting from the spherical form of the earth.[35]

In 1836 Subaji published his own tract in Marathi, entitled *Siddhantasir-omaniprakasa*, which was subsequently translated into Hindi. Here he sought to explain the correct form of astronomy that he had learned from Wilkinson, and he defended this in an unpublished tract called *Avirodhaprakasa*. But although Wilkinson thought that Subaji had become a Copernican, Young argues that something far more complicated happened during this encounter. The title of Subaji's main work, *Siddhan-tasiromaniprakasa*, translates as 'An illumination of Siddhantasiromani, the crest jewel of astronomical systems'. In fact Subaji was merely improving on an established work of astronomy written by Bhaskara, the ancient Indian astronomer.[36] Subaji thus utilized Copernicanism in order to critique the traditions of astronomy in India and to urge their resuscitation in the light of the advances of European science. Young's important work indicates how the arrival of western science and Christianity in India did not lead to hegemony or to the erasure of existing traditions. Instead, by tracing the intellectual works of learned men in India, it is possible to see how new knowledge was utilized to recast traditional knowledge and to redirect it. Young describes this as a history of 'collaboration, interaction and self-differentiation'.[37]

The debate surrounding science and religion in Asia often gained public prominence: local peoples often turned at first to western science as a means of testing Christianity; they saw the two as one package. Eclipses were one class of event that generated such public debate. In northern Siam in August 1868 an American Presbyterian missionary, Daniel McGilvary, used a total solar eclipse as an opportunity to debate with Nan Inta, a man who was known to be religious and studious and who had been educated in Buddhism.[38] Nan Inta had already had some discussions with McGilvary about geography, the shape of the earth, and the nature of eclipses. But McGilvary had failed to convince him. The eclipse allowed McGilvary to present a public proof of his science, and, by predicting the eclipse correctly, the missionary persuaded Nan Inta that his beliefs about eclipses – that they came about when a 'huge monster devour[ed] the sun' – were inaccurate. Nan Inta then began to read about Christianity at great length and was baptized in 1869, subsequently becoming a leader of the north Thai church. McGilvary wrote: 'The explanation of it [the eclipse] seemed to him so natural and beautiful and rational compared with what their books teach, that it led him to a clear and firm foothold on which he feels and knows that he is safe. And now almost daily he uses the same argument to his countrymen'.[39] This conversion story must not be read as the conversion of a 'simple-minded superstitious native' but rather as the outcome of carefully testing both science and Christianity on the basis of evidence. It was an intellectual struggle.

A very similar debate had occurred in Jaffna in northern Sri Lanka in the 1820s but had resulted in a different outcome.[40] Daniel Poor, of the American Board of Commissioners for Foreign Mission, entered into a debate with Vicuvanata Aiyar (1756–1845), an elderly brahmin and astrologer. Poor sent him trigonometric problems to solve, and Vicuvanata sent him an ola, a palm leaf on which was written a physiological problem concerning sneezing. The intellectual exchange carried on in this vein. Poor detected errors in Vicuvanata's almanac, which predicted a lunar eclipse on 20 March 1829. Poor printed a tract that alerted the people in his parish to this error, but Vicuvanata stuck to his original prediction. On the night, in front of a crowd of witnesses, Poor won this contest when the predicted eclipse failed to occur. Poor did his utmost to make Vicuvanata his pupil, but it quickly emerged that Vicuvanata was more interested in improving his almanac by adopting the new science rather than making a radical break with his own traditions of religion and science. Moreover, at the college where Poor taught science his students continued to accept astrology. For instance, when Jonathan Magee, a Tamil student who had converted to Christianity, died in a classroom during the inauspicious fifth day of the waning moon, his schoolmates abandoned the institution, and it had to be closed temporarily. So there was no death-blow to indigenous sciences of the sky, merely an appropriation of new ideas from Europe and their recontextualization within existing traditions. These narrations of the uses of and responses to an eclipse demonstrate the need to be careful in discussing the encounter between sciences and religions.[41] In cases that seem at first to be characterized by the adoption or rejection of new knowledge, a more complicated process of accommodation between different sciences and religions often seems to have occurred.

In addition to Hindu and Buddhist perspectives, it is possible to bring in another religious tradition by drawing on recent work on Islamic science in the modern period. With Islamic science it is important to avoid writing of a unitary tradition; instead there were multiple paths of engagement, which should be contextualized within the modernization of the Middle East in the face of western advances. The reform of the Ottoman empire led to a period of institutional reorganization in the mid-nineteenth century termed *tanzimat*, which saw the opening of numerous schools and academies teaching western science. This in turn led to a programme of reinvigoration for the traditional *madrasa* and the translation of sections of texts on western science into Arabic and Turkish. In parallel with this movement of reform was a set of principles, exemplified for instance by Wahhabism, which sought to return the Middle East to what was said to be pure Islam, and so to reject the West and its sciences. The multiple paths of modernization that arose in this context can be discerned in the growing historiography on this topic. Scholars have identified thinkers who hoped to embrace Christian science in order to forge a westernized or even secularized philosophy, those who sought to modernize Islam in the light of science, and also those who used science in order to bolster traditional Islamic thought.

The classic work of Albert Hourani provided an early commentary on the placement of science in the modernizing propensities of Arabic thought: Middle Eastern intellectuals embraced Christian science, alongside liberal political thought and nationalism, in order to reform the Middle East.[42] For instance Butrus al-Bustani (1819–83) was educated in a Maronite community in Egypt and became closely linked to American Protestant missionaries, whose faith he accepted. Bustani then formed his own school, where the sciences and the Arabic language were taught. He believed that the Middle East could revive itself only by accepting the knowledge of European discoveries, and so from 1876, with the financial help of Khedive Isma'il, he began to issue a vast encyclopaedia, of which eleven volumes were published, full of science, medicine, engineering, and the liberal ideas of Europe.[43] Hourani also paid attention to a generation of Lebanese Christians who in the 1870s adopted the political newspaper and the scientific periodical in order to show Arabs the ideas and inventions of Europe and America. They assumed that the western sciences were universal and that they could readily be communicated in Arabic. One individual who came directly under the sway of these publications was Shibli Shumayyil (1850–1917), a graduate of the Syrian Protestant College. He wrote a small book in 1896, the *Shakwa wa amal,* where he expounded his view of what was wrong with the Ottoman empire. Instead he preferred the ideologies of science, justice, and liberty. For Shumayyil, Huxley, Spencer, and Darwin symbolized all of science; his enthusiasm for evolution was linked to a philosophical materialism.[44] Like Shumayyil, a number of other writers took science on board in order to bolster their positions as either Christians or secularists.

Shumayyil's enthusiasm for Darwin's work can be contextualized within the broader controversy at the Syrian Protestant College about the status of Darwinism. The history of this college shows how the new science provided intellectual resources for conversion from one religion to another, for the reassertion of religious faith, and also, somewhat contradictorily, for the division of existing religious communities. As Marwa Elshakry has recently shown, in 1882, when Edwin Lewis, a Harvard graduate and Professor of Geology and Chemistry, gave the annual graduating speech at the Syrian Protestant College in Arabic and spoke in favour of Darwinism, he unleashed a debate about what counted as good science.[45] His speech was published in *al-muqtataf* or 'The Digest', a journal of 'science and industry' published by the college. Responses and rejoinders soon followed. In the end Lewis had to resign, as did a number of others associated with the college. Darwinism's importance to the missionary movement is underscored here. Yet its ambiguous status within missionary discourse meant that a space was opened for non-European elites to appropriate science for their own ends. For Darwinism did not necessarily lead to Christianity and westernization: some used it as a tool to reform Islam. Thus Husayn al-Jisr (1845–1909), who frequented the college library and served as director of 'The Sultan's School' in Beirut, sought to use Darwin to reinforce Islam by citing several Qu'ranic verses which held that life began in water.

John W. Livingston and S. Irfan Habib also show how Islamic scholars could divorce western science from its Christian framework and lead to a reassertion of Islam. Livingston focusses on an important Egyptian intellectual and political thinker, Rifa'a al-Tahtawi (1801–73). Tahtawi called for Muslim society and in particular al-Azhar, the famous educational institute first founded in the tenth century, to embrace western science. Tahtawi became enamoured of western science while studying in Paris. Livingston argues that the evolution of his thought about scientific method is too complex to classify him as a synthesizer: 'he was an apologist, a reformer and a pragmatist, a man of action helping to educate the modernizing state, while doing what he could to temper modernity with the comforting familiarity of religion'.[46] For instance Tahtawi saw the embrace of western science as a process of repossession of what was originally Islamic. He also urged those with fragile minds, who were not steeped in the Qur'an and sunna, to leave the study of science to others, for their beliefs would become diluted. He accepted various facts about the physical world that were derived from western science and recontextualized them within Sunni thought. It is important to note that he did not aim at a grand synthesis of science and religion but instead adopted a pragmatic and piecemeal acceptance of empirical evidence.

This stance with respect to science and religion is also nicely exemplified by two Indian Muslims: Syed Ahmad Khan (1817–98), a reformer who founded the Aligarh Muslim University and who sought to position

Indian Muslims as loyal to the Raj, and Jamal al-Din al-Afghani (1839–97), who was an anti-imperialist pan-Islamist.[47] Syed Ahmad controversially advocated that the Qur'an be reinterpreted in the light of physical realities; for him religion was not a corpus of tradition but rather had to be remoulded to fit current human experience. Afghani did not seek to reinterpret Islamic theology; instead his anti-imperialism led him to view science not as western but as universal.

Arabic and Islamic engagements with science in the nineteenth century were framed by the long history of science in the Middle East, and also by the felt need to reform and modernize in the face of western imperial expansion. Within this tradition it is difficult to trace a straightforward narrative of the absorption of new ideas from the West or to classify different types of thinker as synthesizers or revivalists. To varying degrees reformers sought to contextualize science within existing frameworks and alternative political goals. In this new age of globalization the multiple intellectual resources open to Islamic and Arabic thinkers meant that different figures were able to forge their own trajectories, ranging from westernization to Islamism. While the world of the Middle East and of Islam more widely, as well as the Hindu and Buddhist cultures of South and South East Asia, had well-institutionalized traditions of education, different historical methods become necessary when we widen our gaze to the regions of the Pacific and Africa. In the Pacific one way in which to appreciate how islanders responded to the scientific instruments, books, and practices that Christian missionaries brought with them is to pay attention to visual images or to read missionary sources against the grain.

For instance Protestant missionaries were emphatic about the need to train islanders to be industrious agriculturalists. But a delegation of evangelicals who visited South Pacific mission stations in the 1820s noted how one inhabitant of the island of Huahine had planted a nail, as a rare object made of metal, hoping that it would bud, blossom, and fruit.[48] Likewise an illustration in a mid-nineteenth-century printed source shows eight Micronesian islanders eating a packet of mail that had landed on shore, thus adopting a very different view of the physicality of paper.[49] It is difficult to decide on the veracity of these accounts and images, yet they suggest how scientific artifacts could have been reinterpreted in local contexts. William Wyatt Gill, the missionary we encountered earlier, compiled a collection of natural history anecdotes used by islanders. For instance one islander announced: 'We poor sinners are like the *titi* – a foolish bird – hiding in the dark noisome haunts of sin'.[50] The use of the *titi* bird here is reminiscent of traditional natural theology tropes in missionary sermons. Yet at the same time the *titi* already possessed significance in Polynesia; for instance in Tahiti a slave was called *titi*. Did the islander then speak of conversion using an already existing tradition of natural historical analogy which was then transposed to a Christian one? In the Pacific the arrival of both Christianity and science did not lead to a straightforward appropriation of new ideas. There was a significant amount of creativity in how Pacific islanders recast existing traditions and responded to the new.

Cultural history is also vital in coming to terms with how Africans responded to the amalgamation of Christianity and science, as demonstrated in Luise White's fascinating work on the history of rumours of blood-sucking in twentieth-century East and Central Africa. White writes of how Africans responded to the medical mission: pills were seen as charms, and the bottles in which lotions were given were not returned. Albert Cook, one of the medical missionaries of the Church Missionary Society, expressed exasperation at how Ugandans responded to his medicines and provided a typical consulting-room dialogue:

DOCTOR: What is the matter with you?
PATIENT: My name is so and so.
DOCTOR: Yes, but what is your disease?
PATIENT: I want medicine to drink.
DOCTOR: Where do you hurt?
PATIENT: I don't want medicine to swallow, but to drink.
DOCTOR (STERNLY):   What is your illness?
PATIENT: Oh it goes all over me, it cries out 'Ka Ka'. Will you listen to the top of my head with your hearing machine etc. etc.?[51]

Using evidence like this, White reinterprets the long queues of patients who attended medical missionary clinics. He writes that they do not signify a real interest in western medicine but rather how these medical objects and remedies were recontextualized in African healing practices.

It is important not to cast the experience of Pacific islanders and Africans in opposition to the inhabitants of South Asia and the Middle East. The general argument that has been proposed is that in all of these regions Christian and scientific practice was not merely appropriated or rejected wholesale. A far more complicated process of accommodation and evolution needs to be traced, where non-Europeans are given both intellectual and cultural agency and where existing local traditions of science and religion are respected. The globalization of science and religion in the wake of the British empire saw different traditions come into more sustained contact than before and provided the resources for different religious and scientific traditions to reinvent themselves. With the emergence of nationalist movements across these territories such newly resurgent ideas became increasingly linked to a shared political programme. For example, as the work of Gyan Prakash shows for India, Hindu nationalists utilized a vocabulary of science in order to bolster their political campaigns.[52] Sciences and religions in the non-European world therefore absorbed the new, went through a long process of negotiation, and then repositioned themselves as distinct ideologies.

TOWARDS A GLOBAL UNDERSTANDING OF SCIENCE AND RELIGION

By tracing a global history of science and religion for territories that loosely came under British influence this chapter has attempted to stretch the boundaries of the traditional Eurocentric and Protestant-focussed history of science and religion. It has provided a general view of some of the common themes that arise when different religious traditions respond to new sciences in the context of colonialism and has pointed to exchange and redefinition as crucial. The evidence offered shows that there was no necessary conflict between sciences and religions. At the same time a simple model of complementarity does not recover the complexity of this story either.

The discussion has focussed on both colonizers and colonized by bringing to view Christian missionaries and non-western elites as examples of the types of individual who might be brought into a global history of science and religion. All of the figures discussed in this chapter – ranging from missionary evangelists to missionary anthropologists, and the *pandits* of South Asia to Pacific islanders – are not those traditionally considered as participants in the history of science and religion. Yet because these individuals lived in the context of colonialism, they had to come to terms with new scientific and religious ideas or redefine existing knowledge. At first glance their biographies may appear rather different from those figures who are better known in the modern history of science and religion, namely clergyman natural historians or pious professional scientists. Yet the scope of a global history of science and religion might be broadened beyond that of this chapter by contextualizing leading figures in the history of European and American science and religion within a larger picture of intellectual patterns and connections across the world.

The geographical ambit of this chapter does not necessarily signal a turn to pluralism but rather to the possibility of drawing out a bigger picture that brings to view the movement of ideas, people, and information. While much of the work in the new global history of science and religion has been restricted to a few specific geographical areas, if a wider perspective is adopted it may be possible to link stories by means of people and artifacts that move across the world. The generalization about science and religion that is proposed in this chapter is represented by the possibility of writing a connected narrative about the intellectual encounters of the British empire. This does not, however, preclude the fact that there were disconnections in the circulation of sciences and religions. Connected histories will need to work alongside comparative ones. Yet a big picture of science and religion may circumvent the fragmentation of the discipline, and for that reason we should work hard at it. Since this chapter has taken a larger view, it has been possible to get a sense of the redefinitions of science and religion in this period of global contact and movement. Sciences and religions had complex engagements, rather than ones characterized only by conflict or complementarity. Yet an argument for complexity should not lead automatically to a dominance of case studies.

The need for more work in the global history of science and religion is underscored by the rich sources that are available for its study: Hindu, Buddhist, and Islamic intellectuals wrote works on science; and the textual and visual archive of the colonizers can be taken apart in order to get to how Pacific islanders and Africans, for instance, repositioned religious science. In all of these ways there are telling signs that the project of writing the history of science and religion for the nineteenth and twentieth centuries has just begun. Such a programme of research, which pays due attention to the whole world and also to all religious and scientific cultures, will no doubt widen our understanding of why different sciences and religions could provide new opportunities and reinforcement to each other. We have only got the first flavour of the global encounter of sciences and religions.

NOTES

1 Sujit Sivasundaram, *Nature and the godly empire: Science and evangelical mission in the Pacific, 1795–1850* (Cambridge: Cambridge University Press, 2005), Conclusion.
2 Sujit Sivasundaram, 'Man, nature and British missionaries in the Pacific, 1820–1880', unpublished MPhil thesis, University of Cambridge (1998), pp. 22–3.
3 Niel Gunson, 'British missionaries and their contribution to science in the Pacific Islands', in Roy M. McLeod and Philip F. Rehbock (eds.), *Darwin's laboratory: Evolutionary theory and natural history in the Pacific* (Honolulu: University of Hawaii Press, 1994), pp. 283–316. See also John Stenhouse,

'Missionary science', in David N. Livingstone and Ronald L. Numbers (eds.), *Modern science in national and international context* (New York: Cambridge University Press, in press).

4 Sivasundaram, 'Man, nature and British missionaries', p. 51. For more on Brown, see Helen Bethea Gardner, *Gathering for God: George Brown in Oceania* (Dunedin: Otago University Press, 2006).

5 Sivasundaram, 'Man, nature and British missionaries', p. 56.

6 Anna Johnston, *Missionary writing and empire, 1800–1860* (Cambridge: Cambridge University Press 2003).

7 Gareth Griffiths, 'Popular imperial adventure fiction and the discourse of missionary texts', in Jamie S. Scott and Gareth Griffiths (eds.), *Mixed messages: Materiality, textuality, missions* (New York: Palgrave Macmillan, 2005), pp. 51–66.

8 Felix Driver, *Geography militant: Cultures of exploration and empire* (Oxford: Oxford University Press, 2001).

9 Details for this paragraph taken from John MacKenzie, *David Livingstone and the Victorian encounter with Africa* (London: National Portrait Gallery, 1996); Clare Pettit, *Dr. Livingstone I presume? Missionaries, journalists, explorers and empire* (London: Profile, 2007); and Tim Jeal, *Livingstone* (London: Yale University Press, 1973).

10 Nicholas Thomas, *Entangled objects: Exchange, material culture and colonialism in the Pacific* (Cambridge, MA: Harvard University Press, 1991).

11 Sujit Sivasundaram, '"A Christian Benares": Orientalism and science in the Serampore Mission of Bengal', *Indian Economic and Social History Review* 44 (2007), 111–45.

12 Annie Coombes, *Reinventing Africa: Museums, material culture and popular imagination in Victorian and Edwardian England* (New Haven, CT: Yale University Press, 1994), pp. 174–86.

13 Ibid., p. 184.

14 See, for instance, Jane Samson, 'Ethnology and theology: Nineteenth-century mission dilemmas in the South Pacific', in Brian Stanley (ed.), *Christian missions and the enlightenment* (Grand Rapids, MI: Eerdmans, 2001), pp. 99–123; Helen Tilley and Robert Gordon (eds.), *Ordering Africa: Anthropology, European imperialism and the politics of knowledge* (Manchester: Manchester University Press, 2007); George Stocking, *After Tylor: British social anthropology, 1888–1951* (London: Athlone, 1996).

15 The following material is drawn from Patrick Harries, 'Anthropology', in Norman Etherington (ed.), *Missions and empire* (Oxford: Oxford University Press, 2005), pp. 238–60.

16 Stanley (ed.), *Christian missions and the enlightenment*.

17 For missionaries and class, see Susan Thorne, *Congregational missions and the making of an imperial culture in nineteenth-century England* (Stanford, CA: Stanford University Press, 1999).

18 Mark W. Graham, '"The enchanter's wand": Charles Darwin, foreign missions, and the voyage of H. M. S. *Beagle*', *Journal of Religious History* 31 (2007), 131–50.

19 Ronald L. Numbers and John Stenhouse (eds.), *Disseminating Darwinism: The role of place, race, religion, and gender* (Cambridge: Cambridge University Press, 1999).

20 See Marwa Elshakry, 'The gospel of science and American evangelism in late Ottoman Beirut', *Past and Present* 196 (2007), 173–214.

21 John Stenhouse, 'Darwinism in New Zealand', in Numbers and Stenhouse (eds.), *Disseminating Darwinism*, pp. 61–90, on p. 65.

22 Norman Etherington, 'Education and medicine', in Etherington, *Missions and empire*, pp. 261–84, esp. p. 279. For more on missionary medicine, see Terence Ranger, 'Godly medicine: The ambiguities of medical mission in South-Eastern Tanzania, 1900–1945', in S. Feierman and J. M. Janzen (eds.), *The social basis of health and healing in Africa* (Berkeley, CA: University of California Press, 1992); M. Worboys, 'The colonial world as mission and mandate: Leprosy and empire, 1900–1940', *Osiris* 15 (2000), 207–18.

23 Megan Vaughan, *Curing their ills: Colonial power and African illness* (Stanford, CA: Stanford University Press, 1991), ch. 3.

24 Udo Bude, 'The adaptation concept in British colonial education', *Comparative Education* 19 (1983), 341–55.

25 David Wright, *Translating science: The transmission of western chemistry into late imperial China* (Leiden: Brill, 2000), ch. 3. For missionary work and science in China, see also Fa-ti Fan, *British naturalists in Qing China: Science, empire and cultural encounter* (Cambridge, MA: Harvard University Press, 2004).

26 Wright, *Translating science*, Appendices 3 and 4.

27 Ibid., p. 78.

28 David N. Livingstone, 'Scientific inquiry and the missionary enterprise', in Ruth Finnegan (ed.), *Participating in the knowledge society: Researchers beyond the university walls* (Basingstoke: Palgrave Macmillan, 2005), p. 51. For a broad narrative of missionary science, see also Stenhouse, 'Missionary science'.

29 Richard Fox Young, *Resistant Hinduism: Sanskrit sources on anti-Christian apologetics in early nineteenth-century India* (Vienna: Institut für Indologie der Universität Wien, 1991); Richard Fox Young and G. P. V. Somaratna, *Vain debates: The Buddhist–Christian controversies of nineteenth-century Ceylon* (Vienna: De Nobili Research Library, 1996); and Richard Fox Young, 'Receding from antiquity: Hindu responses to science and Christianity on the margins of empire, 1800–1850', in Robert Frykenberg (ed.), *Christians and missionaries in India: Cross-cultural communication since 1500* (Grand Rapids, MI: Eerdmans, 2003), pp. 183–222.

30 The material that follows is drawn from Young, *Resistant Hinduism*, ch. 4.

31 See Michael Dodson, 'Re-presented for the pandits: James Ballantyne, "useful knowledge", and Sanskrit scholarship in Benares College during the nineteenth century', *Modern Asian Studies* 36 (2002), 257–98, esp. 271ff.

32 Cited in Young, *Resistant Hinduism*, p. 63.

33 Young, 'Receding from antiquity', pp. 210ff.

34 This description given in ibid., p. 213.

35 Young, *Resistant Hinduism*, pp. 83–4.

36 Young, 'Receding from antiquity', p. 198.
37 Ibid., p. 217. For work that follows Young's lead, see: Michael Dodson, *Orientalism, empire and national culture, India, 1770–1880* (Basingstoke: Palgrave Macmillan, 2007); Indira Viswanathan Peterson, 'Tanjore, Tranquebar and Halle: European science in German missionary education in the lives of two Indian intellectuals in the early nineteenth century', in Frykenberg, *Christians and missionaries*, pp. 93–126. See also Indira Peterson, 'The cabinet of King Serfoji of Tanjore: A European collection in early-nineteenth-century India', *Journal of the History of Collections* 11 (1999), pp. 71–93. My own work also follows that of this group of scholars: see Sivasundaram, 'A Christian Benares'.
38 Herbert R. Swanson, 'Origins of the nineteenth-century transformation of cosmology in Northern Siam: The Nan Inta–McGilvary debates of science and religion', *Journal of the Siam Society* 89 (2001), 32–9.
39 This and the quotations that follow are from Swanson, 'Origins', 35–7.
40 This paragraph relies on R. F. Young and S. Jebanesan, *The Bible trembled: The Hindu–Christian controversies of nineteenth-century Ceylon* (Leiden: Brill), ch. 2.
41 For another account of the uses of an eclipse, see Elshakry, 'The gospel of science', 202–3.
42 Albert Hourani, *Arabic thought in the liberal age, 1798–1939* (Oxford: Oxford University Press, 1932).
43 Ibid., pp. 99–102.
44 Ibid., p. 248.
45 The material for this paragraph draws on Elshakry, 'The gospel of science'.
46 John W. Livingston, 'Western science and educational reform in the thought of Shaykh Rifa'a al-Tahtawi', *International Journal of Middle East Studies* 28 (1996), 543–64, on 554.
47 S. Irfan Habib, 'Reconciling science with Islam in 19th-century India', *Contributions to Indian Sociology* 34 (2000), 63–92, on 64. For a broader, general account of Islam and science encompassing these individuals and others, see Muzaffar Iqbal, *Islam and Science* (Aldershot: Ashgate, 2002).
48 Sivasundaram, *Nature and the godly empire*, p. 161.
49 Vanessa Smith, *Literary culture and the Pacific: Nineteenth-century textual encounters* (Cambridge: Cambridge University Press, 1998), pp. 237–8.
50 Sivasundaram, *Nature and the godly empire*, p. 92.
51 Cited in Luise White, *Speaking with vampires: Rumor and history in colonial Africa* (Berkeley, CA: University of California Press, 2000), p. 97; quoted passage from Cook's diary of 1900.
52 Gyan Prakash, *Another reason: Science and the imagination of modern India* (Princeton, NJ: Princeton University Press, 1999).

CHAPTER 10

The Scopes trial beyond science and religion
Adam R. Shapiro

In the waning days of the 1924–5 school year, John Thomas Scopes, a young teacher filling in for the regular biology teacher in Dayton, Tennessee, assigned reading from Hunter's *Civic biology* to prepare students for their final examination. This came after Tennessee had passed a law in March 1925 outlawing the teaching of evolution. Scopes was put on trial and convicted, and subsequently became a symbol of the (perceived) ongoing warfare between science and religion. Scopes was hailed by some as a martyr to intellectual freedom, compared to the likes of Socrates and Galileo. Often linked with the phrase 'Monkey Trial', the name 'Scopes' also became a label of derision by those who saw in evolution an irreligious and immoral doctrine. It has been immortalized in folk songs, on Broadway, and on the silver screen, and there is no doubt that the Scopes trial remains one of the best-known and most significant events in the history of science and religion in the United States. Because of two men – Clarence Darrow and William Jennings Bryan, whose debate over the truth of the Bible and its relationship to science captivated the country and was reported throughout the world – the Scopes trial has frequently been described as 'the trial of the century'.[1] Even as the twentieth century has given way to the twenty-first, interest in the trial has shown no sign of waning. Controversies over the teaching of evolution in high schools have continued, and both legal rulings and popular perceptions have seen these as originating in Dayton.

At first glance the Scopes 'Monkey' trial appears to be a clear exemplar of the 'conflict thesis'. Once Darwin's *On the origin of species* was published in 1859, the conflict story goes, the findings of biology conflicted with the teachings of scripture, and the Scopes trial, or something like it, was inevitable. In addition to being explained by the conflict thesis, the Scopes trial is also invoked as confirmation of the thesis's validity. If there was no real conflict between evolution and religion, as many have maintained, why was there a Scopes trial? This cycle of self-justification is broken when historical narratives outside those of science and religion are considered. In particular, examining the Scopes trial as an event influenced by trends in biology teaching, education regulation, and book publishing compels not only a rethinking of the trial but also a broadened understanding of the factors that contribute to the history of science and religion. This chapter will explore these factors, in the context of the local politics of Tennessee and its Governor's ambitions for educational reform, to argue for a re-examination of the importance of the Scopes trial to the understanding of science and religion.

THE SIGNIFICANCE OF HUNTER'S 'CIVIC BIOLOGY'

Looked at this way the story of the Scopes trial may well begin in 1923. As that year drew to a close, Tennessee Governor Austin Peay took note of a deadline looming for the people of his state. On 1 September 1924 existing contracts with textbook publishers would expire. On that day the price of schoolbooks would increase by as much as one half. The increase would come as an artifact of a price surge that had actually occurred in 1920 and 1921, when post-war shortages drove up prices. Tennessee had signed a contract in 1919, fixing prices for five years.[2] Neighbouring states were also in the practice of negotiating five-year contracts, but many had cycles that began new adoptions in 1922 or 1923. By the time Peay began to prepare for the upcoming adoption, these states were paying much more than Tennessee for the same textbooks. Come September, it appeared, Tennessee's good fortune would end.[3]

Tennessee's contract was well timed, making the most of the pre-1920 low prices of textbooks. However, its expiration would come at the worst possible moment for the Governor's political plans. Two months after Tennesseans would feel the impact of the price increase, Peay would stand for re-election. He had already presented himself as an advocate of public education and modernizing the state. School reform was to be the defining issue of his 1924 campaign, built upon a platform of increased funding to build more schools, expand the school year, create teaching colleges, and overhaul compulsory public education in a state that ranked among the worst in America for literacy. Aside from teacher salaries, textbooks were the greatest expense for public education. During the lifetime of the five-year contract Tennesseans spent over $2.7 million.[4] As textbooks were bought directly by most parents, it was also the school expense most immediately felt by citizens.[5] A sudden increase in prices might have crippled support for the new taxes and legislation necessary for school reform. While Peay's re-election may not have been jeopardized, the increase would probably have reduced the number of supporters in the legislature and might have compelled the Governor to scale back his ambitions for schools.

And so, as the new year began, Peay, along with his Commissioner of Education and political ally, Perry L. Harned, devised a strategy to avert this political difficulty. On 3 January 1924 Peay wrote:

We must not consider an advance of $33\frac{1}{3}$% in our school books. I will exhaust every means available before consenting to such a contract.

I request you to communicate immediately with the publishers having contracts now with the state and express to them my view that we are entitled, for the school term 1924–1925, to buy our books under existing contracts since the schools will be running before the contracts will expire.[6]

Reasoning that many schools in the state would be opened in August, or early September, any textbooks bought before the 1 September deadline would be available at the prices in the 1919 contract. If textbooks could be bought promptly, no new adoption would be needed until the next school year. In effect Tennessee could squeeze a sixth year out of a five-year adoption.

Peay and Harned did not immediately announce this plan, and as the contract's expiration drew nearer, others began to take note of the potential price increase. In February a legislator from a rural district encouraged Peay to use his 'influence in not changing school books this year, as it will be a heavy expense on the people, especially farmers'.[7] Peay and Harned had not yet publicly announced their plan, in effect (if not intentionally) allowing the perception of a crisis to build before announcing their solution. In March Peay confided to a political supporter, 'I have determined to have no adoption until next year'.[8] As Harned later described it: 'At a meeting of the State Text Book Commission on April 16, 1924, all members being present, it was unanimously decided to defer the adoption of text books until 1925'.[9] Since all members of the Commission were directly appointed by the Governor, the outcome was a foregone conclusion.

Thus a political difficulty was converted into a boon. Voters would not feel the effects of a price increase until after the election, preventing it from becoming an issue against Peay in the election. By delaying the public announcement of this plan until after others had begun to notice the problem, Peay and Harned could present a strategy of coaxing an extra year out of the 1919 contract as proof of their commitment to saving taxpayers money and solidifying their position as champions of school reform. From

1 September 1924 to 30 June 1925 the books adopted in 1919 would be available at increased prices, but early buying and the re-use of previously purchased books meant that very few people would have to buy anything during those nine months.[10] Nearly 90 per cent of students in Tennessee began the school year before 1 September.[11] Estimates of the money saved by Tennesseans during the 1924–5 school year amounted to hundreds of thousands of dollars. In most of the state, parents bought new books from authorized retailers approved by the state. There was no regulation of second-hand books, and many parents took advantage of this in the later years of an adoption. Some urban school districts purchased textbooks which they then provided free for students to use for the year. In most cases the money spent on textbooks came directly out of the pockets of parents.

When Harned wrote an explanation for the postponement that accompanied a published list of interim prices for the 1924–5 school year he not only justified the decision by the money that would be saved under the plan but claimed that it would also be beneficial for new adoptions to occur at the beginning of the scholastic year, 1 July, instead of 1 September, when most students had already begun classes.[12] This allowed Peay and Harned to portray the postponement as a pedagogical benefit as well as an economic one. There were many reasons for postponing the 1924 adoption. It saved taxpayers a huge expense, and it rescued Governor Peay's educational reform. Peay won re-election in 1924 with a mandate to pursue this agenda. For everyone, except perhaps the textbook publishers, the postponement was a good thing. There was one unforeseen consequence that could not have occurred if not for this scheme: the Scopes trial.

Postponing the 1924 adoption left a ten-year-old biology textbook in the hands of Tennessee schoolchildren. In 1919 the State Text Book Commission of Tennessee had adopted George W. Hunter's 1914 book, *A civic biology, presented in problems.*[13] When first published it was a groundbreaking textbook and for many years was a bestseller. By the early 1920s, however, its sales had slipped against newer textbooks from other publishers. By 1924 its publisher, the American Book Company (ABC), had already felt it overdue for revision, and Hunter had begun work on a new manuscript. Its age alone would have been grounds not to readopt the *Civic biology* in Tennessee in 1924 – had an adoption occurred.[14]

The postponement of textbook adoptions in 1924 was in no way intended to alter biology education in particular, but the decision to delay the selection of new textbooks had a significant impact in that field because of the changes in biology textbooks since Hunter's book was first written. Given how significant the Scopes trial has become to the history of science and religion it may seem odd to suggest that if it had not been for the 1924 postponement of textbook adoptions in Tennessee, there might not have been this court case pitting Darwin against the Bible. Of course it is impossible to state with certainty what *might* have happened. But the assumption that the Scopes trial was fundamentally rooted in the incommensurability of science with religion – and was therefore inevitable – is one that was cultivated by the trial's participants and was echoed by those who co-opted the trial to justify later conflicts over evolution.[15] According to the standard 'conflict' view there was nothing unique or particular about Dayton, or about Tennessee, or even about Hunter's *Civic biology*. To accept that a universalized science–religion conflict made the Scopes trial inevitable is to accept the explanation put forward by the trial's participants, who of course accounted for the trial in ways that justified and valorized their own involvement.

In fact there had been a variety of religious responses to theories of evolution. There was no sudden realization in 1925 that Darwin's theories, over half a century old, conflicted with essential truths of religion. Examining the series of events that led to the trial, as opposed to the claims of those who influenced the trial's legacy during and after the fact, helps to explain the confluence of local, state, and national events that led to the historical Scopes trial – in Dayton, Tennessee, in 1925. This was more than an expression of some eternal struggle; the Scopes trial was a specific event, and its occasion relied on several unique factors.

Hunter's book was central to the trial. When he signed the Anti-Evolution Bill into law Governor Peay wrote: 'I can find nothing of consequence in the books now being taught in our schools with which this bill will interfere in the slightest manner'.[16] Yet, just one month before the Scopes trial, William Jennings Bryan wrote to a colleague: 'If you have not read the book in question, "Hunter's Civic Biology", I suggest you get it. It certainly gives us all the ammunition we need'.[17] While Tennessee was still using a textbook from 1914, textbooks published in 1923 and 1924 had adopted a more cautious attitude towards evolution which sought to downplay the novelty or broader implications of Darwin's contributions to biology,[18] and on 2 March 1925, just days before the Anti-Evolution Act was passed, Ginn and Company, one of the largest US textbook publishers, released a new biology textbook that did away with the word 'evolution' after its editor-in-chief solicited Bryan's advice on how to discuss the topic.[19]

The Scopes trial – in Tennessee, in 1925 – cannot be held as confirmation of an inevitable conflict between science and religion. Were it not for many of the contingent circumstances of the textbook politics of

Tennessee at the time, had Peay's political ingenuity not kept his state from adopting a new book in 1924, the anti-evolution law would probably not have been enacted.

Even though there were many people who objected to evolution on religious grounds, the anti-evolution movement was a movement concerning what was taught in schools. In this respect the anti-evolution movement was already winning before Scopes' indictment: winning through less public and more gradual changes in textbooks. There were few places left in 1925 where textbooks as old as Hunter's were still being used. There may not have been anywhere else where a Scopes trial could have happened. Anti-evolution laws passed in other states prior to Tennessee's had prohibited the use of textbooks that taught evolution; the Tennessee law was unique in that it targeted teachers, not textbooks.[20] Even if more states had followed Tennessee's lead, by the time new laws were enacted the issue would have been rendered moot by successfully changing textbooks. The successes of anti-evolution may very well have been concluded without direct confrontation, had Tennessee not been using a book that pre-dated the entire controversy.[21] Of course it is impossible to say with certainty that there would not have been an anti-evolution trial later in another state, but given how much the Scopes trial depended on the unique circumstances of Tennessee in 1925, and how much success the anti-evolution movement had just started to have at the time of the Scopes trial, another anti-evolution trial without Scopes seems unlikely. At the very least the conflict thesis-oriented picture of an anti-evolution trial as 'inevitable' must be rejected. And this same point is further reinforced when we turn to contemporary attitudes to education and the role of the state.

EDUCATION AND THE ROOTS OF THE SCOPES TRIAL

In his memoir Scopes wrote, 'I didn't know, technically, whether I had violated the law or not' until he re-examined the *Civic biology*. 'There's our text, provided by the state. I don't see how a teacher can teach biology without teaching evolution'.[22] Even if Scopes had been presented with a more recent textbook than Hunter's, he may have been correct to think that the teaching of biology could not be done without the teaching of evolution. This was not because evolution was a subject that just happened to occur in the biology curriculum of the early 1920s, but because what it meant for a high-school course in the life sciences to be called 'biology' was something new in the United States at that time. Biology curricula were undergoing significant changes at the national level in the 1910s and 1920s.

The ten years leading up to the Scopes trial saw a dramatic increase in the number of students taking biology classes. While this was in part due to an increase in high-school attendance, the most significant factor affecting this was the replacement of separate courses in botany and zoology (and occasionally human physiology) with a single course in biology.[23] Changes in textbooks reflected and reinforced this development. Almost all high-school textbooks sold as 'biology' before 1914 were structured as if they were two separate books, one of botany, one of zoology. Often, human physiology was also included as a third unit or final chapter to these books. Hunter and his colleagues teaching biology in New York City restructured their courses around the social and economic uses of biology, abandoning the traditional distinctions between plant, animal, and human life in favour of a course that was organized around central concepts common to living things.[24] These included heredity, cellular structure, metabolism, evolution, public health, and the use of biology to improve social conditions.

The *Civic biology*, with its focus on such issues as quarantine, food safety, and the improvement of human society (including a substantial section on eugenics), was geared towards urban schools. This was made clear in the preface. 'This book shows boys and girls living in an urban community how they may best live within their own environment and how they may coöperate with the civic authorities for the betterment of their environment'.[25] The notion of teaching biology differently for urban and rural audiences made sense to educators and to textbook publishers, and so the ABC offered two biology books at the same time. Their second offering, aimed at rural communities, Hunter's 1911 *Essentials of biology*, was organized more closely along the traditional structure of botany, zoology, and physiology, with a final chapter on 'civic biology'.[26] The ABC, the largest textbook publisher of the era, was not the only publisher to follow this strategy.

Yet this marketing strategy collided with a trend in some states, especially in the South, to centralize textbook regulation and strip the power of adoption from local boards. Tennessee passed its first Uniform Textbook Law in 1899, making it one of the earliest Southern states to regulate textbook adoption. In general the states that took over textbook regulation from local school districts did not do so to regulate content but to negotiate for lower prices and prevent local corruption in textbook selection. The primary consideration that drove Governor Peay to postpone the 1924 adoption, the high price of textbooks, was one of the same concerns that had led to state regulation in the first place.

Textbook regulation by states was also seen as a progressive response to the laissez-faire economics and marketing practices of the 'book trust', as the monopolistic ABC was frequently called by its critics. The political movement against unregulated monopolies (championed in his presidential campaigns by William Jennings Bryan) found a successful expression of its policies in statewide textbook adoption.

The 1925 Tennessee legislative session is remembered (if at all) for the passage and enactment of the Anti-Evolution Act, or Butler Act (as it was called after the State Senator who wrote it). At the time, however, the most important matter before the legislature was also part of the progressive impulse to regulate education at a centralized level and to make it more accessible to and compulsory for all school-age children. This General Education Bill consumed the entire session and was passed thanks in large measure to the combined efforts of Harned and Peay. As Charles A. Israel has discussed in his history of the social context of Tennessee prior to the Scopes trial, public education was a disputed institution in the period. Some Evangelicals feared the secularization of society through the instrument of public education, while religious progressives saw education as a means to improve society and fulfil a moral calling. These progressives encouraged religious participation in public education. Encouraging religious participation in the schools was part of the political compromise that allowed earlier compulsory attendance laws to be passed in the State.[27]

Austin Peay was a Baptist progressive, and his General Education Bill reflected this. It was intended to expand education throughout the state, establish a minimum eight-month school year, and provide for the establishment of a high school in every county in the state. Overall the bill would more than quadruple the amount of money spent by the state on education.[28]

This was intended to produce dramatic results. Tennessee was ranked near the lowest of the forty-eight states and the District of Columbia in literacy. Increasing education was seen as vital to preparing students for a future in an urbanizing and industrializing United States. The education bill that Harned and Peay drafted met with resistance in the legislature, where concerns over its social implications, as well as its expense, led to protracted debate and significant compromise.

One particular region of Tennessee whose citizens were largely opposed to the bill was the Cumberland Valley, a rural, mountainous area of middle Tennessee. In 1924 these citizens elected to the State Senate John Washington Butler, the author of the Anti-Evolution Act. Jeanette Keith has observed that Butler's bill was intended as a protest against continued state intrusion into the cultural life of the region. 'Farmers of J. W. Butler's generation believed self-sufficiency a worthy goal;

as Butler said, they wanted the "right kind" of education for their children, the sort that would make youth "thankful that they live on a farm, where they can make what they eat and eat what they make".[29] Butler's objections to evolution were in part religiously motivated, yet those objections found expression in legislation directed against the schools. Before the General Education Bill was proposed, before students in his district would have access to high schools where evolution was taught, Butler's objections had no legislative expression. With the sudden prospect of compulsory high schools in regions of the state in which few people had obtained high-school education, and the perception (reinforced by biology textbooks) that high schools taught a way of life geared towards an urban environment and away from their own rural culture, the General Education Bill was of great concern to the people of the Cumberland Valley. Keith concludes: 'If the Tennessee Monkey Law held any symbolic meaning on the local level, it was a regional reaction to decades of reform culminating in a loss of local control over education'.[30]

When Governor Peay signed the Anti-Evolution Bill into law on 23 March 1925 he asserted: 'The people have the right and must have the right to regulate what is taught in their schools'.[31] Seeing it as 'a distinct protest against an irreligious tendency to exalt so-called science',[32] Peay confidently predicted: 'Probably, the law will never be applied'.[33] Peay was shortly proven wrong, and the application of this law against John Scopes ensured the Butler Act's place in history.

Regardless of whether or not Butler's Act was introduced as a protest against a specific bill or was a reflection of more general dissatisfaction with decades of reform, its passage and signing by Governor Peay were intrinsically linked to the 1925 General Education Bill. A version of the bill was introduced in the State House of Representatives on 6 February 1925. On 9 February it was referred to the Committee on Education, from which it never emerged.[34] A second version was introduced on 18 March and was also referred to the Committee on Education.[35] The new version of the General Education Bill seemed destined to share the fate of the first, when the Anti-Evolution Act was passed by both houses of the legislature and sent to the Governor on 17 March.[36] Although many encouraged the Governor to veto it, he signed it on 23 March. On 25 March the General Education Bill was called from the Committee, and debate began in earnest.[37] After continuous debate for over a week, during which 156 amendments were considered, the bill was passed on 2 April.[38] The Senate passed the bill with an additional 121 amendments on 15 April, and the resultant compromise bill was sent to the Governor the next day, the final day of the legislative session.[39] The General Education Bill became law only through the continuous politicking, compromising, and negotiating by Peay and Harned. Peay's non-veto of the Butler Act was part of that process.

The great number of amendments and the amount of time spent on debate over the General Education Bill show how politically difficult an achievement school reform was in Tennessee. The passage of the bill was a political success for Peay and Harned, one that began at the end of 1923, with the plan to postpone textbook adoptions. The turning point in ensuring the education bill's success came when the second bill was rescued from the Committee on Education, where the previous bill had died. This occurred only after the Governor accepted and signed the Anti-Evolution Bill. In exchange for expanding compulsory public education into rural Tennessee Peay consented to what he thought would be a symbolic protest against state control of school content; his remarks to the legislature upon signing the bill indicate as much.[40] Without this there would have been no education reform. As a consequence of those political compromises the legal conditions for the Scopes trial were created. This unique political and legal environment made it possible for the Scopes trial to occur in the state of Tennessee. Further factors must be considered in locating its occurrence specifically in Dayton, one of the few towns in Tennessee with the particular characteristics needed to give rise to the trial.

'WHY DAYTON, OF ALL PLACES?'

When Tennessee adopted Hunter's *Civic biology* in 1919 it was adopted for all public schools in the state, regardless of a school's size, location, or the local industries of its population. While its focus on the use of biology in urban environments might have been well suited to schools in Memphis, Nashville, or Chattanooga, its use in Dayton was less appropriate. Dayton, the seat of Rhea County, had been a booming town in the 1890s and 1900s, but by 1925 its population had decreased by more than half to just 1,800.[41] This once urbanizing region had become increasingly rural at a time in American history when the exact opposite was happening in most of the country. In this era tensions between urban and rural regions in state politics were not unusual. Those tensions were exemplified in Tennessee, where rural Rhea County was compelled to use a biology textbook that touted the benefits of urban life and prepared students to become city dwellers. Because of Dayton's earlier growth and affluence Rhea was one of the few rural counties that had well-established public high schools at this time. Tennessee had encouraged the growth of high schools for years; it provided funds in 1909 for counties to construct public high schools, although few rural counties did.[42] Rhea County Central High School had been built even before this initiative, in 1906, during the peak of Dayton's industrial boom.[43]

The Scopes trial has usually been presented as a consequence of the incommensurability between fundamentalist Christianity and Darwinian evolution. Even if other legal and cultural factors shaped the specific details of the trial, historians have portrayed it as the 'culmination' of increasing scientific discoveries about human origins on the one side, and fundamentalist religion on the other.[44] That this culmination occurred in Dayton, by this account, was almost accidental and certainly irrelevant to the issues of the trial. The Scopes trial, or something very similar, could have occurred almost anywhere, at any time.

But before the trial was even under way people were asking, 'Why Dayton, of all places?' The town's leading citizens even issued a pamphlet addressing the very question. Although the pamphlet's cover gives its title as 'Dayton's cultural growth: particularly – "agri-cultural!"' the phrase 'Why Dayton, of all places?' was bannered atop each of its twenty-seven pages, and the phrase is often taken as the pamphlet's title.[45] Dayton was portrayed as the typical American town, quoting from Sinclair Lewis's *Main Street*: 'This is America – a town of a few thousand, in a region of fruit and corn and dairies and little groves'.[46] The question was turned around. '"Why Dayton – of *all* places?" You ask! And Dayton answers: "Of all places, *why not Dayton?*"'[47]

Such rhetoric fuelled the desire of trial participants to represent the trial as an epic clash of national, if not universal, significance, and not merely a local issue. The location of the Scopes trial was not a matter of Dayton's peculiarity. Instead, having the trial in Dayton, in Main Street, USA, made the trial universally American – the Scopes trial was worthy of national attention as a matter of American culture. Dayton's supporters also had an eye towards the town's economic revival (the pun of 'agri-cultural!' in the pamphlet's title ironically admitted the town's regression to a rural county seat) and were understandably concerned that the town might be portrayed as provincial and backward; claims that it was quintessentially American could serve to defuse such criticisms. Even those who eagerly portrayed Dayton as an anti-modern backwater, such as *Baltimore Sun* journalist H. L. Mencken, were happy to see nothing peculiar in Dayton specifically. 'Dayton may be typical Tennessee, but it is not all of Tennessee',[48] Mencken wrote, trying to find a 'civilized' contrast in nearby Chattanooga. If not quintessentially American, it was at the very least the epitome of rural America, of Southern America, and representative of the nascent culture clash that the Scopes trial would come to embody. For all parties there was no better answer than: '*Why not Dayton?*' And yet the Scopes trial happened – and perhaps it could only have happened – in the specific town of Dayton.

The lingering use of Hunter's book explains why the Scopes trial almost certainly had to occur in Tennessee, and the effects of statewide adoption of Hunter's urban biology comes close to most completely answering the question: Why Dayton, of all places?

As Edward J. Larson has noted, the citizens of Dayton seized upon the opportunity to host a test of the anti-evolution law as a means to promote their town, incurring the disdain of some throughout the state.[49] But many other places may also have wanted to gain publicity. Shortly after Scopes was indicted, there was an attempt by citizens of Chattanooga to co-opt the publicity of the trial by indicting a schoolteacher of their own in order to attract the media circus to the more accessible, larger town 50 miles to the south-east.[50] This ultimately failed, but Chattanooga only sought a monkey trial after seeing the attention it brought Dayton. Before Scopes's indictment, people in Chattanooga had not had any notion of a test case there.

The anti-evolution trial came to be seen as an expression of the tensions between urban industrial and rural agricultural cultures in America. Dayton was a town that contained elements of both cultures: the jury at the trial consisted almost entirely of farmers. George Rapalleya, the man who first conceived the idea of a test case in Dayton, was a mining engineer.[51] As a town that had experienced the boom and bust of industrialization, and that had begun to reinvent itself as a rural town just as state policies were encouraging greater mobility through the construction of highways and railroads, Dayton was unusual. Yet it was the contrasts of cultures that made it, if not a typical American town, a fitting microcosm of a divided and changing American culture. In this respect the trial in Dayton represented universal themes. These were themes that were also expressed quite specifically in the high-school biology textbooks, as the whole notion of 'civic' biology bespoke the increasing urbanization and industrialization of America. The debate over biology textbooks sold nationally and adopted at the state level brought the ideas of civic biology to places where such cultural change aroused suspicion.

All this explains why the trial's setting in Dayton was no mere accident. This challenges interpretations of the trial that suggest that it came to pass

primarily as the result of a science–religion clash. The interests of participants on all sides of the conflict were to remove any traces of the
peculiarity of Dayton or Tennessee. Daytonians wanted to boost their
town through the claim of being 'Main Street'. The trial's participants
sought to broaden their appeal by recasting the conflict in terms of faith
and reason, of evolution and the Bible, as opposed to the minutiae of
textbook politics and school reform. The news media would have a hard
time explaining the importance of covering a misdemeanour trial in a
small town miles away from widespread consciousness if they could not
frame the contest in the eternal conflict of science and religion. Although
the various agents who made the trial what it was had different aims, and
conflicted with one another, they were united in reducing the role of the
local and the particular in explaining events. After the trial the rhetoric of
the science–religion conflict continued to function as an explanation of
the trial, and in the absence of accounts that emphasized the local and
contingent aspects of its history the Scopes trial could also serve as a
confirming instance of the conflict thesis. The fate of John Scopes was
important not just to the 1,800 people of Dayton but to the world,
because the locality of Dayton itself became universalized.

EDUCATION AND THE BATTLE OVER AMERICAN IDENTITY

In one sense, claiming that Dayton was Main Street, USA, was an attempt
to establish Dayton's character as typically American. At the same time
this claim was also an attempt to establish the character of America by
portraying it as typically Daytonian. As 'Why Dayton, of all places?'
describes the town's origins:

Through the Appalachian trails leading out of the Carolinas and the Virginias
migrated the first white settlers into the land of the Tennessee. Upon the
Cherokees' hunting grounds that rambled over river bottom lands, valleys, ridges
and mountains came the purest strains of sturdy Anglo Saxons, planting their
standards. And their children developed the commonwealth where Dayton grew.
They were all a rugged lot and their convictions were adamant. In these respects
they were no different than the pioneers of America everywhere.[52]

The picture of the American pioneers as rugged settlers of a wilderness, or
pure Anglo-Saxon stock, quintessentially tied to the land and to farming,
presented one view of American identity that was being challenged by
changing demographics in late nineteenth- and early twentieth-century
America. The theme of two conflicting visions of the American nation was

predominant in the political discourse of the era. This was crystallized in the presidential campaign of 1896, in which a young William Jennings Bryan rose to prominence by aligning the issues of business regulation, rural cultural values, and a commitment to global peace. Bryan would become a key participant in the Scopes trial nearly three decades later. The pictures of the American as the independent farmer and the American as the industrial labourer were aligned with contrasting images of the United States that had previously divided Northern and Southern ways of life, and continued to divide Americans over such issues as nativism, anti-trust regulation, and compulsory public education.

Education, as a profitable industry and as a mechanism for social engineering, was central to the larger debates over American identity. The textbook business, which underwent major upheavals during the decades immediately following the Civil War, was one of the first industries in which concerns over monopoly were articulated. The 1876 Supreme Court ruling in Munn *v.* Illinois recognized the right of states to regulate industries that served a public utility.[53] Textbook publishers, serving public education, were regarded as sharing in a civic obligation. Progressives who advocated the expansion of public education warily accepted the role the textbook industry played in driving educational expansion, even while many emphasized a pedagogy that was less reliant upon 'textbook learning'.

The uneasy alliance between textbook publishers and progressives who may have supported industry regulation but who also advocated education expansion could explain the overall lacuna of discussion of the textbook industry in the history of business regulation of this period. While historians of nineteenth-century America have often focussed on such commodities as 'lumber, furniture, shoes, leather goods, petroleum, explosives, glass, paper, iron, steel, copper, brass, and lead'[54] and railroad and oil trusts are standard fare in introductory American history classes, the trade associations that formed among schoolbook publishers predate many of these other industries, and the textbook industry served as a model for other industries whose collusion, interlocking boards, and ultimate consolidation gave rise to the outcry against monopoly.

The rise of all these industries was essential to the shifting demography of the American nation, creating new jobs in urban centres that facilitated both external and internal migration. The new vision of America was not only ethnically and religiously more plural but also more urban and integrated. With the shifting picture of American society towards urbanism and industry came the need for social remedies to incorporate new immigrant groups, train new labourers, and combat public health issues that emerged in the squalor of American cities. Public education was conceived as a mechanism to achieve these goals. This replaced more local pedagogical aims that would come from a traditional nature-study curriculum whose content was shaped by locality. The content of educational fields, such as the new 'biology' course, was crafted to accommodate these social goals. As the textbook industry (like other industries) consolidated, a company's success relied upon having products that could be sold across the country. As a result that educational content, and the social goals embedded within it, became nationalized.

For the rural South, which had experienced economic decline and emigration that could be attributed in part to the rise in the urban-industrial economy, and the urban South, which sought to further industrialize and compete with Northern cities, public education was seen as a means of attaining the modern American worldview. Dayton, the seat of Rhea County, Tennessee, was itself a mixture of the urban and rural South. The complex network of concerns over economy, culture, industry, demography, and education was aligned by competing groups in the Scopes trial and then replaced by the universalizing rhetoric of science-and-religion conflict. The claim of science–religion conflict became self-fulfilling in Dayton when conflicting groups recast their battles in terms of science and religion. This has shaped science and religion in America ever since.

THE SCOPES TRIAL AND THE INTERACTION BETWEEN 'SCIENCE' AND 'RELIGION'

The complex relationship between education, textbook regulation, and ideological pictures of American identity leads to a very different perspective on the Scopes trial and the factors that caused or contributed to it. The trial's chief participants, however, focussed largely on the perceived conflict between science and religion in explaining their presence. 'They did not come here to try this case', Bryan famously declared. '[T]hey came to try revealed religion. I am here to defend it'.[55]

That the trial was about a conflict between science and religion was a view commonly invoked at the time, by the defence team, their expert witnesses, and in media portrayals of the trial. The role of education was marginalized. 'The case itself is not important to education', Darrow stated just days before the trial.[56] At the same time, however, Bryan had portrayed the trial differently: '"This trial", he said, "involves the two great subjects of religion and education, the parents' interest in the religion of the child and the state's right to control the school"'.[57]

As Larson has noted, Bryan believed strongly in political majoritarianism: the right of local communities to determine such matters as education. By this account the significance of the Scopes trial is partly rooted in the fact that it embodied 'the characteristically American struggle between individual liberty and majoritarian democracy, and cast it in the timeless debate over science and religion'.[58] While it is quite true to say that the issue of political autonomy was recast within the framework of science-and-religion, the sides that emerged were not so clear-cut. Bryan defended majoritarianism, while the American Civil Liberties Union (ACLU) – which had offered to pay the expenses of the trial for a teacher willing to break the law – envisioned the law as a violation of teachers' individual liberty. On the other hand, local objections to evolution, culminating in Butler's law, were seen as expressing opposition to statewide majoritarianism dictating local school policy. The struggle between individual liberty and majoritarian democracy was present in the creation of the trial, but in complicated arrangements that did not resolve into a simple polarity between science and religion.

The fact that the legal matter – Scopes's violation of the anti-evolution law – was not in contention also allowed both sides in the trial to use the event for more symbolic disputes. The local politics of education might have been more important had the defence actually been attempting to have Scopes acquitted. Winning on a point of law concerning the politics of textbook adoption would not have had the same impact for these participants. It is worth noting that the ACLU did not become involved in anti-evolution controversies in other states whose laws prohibited textbooks that included evolution, unlike Tennessee's law, which prohibited the teaching of evolution itself.[59] Although the ACLU played an important role in instigating the trial, its power to shape the public perception of the trial and the ways in which issues were presented was mostly lost before the trial began, when John Scopes solicited the addition of Clarence Darrow to the defence team. The ACLU had conceived of the trial as a defence of teachers' personal freedom, not as a science–religion conflict, but many participants, Darrow in particular, shifted this focus. The use of scientific and religious ideas within the confrontational framework of a courtroom, especially Darrow's interrogation of Bryan over the truth of the Bible, made the assertions of science-and-religion conflict self-fulfilling. In an American courtroom there is no room for a middle ground. A position reconciling opposing sides, or arguing for a more complex relationship between interlocutors, has no voice in the oppositional structure of the criminal trial. Ironically the Scopes trial was an unusual criminal trial because the defendant did not seek an acquittal but rather the overturning – on appeal – of the anti-evolution law. With Scopes's guilt practically stipulated, the only issues discussed in the trial were those where the two sides disagreed. The discussion of science and religion had to be one of conflict in the courtroom, otherwise it would have had no bearing on the trial.

Partisans in the Scopes trial, already likely to be committed to positions on the role and control of public education or to the political platforms of such iconic figures as Darrow and Bryan, were given a new framework over which to continue an ongoing conflict. The Scopes trial created a science–religion conflict more than it ever accurately embodied a pre-existing one.

Situating the Scopes trial within this context improves our understanding not only of the trial itself but also of the history of science and religion more generally. The trial has been seen as confirmation of a conflict between science and religion. Historians (as well as philosophers, scientists, and theologians) who oppose a conflict-oriented view of science and religion have had to contend with the fact of the trial, to rationalize it or to otherwise explain it away as an illegitimate expression of a science–religion relationship.

Ian Barbour, for example, while not discussing the trial by name, addresses scientific materialism and biblical literalism, the two positions that had come to symbolize the two sides of the trial. Of the two positions Barbour states: 'each represents a misuse of science. Both positions fail to observe the proper boundaries of science'.[60] This discussion of the two positions allows Barbour to avoid contending with the trial. Implying that both sides in the fray were mistaken about the true relationship between science and religion means that the Scopes trial cannot be held against Barbour as evidence against his own claims of science–religion interaction. By establishing a normative boundary between science and religion Barbour is able to move away from talk of conflict to the more constructive projects of 'dialogue' and 'integration'. The Scopes trial is excluded from the realm of 'proper' science and religion, and a peaceable kingdom is maintained by consigning outliers to the wilderness, where Dayton may be found. The result is a dialogue between science and religion, but it is a dialogue where difficult sciences and religions are excluded by definition.

Stephen Jay Gould's influential articulation of 'Non-Overlapping Magisteria' (NOMA) offers a negotiated disengagement, separating religion and science by 'a longstanding consensus among the great majority of scientific and religious leaders, not a controversial or idiosyncratic resolution'.[61] He claims that although constantly in contact, the domains of scientific and religious concepts are separate, and that the appropriate social response is not one of direct interaction. For Gould, events like the Scopes trial are misguided aberrations, based upon faulty understanding of what the demarcations of science and religion *ought* to be. 'Still, the magisteria do not overlap – but then, neither do spouses fuse in the best of marriages'.[62]

In recent decades historians of science and religion have eschewed the simple notion of conflict in discussing science and religion. This has led to the emergence of a 'complexity thesis' which recognizes that the relationships between science and religion have taken on different valences in different instances.[63] This has gained great currency among historians of science and religion who consign John William Draper and Andrew Dickson White to the role of historiographical straw men, to be burnt in effigy in the footnotes of modern scholarship. In addition to recognizing that science and religion brook no single essential relationship, scholars have also recognized that no essential definition of 'science' and 'religion' can fairly capture the domain of events belonging to such a history. As Peter Harrison has rightly observed: '"Science" and "religion" were not independent entities that might bear some positive or negative relation to each other, and to attempt to identify such connections is to project back in time a set of concerns that are typically those of our own age'.[64] What counts as 'science' or 'religion' is historically bound; understanding the history of science and religion must take into account the boundaries relevant to the historical epoch.

What then should we make of the Scopes trial, considered as a local event shaped significantly by trends that fall outside the categories of both science and religion in this era? One would be hard-pressed to claim that Peay's political manipulation of textbook adoption policies in 1924 had any antecedent in what could reasonably be called either 'science' or 'religion'. Yet, if any events of the twentieth century should be included in the history of science and religion, the Scopes trial must be among them.

An historical understanding of 'science and religion' therefore might entail more than the separate historical understandings of 'science' and of 'religion'.[65] Recognizing the historical contingencies of 'boundaries' is significant, but the science–religion relation may exceed those individual boundaries, just as the relations between two countries are rarely explained only by what is contained within their two borders. Whether they fight, have no relations, are allies, or are neutral towards one another will depend on the rest of the world. Not only in the Scopes trial but more generally, the relationship between science and religion has been and is being evolved by matters extrinsic both to science and to religion. The histories of the book, of education, and of local politics are only some of these.

After conflict and complexity, after setting aside the notion of essential relationships between science and religion, and after setting aside the sense of essential boundaries to 'science' or 'religion' the historical enterprise opens into a broad array of new considerations. The Scopes trial, often thought of as the clearest indication of conflict, illustrates this. It was people – not ideas – that fought in Dayton. The reasons they were fighting were much more complicated than whether ideas they held were incommensurable. To understand why people engaged in the Scopes trial we must understand the particularities of the participants and not simply accept their own accounts of their actions. More broadly the history of science and religion must not restrict itself to scientific and religious ideas when explaining events. It is well accepted that the relationship between scientific and religious ideas is very complex in most historical instances, but to understand events, and the people who participate in them, an even more complicated historical picture needs to be considered.

NOTES

1 Edward J. Larson, 'Law and society in the courtroom: Introducing the trials of the century', *University of Missouri–Kansas City Law Review* 68 (2000), 543–8.

2 P. L. Harned, 'Facts about the state adoption of schoolbooks', unpublished draft of memorandum, p. 5. Governor Austin Peay Papers, Tennessee State Library and Archives, Nashville: Container 98, Folder 5; Bruce P. Shepard to P. L. Harned, 21 March 1924: Peay Papers, Container 98, Folder 5.

3 The states, along with dates of most recent adoption, are as follows: Alabama, 1923; Mississippi, 1920; Arkansas, 1923; Virginia, 1923; North Carolina, 1923; South Carolina, 1923; West Virginia, 1922; and Texas, 1923. Harned to Austin Peay (undated): Peay Papers, Container 98, Folder 5.

4 'Summary text-book sales in Tennessee', undated memorandum: Peay Papers, Container 98, Folder 5.

5 In Chattanooga, Memphis, and Davidson (Nashville) and Knox (Knoxville) Counties, schoolbooks were loaned 'free' to students by the local school boards. Peay to Frank M. Thompson, 9 June 1925: Peay Papers, Container 39, Folder 2.

6 Austin Peay to P. L. Harned, n.d.: Peay Papers, Container 98, Folder 5.

7 Lon C. Hill to Austin Peay, 26 February 1924: Peay Papers, Container 44, Folder 2.

8 Peay to Mrs Neil Wright, 26 March 1924: Peay Papers, Container 59, Folder 2.

9 P. L. Harned, *List and prices of text books adopted in 1919 and prices on the same books from September 1, 1924 to June 30, 1925* (Nashville: State of Tennessee, 1924), p. 3.

10 Shortly after the plan was implemented Harned wrote that 'practically all the books needed for the year were bought before September 1st and that the children here and there needing books since Sept. 1 bought second hand books in the community. Book men report practically no business since September 1st'. Harned to Peay, 16 October 1924: Peay Papers, Container 59, Folder 1.

11 Harned, 'Facts about the state adoption of schoolbooks', p. 4.

12 Harned, *List and prices of text books*, p. 3.

13 George W. Hunter, *A civic biology, presented in problems* (New York: American Book Company, 1914).

14 In addition to the *Civic biology*, W. M. Smallwood *et al.*, *Practical biology* (New York: Allyn & Bacon, 1916) was also adopted in 1919 and was renewed for the 1924–5 school year. Despite being newer and cheaper this book was almost totally unused in the state. Based upon the annual reports of Tennessee high schools, over 90 per cent of students whose biology textbook was indicated used Hunter's book. Based on data compiled from Principals' Annual Reports, 1924–5. Department of Education, Records 1874–1964, Record Group 273. Boxes 66–7. Tennessee State Library and Archives, Nashville. The overwhelming use of the *Civic biology* may well be due to the efforts of ABC sales agents, as well as Hunter's reputation as an author.

15 Consider, as exemplar, Edward J. Larson, *Summer for the gods: The Scopes trial and America's continuing debate over science and religion* (Cambridge, MA: Harvard University Press, 1997). As implied by the subtitle the principal subject of the history is science and religion. (The choice of subtitle was the publisher's and not Larson's. Larson nonetheless situates the origins of the Scopes trial in the conflict, or perception of conflict, between science and religion, especially pp. 11–30.) Earlier histories of the trial also make use of this theme or focus even more directly upon the clash between Darrow and Bryan. See Leslie H. Allen, *Bryan and Darrow at Dayton: The record and documents of the 'Bible–evolution trial'* (New York: Arthur Lee & Co., 1925).

16 Austin M. Peay to Tennessee House, printed in *Journal of the Tennessee House* 64 (1925), 743–5.

17 William Jennings Bryan to W. B. Marrs [sic], 11 June 1925: Clarence Darrow Papers, Box 2, Manuscripts Division, Library of Congress, Washington, DC. W. B. Marr had organized Bryan's 1924 lectures in Nashville on the subject 'Is the Bible true?' On Marr's role, see Kenneth K. Bailey, 'The enactment of Tennessee's antievolution law', *Journal of Southern History* 16 (1950), 475. This letter was apparently taken from Marr's office in 1931 and copied by Ewing C. Baskette, who sent a copy to Clarence Darrow three years later. Enclosing a copy of this and one other letter, Baskette writes: 'I copied as written in the original including the signature … Make what use you please but don't mention Mr. Marr's name as I got this file from his office while I was there about three years ago. I like this kind of stuff. He hasn't missed it so—'. Ewing C. Baskette to Clarence Darrow, 6 January 1934: Clarence Darrow Papers, Box 2, Manuscripts Division, Library of Congress, Washington, DC.

18 For example: 'Contrary to popular opinion, Darwin did not originate the idea of evolution. He only applied a very old doctrine and endeavored to prove that natural selection was the means by which evolution is effected'. Arthur G. Clement, *Living things: An elementary biology* (Syracuse, NY: Iroquois, 1924), p. 455.

19 William Jennings Bryan to C. H. Thurber, 22 December 1923: William Jennings Bryan Papers, Container 38, Manuscripts Division, Library of Congress, Washington, DC.

20 Edward J. Larson, *Trial and error: The American controversy over evolution and creation* (New York: Oxford University Press, 1989), pp. 50–4. After the Tennessee State Supreme Court failed to overturn the anti-evolution law in that state, Tennessee's law became the model for other states.

21 The essays of the *Fundamentals*, published from 1910 to 1915, had already begun to announce some religious objections to Darwinism by the time the *Civic biology* came out in 1914, but none of these essays explicitly linked this to the teaching of Darwinism in schools.

22 John Thomas Scopes and James Presley, *Center of the storm: Memoirs of John T. Scopes* (New York: Holt, Rinehart & Winston, 1967), p. 59. Scopes claims in the memoir that the book had been in use since 1909, not 1919. Whether this is a typographical error or a lack of clarity on Scopes's part, it contributes to the perception that Tennessee was lax in promoting up-to-date education, and it reinforces the perception that anti-evolution was a backlash against an entrenched, rather than a recently introduced, biology pedagogy.

23 William E. Cole, *The teaching of biology* (New York: Appleton, 1934), p. 12.

24 Philip J. Pauly, 'The development of high school biology: New York City, 1900–1925', *Isis* 82 (1991), 662–88.

25 Hunter, *Civic biology*, p. 9.

26 George W. Hunter, *Essentials of biology* (New York: American Book Company, 1911).

27 Charles A. Israel, *Before Scopes: Evangelism, education, and evolution in Tennessee, 1870–1925* (Athens, GA: University of Georgia Press, 2004), esp. pp. 97–127.

28 P. L. Harned to Members of Senate, undated memorandum: Peay Papers, Container 98, Folder 5.

29 Jeanette Keith, *Country people in the new South* (Chapel Hill: University of North Carolina Press 1995), p. 202.

30 Ibid., p. 203.

31 Austin M. Peay to Tennessee House, printed in *Journal of the Tennessee House* 64 (1925), 744.

32 Ibid., 745.

33 Ibid., 744–5.

34 Ibid., 375, 387.

35 Ibid., 682, 708.

36 Ibid., 655.

37 Ibid., 804, 806–7.

38 Ibid., 1049.

39 *Journal of the Tennessee Senate* 64 (1925) 1263, 1290.

40 Austin M. Peay to Tennessee House, printed in *Journal of the Tennessee House* 64 (1925), 744.

41 John T. Moutoux, 'Accused evolution prof most popular man in town', *Knoxville News*, 11 May 1925.

42 Keith, *Country people*, p. 139.

43 Larson, *Summer for the gods*, p. 24.

44 Ibid., p. 14.

45 For examples of 'Why Dayton, of all places?' being referred to as the pamphlet's title, see: Larson, *Summer for the gods*, p. 400; 'Scopes evolution trial information' on the Rhea County website www.rheacounty.com/scopes.html (accessed 7 August 2008).

46 F. E. Robinson and W. E. Morgan, *Dayton's cultural growth: particularly 'Agri-cultural!'* (Chattanooga: Andrews Printery, 1925), p. 2.

47 Ibid., p. 3.

48 H. L. Mencken, 'Tennessee in the frying pan', *Baltimore Sun*, 20 July 1925.

49 Larson, *Summer for the gods*, pp. 93–5.

50 Ibid., pp. 96–7.

51 Ibid., p. 88.

52 Robinson and Morgan, *Dayton's cultural growth*, p. 5.

53 Munn *v*. Illinois, 94 U.S. 113 (1876).

54 Charles W. Carey, Jr, 'Trusts', in Paul Finkelman (ed.), *Encyclopedia of the United States in the nineteenth century*, 3 vols. (New York: Charles Scribner's Sons. 2001), vol. III, p. 314.

55 *The Scopes case*, Official Trial Transcript, Certified by Court Clerk [microfilm] (Wilmington, DE: Michael Glazier, 1978).

56 Darrow quoted in Oliver H. P. Garett, 'Colby enters Scopes case; Darrow chief', *Chattanooga Daily Times*, 10 July 1925, p. 1.

57 [Dateline – St Louis, MO] *Chattanooga Daily Times*, 5 June 1925, p. 1.

58 Larson. *Summer for the gods*, p. 265.

59 It is ironic that the US Supreme Court case that ruled unconstitutional Arkansas's anti-evolution law (identical to Tennessee's) was originally appealed on the basis of an ambiguity of education law – that the state had approved a textbook that, if taught, would have required teachers to violate the anti-evolution law. Yet the opinion in Epperson *v*. Arkansas [393 U.S. 97 (1968)] specifically avoided ruling on these grounds and instead ruled that the law constituted an establishment of religion.

60 Ian Barbour, *Religion in an age of science* (San Francisco: HarperCollins San Francisco, 1990), p. 4.

61 Stephen J. Gould, *Rock of ages: Science and religion in the fullness of life* (New York: Ballantine, 1999), p. 64.

62 Ibid., p. 65. Gould's metaphor here illustrates his misunderstanding that the domain of the ethical, the magisterium of religion, is rooted for many religions in conceptions of the physical and metaphysical. Certainly some religions do hold that, in marriage, spouses fuse, in soul if not in body.

63 John Hedley Brooke states that the term 'complexity thesis' seems to have first been 'used to describe the conclusions in [his] book *Science and religion: Some historical perspectives*'. John Hedley Brooke, 'A call for complexity', *Science and Spirit*, January/February 2006, available at www.science-spirit. org/webexclusives.php?article_id=590

64 Peter Harrison, present volume, pp. 23–49, on p. 26.

65 By contrast Harrison (ibid., p. 41) states that '"science and religion" is primarily a Western problem, for it is here that the respective categories emerged and are most potent'. This formulation implies that 'science and religion' is reducible to the conjunction of the respective categories 'science' and 'religion'.

Science, religion, and the history of the book

Jonathan R. Topham

John Hedley Brooke's *Science and religion: Some historical perspectives* (1991) has had a profound impact on a generation of students of the subject, but my engagement with the book was particularly personal, since at the time it was published I was nearing the end of my doctoral researches under the inspiring tutelage of its author. His emphasis on the 'diversity of interaction' became a central component of my study of the *Bridgewater treatises*, a bestselling series of eight works on the 'Power, Wisdom, and Goodness of God as manifested in the Creation' penned in the 1830s by leading men of science. Whereas Robert M. Young had argued that the series gave paradigmatic expression to a 'relatively homogeneous and satisfactory natural theology' in the period, my study extended Brooke's earlier work on the diversity of natural theology in the early nineteenth century by claiming that the *Bridgewater treatises* developed a range of approaches expressive of the differing theologies and interests of their authors.[1] In addition, my approach drew on Brooke's analysis of the divergent functions that natural theologies fulfilled, ranging from their capacity to evoke awe in religious believers to their role in mediating between different theological positions.[2] However, in pursuing these themes further I also found myself exploring new historiographical avenues. In particular, the notion that the diverse natural theologies of the *Bridgewater treatises* might serve a range of functions for their original readers led me to ask questions about those original readers that gradually led me towards the then still-nascent interdisciplinary field of book history, and much of my subsequent research has been situated in the intersection between these fields.

In the succeeding twenty years the interplay between the histories of the book and of science and religion has developed apace, particularly in regard to nineteenth-century Britain. This chapter offers a useful opportunity to take stock of these developments and to reflect on the value that such an approach might continue to have. In what follows I draw out three aspects of the book-historical turn in the history of science that are of particular value for the history of science and religion. First of all, I revisit my initial insight that a more thoroughly historical approach to books like the *Bridgewater treatises*, which is rigorous in its treatment of readers as well as of authors, greatly extends the scope of historical enquiry to include the public at large, rather than merely religious or scientific specialists. Second, I explore the way in which a book-historical approach contributes to a more general historical movement that examines religious and scientific practices, as well as beliefs. Finally, I return to authors and consider how book history re-emphasizes the financial, vocational, and other motivations that have operated in the production of works on science and religion. My examples relate mostly to nineteenth-century Britain, since this is the focus not only of my own research but also of much of the other work in this area. However, the themes on which I dwell are clearly also relevant to other times and other places.

NOT JUST AUTHORS, BUT READERS

One prominent focus of attention in modern studies of science and religion has naturally been on how the religious commitments of those engaged in scientific research have shaped their researches. As John Hedley Brooke observed in *Science and religion*, historians have identified a great diversity of ways in which, at different times, religious beliefs constituted 'a *presupposition* of the scientific enterprise', provided a '*sanction*' or '*motive*' for engaging in it, or had a role in '*regulating scientific methodology*', providing means of *selecting* between competing theories, and even serving a '*constitutive role*' in the formulation of such theories as William Buckland's flood geology in the 1820s.[3] A further focus of historical attention has been on ecclesiastical and theological responses to key scientific innovations such as the Copernican system of astronomy or Darwin's theory of evolution. Generally, however, the approach here has been to concentrate on the actions of church leaders and on the writings of a small number of clerics, scientists, and other intellectuals whose published interventions have been used to chart the development of the debate. In contrast, the study of how the religious beliefs and practices of people without such status or authority have been affected by developments in the sciences has often been largely disregarded. Yet, as Ronald Numbers has recently argued, historians of science and religion have no good reason to neglect what he calls 'the common people'. Indeed, when such topics as the historical role of science in secularization continue to be of enormous importance to historians, such disregard of the engagement with the sciences of the wider public is clearly unwarrantable.[4] It is in the practice of everyday life that many of the most interesting questions in the history of science and religion are to be answered.

In addressing this historical lacuna, the history of the book has much to offer the historian of science and religion. Indeed, this was one of the motivating factors in my initial engagement with book history while researching the *Bridgewater treatises*. The series had attracted extensive attention as a significant intervention in the history of natural theology, scholars variously claiming that the treatises were either mere restatements of the arguments of William Paley's *Natural theology* (1802) or interesting developments on those arguments. My approach, by contrast, was to use the series as a means of understanding more widely the interplay of scientific and religious concerns in British culture of the period. Rather than focussing solely on the authors and their arguments, I sought to consider the entire circuit or network of communication in which the treatises were enmeshed, including publishers, reviewers, libraries, and readers. In particular, having ascertained that the *Bridgewater treatises* exceeded the expectations of contemporary publishers (who had anticipated a slow and unspectacular sale from books that purported to be contributions to the gentlemanly literature of theology), I addressed the question of why those who bought, borrowed, or otherwise encountered them found them worth reading.

What I discovered was that few valued the *Bridgewater treatises* for their contribution to natural theology strictly defined – that is, as an exercise in inferring God's existence and attributes by the use of 'natural' reason, unaided by God's supposed acts of self-revelation. Rather, readers found them valuable for a range of reasons which were typically neither theological nor evangelistic. Many of those who used them in popular education, for instance, did so because they provided an accessible, authoritative, and above all religiously and politically 'safe' account of the latest findings in the several sciences. Similarly, at a time when new forms of secular 'popular science' publishing, such as the sixpenny pamphlets of the Society for the Diffusion of Useful Knowledge, had led many Christians to become anxious about the effect that such reading matter might have on the religious sensibilities of the faithful, the *Bridgewater treatises* were valued by many religious reviewers as a means of protecting religious sensibilities by directly relating scientific findings to divine agency. Further evidence suggested that many middle-class readers valued these works for their sublime tone and moral safety, which rendered them suitable for the mixed-gender activity of family reading. Viewed, then, from the perspectives of readers, the *Bridgewater treatises* no longer corresponded to the standard histories that represented them as contributions to a developing debate about natural theology. Instead, they provided important and novel evidence of the manner in which religious (and irreligious) readers from a wide range of social and cultural backgrounds engaged with the sciences in the 1830s.[5]

A similar emphasis on the importance of the history of reading to the reinterpretation of well-known episodes in the history of science and religion is found in James Secord's groundbreaking book, *Victorian sensation.* Secord's study sets out to provide for the anonymously published evolutionary blockbuster of early Victorian Britain, *Vestiges of the natural history of creation* (1844), the most comprehensive analysis to date of the reading of 'any book other than the Bible'. He begins by examining the mechanisms by which the book became an acknowledged 'sensation', including the extraordinary process of 'literary replication' in which it was 'advertised, carried on trains, placed in shops, talked about, excerpted, and reviewed'.[6] Then, by exploring how readers engaged with the book within diverse physical and social geographies ranging from London's fashionable elite to the religiously divided city of Edinburgh, and by considering how reading *Vestiges of creation* featured in the developing self-identity of freethinkers, Evangelicals, and others, he provides an astonishingly fine-grained sense of the place of science in the unfolding lives of a wide range of people, both religious and irreligious. What this approach ultimately yields, moreover, is a recasting of the Darwinian revolution as 'an episode in the industrialization of communication and the transformation of reading audiences'. For Secord, the emergence of a mass market for print in the second quarter of the nineteenth century was fundamental to the process by which evolution gained the pivotal role it holds in the public arena, and he considers that the response of readers to *Vestiges of creation* was the 'turning point'.[7] It was in the reading of this book, more than of Darwin's *On the origin of species* (1859), that sweeping narratives of evolutionary progress became central to British culture.

It is not only the interpretation of familiar episodes in standard histories of science and religion that can be transformed by the new focus on readers. In addition, it has led to the uncovering of a large corpus of previously unexamined publications, which have also caused us to reconsider our standard histories. The corpus of works on science and religion familiar to historians has, until recently, been relatively small. Yet scholars interested in the views of Numbers's 'common people' are driven to ask what it was that they read. The answer is rather daunting, at least for the machine-press era, and throws into question the historical validity of our established canon. The output of religious titles in early and mid-nineteenth-century Britain, for instance, dwarfed that of all other subjects, accounting for around one-fifth of the total, yet very few of these books have received historical attention.[8] In the last few years, however, a number of historians have made serious inroads into this previously unexplored territory. A particular impetus has come from the revisionist history of science and evangelical Christianity. Many of the most widely circulated nineteenth-century religious books were issued by evangelical authors and organizations, and scholars seeking to move beyond the simplistic assumption that evangelicalism has been uniformly inimical to science have begun to examine these previously neglected works.

An excellent example is William Astore's study of the Scottish schoolmaster and self-styled 'Christian philosopher', Thomas Dick (1774–1857), whose various publications on science and religion sold extremely widely in early nineteenth-century Britain and America. Dick's mission was to correct both the secularizing trend he perceived in contemporary natural philosophy and the trend among evangelicals to consider the study of nature either irrelevant or irreverent. To this end, Astore recounts, Dick developed a distinctive 'doxological or God-praising theology of nature based upon knowledge of God derived from Scripture (the Revealed Word) and elaborated by studying the natural world as His creation (the Revealed World)'.[9] Through his many books Dick developed this vision of the proper relation of scientific and religious concerns in direct opposition to more secular notions of popular science prevalent in the second quarter of the nineteenth century. Furthermore, Astore argues that Dick's approach did much to foster and shape Evangelical interest in the sciences, particularly in North America.

While Astore focusses exclusively on one author, Aileen Fyfe's important book, *Science and salvation*, considers a range of publications written by a number of authors (Dick included) but published under the auspices of the Religious Tract Society (RTS). Founded in 1799 as part of a more general evangelical drive to use the press to convert the heathen at home as well as abroad, the RTS initially had little secular competition in the supply of cheap reading matter. By the 1820s, however, cheap works of secular 'popular science' had begun to proliferate, and by the 1840s the society felt obliged to respond to what it felt to be a threat to Christianity by issuing its own works on science. These embodied a 'Christian tone', which it was hoped would protect Christians from having their faith worn down by the secular framework of many commercially produced books of popular science. In studying the RTS's scientific output, Fyfe was motivated by a concern to 'gauge attitudes to the sciences and faith as held by laypeople' rather than 'eminent men of science' or 'well-known clergymen'. Moreover, her conclusion is that leading evangelicals in the mid-nineteenth century were concerned about the 'distorting manner' in which scientific discoveries were presented, rather than with 'specific discoveries themselves'.[10] The evidence of these widely circulated books suggests that the supposed antagonism of nineteenth-century evangelicals to the sciences grossly distorts an altogether more subtle position.

The RTS continued to publish on the sciences into the twentieth century, and, as Bernard Lightman has shown in a series of publications culminating in his book, *Victorian popularizers of science*, it was by no means the only publishing house issuing works of popular science imbued with Christian theologies of nature. On the contrary a significant proportion of the most widely read science books in the post-Darwinian era presented the sciences within a Christian framework markedly at odds with the perspective of the secularizing 'young guard' of science typified by Thomas Henry Huxley and John Tyndall. As Lightman observes, the popularity of these books requires us to revise our views of the degree of success that met the campaign for scientific naturalism outlined in Frank Turner's classic article on the 'Victorian conflict between science and religion'.[11] Demonstrating that works like *On the origin of species*, *Vestiges of creation*, and the most popular works of Huxley, Tyndall, and Spencer were significantly outsold by religiously motivated works like Ebenezer Brewer's *Guide to the scientific knowledge of things familiar* (1847) and J. G. Wood's *Common objects of the country* (1858), Lightman concludes that, at least as far as the general reader of the period was concerned, religious themes were far more pervasive in late nineteenth-century science than has been appreciated.

A further body of hitherto largely neglected works now beginning to be subjected to serious historical scrutiny are the productions of what Ralph O'Connor calls the 'biblical literalists' (i.e. the 'so-called "scriptural geologists"') of early nineteenth-century Britain. O'Connor has recently made a compelling case for the need to study these works, pointing out that they constitute 'a valuable resource for the historian wishing to reconstruct public attitudes towards the sciences'. Referring to some of the existing 'claims about what "most people" believed' in regard to the Bible and geology as 'shaky', he urges the necessity for 'a socially comprehensive and theologically nuanced survey of a broad range of literature, from sermons and Bible commentaries to newspapers and diaries'. Moreover, while O'Connor has not himself carried out such a survey, his researches in the literalist corpus reveal that, far from being unambiguously marginalized by the old-earth geology of the gentlemanly specialists, the new-earth geologies of biblical literalists were serious contenders among an array of geologies competing for public support. In particular, he argues that in the 1820s and 1830s the literalists stole a march over the gentlemen of science in exploiting the imaginative potential of geology in works of popular science. Often cheap and widely circulated, such works were enough to cause some old-earth geologists to react with a 'concerted public-relations effort' of their own. In this way, by taking seriously the large and varied readerships of these hitherto neglected works, O'Connor has offered a significant new insight into this pivotal period in the history of geology.[12]

In addition to this bursting of the canon of books on science and religion, the last decade has seen a growing awareness among nineteenth-century scholars of the great bulk of other types of scientific reading matter. Here, James Secord's notion of 'literary replication' is helpful, since it highlights the manner in which works like *Vestiges of creation* became known not solely through their first editions but also through subsequent editions, through a vast range of other printed formats – including advertisements, excerpts, abstracts, and reviews – and also orally, through conversations, lectures, and sermons. Examining the myriad representations of classic texts in the history of science in other, more ephemeral printed formats opens up new vistas on how contemporaries engaged with them.[13] In particular, the vast output of the periodical press in nineteenth-century Britain has increasingly been seen to have important consequences for historians of science and religion, not least through the endeavours of the 'Science in the Nineteenth-Century Periodical' (SciPer) project under the leadership of Geoffrey Cantor and Sally Shuttleworth.[14] Many of the more than 125,000 periodical titles issued in nineteenth-century Britain were religious or (like the High Church *Quarterly Review*) had an identifiable religious alignment, and for many believers such publications constituted a crucial form of reading matter, serving to inform and consolidate their religious identities. However, whereas earlier scholarship tended to see religious periodicals as unproblematic registers of denominational attitudes to the sciences, more recent studies have emphasized the manner in which they embodied debate in which readers themselves were sometimes invited to become actively involved.[15] As we shall see below, religious periodicals provide a particularly valuable means of understanding how believers learned to incorporate the sciences into their quotidian lives.

My argument in this section has been that the methodology of book history, in which readers are seen to be at least as significant as authors, can help to refocus the history of science and religion away from religious and scientific specialists. This not only leads to the development of new interpretations of familiar books like the *Bridgewater treatises, Vestiges of creation,* and Paley's *Natural theology*[16] but also serves to shatter the standard canon of books on 'science and religion', focussing attention on publications that were clearly important from readers' perspectives, even though their authors might have become obscured by subsequent history. Yet the account given in this section has had relatively little to do with the readers themselves. Indeed, much of the recent literature in this area has focussed on the production side of book history – authors and publishers – rather than on reading. While uncovering the popularity of previously disregarded publications helps to develop the external history of reading (who read what, and where?) it leaves the internal history of reading (who read how, and why?) rather underdeveloped. This is the focus of the next section.

NOT JUST BELIEFS, BUT PRACTICES

The emphasis on readers advocated above as a means of expanding the history of science and religion beyond the traditional focus on scientific practitioners, theologians, and churchmen does more than broaden and deepen our understanding of historical debates about scientific and religious beliefs. It also brings to the fore the issue of scientific and, especially, religious practice. The insight that practices might be quite as relevant as beliefs to the history of science and religion has become an increasingly prominent theme in the last two decades as historians of science have turned their attention more generally to the issue of practice. Until recently, however, the focus has been primarily on the effect of religious practices on an individual's scientific work, as in Geoffrey Cantor's pioneering study of Michael Faraday, which showed, among other things, how he 'transferred the Sandemanian social philosophy to science'.[17] With its potential for focussing on a wide range of readers, book history provides an opportunity to extend this concern with practice over a more extensive domain. Indeed, for many religious believers, at least over the last two centuries, science has been encountered primarily through the practice of reading rather than through experimental or observational practices. Moreover, as in the example of the *Bridgewater treatises,* historical actors have often been heavily preoccupied with the question of how reading about science can safely be incorporated within the practice of religious devotion.[18] Thus the history of reading has much to offer in developing an historical understanding of the place of science in everyday religious practice.

It is only over the last decade that this approach has begun to be developed, but a number of productive avenues have already emerged. Most of the work to date focusses on evangelical Christians, which is unsurprising given how pivotal reading was to evangelical practice. The evangelical imperative to convert the heathen at home and abroad motivated a wide range of ventures to promote reading from the 1790s onwards, ranging from elementary education in Sunday and day schools to the distribution of tracts, Bibles, and other publications. For evangelicals, reading was a crucial part of the process by which the individual soul came to know God. For example, as Sujit Sivasundaram has shown, readers of the *Evangelical Magazine* in 1800 were encouraged to measure their progress in sin or grace using a 'spiritual barometer' which was calibrated with such practices as 'Daily perusal of the Bible with prayer' and 'Love of Novels, &c'.[19] James Secord, too, has emphasized the extent to which Evangelicals saw reading as a crucial element of religious self-fashioning. In the religious ferment of mid-nineteenth-century Britain, where libertarian freethinkers vied with their evangelical opponents, Christians had to be taught how to read about science in such a way as to develop, rather than destroy, their faith.[20]

Nineteenth-century evangelicals were particularly concerned about the wellbeing of children, whom they considered particularly vulnerable to inappropriate reading habits. From early in the century they manifested considerable anxiety to train young readers. For instance the first children's magazine in Britain to achieve sustained success was the *Youth's Magazine* (1805–67), a monthly closely associated with the Sunday School Union, which, through its assemblage of moral tales, factual articles, and homilies, provided extensive advice about how to read. One of the critical lessons the magazine sought to enforce was that all secular reading should be infused with scriptural piety. The reading of works of science needed to be incorporated into the life of devotion by associating it with practices of Bible reading, meditation, and prayer – both private and corporate – and religious exhortation. This message was driven home through direct practical advice, through examples of good practice (as in articles that linked scientific and scriptural information), and through moral tales which manifested both the benefits of such practices and the dangers attendant on neglecting them.[21]

Such connections between scientific reading and devotional practices are to be found throughout evangelical and other Christian writings of the nineteenth century.[22] As we have already seen, the popular author

Thomas Dick sought to steer the readers of his scientific texts to turn their minds to God, and some at least of his readers found in them 'the means of opening . . . the beauty and glory of the creation, and the wisdom and goodness of the creator'.[23] Moreover such writings often moved seamlessly from seeking to assist the faithful in the practice of their faith to seeking to introduce others to that faith. As Aileen Fyfe points out, the cheap scientific publications produced by the RTS in the 1840s were not intended primarily for the edification of Christian believers but to convert unbelievers. The 'Christian tone' they embodied consisted of references and reflections that were designed to 'play a pre-evangelical role by making readers think about the claims of Revelation and Christianity, and spurring them on to further investigation and thought', hopefully leading to conversion.[24] By attempting to manage the reading practices of doubtful or unbelieving readers, authors sought to develop in them a habit of religious reflection and enquiry that would lead to faith.

Devotional and apologetic practices were not the only ones that evangelicals considered that science could engage. Historically, one of the defining characteristics of evangelicals has been their campaigning zeal – both in attempting to save souls in home and overseas missions and in attempting to address social deprivations and injustices – and scientific reading could also be relevant here. Taking as his starting point Richard Drayton's suggestion 'that Christian ideologies of man's place in nature lay at the taproot of imperial expansion', Sujit Sivasundaram argues in his study *Nature and the godly empire* that reading about nature played a crucial role in the education and subsequent work of British evangelical missionaries in the Pacific.[25] Similarly readers of the extensive 'Missionary Notices' in the *Wesleyan-Methodist Magazine* during the early years of the century found their commitment to the missionary endeavour confirmed and strengthened by the accounts they read of the peoples, geography, and natural history of the wider world. Such accounts, which 'vividly and charmingly' connected geographical knowledge with 'the struggles and successes of the Kingdom of Christ', also gave a 'fresh stimulus' to the 'desires, exertions, and prayers' of readers in the missionary cause.[26]

A similar activism linked scientific reading with practical concerns in Quaker publications of the mid-nineteenth century, as Geoffrey Cantor has shown. Characterized by a strongly separatist religious ethic, Quakers often manifested considerable reticence about engaging in secular reading, but reading matter that related the sciences to key Quaker campaigns, such as the abolition of the slave trade and the proper treatment of aborigines, was altogether more acceptable. Reading about such matters again furthered practices of religious activism that were highly prized.[27] More generally, the manner in which the sciences might be engaged in different aspects of Christian practice were brought home to readers in the obituaries, biographies, and other forms of exemplary lives that were widely prevalent in the nineteenth-century religious press.[28]

Many of the examples given here derive from the religious press, and the manner in which periodicals served to shape the religious identities of their readers is particularly important for those seeking to understand how religious people came to relate science to their daily religious practice in nineteenth-century Britain. Two features of the periodicals are of particular importance in this regard. First, they were generally aimed at particular religious communities, which, as Geoffrey Cantor points out, acted as 'transmitters of traditions of belief and practice that transcend[ed] the individual'.[29] As a result, they provide particularly valuable evidence of the shared reading and other practices of those communities. Second, because they were aimed at more or less committed members of their respective communities, the periodicals' emphasis was more on the place of science within everyday religious practice than on its place in apologetics, a concern that has perhaps been overemphasized in historical studies of science and Christianity. Thus Sydney Smith, writing in the *Edinburgh Review* for 1808, argued for the importance of the leading religious magazines of the day on the grounds that they 'contain[ed] the opinions and display[ed] the habits' of a great mass of the populace.[30]

There are, however, important caveats to note in regard to the interpretation of religious periodicals. Geoffrey Cantor has observed that within such communities as Anglo-Jewry and the Society of Friends the existence of several periodicals reflected internal divisions, such that the views expressed in the press cannot be assumed accurately to reflect a community's viewpoint.[31] Furthermore, individual periodicals did not present a singular viewpoint; rather, a range of attitudes might find expression, especially on questions that were not fundamental to denominational orthodoxy. Moreover, while readers often contributed letters and articles to the religious press, these can hardly be taken to be representative of the attitudes of readers in general. Indeed, individual readers often read such periodicals against the grain, disagreeing with or misunderstanding the intended readings. In addition, many within religious communities were not readers or auditors of the associated periodicals, and some, indeed, were illiterate. Thus even in a community like Wesleyan Methodism, where the denominational magazine was closely supervised by the upholders of religious orthodoxy, ordinary adherents appropriated scientific ideas in ways that were at odds with more

cautious 'official' attitudes to scientific developments.[32] Once these limitations are appreciated, however, the religious press offers an invaluable body
of evidence concerning the connection of science with everyday religious
practice.

Cantor's observation concerning the divisions within religious communities is addressed to some extent by recent work emphasizing what James
Secord has called 'geographies of reading'. In *Victorian sensation* Secord
examines responses to *Vestiges of creation* in four different locations: London's
high society, middle-class Liverpool, the Anglican university towns of
Oxford and Cambridge, and among the warring factions of Edinburgh's
liberal reformers and Free Church evangelicals. In each of these locations
Secord finds religious communities engaged in readings that, while informed
by more broadly based religious mores, reflect very particular local circumstances. A similar emphasis is found in David Livingstone's impressive
studies of the localized geographies of the reception of Darwinian evolution.
Livingstone's work emphasizes the great differences exhibited in the readings
of scientific works by people of very similar theological or denominational
affiliations when situated in different socio-spatial situations.[33] Thus while
recent periodical studies offer a valuable sense of the connectedness of
religious communities, we must not lose sight of the importance of local
conditions. Indeed, we shall see that this spatial theme is also important in
regard to authorship, which is the focus of the next section.

By directing attention to the place of science in everyday religious
practice, book history has helped open an important new area to historical
consideration. Moreover, in keeping with a more general re-examination
of the interactions of evangelicals with science, this approach has revealed
new ways in which evangelicals and others engaged with and appropriated
the sciences in the practices of daily devotion, missionary endeavour, and
social activism. In addition, however, the new concern with religious
practice addresses a more fundamental aspect of the history of science
and religion, namely the idea that intellectual change ultimately occurs in
the practice of everyday life. Over recent decades historians of science have
come to understand that even thinking is a 'practical activity, intimately
bound up with other kinds of doing'. In the light of this, James Secord
has argued that the intellectual history that used to be told in terms of
'dramatic changes in worldview (the "Darwinian Revolution")' can more
profitably be studied 'by looking at the basic material products of cultural
life and drawing upon techniques developed for studying ordinary
action'.[34] As we have seen, his study of the reading of *Vestiges of creation*
applies this approach to great effect in reinterpreting the 'Darwinian

revolution'. A more extensive investigation of the place of science in the practice of everyday religious life promises further insights into similarly momentous questions.

NOT JUST PIETY, BUT PUDDING

My focus so far in this essay has been on extending the history of science and religion beyond the writings and beliefs of leading religious commentators and practitioners of science. However, the book-historical approach by no means entails abandoning authors in favour of readers. On the contrary, it entails asking new questions about the producers of books – publishers as well as authors – that arise when a more comprehensive view is taken of the network of communication. By taking seriously the financial, vocational, and ideological circumstances in which works on science and religion were produced, the historian is better able to understand the motivations underlying the claims made, and therefore the claims themselves. Historical controversies about science and religion have not infrequently related to such concerns as professional advancement and financial remuneration. For instance – as Frank Turner established many years ago – that great protagonist of the conflict between science and religion, Thomas Henry Huxley, was clearly motivated in part by his concern to carve out a professional identity for the man of science, in contradistinction to the established identity of the clerical gentleman of science. Huxley famously complained in 1852 that science in England did everything except pay; one could earn praise, 'but not pudding'.[35] Yet it was not only anti-Christian authors like Huxley who were interested in pudding. Most of those involved in producing works on science and religion stood to gain professionally or financially, and the focus of book history on the practices of authorship and publishing helps to highlight such concerns.

Even at a fairly basic level, asking questions about the financial or professional context within which the authors of works on science and religion operated can prove surprisingly informative. Take, for instance, the circumstances in which the *Bridgewater treatises* were written. The series was prompted by the munificent bequest of the 8th Earl of Bridgewater, Francis Henry Egerton, and each author was to receive the princely sum of £1,000 for his contribution. At an early stage in the process the leading surgeon and Bridgewater author Charles Bell foresaw that there would be 'great difficulty in reconciling people to such a bequest'. Sure enough, the selection of authors by the embattled President of the Royal Society, Davies Gilbert, and his two episcopal advisors fuelled an already bad-tempered debate concerning the Society's management of patronage and the financial support of working men of science.[36] Many of the reviews revisited the theme once the series began to appear, to the detriment not only of Gilbert but also of the authors. The *Athenaeum*, a moderately reformist weekly, pointed out that the authors' conclusions had been 'supplied by authority' and that they had been 'ordered to search for premises'. Other reviewers thought they could detect 'such marks of carelessness and haste, of languor and indifference, as might be expected in writers who have a given task assigned to them, without much regard to their own inclination'.[37] Indeed, this criticism had some justification. Charles Bell confessed in the preface to his *The hand* (1833) that 'from at first maintaining that design and benevolence were every where visible in the natural world' he had been gradually drawn 'to support these opinions more ostentatiously and elaborately' than he had originally wished. True, he had over many years made reference to divine design in his anatomical teaching – so much so that the *Lancet* suggested that he never touched 'a phalanx and its flexor tendon, without exclaiming, with uplifted eye, and most reverentially-contracted mouth, "Gintilmin, behold the winderful eevidence of *desin*!"' – but this did not fit him to write a theological work on the subject.[38] Needing to fill three hundred pages to earn his thousand pounds, Bell padded his treatise out with seventy pages of somewhat haphazard 'Additional Illustrations'.

Payouts like those experienced by the *Bridgewater* authors do not come around particularly often. However, some of the scientific bestsellers of nineteenth-century Britain were religiously oriented, including Paley's *Natural theology* and Thomas Chalmers's *Astronomical discourses* (1817), and such books could generate significant income for their authors.[39] For many, writing about science and religion was at the same time an employment strategy and a religious vocation. A good example of this is provided by William Astore's study of Thomas Dick. Dick's first calling was to clerical ministry in the Secessionist Church in Scotland but, having committed an act of 'flagrant immorality' (an adulterous affair with his servant, which led to her becoming pregnant), he was removed from office and defrocked.[40] His remorse seems to have been genuine enough, and he considered the subsequent death of the babies of both his servant and his wife to be divine retribution. Over the next two decades, however, Dick built a new vocation, first as a schoolteacher and then increasingly as a public educator and author on scientific subjects. His work as a schoolteacher was initially poorly remunerated, but his other activities served to elevate his reputation and ultimately to provide new sources of income. Astore shows how Dick refashioned himself according to the notion of the 'Christian philosopher' developed in his 1823 bestseller of that title. Advocating that the study of nature should be carried out as a religious activity, Dick sought to recover his moral authority by becoming the exemplar and prophet of this approach. Moreover, he was remarkably successful in doing so, and his reputation among Evangelicals in Britain and North America was ultimately far higher than it would have been had he remained merely a minister. His financial success, however, was more equivocal. Retiring from teaching in 1827 to write on science, religion, and education, his books sold well, but his management of publishing contracts was such that he had ultimately to rely on his reputation for financial relief, initially from admirers, and ultimately from the Civil List.

According to Aileen Fyfe, writing was 'one of the few acceptable ways of making money from one's faith' in mid-nineteenth-century Britain, but for the RTS authors, as for Dick in the above example, the 'balance between faith and finances was a tricky one'.[41] Full-time science writers such as William Martin and Thomas Milner could support themselves and their families by their labour, but they were unable to amass significant savings and were financially vulnerable in times of illness and old age. Moreover, dependent as they were on their writing, such writers adjusted their styles according to publishers' requirements, including modifying the manner in which their scientific exposition related the subject matter to Christianity. Martin, indeed, was prepared to write straightforwardly secular works for publisher Charles Knight, although they were clearly at odds with his evangelical principles. Furthermore, by mid-century the vocational identity of the 'Christian philosopher' who could combine original scientific research with religious leadership was increasingly difficult to sustain. For Milner this was not a problem: a Congregational minister whose ill-health forced him to resign his charge, he found in his career as a mere science writer both adequate income and a satisfying religious vocation. By contrast, Martin had trained as an apothecary and worked in the museum of the Zoological Society for several years, and he was disappointed when his subsequent publications for a general audience failed to reopen the doors to a museum career. Indeed, those like Huxley who sought to fashion a professional identity for the man of science did so in part by denigrating what James Secord calls the 'commercial science' of the likes of Martin and Milner.[42] At the same time, as Bernard Lightman has shown, such scientific writing continued to make an important contribution to the income and vocational identity of prominent Christians into the twentieth century.

Such studies of the practice of authorship thus provide a critical means of re-examining what Frank Turner called the 'professional dimension' of the history of science and religion in nineteenth-century Britain. Moreover, this is also the case for authors far removed from the careers in popular scientific writing pursued by Dick, Martin, and Milner. Indeed, James Secord's focus on 'geographies of reading' in *Victorian sensation* highlights the extent to which the authors of reviews, newspaper articles, pamphlets, and other works were often responding to highly localized conditions and controversies which impinged on individual reputations and career prospects. In a city like Liverpool, Secord shows, interventions in print and speech concerning a controversial book such as *Vestiges of creation* had important consequences for the local standing of clergy, medical practitioners, and men of science. Similarly in the superheated religious politics of Edinburgh, an accusation that Robert Chambers had written the book resulted in his withdrawal from the election for the city's lord provost.[43] Of course the impact of such motives and concerns in shaping the texts that historians study has become a standard feature of the contextual history of science. Yet the more recent studies informed by book history have served to highlight the importance of giving concerted attention to the mixed motives underpinning authorship.

It was not only authors who stood to gain from the production of books. Publishers too – as well as others involved in print communication, such as library owners and booksellers – had financial and other motives for promulgating particular kinds of works. Moreover, if authors have typically been centre-stage in histories of science and religion, publishers have emphatically been in the wings. Yet one of the most striking findings of the recent work on nineteenth-century religious popularizers is the vast sales of many of the books involved and the significant profits that publishers could make from them. Like authors, publishers often had mixed motives. Even those on a mission, like the RTS, had to make their publications commercially viable, and Fyfe shows that the society was 'an efficient Victorian business enterprise'. Similarly, when the devout Church of Scotland elder William Collins struck hard bargains for the works of Thomas Dick, he may have been motivated by a concern to sell them at prices that workers could afford while still turning a profit for himself.[44] Yet, whether religiously or commercially motivated, the decisions of publishers shaped not only the reception but also the contents of the works they published.

The role of the publisher is particularly obvious in the case of the RTS, which, as the instigator of the 'Monthly Series' and other publications, took a very active role in determining what was published, including the choice of subject and author, the implementation of a 'Christian tone', and the appearance and distribution of the finished publications. The prevalence of such large and highly energetic religious publishing houses in nineteenth-century Britain raises many questions about their role in fostering particular views of science. Organizations such as the Sunday School Union, the Wesleyan-Methodist Book Room, and the Society for Promoting Christian Knowledge (SPCK) invite treatment similar to that devoted by Fyfe to the RTS.[45] In addition, however, the activities of the many commercial publishers also warrant investigation. As Bernard Lightman's *Victorian popularizers of science* shows, the great abundance of often religiously inspired books on the sciences that appeared in nineteenth-century Britain was produced within a highly commercialized market-place, and the motives and interests of publishers shaped what appeared in print in important ways.[46]

A particularly instructive illustration of the extent to which publishers have been significant players in the production of works on science and religion comes from Aileen Fyfe's study of the long publishing history of Paley's *Natural theology*. What is most striking about this history is the extent to which the work was beyond the control of its author for so much of the time. Paley died just three years after the publication of his most famous work, and while it continued to appear in largely unchanged form during the term of copyright, by the time that ended in 1816 only around 20,000 copies of the work were in print. Thereafter a series of commercial publishers repeatedly reinvented *Natural theology* in a wide variety of editions, which by the 1880s had between them run to more than 100,000 further copies. In the 1810s and 1820s many editions of the work – as, for instance, those in John Fowler Dove's cheap reprint series, the 'English Classics' – presented it as a 'classic' of natural theology, now published in a smaller format and at cheaper prices to appeal to a middle-class audience. By the 1830s, however, some publishers were modifying the work more fundamentally. Cheap publishers W. & R. Chambers, for instance, issued a 'People's Edition' in 1837, accessible to working-class readers at just 1s. 6d., which transformed the work into a self-conscious contribution to the literature of 'popular science'. This entailed editorial revisions and repackaging by the medically trained journalist Thomas Smibert, who argued in his preface that 'it would not "be easy to point out any other work, professing to handle scientific subjects in a scientific manner that has at once been so satisfactory to the mere man of science, and intelligible to the common reader"'.[47] Even as the harmony of science and faith came more into question later in the century, the work continued to be reissued as a work of popular science. Now, however, it was religious publishers like the

SPCK who found in it a suitable vehicle for their view of modern science, and they found it necessary to engage in more extensive revisions in order to render its science current.

Studies like Fyfe's demonstrate the considerable importance of taking seriously the activities of publishers as well as authors, whether commercially or religiously motivated. It no longer makes sense to treat Paley's *Natural theology* primarily from the perspective of its author's intentions. Book history yields the insight that its cultural meaning should also be understood not only from the perspectives of its readers but also from the perspectives of the many agents in the network of communication who reinvented it over the course of a century. Moreover, this does not apply merely to the editors and publishers of subsequent editions. It also includes those involved in the further processes of 'literary replication' that such works underwent, whether in the excerpts and reviews appearing in periodicals, in the oral discussion in lectures and sermons, or in the controversial exchanges appearing in the correspondence columns and editorials of newspapers. As James Secord has demonstrated, understanding the myriad processes by which such works as *Vestiges of creation* came to the attention of the public, and the motives that lay behind them, is critical in understanding how they came to be involved in changing (or perpetuating) attitudes.

CONCLUSION

In this account I have suggested that the recent interest shown by historians of nineteenth-century science in the history of the book has brought to prominence certain aspects of the historical interactions of science and religion that have previously been relatively neglected. Where previous scholarship tended to focus on leading scientific practitioners and religious commentators, a book-historical approach has enabled historians to expand the focus to a far greater range of individuals and religious groups, encountering the sciences in the widely circulated publications of the industrial age. Where historical interest has typically centred around the interaction of religious and scientific beliefs, a book-historical approach has demonstrated the relevance of the sciences to religious practices, including but extending beyond the practice of reading. Finally, where works relating to science and religion have often been viewed as transparent repositories of the views of their authors, a book-historical approach has helped to uncover how the financial, professional, and other motivations of authors and publishers have also shaped the form, content, distribution, and contemporary meaning of such works. Of course the history of the book is by no means the only approach that yields insights into these questions. On the contrary, it is evident that much remains to be learned from more broadly based studies of religious communities, institutions, and practices, as exemplified by Cantor's *Quakers, Jews, and science*. Nevertheless, the history of the book offers valuable insights in all these respects, and its sources and subjects still remain relatively underexplored.

The consequences of adopting such an approach to the history of science and religion are by no means marginal. By refocussing their attention on the everyday practices of a far wider range of people than have previously been considered, historians can recover the nuts and bolts of the cultural history of science and religion. The history that can be built from them is not only innovative but ultimately more satisfactory. As James Secord's *Victorian sensation* has demonstrated so impressively, a study of the history of reading (in this case of *Vestiges of creation*) can become 'a study of cultural formation in action'.[48] Secord shows that it was in the responses to *Vestiges of creation* of readers who were enmeshed in an industrialized network of print, situated within particular communities, engaged in personal but community-oriented spiritual journeys, and exploring different possible futures for science that the dynamic of historical change took place. It is by exploring this lived history in all its confusing complexity that Secord is able to arrive at a conclusion on an altogether grander scale concerning the process by which evolution came to occupy such a dominant position in British culture. Thus the ambition that the book-historical approach fuels is not merely to discover additional complexity in the history of science and religion as an end in itself. Rather, it is to provide the means to rework such large-scale notions as the 'Darwinian revolution' in the light of a more thorough understanding of how that history occurred in the practice of everyday life.

NOTES

I am grateful to Bill Astore, Geoffrey Cantor, Thomas Dixon, Bernard Lightman, and Ralph O'Connor for their helpful comments on earlier versions of this essay.

1 John Hedley Brooke, *Science and religion: Some historical perspectives* (Cambridge: Cambridge University Press, 1991), p. 19; Robert M. Young, 'Natural theology, Victorian periodicals, and the fragmentation of a common context', in Young, *Darwin's metaphor: Nature's place in Victorian culture* (Cambridge: Cambridge University Press, 1985), pp. 126–63; Jonathan R. Topham, '"An infinite variety of

arguments": The *Bridgewater treatises* and British natural theology in the 1830s', unpublished PhD thesis, University of Lancaster (1993); John Hedley Brooke, 'Natural theology and the plurality of worlds: Observations on the Brewster–Whewell debate', *Annals of Science* 34 (1977), 221–86; Brooke, 'The natural theology of the geologists: Some theological strata', in L. J. Jordanova and Roy S. Porter (eds.), *Images of the earth: Essays in the history of the environmental sciences* (Chalfont St Giles: British Society for the History of Science, 1979), pp. 39–64. I trust that my great debt to both John's teaching and his scholarship is fully evident in my doctoral thesis and subsequent publications.

2 Brooke, 'Natural theology of the geologists'; Brooke, *Science and religion*, pp. 209–13; Brooke, 'Indications of a creator: Whewell as apologist and priest', in Menachem Fisch and Simon Schaffer (eds.), *William Whewell: A composite portrait* (Oxford: Clarendon Press, 1991), pp. 149–73.

3 Brooke, *Science and religion*, pp. 19–33. Italics in original.

4 Ronald L. Numbers, *Science and Christianity in pulpit and pew* (Oxford: Oxford University Press, 2007), p. 11; Jeremy Morris, 'The strange death of Christian Britain: Another look at the secularization debate', *Historical Journal* 46 (2003), 963–76 (esp. 972).

5 Jonathan R. Topham, 'Science and popular education in the 1830s: The role of the *Bridgewater treatises*', *British Journal for the History of Science* 25 (1992), 397–430; Topham, 'Beyond the "common context": The production and reading of the *Bridgewater treatises*', *Isis* 89 (1998), 233–62; Topham, 'Science, natural theology, and the practice of Christian piety in early nineteenth-century religious magazines', in Geoffrey Cantor and Sally Shuttleworth (eds.), *Science serialized: Representations of the sciences in nineteenth-century periodicals* (Cambridge, MA: MIT Press, 2004), pp. 37–66.

6 James A. Secord, *Victorian sensation: The extraordinary publication, reception, and secret authorship of* Vestiges of the natural history of creation (Chicago: Chicago University Press, 2000), pp. 2, 126.

7 Ibid., pp. 4 and 2.

8 Simon Eliot, *Some patterns and trends in British publishing, 1800–1919* (London: Bibliographical Society, 1994), pp. 43–58; Eliot, '*Patterns and trends and the NSTC*: Some initial observations', *Publishing History* 42 (1997), 79–104; 43 (1998), 71–112.

9 William J. Astore, *Observing God: Thomas Dick, evangelicalism, and popular science in Victorian Britain and America* (Aldershot: Ashgate, 2001), p. 46.

10 Aileen Fyfe, *Science and salvation: Evangelical popular science publishing in Victorian Britain* (Chicago: Chicago University Press, 2004), p. 4.

11 Bernard Lightman, *Victorian popularizers of science: Designing nature for new audiences* (Chicago: Chicago University Press, 2007), esp. pp. 39–94; Frank M. Turner, 'The Victorian conflict between science and religion: A professional dimension', *Isis* 69 (1978), 356–76.

12 Ralph O'Connor, 'Young-earth creationists in early nineteenth-century Britain? Towards a reassessment of "scriptural geology"', *History of Science* 45 (2007), 357–403, esp. 360–1, 387–8, and 390. See also O'Connor, *The earth on show:*

Fossils and the poetics of popular science, 1802–1856 (Chicago: University of Chicago Press, 2007), esp. ch. 3.

13 Take, for instance, Suzanne Paylor's finding that among the chief means by which Darwin's evolutionary theorizing became available to working-class readers in late nineteenth-century Britain were the cheap digests of leading secularist Edward Aveling. See Suzanne Paylor, 'Scientific authority and the democratic intellect: Popular encounters with "Darwinian" ideas in later nineteenth-century England with special reference to the secularist movement', unpublished PhD thesis, University of York (2004); Paylor, 'Edward B. Aveling: The people's Darwin', *Endeavour* 29 (2005), 66–71.

14 See Geoffrey Cantor *et al.*, *Science in the nineteenth-century periodical: An electronic index*, v. 3.0, hriOnline 2005–07 at www.sciper.org; Cantor *et al.*, *Reading the magazine of nature: Science in the nineteenth-century periodical* (Cambridge: Cambridge University Press, 2004); Louise Henson *et al.* (eds.), *Culture and science in the nineteenth-century media* (Aldershot: Ashgate, 2004); Cantor and Shuttleworth, *Science serialized.*

15 Alvar Ellegård, *Darwin and the general reader: The reception of Darwin's theory of evolution in the British periodical press, 1859–72*, 2nd edn (Chicago: Chicago University Press, 1990), p. 21; chapters by Sivasundaram, Fyfe, Cantor, and myself in Henson *et al.* (eds.), *Culture and science*; Jonathan R. Topham, 'The *Wesleyan-Methodist Magazine* and religious monthlies in early nineteenth-century Britain', in Cantor *et al.*, *Reading the magazine of nature*, pp. 67–90; Topham, 'Christian piety'.

16 Aileen Fyfe, 'The reception of William Paley's *Natural theology* in the University of Cambridge', *British Journal for the History of Science* 30 (1997), 321–35; Fyfe, 'Publishing and the classics: Paley's *Natural theology* and the nineteenth-century scientific canon', *Studies in the History and Philosophy of Science* 33 (2002), 729–51.

17 Geoffrey Cantor, *Michael Faraday: Sandemanian and scientist* (London: Macmillan, 1991), p. 295. See also Jan V. Golinski, 'The theory of practice and the practice of theory: Sociological approaches in the history of science', *Isis* 81 (1990), 492–505; John Hedley Brooke, 'Religious belief and the content of the sciences', *Osiris* 16 (2001), 3–28, esp. 6–14; Jonathan R. Topham, 'Not thinking about science and religion', *Minerva* 40 (2002), 203–9.

18 Topham, 'Christian piety'.

19 Sujit Sivasundaram, 'The periodical as barometer: Spiritual measurement and the *Evangelical Magazine*', in Henson *et al.* (eds.), *Culture and science*, pp. 43–55.

20 Secord, *Victorian sensation*, pp. 299–355.

21 Jonathan R. Topham, 'Periodicals and the development of reading audiences for science in early nineteenth-century Britain: The *Youth's Magazine*, 1828–37', in Henson *et al.* (eds.), *Culture and science*, pp. 57–69.

22 On the prevalence of such views among High Church Anglicans and rationalist dissenters, see Topham, 'Christian piety'.

23 Quoted in Astore, *Observing God*, p. 153.

24 Fyfe, *Science and salvation*, p. 113.

25 Sujit Sivasundaram, *Nature and the godly empire: Science and evangelical mission in the Pacific, 1795–1850* (Cambridge: Cambridge University Press, 2005).

26 Quoted in Topham, 'Religious monthlies', 81 and 84.

27 Geoffrey Cantor, 'Friends of science? The role of science in Quaker period-icals', in Henson *et al.* (eds.), *Culture and science*, pp. 83–93. See also Cantor, *Quakers, Jews, and science: Religious responses to modernity and the sciences in Britain, 1650–1900* (Oxford: Oxford University Press, 2005).

28 Topham, 'Religious monthlies', 85–90; Geoffrey Cantor, 'Scientific biography in the periodical press', in Cantor *et al.*, *Science in the nineteenth-century periodical*, pp. 216–37.

29 Cantor, *Quakers*, p. 3.

30 [Sydney Smith], '[Review of *Causes of the increase of Methodism and dissension* by R. A. Ingram]', *Edinburgh Review* 11 (1807–8), 341–62, on 342.

31 Cantor, *Quakers*, p. 8.

32 Mark Clement, 'Sifting science: Methodism and natural knowledge in Brit-ain, 1815–1860', unpublished DPhil thesis, University of Oxford (1996), pp. 24–7 and 287.

33 See, for example, David N. Livingstone, 'Science, region, and religion: The reception of Darwinism in Princeton, Belfast, and Edinburgh', in Ronald L. Numbers and John Stenhouse (eds.), *Disseminating Darwinism: The role of place, race, religion, and gender* (Cambridge: Cambridge University Press, 1999), pp. 7–38. For the 'geography of reading', see Livingstone, 'Science, text and space: Thoughts on the geography of reading', *Transactions of the Institute of British Geographers* n.s. 30 (2005), 391–401.

34 Jan Golinski, *Making natural knowledge: Constructivism and the history of science* (Cambridge: Cambridge University Press, 1998), p. 9; Secord, *Victorian sensation*, pp. 520 and 3.

35 Leonard Huxley, *Life and letters of Thomas Henry Huxley*, 2 vols. (London: Macmillan, 1900), vol. I, p. 100; Turner, 'Victorian conflict'.

36 John D. Enys, *Correspondence regarding the appointment of the writers of the Bridgewater treatises between Davies Gilbert and others* (Penryn: privately published, 1877), p. 15; Jonathan R. Topham, 'Authors of the *Bridgewater treatises* (act. c. 1833–1836)', *Oxford Dictionary of National Biography*, online edn, Oxford University Press, May 2008 (www.oxforddnb.com.wam.leeds.ac.uk:80/view/theme/96360); and Topham, 'Infinite variety of arguments'.

37 [Anon.], 'Dr Buckland's *Geology and mineralogy considered*', *Congregational Magazine* 13 (1837), 42–7, on 43; [William Cooke Taylor], '[Review of *Bridgewater treatise*, by William Kirby]', *Athenaeum*, 29 August 1835, 663.

38 [Editorial concerning Joseph Henry Green], *Lancet* 1 (1832–3), 151–5, on 154; Charles Bell, *The hand: Its mechanism and vital endowments as evincing design* (London: William Pickering, 1833), p. xi.

39 *Natural theology* (1802) had sold over 120,000 copies by the 1880s; the *Astronomical discourses* (1817) sold over 20,000 copies within nine months. See Fyfe, 'Publishing and the classics' and Stewart J. Brown, 'Chalmers,

Thomas (1780–1847)', in Colin Matthew (ed.), *Oxford Dictionary of National Biography* (Oxford: Oxford University Press, 2004).

40 Astore, *Observing God*, p. 19.

41 Fyfe, *Science and salvation*, p. 186. See also Fyfe, 'Conscientious workmen or booksellers' hacks? The professional identities of science writers in the mid-nineteenth century', *Isis* 96 (2005), 192–223; and Michael Shortland, 'Hugh Miller's contribution to the *Witness*: 1840–56', in Shortland (ed.), *Hugh Miller and the controversies of Victorian science* (Oxford: Clarendon Press, 1996), pp. 287–300.

42 Secord, *Victorian sensation*, chs. 13 and 14.

43 Ibid., chs. 6 and 8.

44 Fyfe, *Science and salvation*, p. 181; Astore, *Observing God*, pp. 135–7 and 144–6.

45 See Topham, 'Science and popular education'; Topham, 'Reading audiences'; Topham, 'Religious monthlies'.

46 Lightman, *Victorian popularizers of science*. See also Aileen Fyfe and Bernard Lightman (eds.), *Science in the marketplace: Nineteenth-century sites and experiences* (Chicago: Chicago University Press, 2007). On the role of publishers, see Jonathan R. Topham, 'Scientific publishing and the reading of science in nineteenth-century Britain: A historiographical survey and guide to sources', *Studies in History and Philosophy of Science* 31A (2000), 559–612.

47 Fyfe, 'Publishing and the classics', 745.

48 Secord, *Victorian sensation*, p. 3.

PART V

Ways forward

CHAPTER 12

Sciences and religions: what it means to take historical perspectives seriously

Noah Efron

INTRODUCTION: A FIRST ENCOUNTER WITH BROOKE'S HISTORIOGRAPHY

It was by accident that I first encountered *Science and religion: Some historical perspectives* (1991). The monastic scholar's cell I had been assigned as a doctoral student crafting a dissertation proposal was in the university library. A rack of newly acquired books stood by the library entrance, and on my way in each morning I absent-mindedly scanned the fresh arrivals. One morning late in the spring of 1991 my eyes settled on the lime-on-black cover of *Science and religion*. The book had not been there the day before; since it had not yet been catalogued and bar-coded, I could not borrow it. Instead, I settled onto the carpet, where I remained until evening, when my wife, who was studying to be a physician, took me home.

The person she found crumpled on the carpet was different from the one she had kissed goodbye ten hours earlier. I knew immediately that, with this book, my world had shifted on its axis. In 1991 it was still possible for a graduate student to frame a research project asking the same questions as those posed fifty-five years earlier by Robert Merton.[1] In my case, embarking on a dissertation about Jews' attitudes towards sixteenth-century astronomy, I asked whether or not the 'cultural soil' of high central European Ashkenazi Jewish culture was – as Merton had found of seventeenth-century England – 'peculiarly fertile for the growth and spread of science'.[2] Had the rabbis of Rudolfine Prague quashed 'the new science', I asked further, or had they accommodated it? This question, which now seems comically ill-framed, appeared reasonable enough to me then. In 1991 it was still possible for a graduate student to expect in the end to catalogue his findings within Ian Barbour's brisk typology of the possible relationships between religion and science: *Conflict, Harmony, Independence, Dialogue,* or *Integration.*[3] More remarkable still, in 1991 a graduate student could still feel called upon, as I did, to parry Andrew Dickson White's famous *History of the warfare of science with theology in Christendom*; although it had been published ninety-five years earlier, in 1896, its perspective still found purchase in seminar rooms and barrooms.[4] Although many scholars had by then argued that 'science' and 'religion' are not inevitably and irrevocably at odds, doing so again in a previously unexplored context still seemed like a valuable contribution to the history of science and an admirable aim for a dissertation.[5] This was my goal.

All this changed abruptly during that day sprawled on the library floor, although I was not immediately sure just how and why. In the weeks and months that followed, as I tracked down the book's footnotes and polished off its bibliography, I came to realize that John Hedley Brooke was not alone in this new approach, and that his was, as one scholar put it, the canonical expression of a new sort of historiography pursued with vigour by a growing number of scholars.[6] With two decades of hindsight – and after two decades of remarkable research in this vein – one can now see with greater clarity that this new historiography did, in fact, shift the study of science and religion on its axis, leaving those of us who undertake it irrevocably altered.[7] I had from the start understood that Brooke's understated prose had radical implications, but what were they?

A NEW HISTORIOGRAPHY OF SCIENCE AND RELIGION

It had not required great powers of inference, one must admit, to grasp that the book *Science and religion* advocated a new approach to its subject. To start with, the book belied the old adage: it *could* be judged by its cover. Its indefinite and pluralized subtitle – *Some historical perspectives* – was itself a compact and persuasive historiographical argument, making the point with nonpareil efficiency that no single perspective could ever encompass the book's subject matter, and that the aspiration to be comprehensive was misplaced for a subject so complex and varied.

Between the covers of the book Brooke elaborated the point immediately. The relationships between science and religion, he wrote in the introduction, have been 'so extraordinarily rich and complex ... that general theses are difficult to sustain'. 'The real lesson', he continued, 'turns out to be the complexity'.[8] He observed that 'problems arise as soon as one enquires about the relationship between "science" and "religion" in the past. Not only have the boundaries between them shifted with time, but to abstract them from their historical contexts can lead to artificiality as well as anachronism'.[9] Brooke framed his book as a sustained effort to *de-reify* both religion and science, to shake the common assumption that these words refer to enduring entities whose characters have remained intact over the generations. 'We should not talk about either "science" or "religion"', Brooke warned, 'as if they are things in themselves'.[10] In the chapters that follow, Brooke illustrated this point repeatedly, as one generation's natural philosophy was shown to differ from another generation's science, and one generation's Christianity to differ from that of the next. Indeed, these chapters demonstrated that one *individual*'s natural philosophy can differ from that of a colleague, and one *individual*'s religion can differ greatly even from that of a fellow worshipper at the far end of the same pew.

This is a point Brooke has stressed since early in his career. In his now legendary Open University course on Science and Belief, Brooke already observed that nineteenth-century natural theology possessed different meanings for different people. Among other things, he explained, this multiplication of meanings was the result of the frightful ambiguity of the word 'nature', which, according to hair-splitting philosophers, can have no fewer than one hundred meanings! Theoretically, then, there is no reason there should not be a hundred different kinds of 'natural' theology.[11] He wrote this in 1974.

All this complexity, Brooke readily explained, has consequences for anyone seeking to understand the engagements of science and religion. 'One consequence', he wrote with Geoffrey Cantor in *Reconstructing nature*, a book based on their 1995–6 Gifford Lectures at Glasgow, 'is that it becomes extremely difficult, if not impossible, for the historian to sympathize with projects designed to uncover the essence of "science", the essence of "religion" and therefore some timeless, inherent "relationship" between them'.[12] By their very nature 'master-narratives' that insist a single key can unlock the mystery of the history of science and religion are misguided and misleading. A further consequence is that the engagements of science and religion can be understood only by attending to the contexts in which they unfolded: historical contexts, as well as cultural, social, political, economic, and more. This was because different contexts would often produce different sorts of engagement. Still a further consequence was that individuals matter. Sir Isaac Newton's complicated integration of his natural philosophy and his theology says something about mathematics and mechanics in his day, and about the English Church in his day, and about heterodoxy in his day, and about the Royal Society in his day, but along with everything else it tells us something about the uniqueness, idiosyncrasy, courage, and oddity of Newton himself. To generalize from Newton about how science and religion fit together is like fashioning a theory of how paint and canvas go together by gazing at a Jasper Johns. The individual case says something of value about the general question, but it also leaves much unsaid.

In pointing out the senselessness of seeking a general theory, philosopher Alasdair MacIntyre recounted the following parable:

There was once a man who aspired to be the author of the general theory of holes. When asked, 'What kind of hole – holes dug by children in the sand for amusement, holes dug by gardeners to plant lettuce seedlings, tank traps, holes made by road-makers?' he would reply indignantly that he wished for a general theory that would explain all of these.[13]

Reading John Brooke one realizes at once that many of the scholars who had sought to explain the relationship between science and religion had devoted their genius and talent to fashioning a general theory of holes.

In *Reconstructing nature* Brooke and Cantor offered advice about avoiding this general-theory-of-hole-ism and how properly to investigate the engagements of science and religion. Be mindful of context, they counselled. 'Ask what *function* the theology may be playing within the science and vice versa'.[14] Pay careful attention to the rhetoric with which the relationships between religion and science are expressed in each particular context. Instead of focussing on abstract ideas alone, study closely the ways a given individual makes sense of them, in the fuller context of their life and work. Consider not just intellectual matters but also the complicated relationships between practices, behaviours, and rituals associated both with spiritual and scientific devotion (a broadening of attention that both sociologists of religion and sociologists of science have for years advocated with vigour).[15]

This advice can be heeded most fully, Brooke and Cantor continue, if one enquires into history. An historical approach, they write, offers crucial benefits. It dislodges our prejudices: 'it helps us to break out of the tired moulds in which treatments of science and religion are routinely cast'.[16] It also spurs us to debunk familiar pieties: 'If the study of philosophy can be justified because it helps us to recognize bad philosophy, the same is true of history'.[17] When one takes history seriously, they affirm, accounting for the relationships between science and religion 'becomes more complex and unruly; but, we would insist, also more exciting'.[18]

It is here that something is left unsaid. The conclusion that there is something exhilarating in the unruly diversity of history is true enough, as far as it goes. But it is perhaps too sanguine a conclusion, encouraging us to dismiss with a confident wave of the hand difficulties that are real.

For one thing, there is reason to doubt that merely multiplying the complexity of an account renders it better. As the resolution of an account increases, its intelligibility may degrade. Jorge Luis Borges made this point memorably in his parable *On exactitude in science*, in which he described an empire in which:

the Art of Cartography attained such Perfection that the map of a single Province occupied the entirety of a City, and the map of the Empire, the entirety of a Province. In time, those Unconscionable Maps no longer satisfied, and the Carto- graphers' Guilds struck a Map of the Empire whose size was that of the Empire, and which coincided point for point with it. The following Generations, who were not so fond of the Study of Cartography as their Forebears had been, saw that that vast Map was Useless, and not without some Pitilessness was it, that they delivered it up to the Inclemencies of Sun and Winters.[19]

The historian's task, like the cartographer's, is wisely to reduce complexity where it can be reduced without undue violence, and to portray complexity only where it is essential. The notion that complexity, by itself, is an historiographical virtue does not withstand scrutiny. But the recognition of complexity should encourage the search for 'mid-scale patterns', as discussed in Ronald Numbers's chapter below.

One ought immediately to note, however, that although in occasional historiographical asides Brooke does seem to endorse complexity for its own sake, a more comprehensive examination of his writing shows that his view is far more nuanced than this. Brooke well appreciates that it is the task of historians to provide intelligible interpretations of the bloom and buzz of their subjects. He knows too that these interpretations, by their nature, are generalizations that elide great complexity. In his own work, time and again, Brooke himself offers up historical interpretations that, for all their sophisti- cation, wilfully and knowingly halt the infinite regress of multiplying com- plexity. To pick one example among many, he presents a portrait of Sir Isaac Newton that draws together into a cogent narrative much scholarly work about his writing, his life, his colleagues, his social and institutional settings, and so forth. In his own research Brooke does not amplify the complexity of the accounts he provides for the sake of amplifying complexity.

It may be that the complexity that Brooke advocates is not, in the end, mere complexity of the account itself, a mechanical multiplication of factors taken into account. It may be that the complexity Brooke seeks is not *narrative* complexity at all but *moral* complexity.

In the two decades since *Science and religion* was received with near- universal acclaim a great number of books and essays have been published each year seeking still to identify something timeless in the nature of the relationship between 'science' and 'religion'. Among these are bestselling polemics like Richard Dawkins's *The God delusion* and Daniel Dennett's

Breaking the spell,[20] but also more serious inquiries.[21] Interfaith gatherings find scholars of different religious traditions called upon to present their faith's 'attitude' towards science: the Muslim 'view', or the Jewish 'view', or the Hindu 'view', as though each tradition offers a single and enduring approach. The approach that Brooke has called for may be canonical for historians, and is admired by all, but it is also ignored by a great many of those most interested in understanding the engagements of what they still simply think of as 'science and religion'. Why is this?

When Brooke's counsel is sidestepped, it is not evaded out of weakness of will or intellect. It is not overlooked because people are lazy or uncomprehending. Many people of insight and considerable wisdom continue to advocate what literary critics call 'master-narratives'. In the less discriminating of these narratives science frees itself from the shackles of religion; alternatively science is nurtured by wise churchmen.[22] In somewhat more discriminating narratives religious beliefs and scientific theories may be seen as conflicting, independent, in dialogue, or integrated (to recall Ian Barbour's famous typology). Such narratives retain their force because they produce things of value (to some, at least). For one thing, master-narratives allow simple lessons or morals to be drawn from accounts of past events; by contrast, the sort of 'complexity' advocated by Brooke does not encourage such easy moralizing.

Consider this point from the following angle. It is true, as Brooke and Cantor wrote, that when one takes history seriously, accounting for the relationships between science and religion 'becomes more complex and unruly'.[23] While it was not their purpose, they explained, 'to dissolve the great issues that have been debated under the banner of "science and religion" into fragments of local history',[24] this may be one consequence of the approach they advocate. Focussing on the historically specific, the contingent, the unique, the *sui generis* makes it difficult to bring any given moment in time and space to bear on any other moment. It also makes it difficult to engage in productive dialogue across boundaries of faith and often even within a single faith. Where we once thought we were all speaking about the same things, we must now recognize that we are not. Taking history seriously also makes it difficult to extract moral or spiritual guidance from our research, which is the reason many others enquire into the nature of science and religion. If there is any sense at all to the old saw that 'the past is a foreign country', what can it tell us about how to make our way in our own home?[25] 'The greatest lesson of history', I was told on my very first day of graduate school, 'is that history teaches no great lessons at all'.[26]

This is the challenge of taking history seriously and of seeking to render its subjects more complex. Doing so calls into doubt the relevance of one thing for the next: the past for the present, one tradition for another, one individual's worldview for another's. As Brooke himself noted, taking history seriously leaves as the main message, perhaps the sole message, the diversity of past attitudes and approaches. He claimed that 'The real lesson turns out to be the complexity' and 'The value [of history] may consist precisely in the fact that there is multiplicity'.[27] And this may well demoralize anyone who turns to the study of science and religion not purely as an academic pursuit but in order to make some sense of their lives, their world, their work, their God: 'demoralize' in the literal sense of removing the 'moral of the story' from history, as well as greatly diminishing the power to moralize history. If we accept – as I do – that Maimonides' natural philosophy has little in common with today's science, and if we accept – as I do – that Maimonides' Judaism was different in important ways from today's Judaism, then we strain to see what we can learn from Maimonides' example.

MacIntyre once asked, 'Is understanding religion compatible with believing?' and concluded that it was not.[28] While one may disagree with MacIntyre's conclusion, it is hard to doubt that explaining one or another attitude towards the intercourse of science and religion by *historicizing* it makes it harder, not easier, to credit that attitude as true and proper in some deep sense.[29] There is a gap between those who try 'to understand' the engagements of science and religion, and those who try 'to engage' science and religion. Often there is more than a gap: sometimes there is an antagonism. Many believers experience something corrosive in such explanations, and the same can be said for at least some historians and social scientists.[30] And there is likewise something corrosive about finding the real message of the engagements of religion and science to be the multiplicity itself.

In his contribution to this volume Peter Harrison asserts that historical accounts may contribute to contemporary discussions of religion and science by drawing attention to the circumstances in which the categories of the present discussion arose. This assertion is in the spirit of the historiography that John Brooke has described and advanced, and that is shared today by many historians of science and religion. But the appeal of such an assertion, and perhaps its plausibility, may wane as one makes one's way from the history department seminar room to the sanctuary or, for that matter, to the laboratory. For any deeply religious person for whom religion contains the Truth of ages, or for anyone deeply committed to science for whom science contains an ageless truth, learning that both science and religion as we know them are constantly changing products of constantly changing historical contexts provides neither aid nor solace. And for those who feel in the smithy of their souls that they grasp a timeless wisdom – by virtue of revelation or by virtue of the scientific method – such an assertion can only seem like the niggling pedantry of a spineless and misguided naïf unable to recognize what is self-evidently true.

It is perhaps for such people that Brooke's counsel to seek complexity is most full-throatedly intended, and it is perhaps for such people that this counsel is most vexing. Brooke's observation that the history of religion and science is so complex and unstable as to defy generalization is first and foremost an observation about the lessons one ought properly to draw from the history of religion and science. As Brooke describes this history, it does not lend support to timeless wisdoms. It does not ratify religious beliefs or scientific beliefs or any given notion about the relationship between the two. The sort of complexity Brooke advocates is not the sort that shows that history is too exquisitely variegated to support generalization. Indeed, it is the sort that supports with bold certainty the generalization that orthodoxies of all sorts do not have history on their side and ought best to be avoided.

The novelty of this position may be less apparent now than it was when *Science and religion* was first published, but it remains significant. To this day, as in the past, many studies of the relationship between science and religion remain embedded in polemics. 'The rise of science was achieved by deeply religious Christian scholars', writes sociologist Rodney Stark,[31] and the world is a far better place for it:

Christianity created Western Civilization. Had the followers of Jesus remained an obscure Jewish sect, most of you would not have learned to read and the rest of you would be reading from hand-copied scrolls. Without a theology committed to reason, progress, and moral equality, today the entire world would be about where non-European societies were in, say, 1800: A world with many astrologers and alchemists but no scientists. A world of despots, lacking universities, banks, factories, eyeglasses, chimneys, and pianos. A world where most infants do not live to the age of five and many women die in childbirth – a world truly living in 'dark ages'.[32]

The history of science and Christianity, Stark insists, demonstrates the superiority of Christianity.

Pulitzer prize-winning journalist Chris Hedges, author of *American fascists: The Christian right and the war on America*, draws from this history precisely the opposite conclusion, arguing that it shows that Christianity:

must discredit the rational disciplines that are the pillars of the Enlightenment to abolish the liberal polity of the Enlightenment. This corruption of science and law is vital in promoting the doctrine. Creationism, or 'intelligent design', like Eugenics for the Nazis, must be introduced into the mainstream as a valid scientific discipline to destroy the discipline of science itself.[33]

One implication of Brooke's historiography is that all such polemics are bound to over-generalize, reifying ever-shifting social phenomena of exquisite complexity and holding them static, thereby doing violence to the history upon which they base their claims. If this is so, then Brooke's own conclusion that 'the real lesson turns out to be the complexity' may be in need of expansion. The real lesson of Brooke's historiography may be that the variety and complexity and pliability of the relationships between various religious sensibilities and various scientific endeavours nullify all attempts to draw fast conclusions about either religion or science. In this light, when Brooke writes that the value of recounting this complex history 'may consist precisely in the fact that there is multiplicity',[34] the value to which he alludes may be that this complex history invalidates the uncivil polemical uses to which the history of religion and science has so often in the past been put, demonstrating now the superiority of this or that religion, now its inferiority. The value may be that respecting the complexity of the history of religion and science demands that the historian respect the complexity and fullness of the individuals who people that history. The *real* lesson, then, turns out not to be the complexity itself but the decency it demands of the historian dedicated to providing for the complexity an adequate account. The *real* lesson turns out to be a moral one.[35]

DECENCY AND HISTORIOGRAPHY

Consider John Wesley, the founder of Methodism, as an illustration. In a carefully crafted 1953 essay in the journal *Isis*, abundant in fine detail and understandably long-considered canonical, Robert Schofield found that:

The result of any specific study of Wesley's science was probably bad. The personal and religious bias from which Wesley approached scientific matters caused him to neglect, or even depreciate, the elements in science which lead to its advance ... The most serious fault is, however, Wesley's attitude toward theory ... He repeatedly emphasized the inevitableness of man's ignorance ... In scientific questions ... he encouraged [the rejection of rational explanation] among his followers.[36]

In *Science and religion* Brooke consults the same sources and cites the same facts, but interprets them differently:

In Wesley one sees how a deeply pious man could be an enthusiast for certain types of science, and a sharp critic of others ... He found elaborate theorizing presumptuous. It was the incomprehensible in nature that nourished his piety ... Wesley was drawn to those aspects of science that offered help to humanity. In [his] natural theology, Wesley placed a high value on the study of nature precisely because it promoted a sense of awe and humility toward its divine author ... The lesson that Wesley's many readers would have absorbed was that a science of nature, not bedevilled by arrogant theorizing, could offer rational support for Christian piety – revealing, as it appeared to do, a marvellous organization and adaptation within the created order.[37]

Schofield's and Brooke's accounts are both careful history. What separates Brooke's from the earlier one is his premise that Wesley's beliefs and his actions follow a logic that can be understood even from the remove of generations. What Schofield dismissed as 'personal and religious bias' and 'a fault' becomes, in Brooke's telling, a recoil at the haughty claim to have captured everything in a single theory. What was ignorance to Schofield becomes for Brooke an admirable alchemy of scepticism and humility. A forbidding and close-minded autocrat becomes a complicated man of searching probity. Brooke's portrayal is by no means entirely positive, but what it is, is entirely *human*.

What stirred me that first day on the library floor two decades ago was not so much that Brooke had taken the complexity of history seriously but the way in which he took the complexity of history seriously. Brooke's history proceeds from the axiom that, as Clifford Geertz once put it, 'human beings, gifted with language and living in history, are, for better or worse, possessed of intentions, visions, memories, hopes, and moods, as well as of passions and judgments, and these have more than a little to do with what they do and why they do it'.[38] It approaches its subjects with respect. It treats them with dignity. It applies compassion and empathy and sympathy and imagination painstakingly to understand the lives of its subjects. And it does this delicately and with humility.

This is the real lesson of the approach Brooke advocates, and it is a lesson that I think appeals deeply also to theologians and philosophers, to devout Christians and devout atheists, including even those whose attitude towards history is understandably ambivalent. The real lesson of Brooke's historiography is that history done right must enlarge not just our knowledge but our spirit, so that we can enter the worlds of others, worlds we have never known ourselves. And this is why history as Brooke has written it does not, unlike much history these days, crumble 'into mere fragments of local history'.[39] Because history as Brooke practises it expands our moral universe – tentatively, imperfectly, but surely – until we can begin to understand localities far from our own. Describing how 'even those scientific practices that superficially seem far removed from religious incursion can be lodged in programmes that impinge on religious sensibilities', Brooke noted that 'John Ruskin was finally disillusioned with science in Oxford when, from the lecture theatre adjacent to his own, he heard the cries of a screaming cat'.[40] This observation, that the cry of a vivisected animal might spark sympathies the roots of which reach back to a spiritual education never fully erased by years of rational training, reminds us that the subjects of our histories were more than just repositories of abstract ideas. John Ruskin feels as well as thinks; in Brooke's presentation, he is human.

Considering the remarkable career of Mary Somerville, Brooke casts doubt on the common view that she was stymied at every turn by the 'masculine clerical regime [that] dominated the physical sciences'. True, Brooke observes, Somerville's sex impeded her education and prevented her from attacking her research with a single-minded determination that precluded familial and social obligations. ('A man', Brooke quotes Somerville, 'can always command his time under the plea of business, a woman is not allowed any such excuse'.) Equally true, Somerville's uncle – a minister of the kirk at Jedburgh – had noticed her genius and nurtured it, teaching her Latin, reading Virgil together 'for an hour or two every morning before breakfast', as Somerville later remembered. In time she found encouragement from John Herschel and three scientifically able clergymen – John Playfair, George Peacock, and William Whewell. Brooke's point is not that gender was not an impediment. It is that if you look more closely at a story in which gender was an impediment, and perhaps in part because the 'masculine clerical regime' was well schooled in discounting the talents of women, you may still find a minister uncle patiently and proudly reviewing Latin conjugation with his young niece, and you may find some of the greatest male intellects of the day rightly treating a female as their equal. Abstractions like the 'masculine clerical regime' may have their place in writing the history of science and religion, Brooke easily admits. But only if they are set alongside descriptions of moments of human particularity as well; for instance, an uncle sees in the eyes of his niece a spark and resolves to usher her into the republic of letters.[41]

It is for this reason that when a rigorous, critical study of John Brooke's historiography is produced, as I am sure it will be, his insistence that complexity not be overlooked will be only one part of it, and not its defining feature. It will find that Brooke cannot easily be located on the map of contemporary historiography: neither postmodern, nor pre-postmodern, not comfortably bearing any of the normal adjectives that modify historian (intellectual, social, cultural, and so on), but in some ways embracing them all. It will also describe the method behind his uncanny ability to uncover the humanity of his subjects, discovering their 'intentions, visions, memories, hopes, and moods', as well as their 'passions and judgments'. We do not yet have a name for his historiography; for those of us who have grown as historians in his shadow, the influence of Brooke's example is difficult to exaggerate.

Reading Brooke on that first day I could already understand that to ask of those sixteenth-century rabbis whose books and letters I had begun to read whether they were for astronomy or against it was to miss the fact that these were men of exquisite curiosity and intellectual dexterity. It was to miss the fact that they treated books and ideas with great seriousness of purpose. It missed their raging ambivalence about the wisdom of Christian scholars – brilliant and fearsome at once – among whom they lived. It missed the complexity of their attitudes towards their Sephardic forebears who had engaged in astronomy with vigour. It missed the fact that, as printed books grew cheaper and more plentiful, their libraries had become overstuffed with new books, containing new attitudes and new theories, a heady moment, but one that threw into doubt what their teachers had told them, and what they must tell their students and children. It missed the fact that they were complicated people living in complicated times with complicated hopes and ideals. In short, as I learned that day from Brooke's book, it missed *everything* that matters.

Science and religion demonstrated on each page that while different people in different circumstances make different sense of the worlds they inhabit – the material world and the spiritual world – with a patient ear, an open mind, a probing heart, and moral imagination it is possible to come to understand – imperfectly but dependably – what this different sense is. It demonstrated that there may be one hundred kinds of natural theology, and many more ways to make sense of heaven and earth, and that this is never the end of the story but always only its beginning.

It is owing to this insight above all that John Brooke helped to change the way a generation of scholars have understood science and religion, above all perhaps an awe-struck graduate student crumpled and content on his library carpet.

NOTES

1 Robert K. Merton's 1936 Harvard dissertation was first published as 'Science, technology and society', *Osiris* 4 (1938), 360–632. The quoted text is from the final sentence of his dissertation, on 597.

2 Ibid., 598.

3 Ian G. Barbour, *Science and religion: New perspectives on the dialogue* (London: SCM Press, 1986), ch. 1 ('Ways of relating science and religion').

4 Andrew Dickson White, *A history of the warfare of science with theology in Christendom* (London: Macmillan, 1896).

5 Merton himself had done so, of course. He was joined by several historians of stature and influence, the most prominent among them being Reijer Hooykaas, *Religion and the rise of modern science* (Grand Rapids, MI: Eerdmans, 1972) and Stanley L. Jaki, *The savior of science* (Washington, DC: Regnery Gateway, 1988).

6 For excellent examples of this new historiography, by many of its best practitioners, see the essays in David C. Lindberg and Ronald L. Numbers (eds.), *God and nature: Historical essays on the encounter between Christianity and science* (Berkeley, CA: University of California Press, 1986).

7 More recent examples of scholarship in this vein include: Peter Harrison, *The Bible, Protestantism, and the rise of natural science* (Cambridge: Cambridge University Press, 1998); Harrison, *The fall of man and the foundations of science* (Cambridge: Cambridge University Press, 2007); Margaret J. Osler, *Divine will and the mechanical philosophy: Gassendi and Descartes on contingency and necessity in the created world* (Cambridge: Cambridge University Press, 1994); Osler, *Rethinking the scientific revolution* (Cambridge: Cambridge University Press, 2000); Matthew Stanley, *Practical mystic: Religion, science, and A. S. Eddington* (Chicago: University of Chicago Press, 2007); Geoffrey Cantor, *Quakers, Jews, and science: Religious responses to modernity and the sciences in Britain, 1650–1900* (Oxford: Oxford University Press, 2005).

8 John Hedley Brooke, *Science and religion: Some historical perspectives* (Cambridge: Cambridge University Press), p. 5.

9 Ibid., p. 16.

10 Ibid., pp. 36–7.

11 John Hedley Brooke, *New interactions between theology and natural science* (London: Open University, 1974), pp. 8–9.

12 John Hedley Brooke and Geoffrey Cantor, *Reconstructing nature: The engagement of science and religion. The 1995–6 Gifford Lectures at Glasgow* (Edinburgh: T & T Clark, 1998), p. 8.

13 Alasdair C. MacIntyre, 'Is a science of comparable politics possible?', in MacIntyre, *Against the self-images of the age: Essays on ideology and philosophy* (London: Duckworth, 1971), pp. 260–79, on p. 260.

14 Brooke and Cantor, *Reconstructing nature*, p. 26.

15 Ibid., pp. 22–31.

16 Ibid., p. 36.

17 Ibid., p. 35.

18 Ibid., p. 69.

19 Jorge Luis Borges, *Collected fictions* (New York: Penguin, 1999), p. 325.

20 Richard Dawkins, *The God delusion* (Boston, MA: Houghton Mifflin, 2006); Daniel C. Dennett, *Breaking the spell: Religion as a natural phenomenon* (New York: Viking, 2006).

21 Recent examples include: Frank J. Tipler, *The physics of Christianity* (New York: Doubleday, 2007); Patrick Hugh Byrne, *The dialogue between science and religion: What we have learned from one another* (Scranton, PA: University of Scranton Press, 2005); Cornelius G. Hunter, *Science's blind spot: The unseen religion of scientific naturalism* (Grand Rapids, MI: Brazos Press, 2007); Muzaffar Iqbal, *Science and Islam* (Westport, CT: Greenwood Press, 2007); J. C. Polkinghorne, *Quantum physics and theology: An unexpected kinship* (New Haven, CT: Yale University Press, 2007).

22 The term 'master-narrative' first appeared in Jean-François Lyotard, *La condition postmoderne: Rapport sur le savoir* (Paris: Éditions de Minuit, 1979). In the thirty years since Lyotard's analysis, contentious debate about the legitimacy of 'master-narratives' or 'grand narratives' has enlivened every narrative discipline, including literature, history, anthropology, and sociology.

23 Brooke and Cantor, *Reconstructing nature*, p. 69.

24 Ibid., p. 25.

25 'The past is a foreign country' is the first sentence of a novel: L. P. Hartley, *The go-between* (London: Hamilton, 1953). This line has since been adopted, interpreted, and debated by historians too many times to count, and given sustained scholarly attention in David Lowenthal, *The past is a foreign country* (Cambridge: Cambridge University Press, 1985).

26 It was only some years later that I learned that this bit of graduate-school wisdom had been cribbed from Hegel, who is said to have declared in 1830 that 'the only thing we learn from history is that we learn nothing from history'.

27 Brooke, *Science and religion*, p. 5.

28 Alasdair MacIntyre, 'Is understanding religion compatible with believing?', in Bryan R. Wilson (ed.), *Rationality* (Oxford: Blackwell, 1970), pp. 62–77. For a more recent discussion of the issue MacIntyre raised, see D. Wiebe, 'Does understanding religion require religious understanding?', in R. T. McCutcheon (ed.), *The insider/outsider problem in the study of religion: A reader* (London: Cassell, 1999), pp. 260–73.

29 For a recent enquiry into the challenge that historicism presents to religious belief, see Sheila Greeve Davaney, *Historicism: The once and future challenge for theology: Guides to theological inquiry* (Minneapolis: Fortress Press, 2006). For a riveting discussion of the issue within the Catholic Church, see Paul L. Williams, *Historicism and faith: Proceedings of the Fellowship of Catholic Scholars* (Scranton, PA: Northeast Books, 1980). For an account of the

nineteenth-century roots of historicism and the history of the ambivalence it has inspired among theologians, see Thomas A. Howard, *Religion and the rise of historicism: W. M. L. De Wette, Jacob Burckhardt, and the theological origins of nineteenth-century historical consciousness* (Cambridge: Cambridge University Press, 2000).

30 Sociologist of religion Robert Segal has argued with obvious satisfaction that an 'explanation of religious belief would, if adequate, challenge one commonly used justification for the truth of religious belief: its supernatural source … Many would appeal to what they deem the supernatural origin of their belief: miracles, revelation or the experience of God. For the social sciences to account for that origin naturally would be to undermine its use as justification for the belief in the reality of God.' Segal, 'The social sciences and the truth of religious belief', *Journal of the American Academy of Religion* 48 (1980), 403–13, on 403. Stronger still was the judgement of Ian Hamnett, who wrote that 'The sociology of religion is, in fact, the sociology of error … In the case of religion … the problem that activates the sociological machinery is really: how can people possibly believe *that?*' Ian Hamnett, 'Sociology of religion and sociology of error', *Religion* 3 (1973), 1–12, on 1–2.

31 Rodney Stark, *For the glory of God: How monotheism led to reformations, science, witch-hunts and the end of slavery* (Princeton, NJ: Princeton University Press, 2003), p. 12. Other popular, and more scholarly, expressions of this view include Hooykaas, *Religion and the rise of modern science* and Jaki, *Savior of science.*

32 Stark, *For the glory of God*, p. 233.

33 www.theocracywatch.org/chris_hedges_nov24_04.htm (accessed 18 August 2008).

34 Brooke, *Science and religion*, p. 5.

35 Thomas Dixon, reviewing Brooke and Cantor, *Reconstructing nature*, made a similar point: 'Given that they themselves illustrate, ingeniously and repeatedly, how theology, science and history can all be used as apologetic tools in the service of religious causes, the reader is bound to speculate about the possible apologetic motives behind the writing of *Reconstructing Nature* … The text is infused with a spirit of rationalism, religious toleration and pluralism. Although this book is certainly a very subtle and sophisticated piece of apologetics, it is a piece of apologetics all the same.' *Religion* 34 (2004), 161. It may be too much to characterize Brooke's and Cantor's historiography as 'apologetic', but Dixon is right that it advances a moral agenda.

36 Robert E. Schofield, 'John Wesley and science in 18th century England', *Isis* 44 (1953), 331–40, on 338–40.

37 Brooke, *Science and religion*, pp. 189–91.

38 Clifford Geertz, *After the fact: Two countries, four decades, one anthropologist: The Jerusalem–Harvard Lectures* (Cambridge, MA: Harvard University Press, 1995), p. 127.

39 Brooke and Cantor, *Reconstructing nature*, p. 25.

40 John Hedley Brooke, 'Religious belief and the content of the sciences', *Osiris* 16 (2001), 3–28, on 8.

41 John Hedley Brooke, 'Presidential address: Does the history of science have a future?', *British Journal for the History of Science* 32 (1999), 1–20, on 9–19.

CHAPTER 13

Simplifying complexity: patterns in the history of science and religion

Ronald L. Numbers

In 1991 John Hedley Brooke launched what I have dubbed the 'complexity thesis' in a review of his landmark book *Science and religion: Some historical perspectives*, the most important contribution to the historiography of the field since the appearance of Andrew Dickson White's *History of the warfare of science with theology in Christendom* nearly a century earlier. Avoiding the simplistic formulas of the past, Brooke revelled in the rich complexity and diversity of interplay between science and Christianity. He described a thoroughly entangled relationship, with religious beliefs not only providing 'presupposition, sanction, even motivation for science' but also regulating 'discussions of method' and playing 'a selective role in the evaluation of rival theories'.[1] As all right-thinking historians of science and religion now concede, he was correct. But he left many feeling emotionally and intellectually unsatisfied, because, to be blunt, Brooke's complexifying history seems to have little to recommend it besides its truth.

John Brooke is a self-described historical voyeur. 'I like to stand back from the heated polemics', he confesses, 'and examine the enormous diversity and richness in the debate'. Fortunately for him he does not suffer this vice in isolation. Thus he has avoided the fate of many scholars who eschew notoriety for insight and accuracy. Not long ago one American intellectual suggested that 'Historians who offer "multicausal explanations" – and use phrases like that – do not last, while those who discover the hidden wellspring of absolutely everything are imitated and attacked but never forgotten'. This volume, however, is testimony to the fact that Brooke, for one, will not soon be forgotten.[2]

During the past decade and a half, prospecting for historical complexity has become something of a rush among historians of science and religion, myself included. (In a recent book I proudly announced my intention of contributing to 'the ongoing complexification of the science-and-religion narrative').[3] The history of the evolution controversies offers a striking example of what has occurred. The neo-conflictist David L. Hull insisted as late as 1974, but well before Brooke's masterpiece, 'that almost all the early proponents of Darwinism were atheistic materialists – or their near relatives'. Five years later, in an influential attack on the warfare thesis, the neo-harmonist James R. Moore claimed that only 'those whose theology was distinctly orthodox' – that is, Calvinist – could embrace true-blue Darwinism.[4] Publishing in the wake of Brooke, though betraying no direct influence, the complexifier David N. Livingstone began denying the very existence of a distinctly orthodox response to Darwinism and arguing that Calvinist reactions varied dramatically from place to place.[5]

But outside a small circle of experts the turn to complexity has left most people yawning or, worse yet, unconvinced. Despite the efforts of Brooke and his disciples untold numbers still swear by the warfare and harmony theses. There may be little we can do about such obstinacy in the face of overwhelming evidence to the contrary; but without abandoning the gospel of complexity and retreating to uncomplicated master-narratives we can – and, I believe, should – search for mid-scale patterns, whether epistemic or social, demographic or geographical, theological or scientific. This is a quest, I am happy to say, that Brooke himself heartily endorses.[6] In the remainder of this chapter I shall therefore contribute to this task by offering five such mid-scale generalizations, addressing what I call naturalization, privatization, secularization, globalization, and radicalization.

NATURALIZATION

The most discernable – and historically significant – pattern relates to the naturalization of scientific discourse during the past two hundred years or so. Although many students of nature since antiquity had expressed a strong preference for natural over supernatural explanations, within the modern period it was not until the late eighteenth and early nineteenth centuries that the idea emerged that 'science', unlike natural philosophy, should disallow appeals to the supernatural. On this view, regardless of one's theological convictions, supernatural interventions had no place in the practice of science. Much later this attitude came to be known as methodological naturalism.[7] Natural philosophers had often expressed a preference for natural causes, but few, if any, had ruled out appeals to God. In contrast, virtually all scientists (a term coined in the 1830s but not widely used until the late nineteenth century), whether Christian or not, came by the mid-nineteenth century to agree that God-talk lay beyond the boundaries of science.[8]

As early as 1800 a contributor to the *Medical Repository*, America's first medical magazine, applauded the growing tendency to refrain from invoking divine intervention in explaining the workings of nature, noting that 'the modesty of science has given up the investigation of the first cause as beyond its comprehension'. While acknowledging that some events might have resulted from 'an immediate act of Deity', the anonymous author believed that 'we should not dignify this [kind of explanation] with the name either of philosophy, science, or even of history'. Yale's Evangelical Benjamin Silliman, founder of the *American Journal of Science*, unashamedly embraced the rule of limiting scientific explanations to physical causes known to exist in nature. 'Our advancement in natural science is not dependent upon our faith', he wrote in 1842. 'All the problems of physical science are worked out by laborious examination, and strict induction'.[9]

Such enthusiasm for banishing supernaturalism from science was possible only because Christian men of science typically attributed the laws of nature that they discovered to God, something that even Charles Darwin felt the need to do in the closing paragraphs of *On the origin of species* in 1859. Thus naturalized science continued – if only silently – testifying to God's existence. Not surprisingly the practice of such methodological naturalism did not meet with universal approbation. 'Physical science, at the present day, investigates phenomena simply as they are in themselves', observed a contributor to the *Biblical Repertory and Princeton Review* in 1860. 'This, if not positively atheistic, must be of dangerous tendency. Whatever deliberately omits God from the universe, is closely allied to that which denies him'.[10]

Christian men of science stressed their religious contributions as much, it seems, to enhance the public image of science as to establish a metaphysical claim. In the workaday world of science, in the field, and in the laboratory, natural theology played a minuscule role. Following up on Ralph Waldo Emerson's call for a 'metaphysics of conchology', the historian Neal C. Gillespie tracked down over 135 books and articles on shells written before 1859 by more than 60 British and American conchologists. Despite the amazing architecture and beauty of shells, few of the naturalists alluded to the argument from design. This finding led Gillespie to conclude that, well before Darwin's notorious attack on intelligent design, 'natural theology of any kind, despite its strong grip on men's minds as a world view, had virtually ceased to be a significant part of the day-to-day practical explanatory structure of natural history'.[11]

Even the great naturalist Louis Agassiz struggled with drawing acceptable boundaries for science. In his *Essay on classification*, published in 1857, he defended the special creation of species and asserted that 'the facts of nature' provided 'direct proof of the existence of a thinking God', although he admitted that some would regard this claim as 'very unscientific'. He went on to explain:

I am well aware that even the most eminent investigators consider the task of science at an end, as soon as the most general relations of natural phenomena have been ascertained. To many the inquiry into the primitive cause of their existence seems either beyond the reach of man, or as belonging rather to philosophy than to physics. To these the name of God appears out of place in a scientific work, as if the knowledge of secondary agencies constituted alone a worthy subject for their investigations, and as if nature could teach nothing about its Author. Many, again, are no doubt prevented from expressing their conviction that the world was called into existence and is regulated by an intelligent God, either by the fear of being supposed to share clerical or sectarian prejudices; or because it may be dangerous for them to discuss freely such questions without acknowledging at the same time the obligation of taking the Old Testament as the standard by which the validity of their results is to be measured. Science, however, can only prosper when confining itself within its legitimate sphere.

Yet Agassiz had his limits. Years later, when a newly appointed junior colleague vowed to 'strike a sturdy blow for Religion' in the classroom, Agassiz quashed the effort. 'My convictions are recorded in the Essay on Classification & there need be no question about them', he wrote, 'but I hardly think that these topics belong to the lecture room beyond a general discussion of principles, which do not yet constitute Religion; at least as practiced in this country, where every body is expected to subscribe to some particular tenets, & tenet teaching is no part of science'.[12]

   In his revolutionary essay *On the origin of species* Darwin aimed primarily 'to overthrow the dogma of separate creations' and to extend the domain of natural law throughout the organic world. He succeeded spectacularly – not because of his clever theory of natural selection (which few biologists thought sufficient to account for evolution), nor because of the voluminous evidence of organic development that he presented, but because, as one Christian reader bluntly put it, there was 'literally nothing deserving the name of Science to put in its place'. The American geologist William North Rice, an active Methodist, made much the same point. 'The great strength of the Darwinian theory', he wrote in 1867, 'lies in its coincidence with the general spirit and tendency of science. It is the aim of science to narrow the domain of the supernatural, by bringing all phenomena within the scope of natural laws and secondary causes'.[13]

In reviewing *On the origin of species* for the *Atlantic Monthly*, the Harvard botanist Asa Gray forthrightly addressed the question of how he and his colleagues had come to feel so uncomfortable with a 'supernatural' account of speciation. 'Sufficient answer', he explained, 'may be found in the activity of the human intellect, "the delirious yet divine desire to know", stimulated as it has been by its own success in unveiling the laws and processes of inorganic Nature'. Minds that had witnessed the dramatic progress of the physical sciences in recent years simply could not 'be expected to let the old belief about species pass unquestioned'. Besides, he later explained, 'the business of science is with the course of Nature, not with interruptions of it, which must rest on their own special evidence'. Organic evolution, echoed his friend George Frederick Wright, a geologist and ordained Congregational minister, accorded with the fundamental principle of science, which states that 'we are to press known secondary causes as far as they will go in explanation of facts. We are not to resort to an unknown cause for explanation of phenomena till the power of known causes has been exhausted. If we cease to observe this rule there is an end to all science and all sound sense'. Since Darwin had shown that 'known causes' could at least potentially explain the origin of species, God should not be resorted to.[14]

By the late twentieth century nothing characterized science more than its rejection of appeals to God in explaining the workings of nature. Numerous scientists, philosophers of science, and science educators made this claim. In 1982 a US federal judge, eager to distinguish science from other forms of knowledge, especially religion, spelled out 'the essential characteristics of science'. At the top of his list appeared the notion that science must be 'guided by natural law'. No statement, declared the judge, could count as science if it depended on 'a supernatural intervention'. Five years later the US Supreme Court affirmed the judge's reasoning.[15]

Naturalistic methods reigned supreme within the scientific community, and even devout Christian scientists scarcely dreamed of appealing to the supernatural when actually doing science. 'Naturalism rules the secular academic world absolutely, which is bad enough', lamented one concerned layman. 'What is far worse is that it rules much of the Christian world as well'. Even the founders of scientific creationism, who brazenly rejected so much of the content of modern science, acknowledged naturalism as the legitimate method of science. Because naturalists narrowed the scope of science to exclude questions of origins, they typically limited it to the study of 'present and reproducible phenomena' and left God and miracles to religion. Given the consensus on naturalism, it came as something of a surprise in the late 1980s and 1990s when a small group of so-called theistic scientists and camp followers unveiled plans 'to reclaim science in the name of God'. They launched their offensive by attacking methodological naturalism as atheistic – or, as one partisan put it, 'absolute rubbish' – and by asserting the presence of intelligent design (ID) in the universe.[16]

Significantly, the most spirited debate over ID and scientific naturalism took place among conservative Christian scholars. Having long since come to terms with doing science naturalistically, reported the editor of the Evangelical journal *Perspectives on Science and Christian Faith*, 'most evangelical observers – especially working scientists – [remained] deeply skeptical'. Although supportive of a theistic worldview, they balked at being 'asked to add "divine agency" to their list of scientific working tools'.[17] For this and other reasons ID theorists largely failed in their effort to change the way science is practised.

PRIVATIZATION

A second clear pattern relates to the increasing privatization of religious views, by which I mean the shift of God-talk from scientific to religious literature. Despite the near-universal acceptance of methodological naturalism, the vast majority of scientists, at least in the United States, remained Christians or theists. The extensive 'retreat' of religion into the non-professional world resulted from a diverse array of factors, including such religious ones as a desire to quarantine sectarian differences and to avoid crossing confessional lines. The secularizing agenda of non-believers may have contributed to the process but not in a major way. The deletion of religious references from scientific works – by both Christians and unbelievers – went hand in hand with the depersonalization of scientific rhetoric, such as avoiding the first person and adopting the passive voice.[18]

The distinguished biologist and sometime historian Ernst Mayr once asserted that Charles Darwin's *On the origin of species* 'almost single-handedly effected the secularization of science'. I only wish that the process were that easily explained. Few contemporaries left any record about either the process or the motivations behind it. One of the few I have found comes from the merchant-naturalist Samuel Elliott Coues. In 1860 he published an essay on geological and meteorological phenomena, *Studies of the earth*, which listed fourteen ways of calculating the distance of the sun from the earth. In presenting the fourteenth method, based on the structure of the heavens and earth given in the first chapter of Genesis, Coues noted self-consciously: 'The author was advised by a friend to omit the fourteenth method . . . on the ground that the method would be deemed altogether unsatisfactory; and also, because a reference should never be made in scientific works to the Bible'. He conceded that the Bible primarily revealed spiritual matters but asked readers to remember 'that the Prophets and Patriarchs were the astronomers of their times'. This note caught the attention of a contributor to the *Princeton Review*, who interpreted it as a disturbing sign of increasing secularity.[19]

By the 1880s, then, references to God were seldom appearing in the increasingly specialized literature of science, and scientists were saying less about their religious convictions. 'For the most part', the Princeton astronomer Charles A. Young explained, scientists did 'not *publicly* take *any* position with reference to Christianity in their scientific intercourse and study'. The 'scientific etiquette of the day', as David L. Hull has termed it, dictated that even in public debates over evolution scientists avoided dragging religion into the discussion. In 1885 the science popularizer John Fiske remarked that scientific texts were 'no proper place' to refer to the Divine Architect or the Great Designer. That same year Enoch Fitch Burr, a scientifically trained Congregational minister who wrote numerous popular works on science and religion, contrasted the new policy which declared that it was 'not scientific to mix up science and religion in the same book' with the views of the 'most eloquent expounder of science in this country during the last generation', Benjamin Silliman:

I can truly declare that in the study and exhibitions of science to my pupils and fellow men I have never forgotten to give all honor and glory to the infinite Creator—happy if I might be the honored interpreter of a portion of his works and of the beautiful structure and beneficent laws discovered therein by the labors of many illustrious predecessors.

Advocates of privatization argued that it would 'be for the comfort and advantage of both' science and religion. But Burr suspected that such separation would make 'God himself . . . unscientific, for he has so largely and legibly written himself into that Book of Nature that contains all the sciences that even the heathen "are without excuse for not reading his eternal power and godhead in the things that are made"'.[20]

The Evangelical physicist Howard J. Van Till, one of the foremost advocates of theistic evolution during the late twentieth century, has argued that doing science 'can be as religiously neutral as dialing a telephone' – so much so that scientific publications in professional journals seldom betray their authors' religious allegiances. 'One could, for example, read the *Astrophysical Journal* for days on end', claims Van Till, 'without detecting

the religious commitments of any authors, many of whom are Christians.'
To discover religious values one had to turn to popular literature written
for a lay audience. Addressing the public rather than their peers, scientists
'usually choose to speak as complete persons, and therefore not only
report the technical results of natural science but also seek to place those
scientific results in the framework of their worldview'.[21]

SECULARIZATION

Although the evidence is sketchy, a third trend relates to the increasing
loss of faith among scientists, especially the best ones. Over the years
many scientists not only privatized their religious beliefs but abandoned
them altogether. Some, such as Charles Darwin, did so for largely non-
scientific reasons (relating to the deaths of his father and daughter Annie).
For others, however, science itself played a role.[22]

Opinion surveys did not become available before the early twentieth
century, but my own retrospective assessment of the religious beliefs of
the leading American biologists, geologists, and anthropologists in the
years 1863–1900 shows that three-quarters of them remained theists, the
overwhelming majority identifying themselves as Christians. Similarly
an informal survey in the early 1880s – the sample of eight scientists comprising six American, one Canadian, and one British – elicited testimonies of
widespread support for Christianity. To the question of whether scientists
were hostile to Christianity, the University of California's Joseph LeConte
replied that although British and Americans were not, it might be different 'on the continent of Europe, and especially in Germany', where
Christianity was so intertwined with politics. Speaking for the British,
Peter Guthrie Tait of Edinburgh offered much the same observation, that
'*indifference* rather than *hostility* would be the proper word here'. The
Princeton astronomer Charles A. Young, although surmising that the
majority of scientists gave 'the subject the go-by', reported that among
his colleagues 'only a small (but rather noisy) minority were decidedly
hostile to Christianity'. Likewise the Canadian, Presbyterian John William
Dawson suspected that 'only a small minority of scientific men are *hostile* to
Christianity'. James Dwight Dana, America's leading geologist, admitted
that recent scientific encroachments on common understandings of Genesis
and speculations 'with regard to the origin of life and of mind and man'
had, 'beyond question, increased doubt', but he expressed confidence that
'the whirlwind is passing'.[23]

Anecdotal evidence from the 1920s suggests that many American scientists remained personally religious. During the anti-evolution agitation of the 1920s, for instance, members of the scientific community repeatedly went out of their way to assert the harmony of evolution and Christianity. As Edward B. Davis has recently shown, such stellar scientists as Robert Millikan, Arthur Holly Compton, Kirtley Mather, and Michael Pupin each contributed to the mass-circulated pamphlets in the 'Science and Religion Series' underwritten by the Rockefeller Foundation. The Tennessee Academy of Sciences, in a brief submitted in connection with the appeal of the Scopes decision in 1926, declared that 'Innumerable numbers of our greatest Christian scientists, philosophers, educators and ministers firmly believe in the truth of the origin of man as taught by evolution'.[24]

On the eve of the First World War the American psychologist James Leuba conducted a pioneering survey of 1,000 American men of science and found that 41.8 per cent affirmed belief in a personal God 'to whom one may pray in expectation of receiving an answer'. Because he did not ask how many endorsed a less personal divinity, such as a God who did not answer intercessory prayers, it is impossible to determine the percentage of theists. Of the same group, 50.6 per cent subscribed to the notion of individual human immortality. In general the more distinguished the scientist, the greater the likelihood of disbelieving in these 'two fundamental dogmas' of Christianity: only 27.7 per cent of his 'greater' scientists believed in a personal God and 35.2 per cent in human immortality. Belief was lower among biological scientists than among physical scientists and, as subsequent surveys showed, lowest of all among social scientists, such as psychologists and sociologists. Although this data did not indicate a simple relationship between science and religious faith, it led Leuba to predict that there would be a growth in scepticism as more and more Americans encountered science.[25]

Eighty years later, however, Edward Larson and Larry Witham replicated his survey and discovered virtually no additional loss of faith among ordinary scientists. Using the same crude instrument Leuba had employed, they found that approximately four in ten American scientists (39.3 per cent) continued to embrace a prayer-answering God, while 38.0 per cent believed in an afterlife. A follow-up survey of the country's most distinguished scientists (all fellows of the elite National Academy of Sciences) revealed that only 7.0 per cent believed in a personal God and 7.9 in personal immortality.[26]

Indeed, one of the most interesting – and perhaps significant – recent developments has been the embrace of an amorphous 'spirituality' by large segments of the public, scientists and laypersons alike. In an ongoing study of 'Religion among academic scientists' the American sociologist Elaine Howard Ecklund has discovered that 34 per cent of the 1,600 scientists surveyed identified with atheism, 30 per cent with agnosticism. (The corresponding figures for the general public are 3 and 5 per cent, respectively.) The truly surprising finding is the high level of spirituality among scientists. About 66 per cent of the natural scientists and 69 per cent of the social scientists consider themselves 'spiritual' people. Included among the self-identified spiritual are more than 22 per cent of the atheists and 27 per cent of the agnostics. These counterintuitive findings led Ecklund to conclude 'that, for some scientists, rather than science replacing religion, *spirituality* may be replacing religion'. And, for most, spirituality is a very private thing.[27]

GLOBALIZATION

For years I (and others) have struggled to discover any pattern to the way that science and religion may have varied from place to place – and especially to determine in which ways the American experience may have been distinctive. It is self-evident that the history of science and religion among Catholics in Spain, France, and Italy differed from that of Anglicans in Britain or the Orthodox in Russia, and that the various European experiences have even less in common with the Hindus of India, the Muslims of Iran, and the atheists of China.[28]

But how much more can we say? Historians of science and religion generally know more about responses to Darwinism than any other topic. However, as the philosopher of science David L. Hull noted in 1984, no one has yet demonstrated a correlation 'between the reception of Darwin's theory around the world and the larger characteristics of these societies'.[29] Thomas Glick tried and failed in *The comparative reception of Darwinism*, as did John Stenhouse and I in *Disseminating Darwinism*.

We know that theology has sometimes made a difference. In a new introduction to his meticulously researched *Darwinism and the divine in America* (1988), Jon H. Roberts has argued that 'the great majority of American Protestant thinkers who remained committed to orthodox formulations of Christian doctrine actually rejected Darwinism; indeed, they denounced the theory of organic evolution in *any* guise that described speciation in terms of naturalistic agencies'. The 'crucial determinant', he maintains, 'was their conviction that the theory of organic evolution could not be reconciled with their views of the origin, nature, and "fall" of man, the nature and basis of moral judgment, and a number of other doctrines—all based on their interpretation of the Scriptures'. My own research bears this out. I have also found that although mainstream Protestants often used arguments interchangeably in critiquing Darwinism, as one moves from the Protestant centre to the periphery occupied by such groups as Pentecostals and Seventh-Day Adventists, one finds unique theological teachings taking on greater significance.[30]

Given the theological heterogeneity of Protestantism, it is not surprising to find a range of responses to evolution. But even in the hierarchical Roman Catholic Church, where one might expect relative uniformity, we also find diversity. Catholics have agreed on little other than the belief that evolution, if it occurred, has been guided by God and has not included the origin of humans (especially the soul) by purely natural means. In an early essay on 'varieties' of Catholic reactions to Darwinism, Harry W. Paul contrasted 'the power Catholicism was able to exert against Darwinism in Spain' with its virtual impotence in Italy. Even more telling, however, are the revelations coming out of the recently opened Vatican archives of the Congregation for the Doctrine of the Faith, which hold the records of the old Congregations of the Holy Office and of the *Index of prohibited books*. In researching their book, *Negotiating Darwin: The Vatican confronts evolution, 1877–1902* (2006), Mariano Artigas, Thomas F. Glick, and Rafael A. Martinez discovered six instances in which the Vatican dealt with complaints about Catholic evolutionists, two of the accused coming from Italy, two from England, and one each from France and the United States. These complaints resulted in no official condemnation of evolution, although some individual works were proscribed and placed on the *Index*. (In one case the Pope vetoed a prohibition against evolution recommended by the Cardinals.) The historians detected no common response, no 'fixed agenda'. The strongest opposition to Darwinism did not come from the Vatican itself but from *La Civiltà Cattolica*, an unofficial but influential Catholic journal.[31]

After studying the reception of evolution in the predominantly Catholic cultures of Latin America, where the church hierarchy widely regarded Darwin as the 'great enemy', Glick identified 'centralization of power' rather than cultural isolation as the 'crucial variable' in determining how various countries responded to evolution. In contrast to the largely Protestant United States, where church and state remained constitutionally separate and Protestant sects competed openly, the more centrally controlled Latin American countries presented an environment relatively inhospitable to new ideas. Nevertheless Pietro Corsi has warned historians discussing Catholicism not to let the hierarchy's opposition to evolution lead to a view of Roman Catholic theology as 'a monolithic structure of doctrines and beliefs, free from conflicts and tensions'. In the Catholic countries of Italy and France, he argues, 'the official voice of the Church – or its silence – did not prevent individual Catholics or groups of Catholic intellectuals from holding strong views that differed from those of the keepers of the dogma'.[32]

Virtually everything I have written so far in this section could be taken to support the 'complexity thesis'. The one generalization I feel confident making is that during the past fifteen years or so the so-called 'science-and-religion dialogue' has spread around the world. A clear (but unexpected) example of this has been the recent globalization of the anti-evolution movement. Despite growing evidence to the contrary, evolutionists in the late twentieth and early twenty-first centuries have clung to the belief that creationism could be geographically contained. In 1986 the usually reliable American palaeontologist and anti-creationist Stephen Jay Gould, then visiting Auckland, assured New Zealanders that they had little to fear from scientific creationism. Because the movement was so 'peculiarly American', he thought it stood little chance of 'catching on overseas'. Fourteen years later he was still assuring listeners that creationism was not contagious. 'As insidious as it may seem, at least it's not a worldwide movement', he said reassuringly. 'I hope everyone realizes the extent to which this is a local, indigenous, American bizarrity'.[33] Although Gould remained oblivious to it, the worldwide growth of creationism by 2000 had already proved him wrong. Anti-evolutionism had become a global phenomenon, as distinctively American in its origins and yet also as readily exportable as hip-hop and blue jeans. In the past few decades it has quietly spread from America throughout the world and from Evangelical Protestantism to Catholicism, Eastern Orthodoxy, Islam, Judaism, and even Hinduism.

In recent years the movement's most robust institution has been Answers in Genesis (AiG), a Kentucky-based operation (located just south of Cincinnati) begun in 1994 by the Australian Ken Ham. A sometime biology teacher and a charismatic public speaker with a 'machine-gun style of delivery', Ham helped to organize the Creation Science Foundation (CSF) in Australia before joining the staff of the Institute of Creation Research (ICR), where he enjoyed spectacular success with his 'Back to Genesis' seminars. After seven years with the ICR he left to establish AiG as an 'outreach' of the CSF. As creationism's newest star he packed in audiences almost everywhere he went, speaking to well over 100,000 people a year. In less than a decade he and his AiG colleagues had created a network of AiG organizations in Australia, New Zealand, Canada, the United Kingdom, Japan, and South Africa, with Cincinnati as the hub. The organization distributed books in Afrikaans, Albanian, Chinese, Czech, English, French, German, Hungarian (Magyar), Italian, Japanese, Polish, Portuguese, Romanian, Russian, and Spanish, and maintained websites in Danish, Dutch, Greek, and Korean as well. Its popular *Creation* magazine appeared in Spanish as *Creación*, while its technical counterpart, *TJ: The In-Depth Journal of Creation*, became 'the world's premier refereed Creation publication'. Its 90-second radio spots, *Answers ... with Ken Ham*, could be heard on approximately 700 English-language stations around the globe. It employed scores of skilled employees and in 2007 opened a $25-million, state-of-the-art creation museum in Kentucky, funded by repeated appeals to the creationist community.[34]

At first few observers noticed the spread of creationism outside the United States. However, in 2000 the British magazine *New Scientist* devoted a cover story to warning the public that it was time to 'Start worrying now', because 'from Kansas to Korea, Creationism is flooding the earth'. Although the unexpected development seemed almost 'beyond belief', the magazine described creationism as 'mutating and spreading' around the world, 'even linking up with like-minded people in the Muslim world'. Just five years later representatives from national academies of science around the world joined in signing a statement supporting evolution and condemning the global spread of 'theories not testable by science'.[35] Contrary to almost all expectations, geographical, theological, and political barriers had failed to contain creationism.

RADICALIZATION

A final pattern worth noting dates from the latter half of the nineteenth century, which witnessed a marked intensification of the debates about science and religion and which saw extremists – on both sides – elevated to positions of high visibility. In the United Kingdom the Irish physicist John Tyndall and the English naturalist Thomas Henry Huxley led the way with their screeds against organized religion, while in the United States the historical polemicists Andrew Dickson White and John William Draper rushed to defend science against alleged clerical attacks. Although one would scarcely have gathered it from the ensuing hubbub in the popular press, moderate harmonizers greatly outnumbered zealots, even in the scientific community.[36]

In the 1920s the press elevated the infamous Scopes trial in small-town Tennessee into 'the trial of the century', while largely ignoring the fact that most legislatures in the American South refused to ban the teaching of human evolution. Similarly in recent years we have been regaled with accounts of the 'evolution wars' between ID theorists and mainstream scientists, with little mention made of the minuscule support for ID among practising scientists and the virtual absence of peer-reviewed scientific publications supportive of ID.[37] Reprising the roles of Tyndall and Huxley have been the British biologist Richard Dawkins and the American philosopher Daniel Dennett. Dawkins, Britain's number-one public intellectual (according to one magazine poll), has repeatedly gone out of his way to bait and belittle religious believers, especially creationists, whom he has described as 'ignorant, stupid or insane'. To the consternation of even liberal Christians, Dawkins has diagnosed religious faith 'as a kind of mental illness' and as 'the great cop-out, the great excuse to evade the need to think and evaluate evidence'. On one occasion he described religious faith as 'one of the world's great evils, comparable to the smallpox virus but harder to eradicate'.[38] Dennett despised creationists, arguing that 'there are no forces on this planet more dangerous to us all than the fanaticisms of fundamentalism' and calling for 'caging' those who would deliberately misinform children about the natural world, just as one would cage a threatening wild animal.[39] In the Sermon on the Mount Jesus blessed 'the meek: for they shall inherit the earth' (Matthew 5:5). Perhaps some day they will, but they seem unlikely ever to inherit the celebrity that assertive ideologues do.

CLOSING THOUGHTS

The five themes I have identified in this chapter represent a modest beginning towards (re-)simplifying the increasingly complex story of the historical relationship between science and religion that has emerged in the past three decades or so. Non-Americanists, for example, would no doubt generate a somewhat different list. And scholars who focus on non-Christian traditions would almost certainly do so. But after Brooke and like-minded colleagues have so assiduously deconstructed the simplistic narratives of the past, it is difficult to imagine any serious scholar trying to reconstruct them. I do hope, however, that a search for mid-scale patterns, such as the ones I have identified, will be linked in the future with continuing efforts to explore the uniqueness of past engagements involving science and religion.

NOTES

1 John Hedley Brooke, *Science and religion: Some historical perspectives* (Cambridge: Cambridge University Press, 1991), p. 33. For an earlier assessment of the historical relationship between science and Christianity that similarly portrayed 'a complex and diverse interaction that defies reduction to simple "conflict" or "harmony"', see David C. Lindberg and Ronald L. Numbers (eds.), *God and nature: Historical essays on the encounter between Christianity and science* (Berkeley and Los Angeles, CA: University of California Press, 1986), p. 10. See also John Hedley Brooke and Geoffrey Cantor, *Reconstructing nature: The engagement of science and religion. The 1995–6 Gifford Lectures at Glasgow* (Edinburgh: T & T Clark, 1998); Brooke, 'A call for complexity', available at www.science-spirit.org. On Brooke and 'the complexity thesis', see Ronald L. Numbers, review of *Science and religion*, by John Hedley Brooke, *Metascience*, new ser. 1 (1992), 35–9, at 36.

2 'Questions of design and purpose: Science and religion at Oxford', *University of Oxford Annual Review 2000–1*, p. 6, quoting Brooke; Mark Lilla, 'Mr. Casaubon in America', *New York Review of Books*, 28 June 2007, 29.

3 Ronald L. Numbers, *Science and Christianity in pulpit and pew* (New York: Oxford University Press, 2007), p. 9. See also Lindberg and Numbers, *God and nature*; David C. Lindberg and Ronald L. Numbers (eds.), *When science and Christianity meet* (Chicago: University of Chicago Press, 2003).

4 James R. Moore, *The post-Darwinian controversies: A study of the Protestant struggle to come to terms with Darwin in Great Britain and America, 1870–1900* (Cambridge: Cambridge University Press, 1979), p. ix; David L. Hull, 'Darwinism and historiography', in Thomas F. Glick (ed.), *The comparative reception of Darwinism* (Austin: University of Texas Press, 1974), pp. 388–402, at p. 391.

5 David N. Livingstone, 'Science, region, and religion: The reception of Darwinism in Princeton, Belfast, and Edinburgh', in Ronald L. Numbers and John Stenhouse (eds.), *Disseminating Darwinism: The role of place, race, religion, and gender* (Cambridge: Cambridge University Press, 1999), pp. 7–38; Peter Monaghan, interview with David Livingstone, *Chronicle of Higher Education*, 19 September 2003, A19. See also Livingstone, 'Darwinism and Calvinism: The Belfast–Princeton connection', *Isis* (1992), 408–28; Livingstone, *Putting science in its place: Geographies of scientific knowledge* (Chicago: University of Chicago Press, 2003), esp. pp. 116–23.

6 Jon H. Roberts, 'The idea that wouldn't die: The warfare between science and Christianity', *Historically Speaking* 4 (February 2003), 21–4; John Hedley Brooke, 'Science, religion, and historical complexity', *Historically Speaking* 8 (May–June 2007), 10–13. Brooke and two dozen colleagues have recently contributed to an attempt to educate the masses: Ronald L. Numbers (ed.), *Galileo goes to jail and other myths about science and religion* (Cambridge, MA: Harvard University Press, 2009).

7 The phrase 'methodological naturalism' seems to have been coined by the philosopher Paul de Vries, then at Wheaton College, who introduced it at a

conference in 1983 in a paper subsequently published as 'Naturalism in the natural sciences', *Christian Scholar's Review* 15 (1986), 388–96. De Vries distinguished between what he called 'methodological naturalism', a disciplinary method that says nothing about God's existence, and 'metaphysical naturalism', which 'denies the existence of a transcendent God'. For a history of methodological naturalism, on which much of this section is based, see Ronald L. Numbers, 'Science without God: Natural laws and Christian beliefs', in Lindberg and Numbers, *Science and Christianity*, pp. 265–85.

8 Andrew Cunningham, 'Getting the game right: Some plain words on the identity and invention of science', *Studies in History and Philosophy of Science* 19 (1988), 365–89. See also Sydney Ross, 'Scientist: The story of a word', *Annals of Science* 18 (1962), 65–85, which dates the earliest use of the term 'scientist' in print to 1834. Whewell had first used the term in an address to the British Association for the Advancement of Science in the previous year.

9 Review of James Tytler, *A treatise on the plague and yellow fever*, in *Medical Repository* 3 (1800), 373–9, on 376; Benjamin Silliman, 'Address before the Association of American Geologists and Naturalists, assembled at Boston, April 24, 1842', *American Journal of Science* 43 (1842), 217–50, on 218.

10 [James Read Eckard], 'The logical relations of religion and natural science', *Biblical Repertory and Princeton Review* 32 (1860), 577–608, esp. 577 (atheistic). For similar complaints about the naturalization of science, see William D. Whitney, 'Is the study of language a physical science?', *North American Review* 101 (1865), 434–74; [C. A. Aiken], 'Whitney on language', *Princeton Review* 40 (1868), 263–92, quotation on 270 (incredulous). I am indebted to Jon Roberts for identifying Eckard and to Steve Alter for identifying Aiken.

11 Walter H. Conser, Jr, *God and the natural world: Religion and science in Antebellum America* (Columbia: University of South Carolina Press, 1993), p. 9 (Hitchcock); A[lexander] Winchell, *Creation: The work of one intelligence, and not the product of physical forces* (Ann Arbor, MI: Young Men's Literary Assn, 1858), p. 3; Neal C. Gillespie, 'Preparing for Darwin: Conchology and natural theology in Anglo-American natural history', *Studies in History of Biology* 7 (1984), 93–145, esp. 94–5.

12 Louis Agassiz, *Essay on classification*, ed. Edward Lurie (Cambridge, MA: Harvard University Press, 1962), p. 12; Ronald L. Numbers, *The creationists: From scientific creationism to intelligent design* (Cambridge, MA: Harvard University Press, 2006), p. 20 (tenet teaching).

13 Charles Darwin, *The descent of man, and selection in relation to sex*, 2 vols. (London: Murray, 1871), vol. I, pp. 152–3; S. R. Calthrop, 'Religion and evolution', *Religious Magazine and Monthly Review* 50 (1873), 205; [W. N. Rice], 'The Darwinian theory of the origin of species', *New Englander* 26 (1867), 608.

14 Asa Gray, *Darwiniana: Essays and reviews pertaining to Darwinism* (New York: D. Appleton & Co., 1876), pp. 78–9, from a review first published in 1860 (sufficient answer); Asa Gray, *Natural science and religion: Two lectures delivered to the Theology School of Yale College* (New York: Charles Scribner's Sons, 1880), p. 77 (business of science); George F. Wright, 'Recent works

bearing on the relation of science to religion: No. II', Bibliotheca Sacra 33 (1876), 480.

15 Opinion of Judge William R. Overton in McLean *v.* Arkansas Board of Education, in Marcel C. La Follette (ed.), *Creationism, science, and the law: The Arkansas case* (Cambridge, MA: MIT Press, 1983), p. 60. See also Michael Ruse, 'Creation-Science is not science', ibid., pp. 151–4; Stephen Jay Gould, 'Impeaching a self-appointed judge', *Scientific American* (July 1992), 118–20; Gould, *Science and creationism: a view from the National Academy of Sciences* (Washington, DC: National Academy Press, 1984), p. 8; Gould, *Teaching about evolution and the nature of science* (Washington, DC: National Academy Press, 1998), ch. 3.

16 Phillip E. Johnson, 'Foreword' to J. P. Moreland (ed.), *The creation hypothesis: Scientific evidence for an intelligent designer* (Downers Grove, IL: InterVarsity Press, 1994), pp. 7–8; Larry Vardiman, 'Scientific naturalism as science', *Impact* 293, inserted in *Acts & Facts* 26 (November 1997); Paul Nelson at a conference on 'Design and its critics', Concordia University Wisconsin, 24 June 2000. On scientific creationists and naturalism, see Numbers, *Creationists*, pp. 107–8, 113–14, 232–3.

17 J. W. Haas, Jr, 'On intelligent design, irreducible complexity, and theistic science', *Perspectives on Science and Christian Faith* 49 (March 1997), 1.

18 This discussion is extracted from Numbers, *Science and Christianity*, pp. 132–4. Some Lutherans, for example, insisted on strictly secular scientific meetings because their beliefs precluded even 'joint prayer with those not on the same confessional basis'; see Numbers, *Creationists*, p. 131. On the privatization of religion and secularization, see Thomas Luckmann, *The invisible religion: The problem of religion in modern society* (New York: Macmillan 1967). On the privatization of religious beliefs among scientists, see also Nicolaas A. Rupke, 'Introduction: Telling lives in science and religion', in Rupke (ed.), *Eminent lives in twentieth-century science and religion* (Frankfurt-am-Main: Peter Lang, 2007), pp. 20–1.

19 Ernst Mayr, *What evolution is* (New York: Basic Books, 2001), p. 9; Samuel Elliott Coues, *Studies of the earth: An essay on the figure and surface-divisions of the earth, its geological and meteorological phenomena, and astronomical elements* (Washington, DC: Philip & Solomons, 1860), pp. 68–9, 76; [Eckard], 'Logical relations of religion and natural science', 578.

20 David L. Hull, 'Darwinism and historiography', in Thomas F. Glick (ed.), *The comparative reception of Darwinism* (Austin: University of Texas Press, 1974), p. 393; John Fiske, *The idea of God as affected by modern knowledge* (Boston, MA: Houghton, Mifflin, 1885), p. 119; Lemuel Moss, 'Present relation of scientific thought to Christianity', *Baptist Quarterly Review* 4 (1882), 1–25, quotation on 30 (Young); Enoch Fitch Burr, *Celestial empires* (New York: American Tract Society, 1885), preface, no pagination. Burr left the 'eloquent expounder' unnamed, but Judith Ann Schiff has identified him as Silliman in 'Old Yale: Learning by doing', *Yale Alumni Magazine* 64 (November 2000), 80.

21 Howard J. Van Till, *The fourth day: What the Bible and the heavens are telling us about the Creation* (Grand Rapids, MI: Eerdmans, 1986), p. 209.

22 James Moore, 'Myth 16: That evolution destroyed Darwin's faith in Christianity – until he reconverted on his deathbed', in Numbers, *Galileo goes to jail*, pp. 142–51. See also John Hedley Brooke, 'Myth 25: That modern science has secularized western culture', ibid., pp. 224–34.

23 Moss, 'Present relation of scientific thought', 16–35; Ronald L. Numbers, *Darwinism comes to America* (Cambridge, MA: Harvard University Press, 1998), p. 41. This retrospective survey is based on the eighty biologists, geologists, and anthropologists elected to the National Academy of Sciences after its founding in 1863. I was unable to identify the religious affiliations of twenty-seven of the eighty. On European surveys of the beliefs of scientists, see Rupke, 'Introduction', 16–19. This section is extracted from Numbers, *Science and Christianity*, pp. 134–5.

24 Edward B. Davis, 'Science and religious fundamentalism in the 1920s', *American Scientist* 93 (2005), 253–60; 'Brief and argument of the Tennessee Academy of Sciences as Amicus Curiae', Scopes *v.* State, 154 Tenn. 105 (1926), as quoted in Edward J. Larson, *Summer for the gods: The Scopes trial and America's continuing debate over science and religion* (New York: Basic Books, 1997), p. 214. See also Edwin Slosson, 'Evolution – The conference method of study', Kirtley F. Mather Papers, Harvard University Archives.

25 James H. Leuba, *The belief in God and immortality: A psychological, anthropological and statistical study* (Boston, MA: Sherman, French, and Co., 1916).

26 Edward J. Larson and Larry Witham, 'Scientists are still keeping the faith', *Nature* 386 (1997), 435–6; Larson and Witham, 'Leading scientists still reject God', *Nature* 394 (1998), 313. See also Larson and Witham, 'Scientists and religion in America', *Scientific American* 281 (September 1999), 89–93. On earlier surveys, see Russell Heddendorf, 'Religious beliefs of scientists', *Journal of the American Scientific Affiliation* 23 (1971), 10–11; Rodney Stark, Laurence R. Iannaccone, and Roger Finke, 'Religion, science, and rationality', *American Economic Review* 86 (1996), 433–7. Stark *et al.* report that a Carnegie Commission survey of 60,000 academics in 1969 found that 55 per cent of physical and life scientists regarded themselves as religious, over 40 per cent attending church regularly. Social scientists, especially anthropologists and psychologists, were less religious.

27 Elaine Howard Ecklund, 'Religion and spirituality among university scientists', 5 February 2007, available at http://religion.ssrc.org/reforum/Ecklund. See also Ecklund and Christopher P. Scheitle, 'Religion among academic scientists: Distinctions, disciplines, and demographics', *Social Problems* 54 (2007), 289–307; Ecklund, *Waging peace on the science and religion battleground* (New York: Oxford University Press, in press).

28 For an effort at broadening 'science and religion' beyond 'science and Christianity', see John Hedley Brooke and Ronald L. Numbers (eds.), *Science and religion around the world* (New York: Oxford University Press, 2010).

29 David L. Hull, 'Evolutionary thinking observed', *Science* 223 (1984), 923–4.

30 Jon H. Roberts, *Darwinism and the divine in America: Protestant intellectuals and organic evolution, 1859–1900* (Notre Dame, IN: University of Notre Dame Press, 2001; first published in 1988), p. x; David N. Livingstone, *Darwin's forgotten defenders: The encounter between evangelical theology and evolutionary thought* (Grand Rapids, MI: Eerdmans, 1987); Ronald L. Numbers, *The creationists* (New York: Knopf, 1992), pp. 7–36; Numbers, *Darwinism comes to America*, pp. 24–48. Livingstone detects less hostility towards theistic evolution than Roberts and I do. See also Jon H. Roberts, 'Darwinism, American Protestant thinkers, and the puzzle of motivation', in Numbers and Stenhouse, *Disseminating Darwinism*, pp. 145–72. Regarding Seventh-Day Adventists and Pentecostals, see Numbers, *Darwinism comes to America*, chs. 5 and 6.

31 Harry W. Paul, 'Religion and Darwinism: Varieties of Catholic reaction', in Glick, *Comparative reception of Darwinism*, pp. 403–36, quotation on p. 408; Mariano Artigas, Thomas F. Glick, and Rafael A. Martinez, *Negotiating Darwin: The Vatican confronts evolution, 1877–1902* (Baltimore, MD: Johns Hopkins University Press, 2006). On the reaction of Catholics to evolution, see also Thomas F. Glick, 'The reception of Darwinism in Uruguay', in Glick, Miguel Angel Puig-Samper, and Rosaura Ruiz (eds.), *The reception of Darwinism in the Iberian world: Spain, Spanish America and Brazil* (Dordrecht: Kluwer Academic Publishers, 2001), pp. 29–52, especially pp. 43–7; John Lyon, 'Immediate reactions to Darwin: The English Catholic press' first reviews of the *Origin of Species*', *Church History* 41 (1972), 78–93; Jacob W. Gruber, *A conscience in conflict: The life of St George Jackson Mivart* (New York: Columbia University Press, 1960); Noor Giovanni Mazhar, *Catholic attitudes to evolution in nineteenth-century Italian literature* (Venice: Istituto Veneto di Scienze, Lettere ed Arti, 1995); Harry W. Paul, *The edge of contingency: French Catholic reaction to scientific change from Darwin to Duhem* (Gainesville: University Presses of Florida, 1979); R. Scott Appleby, 'Exposing Darwin's "hidden agenda": Roman Catholic responses to evolution, 1875–1925', in Numbers and Stenhouse, *Disseminating Darwinism*, pp. 173–208; Ralph E. Weber, *Notre Dame's John Zahm: American Catholic apologist and educator* (Notre Dame, IN: University of Notre Dame Press, 1961).

32 Glick, 'Reception of Darwinism in Uruguay', quotations on p. 47 (enemy) and p. 52 (crucial variable); Pietro Corsi and Paul J. Weindling, 'Darwinism in Germany, France and Italy', in David Kohn (ed.), *The Darwinian heritage* (Princeton, NJ: Princeton University Press, 1985), pp. 683–729, quotation on pp. 725–6.

33 'Creationism in NZ "Unlikely"', *NZ Herald*, 3 July 1986, p. 14 (Gould), clipping courtesy of Carol Scott; *Wisconsin State Journal*, 7 May 2000, p. 2A. For similar statements, see Richard C. Lewontin, Introduction to Laurie R. Godfrey (ed.), *Scientists confront creationism* (New York: W. W. Norton, 1983), p. xxv; Michael Ruse, *The evolution–creation struggle* (Cambridge, MA: Harvard University Press, 2005), p. 5; and Edward O. Wilson, quoted in Nicholas Wade, 'Long-ago rivals are dual impresarios of Darwin's oeuvre',

New York Times, 25 October 2005, p. D2. For a creationist response to Gould, see Frank Sherwin, 'Can creation science be found outside America?', *Acts & Facts* 30 (March 2001), 4.

34 Interview with Ken Ham, 7 December 2001; '*Creation* in other languages!', *Answers Update* 2 (March/April 2000), 4; Katia Berra, 'Expanded international outreach!', ibid., 8 (April 2001), 11; 'All but Antarctica!', ibid., 8 (September 2001), 11; 'AiG launched in South Africa!', ibid., 9 (August 2002), 9. See also Francis X. Clines, 'Creationist captain sees battle "hotting up"', *New York Times*, 1 December 1999, p. A15; and www.answersingenesis.org

35 Debora MacKenzie, 'Unnatural selection', *New Scientist*, 22 April 2000, 35–9, plus the cover of the 22 April 2000 issue and an editorial on p. 3; Interacademy Panel on International Issues, 'IAP statement on the teaching of evolution', December 2005, personal copy. See also Michael Gross, 'US-style creationism spreads to Europe', *Current Biology* 12 (2002), R265–6; Ulrich Kutschera, 'Darwinism and intelligent design: The new anti-evolutionism spreads in Europe', *NCSE Reports* 23 (September–December 2003), 17–18.

36 For a more extended discussion of this phenomenon, see Ronald L. Numbers, 'Aggressors, victims, and peacemakers: Historical actors in the drama of science and religion', in Harold Attridge (ed.), *The science and religion debate: Why does it continue?* (New Haven, CT: Yale University Press, in press). Huxley himself described one of his attacks on 'Theology & Parsondom' as a 'screed'; see Adrian Desmond, *Huxley: From devil's disciple to evolution's high priest* (Reading, MA: Addison-Wesley, 1997), p. 253.

37 Some of the attention the press devoted to creationism and ID stemmed from its quest for 'balance', regardless of merit. On this tendency, see Chris Mooney, 'Blinded by science: How "balanced" coverage lets the scientific fringe hijack reality', *Columbia Journalism Review* 43 (November–December 2004), 26–35; Mooney and Matthew C. Nisbet, 'Undoing Darwin', ibid., 44 (September–October 2005), 31–9. On evolution in the South, see Ronald L. Numbers and Lester D. Stephens, 'Darwinism in the American South', in Numbers and Stenhouse, *Disseminating Darwinism*, pp. 123–43.

38 Richard Dawkins, Review of Maitland A. Edey and Donald C. Johanson, *Blueprints: Solving the mystery of evolution*, New York Times, 9 April 1989, section 7, p. 34 (ignorant); Dawkins, 'Is science a religion?', *The Humanist* 57 (January–February 1997), 26–9, smallpox quotation on 26; Alister McGrath, *Dawkins' God: Genes, memes, and the meaning of life* (Oxford: Blackwell, 2005), p. 84 (mental illness and cop-out); Dawkins, *The God delusion* (Boston, MA: Houghton Mifflin, 2006), pp. 66–9.

39 Daniel C. Dennett, *Darwin's dangerous idea: Evolution and the meaning of life* (New York: Simon and Schuster, 1995), pp. 515–16, 519–21.

CHAPTER 14

What shall we do with the 'Conflict Thesis'?

Geoffrey Cantor

INTRODUCTION

John Rutty, a Dublin apothecary, maintained a diary for some twenty years, beginning in 1753. Every day he reflected on the state of his soul and the religious significance of his various experiences. We know a great deal about the state of Rutty's soul because in 1776, the year after his death, a number of his fellow Quakers published his diary under the title *A spiritual diary and soliloquies*. The *Spiritual diary* is a fascinating document which provides the historian with an entrée into the intimate religious thoughts and feelings of an eighteenth-century Quaker. We also know that Rutty had a thriving medical practice and published works on gallstones, on mineral waters, on the weather, and on the natural history of Dublin, and he even wrote a *materia medica*. For the historian of science and religion what is most striking is the large number of entries in which Rutty exposed his deep ambivalence about his pursuit of medicine and science. The following three diary entries characterize his attitude to science and medicine:

Physick is less precious in my view, having for its object the welfare of the mortal body only: Lord, raise up the *medicina mentis* [the medicine of the soul].

Lord, remember not the sin of my youth and age, even that of idolizing nature! O give me now to redeem the time, the precious time!

Now is the snare laid in natural science: Lord, grant that it may be in vain![1]

In these and many similar passages, which are loaded with biblical resonances, we see Rutty assailed by inner conflict as he was repeatedly pulled between the opposing poles of the pursuit of science and of the pure spiritual life. He was never satisfied that he had adequately achieved a state of grace, and yet he was not able to relinquish his abiding enthusiasm for scientific investigations. He had one foot in the world of those quietist Quakers who sought to live a simple life of religious purity, but his other foot was firmly placed in the Dublin Enlightenment.[2]

These entries from Rutty's diary raise two salient issues. The first concerns sources. Diaries and letters make visible certain aspects of science and of religion and of their interrelation that rarely find expression in other sources, particularly works intended for the press. Thus in my research on Quakers I found a number of expressions of a tension between science and religion principally in diaries and correspondence, and occasionally in testimonies – short biographies of recently deceased Quakers that often reveal their spiritual struggles.[3] Such issues hardly ever surfaced in other Quaker publications; indeed, one can find no indication of Rutty's inner turmoil in his scientific writings. Therefore the historian needs to be aware that expressions of anxiety may be confined principally to certain types of literary source.

Second, the short passages I have quoted from Rutty's *Spiritual diary* make manifest one specific form of conflict between science and religion. It is not our usual notion of conflict, as instantiated in the 'Conflict Thesis', of warfare between opposing armies, one fighting in the cause of science, the other in the cause of religion. Instead Rutty experienced an inner conflict in trying to be both a pious Quaker and a man of science. This is an issue that is not confined to Rutty nor to Quakers but is one that has recurred very frequently in the domain of science and religion during the past four centuries. In this chapter I shall reflect further on the roles that conflict can play in the science–religion domain and suggest that the historian needs to embrace certain notions of conflict, but without returning to the tired, old 'Conflict Thesis'. Thus I want to reinstate the notion of conflict but in a richer and more historically sensitive form.

To achieve this I shall first outline the traditional strong version of the 'Conflict Thesis' and the criticisms that have been mounted against it; then I shall examine how individuals address conflicting claims. That will be the longest section and will form the crux of my argument. Then, rather more briefly, I shall sketch some of the issues implicit in describing publicly visible conflicts over matters of science and religion.

THE CONFLICT THESIS REVISITED

We now need to analyse the 'Conflict Thesis' itself and appreciate how it has been understood. First, it should be noted that there is no consensus over precisely the nature of the conflict, and many different versions have been proposed, as indicated by Colin Russell's contribution to Gary B. Ferngren's *Encyclopedia* of the history of science and religion.[4] Russell suggests that the 'Conflict Thesis' applies to four distinct areas. The first he calls epistemological and refers to instances of conflict between the world-view of religion and that of science. The second version refers to those conflicts that occur when different methodologies are employed in science and in religion. Third, it refers to conflict over values, especially when dealing with medicine and the applied sciences. Fourth, it refers to social conflict between groups, for example the conflict that ensued when a group of scientific naturalists sought to wrest power from the Established Church in Victorian Britain. (I shall return to this type of conflict in the fourth section, below.) We can easily extend Russell's list. However, in discussing conflict between science and religion, Russell has identified potential sites of conflict, implicitly acknowledging that in these areas there is no necessity for any actual conflict. Thus, for example, over and against examples where there have been methodological conflicts (his second category) there have been many instances where no such conflict has occurred. For example Galileo sought to emphasize the methodological differences between science and religion, rather than their conflict, while Newton saw these methodologies as overlapping and mutually supporting. As an historian Russell has empha-sized the contingency of conflict, rather than the necessity.

In contrast to Russell's argument, there exists the strong version of the 'Conflict Thesis' that posits a *necessary* conflict between science and religion – this version will be referred to as CT hereafter. It provides a master-narrative in which science is portrayed as inevitably pitted against religion, because of some essential difference between the two. Reconciliation is not possible, and this opposition is played out in history. Classic versions were published in John William Draper's *History of the conflict between religion and science* (1875) and Andrew Dixon White's *A history of the warfare of science with theology in Christendom* (1896).[5] In Draper's oft-quoted for-mulation: 'The history of Science is ... a narrative of the conflict of two contending powers, the expansive force of the human intellect on one side, and the compression arising from traditional faith and human interests on the other'.[6] Throughout the ensuing century this thesis has become part of our general culture, and it continues to be repeated *ad nauseam* in the popular media and even in academic contexts. In our own day Richard Dawkins, among others, takes this conflict as axiomatic. For him science is rational and based on empirical evidence; religion is irrational and not founded on evidence. 'Science', he writes, 'is based upon verifiable evidence. Religious faith not only lacks evidence, its independence from evidence is its pride and joy, shouted from the rooftops'.[7] Having adopted such simplistic characterizations he has no difficulty in arguing that these two activities are necessarily in conflict.

One of the major tasks of historians of science over the last two decades has been to criticize CT and similar master-narratives. John Hedley Brooke has been the most prominent revisionist, and he and several other historians have argued that this strong version of CT – as in the Draper and Dawkins examples – incorporates untenable and often highly partial notions of both science and religion. Thus in his path-breaking 1991 book Brooke wrote: 'The fundamental weakness of the conflict thesis is its tendency to portray science and religion as hypostatized forces, as entities in themselves'.[8] To view the history of science and religion using such crude *a priori* notions of both science and religion is to distort our understanding of the past. CT – at least in this version – is plainly untenable. But where do we go from here?

Immediately following the earlier quotation from Brooke, he proposes that both science and religion 'should rather be seen as complex social activities involving different expressions of human concern, the same individuals often participating in both'.[9] The emphasis here is the historian's concern with what people do, not with some inadequate essentialist view of what constitutes either science or religion. But notice, too, that Brooke describes these activities as 'complex'. This takes us to an argument from history that has often been used against CT. As David Lindberg and Ronald Numbers point out in their *God and nature* volume of 1986 and more recently in the introduction to their *When science and Christianity meet* (2003), the researches of historians demonstrate the immense diversity and complexity of the issues and arguments used by historical actors when discussing matters of science and religion. As Lindberg and Numbers wrote of their 1986 volume, 'almost every chapter portrays a complex and diverse interaction that defies reduction to simple "conflict" or "harmony"'.[10] In rejecting these theses they urge the historian to encompass what some have called the 'Complexity Thesis'.[11] In this and similar analyses,[12] a sharp contrast is drawn between two historiographies: while CT involves a species of Whig history,[13] which attempts to understand the past using present-day categories that are inappropriate for understanding the past, contextualist history aims to understand historical actors from the perspective of their own historical contexts and does not judge them by present-day – and thus inappropriate – criteria. On this account contextualist historians emerge triumphant; they are good listeners and seek to understand the arguments and motivations of historical actors on their own terms. They appreciate the complexity of history. By contrast Whig historians are autocratic and are deaf to periods other than their own and merely shoehorn the past – including the history of the science–religion relationship – into pre-formed boxes. CT is therefore a creation of Whig history.

However, is the situation really that simple? Have we perhaps been trading in our own stereotypes? Is the choice really between the naïve and unacceptable version of CT – from which we recoil in horror – and the new contextualist history? Perhaps, too, having set the agenda for discussing science and religion, Dawkins and others have thereby forced revisionist historians into an over-reactive mode. It is true that there are powerful arguments against the strong version of CT. However, have we over-reacted to the very notion of conflict? Are there weaker accounts of conflict that are commensurable with good historical practice?

I shall suggest below how we might reconceptualize two forms of conflict involving science and religion. Before entering into this discussion it may be helpful to note that students of social conflict, especially warfare, recognize that there are many different types of conflict and many ways in which they can be analysed. As one commentator has noted, 'conflict can be apprehended as a potentiality or a situation, as a structure or a manifestation, as an event or a process'.[14]

HOW MIGHT WE RECONCEPTUALIZE CONFLICT?

The earlier quotations from John Rutty's *Spiritual diary* provide evidence of his internal conflict over issues of science and religion. Rutty was clearly experiencing a deep spiritual torment in confronting these two crucial but, to him, incompatible aspects of his life. These diary entries contain a strong emotional charge indicating the depth of his turmoil. As Thomas Söderqvist, an historian who writes on scientific biography, has recently emphasized, it is important to appreciate the deep passions experienced by scientists when choosing and engaging with their scientific projects. Drawing on Søren Kierkegaard's philosophy of existentialism, Söderqvist argues that biographers need to structure their accounts of scientists' lives round such existential themes.[15] While Söderqvist uses existentialism in a modern secular context, it should be remembered that Kierkegaard himself was centrally concerned with the individual's conflicts over religion and issues of faith. Although the ensuing discussion does not draw specifically on existentialism, an existentialist framework helps us appreciate that the tensions between science and religion usually generate deep and unsettling emotions. This is one reason the notion of conflict should be accorded a central role in our understanding of science–religion relations; other reasons will become clear as we proceed.

I now intend to expand this discussion well beyond the example of Rutty and to suggest that we are in fact dealing with a frequently recurring phenomenon. Like Rutty, many individuals have encountered what we might call tensions or conflicts arising from their joint engagements with science and religion. In Rutty's case the conflict was between the practice of science and his religious duty as a pious Quaker. In other cases the tension may be between specific aspects of science – for example, the moving earth postulated by Copernicus's theory – and specific aspects of religious thought – such as the biblical passage in which Joshua commanded 'sun, stand thou still upon Gibeon' (Joshua 10:12).

To help us analyse such tensions I want to make use of a rather slimmed-down version of Leon Festinger's theory of cognitive dissonance, which he framed in the 1950s after studying how members of a doomsday cult responded when their prediction of the date of the end of the world failed to be confirmed. The term 'cognitive dissonance' can be defined as the incompatibility between two cognitions – a cognition being rather widely defined as any element of knowledge. 'Dissonance produces discomfort'. The theory of cognitive dissonance goes on to postulate that confronted by such dissonant cognitions the mind is forced to gain or invent new thoughts or beliefs, or to modify existing ones, in order to reduce the dissonance (or conflict) between cognitions.[16] For our purpose there are two crucial features of the theory, the first being the initial conflict itself, which is accompanied by an emotional charge. This occurs in many situations, not just with respect to science and religion. Indeed, scientists repeatedly encounter conflicts within their science, for example when a scientist's prediction from a theory fails to be confirmed. At a more elevated level we might cite Albert Einstein's awareness of the deep incompatibility between electromagnetism and the general theory of relativity. Likewise, he possessed a strong aversion to the statistical understanding of quantum mechanics, which he viewed as incompatible with his notion of the laws of nature. Thus he complained to one correspondent: 'I find the idea that there should not be laws for being, but only laws for probabilities, simply monstrous (a nauseatingly indirect description)'.[17] Individuals also repeatedly experience similar conflicts within their religious lives. For example Charles Darwin was much exercised by the doctrine of eternal damnation following the death of his father in 1848. He could not accept that his father would be subjected to eternal torment – that 'damnable doctrine', as Darwin described it – just because his father was not a true believer.[18] This dissonance played a significant role in Charles Darwin's loss of faith.

The type of conflict I have been discussing is a recurrent phenomenon not only in the science–religion domain but also within science and also within religion; indeed, it occurs in other intellectual disciplines. There is a distinction to be drawn between potential conflicts (which exist in the realm of ideas in themselves) and the recognition of conflict. Doubtless for much of the time we are unaware of the potential dissonances within our lives. As an historian I am primarily interested in the perceived dissonances. These can be highly individualistic; for example most of Einstein's contemporaries in the physics community did not appreciate his perception of the conceptual rupture between electromagnetism and relativity theory.

A second pertinent issue arising from Festinger's theory is the claim that people attempt to frame new thoughts or beliefs, or to modify existing beliefs, in order to reduce the dissonance between cognitions. To quote Festinger's empirical study of the doomsday cult, he comments that following the discomfort produced by dissonance 'there will arise pressure to reduce or eliminate the dissonance. Attempts to reduce dissonance represent the observable manifestations that dissonance exists'.[19] There are many ways to reduce or eliminate dissonance. To take one example that features prominently in the history of science–religion interactions, science and religion can be consigned to separate, non-interacting domains – what Ian Barbour would call an *Independence* strategy – so that immediate dissonance is avoided. This example has one interesting implication: rather than seeing Barbour's *Conflict* and *Independence* strategies[20] as totally separate, viewed through Festinger's lens we see them both as responses to underlying tensions – a point to which I shall return.

Let me now work through one example in more detail with the help of Kenneth Howell's analysis of the conflicts over astronomy and theology in the early modern period. From early in his astronomical career the Danish astronomer Tycho Brahe had become convinced that both the Ptolemaic and Copernican systems were observationally inadequate. Yet he was increasingly attracted to the Copernican theory because it provided a more satisfactory account of the natural ordering of the planets. Copernicus attributed three motions to the earth – the diurnal spin, the annual transit round the sun, and the annual tilting motion of its axis. But, as Tycho states, attributing motion to the earth 'openly contradicts Sacred Scripture in not a few places'. It should also be remembered that there was no empirical support for the motion of the earth, and therefore 'Sacred Scripture' was commensurate with Tycho's understanding of the physics of a stationary earth. Here we see a whole series of unresolved tensions arising between the two astronomical theories under consideration, the empirical evidence, notions of simplicity, and Tycho's understanding of the Bible. After some time he achieved a form of resolution, which he reported to a contemporary in a letter of 1588:

So when I had turned this matter over in my mind in various ways, I carefully considered the [possibility] of another set of hypotheses. At first, I seemed to struggle against impossible odds when unexpectedly it occurred to me that if the sun is situated as the center of the five planets and yet revolves yearly around the earth which is at rest ... [the problems are overcome].

Confronted by these several tensions – note his *struggle* – Tycho eventually resolved them by framing a new astronomical system (which bears his name). Unlike the Copernican system, the Tychonic was commensurate with the biblically sanctioned view of a stationary earth.[21]

One historian who has made effective use of a more elaborated form of Festinger's theory of cognitive dissonance in discussing the history of science and religion is James Moore. In his *Post-Darwinian controversies* (1979) Moore examines a number of Protestant writers who tried to make sense both of their religion and also of the new and challenging idea of organic evolution. He notes that some writers abandoned Christianity while holding firm to evolution, whereas others maintained their religion while jettisoning Darwin's theory. Yet for Moore the historically interesting individuals are those who made more sophisticated moves towards a resolution, while retaining significant parts of both their religion and the challenging theory of evolution. But in achieving a new synthesis they had also to reject or modify parts of each.

A particularly complex and fascinating example discussed by Moore is the Catholic zoologist St George Jackson Mivart, who aligned himself with Darwin and Huxley soon after the publication of *On the origin of species* (1859). He suffered increasing torment in trying to resolve the conflict between Darwin's theory and his religious commitments. The partial resolution he reached in his 1871 book, *On the genesis of species*, involved rejecting natural selection as the primary mechanism for evolution; instead he attributed to organisms certain intrinsic powers. For this heresy he suffered at the hands of the Darwinians, and to add to his tribulations he was later excommunicated by the Catholic Church.[22]

Drawing on these examples, the scenario I am suggesting is as follows. Individuals try to make sense of their experience, which for each individual includes knowledge or beliefs concerning many diverse aspects of both religion and science. Individuals may perceive tensions within religion (such as the existence of evil in a world created by a benevolent Creator) and also within their view of science (such as light sometimes behaving like a wave and in other circumstances like a particle). Moreover, conflicts, tensions, dissonances, or whatever you want to call them are likely to occur between a person's understanding of science and of religion. Historical actors who recognize these tensions will often try to minimize them (especially if the tensions lead to distress), one strategy being to frame a relevant problem for which a solution can be sought.

My argument assumes that there will at any time be numerous potential tensions between science and religion, at least some of which will be actualized in informed individuals. The range and intensity of these dissonances will depend on the actor's own religious and scientific commitments; those who take an intelligent interest in one or both topics are most likely to experience such dissonances. Certain kinds of religious movement may also accentuate or resolve tensions; for example dogmatic forms of religion may both recognize a conflict with science but also provide their followers with easy ways of avoiding any confrontations. Again, I would hypothesize that new large-scale theories in science that make strong ontological and epistemological claims – such as Newtonian mechanics or Darwin's theory of evolution – are likely to create many fresh tensions.

One of my intuitions is that conflicts of the kind I have been discussing are thick on the ground because science has very effectively generated its own facts, methods, practices, and theories. From the seventeenth century onwards science has gained a fair degree of autonomy from both religion and philosophy, and this increasing historical separation of science and religion has fuelled the potential for conflict. Although the precise nature of any perceived conflict will depend on the historical actor and context, we see certain conceptually important themes, such as the challenge of materialism, recurring throughout the early modern and modern periods.

The view of conflict that I am advancing adds an important new dimension to discussions of science and religion and differs significantly from the hackneyed CT. That thesis portrays conflict solely in a negative light and assumes that it must be destructive, one side being the winner, the other the loser. The current confrontation between evolutionists and Christian creationists seems to be of this kind, since it has produced much heat and anger but so far very little light. However, both from a philosophical and a psychological standpoint the type of conflict I have been discussing should be viewed very differently. As theorists of social conflict have noted, some forms of conflict can indeed be destructive, but conflict is also necessary for change, for example in helping to sweep away a corrupt regime. In the context of science and religion, conflict has been the engine of change, even perhaps of what we might call progress. As one conflict

theorist writes: 'Our very experience presupposes conflict in its generation, and our knowledge, apart from its apriori categories, is based on
such conflict. Man's learning about himself, others, and reality, his growth
and development, and his increasing ability to create his own heaven or
hell, comes through conflict'.[23] Internal conflict is necessary for any
innovation in science, in religion, but also in the science–religion domain.

A more philosophical gloss can be given to the above discussion by citing
the philosophies of science of Karl Popper and Larry Laudan, who both
emphasize problem-solving as a crucial part of science and also the role
of dissonance in framing such problems.[24] Problem-solving is crucially
important not only to science but also to religion. Although certain dogmatic forms of religion have innate resistance to change, many religions
include critical traditions that sanction change. New religious movements
arise by addressing the dissonances of the old. For example, in his wonder-
fully entitled *Rational rabbis* Menachem Fisch identified two strands within
the history of Judaism – one authoritarian and the other anti-authoritarian.
Proponents of the latter were good Popperians in the sense that they argued
over interpretations of the Torah and of rabbinic commentaries. From their
arguments came new insights and understandings.[25]

The view I have been advancing has another interesting implication for
our understanding of science–religion interrelations. In his well-known
taxonomy of science–religion interactions Ian Barbour identifies *Conflict*
as separate from *Dialogue* (where there is some sharing between science and
religion).[26] However, rather than portraying *Conflict* as being opposed to
Dialogue, I would argue for a dialectical relationship between *Conflict* and
Dialogue, such that *Conflict* can lead to *Dialogue*, and *Dialogue* to *Conflict*.
From this standpoint, conflict can be intellectually constructive.

The arguments advanced in this chapter also make me wary of the
claim that science and religion are in harmony. As noted above, this view,
if propounded in a simple form, is subject to criticisms similar to those
that have been made of CT. Moreover, the view that science and religion
exist in necessary harmony seems to me a rather saccharine view and not
intellectually generative. However, if this harmony is the hard-won outcome of conflict, then it may have some virtue.

SOCIAL CONFLICTS

The preceding discussion has focussed on individuals and how they
manage inner conflicts over issues of science and religion. We now move
to consider briefly how these conflicts emerge in the public domain and
are mobilized by social groups; that is, how they become controversies.

There are many routes by which a conflict can become a controversy. Festinger gives one example: he argues that one way to reduce dissonance is to reject compromise and instead try to convince others of the correctness of one's own system. He used this explanation to account for the members of his doomsday cult forming an isolated but socially cohesive group whose members were convinced of the truth of their own beliefs and stood opposed to all doubters.[27] This social process creates insiders and outsiders and operates through power relations. As theorists of conflict emphasize, conflict involves just this exercise of power, where opposing groups – each with its own set of commitments – seek to achieve incompatible goals.

This is not the place to categorize the different kinds of social conflict, but in any particular case it is important to establish precisely the roles played both by science and by religion. One difficulty with CT is that it asserts that the lines are to be drawn with science on one side and religion on the opposing side. However, what has emerged from a number of historical case studies is that in many instances this is not the case; instead the alignments are usually far more complex. For example the protagonists may hold very different notions not only of science but also of religion. Thus in the early years of its existence the British Association for the Advancement of Science came under attack from the Dean of York, William Cockburn, who claimed that some of those attending the Association had 'deeper thoughts of evil – hoping to invalidate our trust in a religion which is opposed to all their passions and their vices'. He particularly railed against contemporary geologists. This controversy between the Dean and the British Association geologists would appear at first sight to be an example of the conflict between science and religion, the Dean fighting the irreligious geologists. However, this case looks very different if we remember that the leading geologists whom Cockburn was attacking were themselves Anglican clergy – like the Reverend William Buckland, the Reverend Adam Sedgwick, and the Reverend William Conybeare. Thus we are not faced with an example of science *versus* religion, but of a conservative Anglican committed to Mosaic geology *versus* a group of liberal Anglicans upholding new theories and practices in geology.[28]

There is, however, one type of conflict that deserves particular attention. To appreciate its significance we need to focus on the mid-Victorian period, and especially the 1870s, when the notion of conflict began to take on a new meaning. One of the first books to be structured on the idea of a 'preordained and necessary' conflict between two opposing worldviews was John William Draper's three-volume *History of the American Civil War*

(1868–70), in which he attributed to climate the creation of two hostile groups of states, the North and the South, the former being committed to freedom, the latter to slavery. Draper quoted approvingly a famous speech in which Senator William H. Seward had predicted the Civil War as the outcome of 'an irrepressible conflict between [these] opposing and enduring forces'.[29] This book of Draper's was published just a few years before the publication of his *History of the conflict between religion and science* in which he likewise postulated a 'preordained and necessary' conflict, but this time between science and religion. It appeared very shortly after John Tyndall's famous presidential address before the British Association in Belfast, for which Tyndall was widely criticized for endorsing materialism and therefore atheism. As Frank Turner has noted, 'no single incident in the conflict of science and religion raised so much furore' as Tyndall's address.[30]

The close temporal connection between Tyndall's address and Draper's *History of the conflict between religion and science* suggests that the strong version of CT only took root in the 1870s, and that from the 1870s science became a weapon to be wielded in public attacks on religion. One example of this deployment of science occurred at the 1927 meeting in Leeds of the British Association. The president that year was the palaeoanthropologist Arthur Keith, who was active in the Rationalist Press Association. Keith deliberately used his presidential address, entitled 'Darwin's theory of man's descent as it stands today', to excite religious controversy. He argued that evolution is a purely mechanistic process, such that hominids were the result of numerous small local modifications and had not emerged by a process of progressive change. Moreover, since these modifications could not be predicted, there was no overall plan. Keith exploited this high-profile lecture at the British Association not only to argue for the importance of Darwin's theory in enabling us to trace the common ancestry we share with the anthropoid ape but also to refute the view of man's special creation. Indeed, he opened his address by referring back to the 1858 British Association meeting, which was also held in Leeds, when 'the first verbal shot' had been fired 'of that long and bitter strife which ended in the overthrow of those who defended the Biblical account of man's creation and in a victory for Darwin'.[31] Keith's address was calculated to infuriate the clergy – and it did. In much the same way Richard Dawkins, Peter Atkins, and others have in our own day evoked the power and authority of science to attack religion.

In the eighteenth and early nineteenth centuries religion – specifically, Christianity – came under attack from sceptics and radicals, including

David Hume, Baron d'Holbach, and Thomas Paine, who criticized central aspects of religion as being contrary to reason. There have also been many examples of Christians who considered that certain sciences were corrosive to religion; for example John Hutchinson (who wrote several anti-Newtonian works in the 1720s and 1730s) and his followers mounted attacks on Newton's science and especially on the notion of action at a distance, which they considered to be contrary to revelation. Yet, as Frank Turner argues in his chapter of this volume, a number of developments in both science and Christianity especially during the third quarter of the nineteenth century conspired to give the discourse of conflict a far higher cultural profile and extensive popularity. It was widely recognized that the generally supportive relationship between science and religion that had existed a generation earlier had come under considerable strain, even by those who sought to heal the rift. In the 1860s and 1870s the discourse of conflict had achieved a previously unattained level of social legitimacy, aided by those like Huxley and Tyndall who saw the Church as an impediment to scientific progress. Keith's 1927 British Association address and Dawkins's attacks on religion in the name of science build on these mid-Victorian perceptions. Thus CT itself possesses a history and one that has been part of the history of science and religion over the last 150 years.

CONCLUDING REMARKS

Some years ago I asked a friend who is both a scientist and a member of an Ultra-Orthodox Jewish community how he coped with these two aspects of his life. He replied, 'With exquisite difficulty'. I do not think we should lose sight of either the difficulty or the subtlety of the conflicts that inhabit the science–religion domain. While historians have rightly rejected strong versions of CT, I have argued in this chapter that we should not overlook the recurrent conflicts between science and religion in the modern period. I have particularly pointed to inner conflicts that litter the field and also those that manifest themselves in overheated public controversies. In so doing I want to recover the importance of at least certain types of conflict as necessary for the creative engagement of science and religion.

The argument of this chapter also challenges some of the most frequently articulated responses both by members of religious communities and by atheists. For the former the coherence between science and their own religious positions is often taken as a vindication of (their) religion, and they strive to demonstrate the harmony between science and (their) religion. However, my argument implies that the absence of any kind of conflict should not be taken as a feather in religion's cap. Instead the absence of conflict may well indicate the lack of critical awareness on the part of such religious people. Their religion may be intellectually stagnant. On the other hand, the atheist who views all forms of conflict between science and religion as arguments against religion should not see this as evidence of the victory of atheism. My argument instead implies that any self-critical religious tradition would expect the kind of tension discussed in the third section of this chapter. Indeed, far from undermining religion, such tensions seem necessary for its intellectual development.

But there is one final issue I want to raise. Historians have become used to referring to CT as a myth. The word 'myth' has been used in two very different ways: a myth can be taken as a false belief, or, in the anthropological sense, it is a story that members of a social group take to be true. Most historians criticize CT as a myth of the first kind – it is simply false. Yet I am more concerned with how CT has operated as a cultural construct. This raises some challenging questions for the historian. If I am correct in suggesting that CT gained prominence in the 1870s, why were books like Draper's and White's so influential? And what has sustained this myth for the last century and a half? What functions does it perform? And, lastly, why has it proved so difficult for us – the revisionist historians – to eradicate? Perhaps there is more to the 'Conflict Thesis' than we think.

NOTES

I would like to express my deep appreciation to Barbara Cantor, Thomas Dixon, Chris Kenny, Bernie Lightman, Ron Numbers, Matthew Stanley, and Jon Topham for their helpful comments on earlier versions of this chapter.

1 John Rutty, *A spiritual diary and soliloquies*, 2nd edn, 2 vols. (London: James Phillips, 1776), vol. I, pp. 86, 256, and 276. These entries are dated 8th of the second month 1756, 13th of the fourth month 1760, and 12th of the tenth month 1760.
2 Rutty is discussed in my *Quakers, Jews, and science: Religious responses to modernity and the sciences in Britain, 1650–1900* (Oxford: Oxford University Press, 2005), pp. 243–4.
3 For example, [W. Allen], *Life of William Allen, with selections from his correspondence*, 3 vols. (London: Gilpin, 1846–7) and [Anon.], *A memoir of John Barlow* (London: Friends' Tract Society, 1889).
4 Colin A. Russell, 'The conflict of science and religion', in Gary B. Ferngren *et al.* (eds.), *The history of science and religion in the western tradition: An encyclopedia* (New York and London: Garland, 2000), pp. 12–16.

5 John William Draper, *History of the conflict between religion and science* (London: Henry S. King & Co., 1875) and Andrew Dixon White, *A history of the warfare of science with theology in Christendom*, 2 vols. (New York: D. Appleton & Co., 1896). James R. Moore discusses the history of the 'Conflict Thesis' in his *The post-Darwinian controversies: A study of the Protestant struggle to come to terms with Darwin in Great Britain and America, 1870–1900* (Cambridge: Cambridge University Press, 1979), pp. 19–49.

6 Draper, *History*, p. 8.

7 Richard Dawkins, 'Is science a religion?', *The Humanist* 57 (January–February 1997), available at http://www.thehumanist.org/humanist/articles/dawkins.html

8 John Hedley Brooke, *Science and religion: Some historical perspectives* (Cambridge: Cambridge University Press, 1991), p. 42.

9 Ibid.

10 Introduction to David C. Lindberg and Ronald L. Numbers (eds.), *God and nature: Historical essays on the encounter between Christianity and science* (Berkeley and Los Angeles, CA: University of California Press, 1986), p. 10; Introduction to Lindberg and Numbers (eds.), *Science and Christianity* (Chicago: University of Chicago Press, 2003), pp. 1–5. Some writers have coined the term 'Harmony Thesis' in postulating the complete coherence between science and religion. It is open to the same objections as CT is.

11 I'm not sure whether the recognition of historical complexity deserves to be called a thesis; the claim that we see 'complexity' in history sheds little light on the specific question of how science and religion interrelate. Moreover the discovery of 'complexity' is not confined to the historical study of science and religion. In every branch of history with which I am familiar, historians have forsaken Whiggish narratives and instead pursued contextualism by examining closely the primary sources and have found that master-narratives are inadequate and that the situation turns out to be far more complex. See also John Hedley Brooke, 'A call for complexity', *Science and Spirit*, January–February 2006, available at http://www.science-spirit.org/webexclusives.php?article_id=590

12 For example, David B. Wilson, 'The historiography of science and religion', in Ferngren *et al.*, *History of science and religion*, pp. 3–11.

13 The classic analysis of Whig history is Herbert Butterfield, *The Whig interpretation of history* (London: G. Bell, 1931). As Nick Jardine notes ('Whigs and stories: Herbert Butterfield and the historiography of science', *History of Science* 41 (2003), 125–40) it became commonplace in the 1960s and 1970s for historians of science to repudiate attempts to read history as a triumphalist accretion of knowledge. However, it is now recognized that a more sophisticated position needs to be adopted between past and present and that a simple opposition to Whiggism is not adequate.

14 R. J. Rummel, *Understanding conflict and war. Vol. II, The conflict helix* (Beverly Hills, CA: Sage, 1976), p. 237.

15 Thomas Söderqvist, 'Essential projects and existential choice in science: science biography as an edifying genre', in Michael Shortland and Richard

Yeo (eds.), *Telling lives in science: Essays on scientific biography* (Cambridge: Cambridge University Press, 1996), pp. 45–84.

16 Leon Festinger, Henry W. Riecken, and Stanley Schachter, *When prophecy fails* (Minneapolis: University of Minnesota Press, 1956), p. 26; Festinger, *A theory of cognitive dissonance* (Stanford, CA: Stanford University Press, 1957).

17 John Stachel, 'Einstein and the quantum: Fifty years of struggle', in Stachel, *Einstein from 'B' to 'Z'* (Boston, MA: Birkhauser, 2002), pp. 367–402, on p. 374.

18 Nora Barlow (ed.), *The autobiography of Charles Darwin* (London: Collins, 1958), p. 87.

19 Festinger, Riecken, and Schachter, *When prophecy fails*, p. 26.

20 Ian G. Barbour, *Science and religion: Historical and contemporary issues* (San Francisco: HarperSanFrancisco, 1997), pp. 77–105. See also Mikael Stenmark, *How to relate science and religion: A multidimensional model* (Grand Rapids, MI: Eerdmans, 2004); Geoffrey Cantor and Chris Kenny, 'Barbour's four-fold way: Problems with his taxonomy of science–religion relationships', *Zygon* 36 (2001), 763–79.

21 Kenneth J. Howell, *God's two books: Copernican cosmology and biblical interpretation in early modern science* (Notre Dame, IN: University of Notre Dame Press, 2002), pp. 73–97, esp. p. 85.

22 Moore, *Post-Darwinian controversies*, pp. 14–16 and 110–22. On Mivart and his *On the genesis of species* (London: Macmillan, 1871), see also Jacob W. Gruber, *A conscience in conflict: The life of St George Jackson Mivart* (New York: Columbia University Press, 1960).

23 Rummel, *Understanding conflict and war*, vol. II, p. 238.

24 Karl Popper, *All life is problem solving* (London: Routledge, 1999); Larry Laudan, *Progress and its problems: Towards a theory of scientific growth* (London: Routledge and Kegan Paul, 1977).

25 Menachem Fisch, *Rational rabbis: Science and Talmudic culture* (Bloomington and Indianapolis: University of Indiana Press, 1997).

26 Barbour, *Science and religion*, pp. 77–105.

27 Festinger, Riecken, and Schachter, *When prophecy fails*, pp. 193–315.

28 My discussion draws on Jonathan Topham's paper '"The dangers of peripatetic philosophy": Contesting geology at the early BAAS', delivered at the British Association meeting in York, September 2007. My sincere thanks to Dr Topham for generously allowing me to draw on his researches. The quotation is from William Cockburn, *Remarks on the geological lectures of F. J. Francis* (London: J. Hatchard & Son, 1839), p. 16.

29 John William Draper, *History of the American Civil War*, 3 vols. (New York: Harper & Brothers, 1868–70), vol. I, pp. 17–38, esp. p. 31.

30 Frank Turner, *Contesting cultural authority: Essays in Victorian intellectual life* (Cambridge: Cambridge University Press, 1993), p. 196.

31 'The British Association', *The Times*, 1 September 1927, p. 7.

Select bibliography

This bibliography, starting with the principal publications of John Hedley Brooke, is arranged thematically and is intended to provide helpful starting points for further reading on the topics covered in this volume. Accordingly, it primarily recommends works on the history of engagements between science and religion since the seventeenth century. It includes some but by no means all of the works referred to in each chapter above, which are fully referenced in footnotes, and also additional material not cited above.

PRINCIPAL PUBLICATIONS BY JOHN HEDLEY BROOKE

(His edited volumes are included in 'Edited collections and encyclopaedias', below.)

John Hedley Brooke 1977 'Natural theology and the plurality of worlds: Observations on the Brewster–Whewell debate', *Annals of Science* 34, 221–86.

'Richard Owen, William Whewell and the *Vestiges*', *British Journal for the History of Science* 10, 132–45.

1979 'The natural theology of the geologists: Some theological strata', in L. Jordanova and R. Porter (eds.), *Images of the earth*, Chalfont St Giles: British Society for the History of Science monograph no. 1, 1979, pp. 39–64. 2nd rev. edn, 1997, pp. 53–74.

'Nebular contraction and the expansion of naturalism', *British Journal for the History of Science* 12, 200–11.

1985 'The relations between Darwin's science and his religion', in John R. Durant (ed.), *Darwinism and divinity: Essays on evolution and religious belief*, Oxford: Blackwell, pp. 40–75.

1987 'Joseph Priestley and William Whewell, apologists and historians of science: A tale of two stereotypes', in R. Anderson and C. Lawrence (eds.), *Science, medicine and dissent: Joseph Priestley*, London: Wellcome Foundation and Science Museum, pp. 11–27.

'Why did the English mix their science and their religion?', in S. Rossi (ed.), *Science and imagination in 18th-century British culture*, Milan: Edizioni Unicopli, pp. 57–78.

1988 'The God of Isaac Newton', in J. Fauvel, R. Flood, M. Shortland, and R. Wilson (eds.), *Let Newton be!*, Oxford: Oxford University Press, pp. 169–83.

1989 'Science and the fortunes of natural theology: Some historical perspectives', *Zygon* 24, 3–22.

'Science and the secularisation of knowledge: Perspectives on some 18th-century transformations', *Nuncius: Annali di Storia della Scienza* 4, 43–65.

'Scientific thought and its meaning for religion: The impact of French science on British natural theology, 1827–1859', *Revue de Synthèse* 4, 33–59.

1990 'Between science and theology: The defence of teleology in the interpretation of nature, 1820–1876', *Proceedings of the 19th-century Working Group of the American Academy of Religion* 16, 80–94. Republished in the *Journal for the History of Modern Theology* 1 (1994), 47–65.

'Science and religion', in G. Cantor, J. Christie, J. Hodge, and R. Olby (eds.), *A companion to the history of modern science*, London: Routledge, pp. 763–82.

'"A sower went forth": Joseph Priestley and the ministry of reform', in A. Truman Schwarz and J. G. McEvoy (eds.), *Motion toward perfection: The achievement of Joseph Priestley*, Boston, MA: Skinner House, pp. 21–56.

1991 'Indications of a creator: Whewell as apologist and priest', in M. Fisch and S. Schaffer (eds.), *William Whewell: A composite portrait*, Oxford: Clarendon Press, pp. 149–73.

Science and religion: Some historical perspectives, Cambridge: Cambridge University Press. (Foreign language editions include Chinese, Greek, Portuguese, Romanian, and Russian translations.)

1992 'Natural law in the natural sciences: The origins of modern atheism?', *Science and Christian Belief* 4, 83–103.

1995 *Thinking about matter: Studies in the history of chemical philosophy*, Aldershot: Ashgate.

1996 'Like minds: The god of Hugh Miller', in Michael Shortland (ed.), *Hugh Miller and the controversies of Victorian science*, Oxford: Oxford University Press, pp. 171–86.

'Religious apologetics and the transmutation of knowledge: Was a chemico-theology possible in 18th- and early-19th century Britain?', in van der Meer (ed.), *Facets of faith and science*, vol. IV, pp. 215–29.

'Religious belief and the natural sciences: Mapping the historical landscape', in van der Meer (ed.), *Facets of faith and science*, vol. I, pp. 1–26.

'Science and theology in the enlightenment', in Richardson and Wildman (eds.), *Religion and science*, pp. 7–27.

1997 'L'essor d'une culture scientifique', in H. McLeod, S. Mews, and C. d'Haussy (eds.), *Histoire religieuse de la Grande-Bretagne*, Paris: Les Éditions du Cerf, pp. 261–85.

1998 *Reconstructing Nature: The engagement of science and religion. The 1995–6 Gifford Lectures at Glasgow*, Edinburgh: T & T Clark. Jointly authored with Geoffrey Cantor.

1999 'The history of science and religion: Some evangelical dimensions', in Hart, Livingstone, and Noll (eds.), *Evangelicals and science*, pp. 17–40.

'Presidential address: Does the history of science have a future?', *British Journal for the History of Science* 32, 1–20.

2000 '"Wise men nowadays think otherwise": John Ray, natural theology and the meanings of anthropocentrism', *Notes and Records of the Royal Society* 54, 199–213.

2001 'Religious belief and the content of the sciences', in Brooke, Osler, and van der Meer (eds.), *Science in theistic contexts* pp. 3–28.

'Science and secularization', in L. Woodhead (ed.), *Reinventing Christianity*, Aldershot: Ashgate, pp. 229–38.

'The Wilberforce–Huxley debate: Why did it happen?', *Science and Christian Belief* 13, 127–41.

2002 'The changing relations between science and religion', in H. Reagan and M. Worthing (eds.), *Interdisciplinary perspectives on cosmology and biological evolution*, Adelaide: Australian Theological Forum, pp. 3–18.

'Darwin and Victorian Christianity', in Gregory Radick and Jonathan Hodge (eds.), *The Cambridge companion to Darwin*, Cambridge: Cambridge University Press, pp. 192–213.

2003 'Detracting from divine power? Religious belief and the appraisal of new technologies', in Celia Deane-Drummond and Bronislaw Szerszynski (eds.), *Reordering nature: Theology, society and the new genetics*, London: T & T Clark, pp. 43–64.

'Improvable nature?', in Willem Drees (ed.), *Is nature ever evil?: Religion, science and value*, London: Routledge, pp. 149–69.

'Science and religion', in Roy Porter (ed.), *The Cambridge history of science: Vol. IV Eighteenth-century science*, Cambridge: Cambridge University Press, pp. 741–61.

2004 'Science and dissent: Some historiographical issues', in Wood (ed.), *Science and dissent*, pp. 19–37.

2005 'Darwin, design, and the unification of nature', in Proctor (ed.), *Science, religion, and the human experience*, pp. 165–83.

'Joining natural philosophy to Christianity: The case of Joseph Priestley', in Brooke and Maclean (eds.), *Heterodoxy*, pp. 319–36.

'Learning from the past', in Christopher Southgate (ed.), *God, humanity and the cosmos*, London: T & T Clark, pp. 63–81.

2006 'Contributions from the history of science and religion', in Clayton and Simpson (eds.), *Oxford handbook* pp. 293–310.

'Darwin and God: Then and now', *Harvard Divinity Bulletin*, Autumn 2006, 76–85.

'Friends and enemies: Breaking down the dichotomies', *Modern Believing* 47 (no. 4), 5–16.

'"If I were God": Einstein and Religion', *Zygon* 41, 941–54.

'Science and the self: What difference did Darwin make?', in F. Leron Shults (ed.), *The evolution of rationality: Interdisciplinary essays in Honor of J. Wentzel Van Huyssteen*, Grand Rapids, MI: Eerdmans, pp. 253–73.

'The search for extra-terrestrial life: Historical and theological perspectives', *Omega: Indian Journal of Science and Religion* 5 (no. 1), 6–22.

2007 'La ciencia en los Unitarios', in José Montesinos and Sergio Toledo (eds.), *Ciencia y religion en la edad moderna*, La Orotava: Fundación Canaria Orotava de Historia de la Ciencia, pp. 253–71.

'Overtaking nature? The changing scope of organic chemistry in the nineteenth century', in Bernadette Bensaude-Vincent and William R. Newman (eds.), *The artificial and the natural: An evolving polarity*, Cambridge, MA: MIT Press, pp. 275–92.

2009 '"Laws impressed on matter by the deity"? The *Origin* and the question of religion', in Michael Ruse and Robert J. Richards (eds.), *The Cambridge companion to the 'Origin of Species'*, Cambridge: Cambridge University Press, pp. 256–74.

(forthcoming) 'Science and secularization', in P. Harrison (ed.), *The Cambridge companion to science and religion*, Cambridge: Cambridge University Press.

EDITED COLLECTIONS AND ENCYCLOPAEDIAS

Brooke, John H., and E. Ihsanoglu (eds.), *Religious values and the rise of science in Europe*, Istanbul: Research Centre for Islamic History, Art and Culture, 2005.

and Ian Maclean (eds.), *Heterodoxy in early modern science and religion*, Oxford: Oxford University Press, 2005.

M. J. Osler, and J. van der Meer (eds.), *Science in theistic contexts: Cognitive dimensions*, Chicago: University of Chicago Press, 2001.

and Ronald L. Numbers (eds.), *Science and religion around the world*, New York: Oxford University Press, 2010.

Clayton, Philip, and Zachary Simpson (eds.), *The Oxford handbook of religion and science*, Oxford: Oxford University Press, 2006.

Ferngren, Gary B. (ed.), *Science and religion: A historical introduction*, Baltimore, MD: Johns Hopkins University Press, 2002.

et al. (eds.), *The history of science and religion in the western tradition: An encyclopedia*, New York and London: Garland, 2000.

Harrison, Peter (ed.), *The Cambridge companion to science and religion*, Cambridge: Cambridge University Press, (forthcoming).

Hart, D., D. Livingstone, and M. Noll (eds.), *Evangelicals and science in historical perspective*, Oxford: Oxford University Press, 1999.

Killeen, Kevin, and Peter Forshaw (eds.), *The Word and the world: Biblical exegesis and early modern science*, London: Palgrave Macmillan, 2007.

Knight, David, and Matthew Eddy (eds.), *Science and beliefs: From natural philosophy to natural science*, Aldershot: Ashgate, 2005.

Lindberg, David C., and Ronald L. Numbers (eds.), *God and nature: Historical essays on the encounter between Christianity and science*, Berkeley, CA: University of California Press, 1986.

When science and Christianity meet, Chicago: University of Chicago Press, 2003.

Numbers, Ronald L. (ed.), *Galileo goes to jail and other myths about science and religion*, Cambridge, MA: Harvard University Press, 2009.

Proctor, James D. (ed.), *Science, religion, and the human experience*, New York: Oxford University Press, 2005.

Richardson, W. Mark, and Wesley J. Wildman (eds.), *Religion and science: History, method and dialogue*, London: Routledge, 1996.

van der Meer, Jitse (ed.), *Facets of faith and science*, 4 vols., New York: University Press of America, 1996.

van Huyssteen, J. Wentzel (ed.), *Encyclopedia of science and religion*, 2 vols., New York: Macmillan, 2003.

Wood, Paul (ed.), *Science and dissent in England 1688–1945*, Aldershot: Ashgate, 2004.

OVERVIEWS AND GENERAL WORKS

Dixon, Thomas, *Science and religion: A very short introduction*, Oxford: Oxford University Press, 2008.

Livingstone, David N., *Adam's ancestors: Race, religion, and the politics of human origins*, Baltimore, MD: Johns Hopkins University Press, 2008.

McGrath, Alister E., *Science and religion: An introduction*, Oxford: Blackwell, 1999.

Numbers, Ronald L., *Science and Christianity in pulpit and pew*, New York: Oxford University Press, 2007.

Olson, Richard, *Science and religion, 1450–1900: From Copernicus to Darwin*, Westport, CT: Greenwood Press, 1994.

Russell, Colin A., *Cross-currents: Interactions between science and faith*, Leicester: Inter-Varsity, 1985.

Taylor, Charles, *A secular age*, Cambridge, MA: Belknap Press of Harvard University Press, 2007.

PARTICULAR (NON-PROTESTANT) RELIGIOUS TRADITIONS

a) Hinduism and Buddhism

Bayly, C. A., *Empire and information: Intelligence gathering and social communication in India, 1780–1870*, Cambridge: Cambridge University Press, 1996.

Dodson, Michael, 'Re-presented for the Pandits: James Ballantyne, "useful knowledge", and Sanskrit scholarship in Benares College during the nineteenth century', *Modern Asian Studies* 36 (2002), 257–98.

Orientalism, empire and national culture: India, 1770–1880, Basingstoke: Palgrave Macmillan, 2007.

Killingley, Dermot, 'Hinduism, Darwinism and evolution in late nineteenth-century India', in David Amigoni and Jeff Wallace (eds.), *Charles Darwin's The origin of species: New interdisciplinary essays*, Manchester: University of Manchester Press, 1995, pp. 174–202.

Lopez, Donald S., *Buddhism and science: A guide for the perplexed*, Chicago: University of Chicago Press, 2008.

Sivasundaram, Sujit, '"A Christian Benares": Orientalism and science in the Serampore Mission of Bengal', *Indian Economic and Social History Review* 44 (2007), 111–45.

Young, Richard Fox, *Resistant Hinduism: Sanskrit sources on anti-Christian apologetics in early nineteenth-century India*, Vienna: Institut für Indologie der Universität Wien, 1991.

'Receding from antiquity: Hindu responses to science and Christianity on the margins of Empire, 1800–1850', in Robert Frykenberg (ed.), *Christians and missionaries in India: Cross-cultural communication since 1500*, Grand Rapids, MI: Eerdmans, 2003, pp. 183–222.

and G. P. V. Somaratna, *Vain debates: The Buddhist–Christian controversies of nineteenth-century Ceylon*, Vienna: De Nobili Research Library, 1996.

b) Islam

Ben-Zaken, Avner, 'Heavens of the sky and the heavens of the heart: The Ottoman cultural context for the introduction of post-Copernican astronomy', *British Journal for the History of Science* 37 (2004), 1–28.

Daiber, Hans, 'Science and technology versus Islam: A controversy from Renan and Afghani to Nasr and Needham and its historical background', *Annals of Japan Association for Middle East Studies* 8 (1993), 169–80.

Edis, Taner, *An illusion of harmony: Science and religion in Islam*, New York: Prometheus Books, 2007.

Gutas, Dimitri, 'The study of Arabic philosophy in the twentieth century: An essay on the historiography of Arabic philosophy', *British Journal of Middle Eastern Studies* 29 (2002), 5–25.

Huff, Toby E., *The rise of early modern science: Islam, China, and the West*, Cambridge: Cambridge University Press, 1993.

Ragep, F. J., 'Duhem, the Arabs and the history of cosmology', *Revue de Synthèse* 83 (1990), 201–14.

Sabra, A. I., 'The appropriation and subsequent naturalisation of Greek science in medieval Islam', *History of Science* 25 (1987), 223–43.

Saliba, George, *Islamic science and the making of the European Renaissance*, Cambridge, MA: MIT Press, 2007.

Tibi, Bassa, 'The worldview of Sunni Arab fundamentalists: Attitudes towards modern science and technology', in M. E. Marty and R. S. Appleby (eds.), *Fundamentalisms and society: Reclaiming the sciences, the family, and education*, Chicago: University of Chicago Press, 1993, pp. 73–102.

c) Judaism

Cantor, Geoffrey, *Quakers, Jews, and science: Religious responses to modernity and the sciences in Britain, 1650–1900*, Oxford: Oxford University Press, 2005.

and Marc Swetlitz (eds.), *Jewish tradition and the challenge of Darwinism*, Chicago: University of Chicago Press, 2006.

Charpa, Ulrich, and Ute Deichmann (eds.), *Jews and sciences in German contexts: Case studies from the 19th and 20th centuries*, Tübingen: Mohr Siebeck, 2007.

Efron, Noah J., *Judaism and science: A historical introduction*, Westport, CT: Greenwood Press, 2007.

Fisch, Menachem, *Rational rabbis: Science and Talmudic culture*, Bloomington, IN: Indiana University Press, 1997.

Hollinger, David A., *Science, Jews, and secular culture: Studies in mid-twentieth-century American intellectual history*, Princeton, NJ: Princeton University Press, 1996.

Ruderman, David B., *Jewish thought and scientific discovery in early modern Europe*, New Haven, CT: Yale University Press, 1995.

d) Roman Catholicism

Artigas, Mariano, Thomas F. Glick, and Rafael A. Martinez, *Negotiating Darwin: The Vatican confronts evolution, 1877–1902*, Baltimore, MD: Johns Hopkins University Press, 2006.

Finocchiaro, Maurice A., *Retrying Galileo, 1633–1992*, Berkeley, CA: University of California Press, 2007.

Harris, Ruth, *Lourdes: Body and spirit in a secular age*, London: Allen Lane, 1999.

Heilbron, J. L., *The sun in the church: Cathedrals as solar observatories*, Cambridge, MA: Harvard University Press, 1999.

Hess, Peter M. J., and Paul L. Allen, *Catholicism and science*, Westport, CT: Greenwood Press, 2008.

McMullin, Ernan (ed.), *The Church and Galileo*, Notre Dame, IN: University of Notre Dame Press, 2005.

Mullin, Robert B., *Miracles and the modern religious imagination*, New Haven, CT: Yale University Press, 1996.

O'Leary, Don, *Roman Catholicism and modern science: A history*, New York: Continuum, 2006.

Turner, Frank, *John Henry Newman: The challenge to evangelical religion*, New Haven, CT: Yale University Press, 2002.

THE EARLY MODERN PERIOD

Barker, Peter, and Bernard R. Goldstein, 'Theological foundations of Kepler's astronomy', *Osiris* 16 (2001), 88–113.

Cohen, I. Bernard (ed.), *Puritanism and the rise of modern science: The Merton thesis*, New Brunswick, NJ: Rutgers University Press, 1990.

Dear, Peter, *Revolutionizing the sciences: European knowledge and its ambitions, 1500–1700*, Basingstoke: Palgrave, 2001.

Finocchiaro, Maurice A. (ed. and trans.), *The Galileo affair: A documentary history*, Berkeley, CA: University of California Press, 1989.

Force, James E., and Richard H. Popkin, *Essays on the context, nature, and influence of Isaac Newton's theology*, Dordrecht: Kluwer Academic, 1990.

Funkenstein, Amos, *Theology and the scientific imagination*, Princeton, NJ: Princeton University Press, 1986.

Harrison, Peter, *The Bible, Protestantism, and the rise of natural science*, Cambridge: Cambridge University Press, 1998.

'Physico-theology and the mixed sciences: Theology and early modern natural philosophy', in Peter Anstey and John Schuster (eds.), *The science of nature in the seventeenth century*, Dordrecht: Springer, 2005, pp. 165–83.

The fall of man and the foundations of science, Cambridge: Cambridge University Press, 2007.

Heilbron, J. L., *The sun in the church: Cathedrals as solar observatories*, Cambridge, MA: Harvard University Press, 1999.

Hooykaas, R., *Religion and the rise of science*, Grand Rapids, MI: Eerdmans, 1972.

Howell, Kenneth J., *God's two books: Copernican cosmology and biblical interpretation in early modern science*, Notre Dame, IN: University of Notre Dame Press, 2002.

Iliffe, Rob, *Newton: A very short introduction*, Oxford: Oxford University Press, 2007.

Israel, Jonathan I., *Radical enlightenment: Philosophy and the making of modernity, 1650–1750*, Oxford: Oxford University Press, 2001.

Enlightenment contested: Philosophy, modernity, and the emancipation of man 1670–1752, New York: Oxford University Press, 2006.

Lindberg, David C., 'Galileo, the Church, and the cosmos', in Lindberg and Numbers (eds.), *When science and Christianity meet*, pp. 33–60.

McMullin, Ernan (ed.), *The Church and Galileo*, Notre Dame, IN: University of Notre Dame Press, 2005.

Oakley, Francis, *Omnipotence, covenant, and order: An excursion in the history of ideas from Abelard to Leibniz*, Ithaca, NY: Cornell University Press, 1984.

Osler, Margaret J., *Divine will and the mechanical philosophy: Gassendi and Descartes on contingency and necessity in the created world*, Cambridge: Cambridge University Press, 1994.

'Mixing metaphors: Science and religion or natural philosophy and theology in early modern Europe', *History of Science* 3 (1998), 91–113.

(ed.), *Rethinking the scientific revolution*, Cambridge: Cambridge University Press, 2000.

Shapin, Steven, *The scientific revolution*, Chicago: University of Chicago Press, 1996.

Snobelen, Stephen, 'Isaac Newton, heretic: The strategies of a Nicodemite', *British Journal for the History of Science* 32 (1999), 381–419.

'"God of Gods and Lord of Lords": The theology of Isaac Newton's General Scholium to the *Principia*', *Osiris* 16 (2001), 169–208.

'To discourse of God: Isaac Newton's heterodox theology and his natural theology', in Wood (ed.), *Science and dissent*, pp. 39–62.

Westfall, Richard S., *Science and religion in seventeenth-century England*, New Haven, CT: Yale University Press, 1958.

THE NINETEENTH CENTURY

Astore, William J., *Observing God: Thomas Dick, evangelicalism, and popular science in Victorian Britain and America*, Aldershot: Ashgate, 2001.

Barton, Ruth, 'John Tyndall, pantheist: A rereading of the Belfast Address', *Osiris* 3 (1987), 111–34.

Cantor, Geoffrey, *Michael Faraday: Sandemanian and scientist*, London: Macmillan, 1991.

Dixon, Thomas, *From passions to emotions: The creation of a secular psychological category*, Cambridge: Cambridge University Press, 2003.

  'Looking beyond "The Rumpus about Moses and Monkeys": Religion and the sciences in the nineteenth century', *Nineteenth Century Studies* 17 (2003), 25–33.

  The invention of altruism: Making moral meanings in Victorian Britain, Oxford: Oxford University Press, 2008.

Fichman, Martin, *An elusive Victorian: The evolution of Alfred Russel Wallace*, Chicago: University of Chicago Press, 2004.

Fyfe, Aileen, 'The reception of William Paley's *Natural theology* in the University of Cambridge', *British Journal for the History of Science* 30 (1997), 321–35.

  'Publishing and the classics: Paley's *Natural theology* and the nineteenth-century scientific canon', *Studies in the History and Philosophy of Science*, 33 (2002), 433–55.

  Science and salvation: Evangelical popular science publishing in Victorian Britain, Chicago: University of Chicago Press, 2004.

  'Science and religion in popular publishing in nineteenth-century Britain', in Peter Meusburger *et al.* (eds.), *Clashes of knowledge: Orthodoxies and heterodoxies in science and religion*, Dordrecht: Springer Science, 2008, pp. 121–32.

Gregory, Frederick, *Scientific materialism in nineteenth-century Germany*, Dordrecht: Reidel, 1977.

  Nature lost?: Natural science and the German theological traditions of the nineteenth century, Cambridge, MA: Harvard University Press, 1992.

Lightman, Bernard, *The origins of agnosticism: Victorian unbelief and the limits of knowledge*, Baltimore, MD: Johns Hopkins University Press, 1987.

  'Victorian sciences and religions: Discordant harmonies', *Osiris* 16 (2001), 343–66.

  'Scientists as materialists in the periodical press: Tyndall's Belfast Address', in Geoffrey Cantor and Sally Shuttleworth (eds.), *Science serialized: Representations of the sciences in nineteenth-century periodicals*, Cambridge, MA: MIT Press, 2004, 199–238.

  Victorian popularizers of science: Designing nature for new audiences, Chicago: University of Chicago Press, 2007.

Moore, James, 'Herbert Spencer's henchmen: The evolution of Protestant liberals in late nineteenth-century America', in John Durant (ed.), *Darwinism and divinity: Essays on evolution and religious belief*, Oxford: Blackwell, 1985, pp. 76–100.

O'Connor, Ralph, 'Young-earth creationists in early nineteenth-century Britain? Towards a reassessment of "scriptural geology"', *History of Science* 45 (2007), 357–403.

Roberts, Jon H., and James Turner, *The sacred and the secular university*, Princeton, NJ: Princeton University Press, 2000.

Sivasundaram, Sujit, *Nature and the godly empire: Science and evangelical mission in the Pacific, 1795–1850*, Cambridge: Cambridge University Press, 2005.

Topham, Jonathan R., 'Science and popular education in the 1830s: The role of the Bridgewater treatises', *British Journal for the History of Science* 25 (1992), 397–430.

'Beyond the "common context": The production and reading of the Bridgewater treatises', *Isis* 89 (1998), 233–62.

'Science, natural theology, and the practice of Christian piety in early nineteenth-century religious magazines', in Geoffrey Cantor and Sally Shuttleworth (eds.), *Science serialized: Representations of the sciences in nineteenth-century periodicals*, Cambridge, MA: MIT Press, 2004, pp. 37–66.

Turner, Frank M., *Between science and religion: The reaction to scientific naturalism in late Victorian England*, New Haven, CT: Yale University Press, 1974.

'The Victorian conflict between science and religion: A professional dimension', *Isis* 49 (1978), 356–76.

Contesting cultural authority: Essays in Victorian intellectual life, Cambridge: Cambridge University Press, 1993.

John Henry Newman: The challenge to evangelical religion, New Haven, CT: Yale University Press, 2002.

Welch, Claude, 'Dispelling some myths about the split between theology and science in the nineteenth century', in Richardson and Wildman (eds.), *Religion and science*, pp. 29–40.

Wilson, David, 'Victorian science and religion', *History of Science* 15 (1977), 52–67.

Yeo, Richard, 'The principle of plenitude and natural theology in nineteenth-century Britain', *British Journal for the History of Science* 19 (1986), 273–81.

Young, Robert M., 'Natural theology, Victorian periodicals, and the fragmentation of a common context', in Young, *Darwin's metaphor: Nature's place in Victorian culture*, Cambridge: Cambridge University Press, 1985, pp. 126–63.

THE TWENTIETH CENTURY

Bowler, Peter J., *Reconciling science and religion: The debate in early twentieth-century Britain*, Chicago: University of Chicago Press, 2001.

Dillistone, F. W., *Charles Raven: Naturalist, historian, theologian*, London: Hodder and Stoughton, 1975.

Gilbert, James, *Redeeming culture: American religion in an age of science*, Chicago: University of Chicago Press, 1997.

Hayward, Rhodri, *Resisting history: Popular religion and the invention of the unconscious*, Manchester: Manchester University Press, 2007.

Hollinger, David A., *Science, Jews, and secular culture: Studies in mid-twentieth-century American intellectual history*, Princeton, NJ: Princeton University Press, 1996.

Jammer, Max, *Einstein and religion: Physics and theology*, Princeton, NJ: Princeton University Press, 1999.

Moore, James R., 'R. A. Fisher: A faith fit for eugenics', *Studies in History and Philosophy of Biological and Biomedical Sciences* 38 (2007), 110–35.

Richards, Graham, 'Psychology and the Churches in Britain, 1919–1939', *History of the Human Sciences* 13 (2000), 57–84.

Roberts, Jon H., 'Psychoanalysis and American Christianity, 1900–1945', in Lindberg and Numbers (eds.), *When science and Christianity meet*, pp. 225–44.

Rupke, Nicolaas A. (ed.), *Eminent lives in twentieth-century science and religion*, Frankfurt am Main: Peter Lang, 2007.

Stanley, Matthew, *Practical mystic: Religion, science, and A. S. Eddington*, Chicago: University of Chicago Press, 2007.

DARWINISM, EVOLUTION, AND CREATIONISM

Artigas, Mariano, Thomas F. Glick, and Rafael A. Martinez, *Negotiating Darwin: The Vatican confronts evolution, 1877–1902*, Baltimore, MD: Johns Hopkins University Press, 2006.

Bowler, Peter J., *Monkey trials and gorilla sermons: Evolution and Christianity from Darwin to intelligent design*, Cambridge, MA: Harvard University Press, 2007.

Brown, Andrew, *The Darwin wars*, London: Simon and Schuster, 1999.

Cantor, Geoffrey, and Marc Swetlitz (eds.), *Jewish tradition and the challenge of Darwinism*, Chicago: University of Chicago Press, 2006.

Clark, Constance A., *God or gorilla: Images of evolution in the Jazz Age*, Baltimore, MD: Johns Hopkins University Press, 2008.

Desmond, Adrian, and James R. Moore, *Darwin's sacred cause: Race, slavery and the quest for human origins*, London: Allen Lane, 2009.

Durant, John R. (ed.), *Darwinism and divinity: Essays on evolution and religious belief*, Oxford: Blackwell, 1985.

Ellegård, Alvar, *Darwin and the general reader: The reception of Darwin's theory of evolution in the British periodical press, 1859–72*, 2nd edn, Chicago: Chicago University Press, 1990.

James, Frank, 'An "open clash between science and the Church"? Wilberforce, Huxley, and Hooker on Darwin at the British Association, Oxford, 1860', in Knight and Eddy (eds.), *Science and beliefs*, pp. 171–93.

Killingley, Dermot, 'Hinduism, Darwinism and evolution in late nineteenth-century India', in David Amigoni and Jeff Wallace (eds.), *Charles Darwin's The origin of species: New interdisciplinary essays*, Manchester: University of Manchester Press, 1995, pp. 174–202.

Larson, Edward J., *Summer for the gods: The Scopes trial and America's continuing debate over science and religion*, New York: Basic Books, 1997.

    Trial and error: The American controversy over creation and evolution, 3rd edn, Oxford: Oxford University Press, 2003.

Livingstone, David N., *Darwin's forgotten defenders: The encounter between evangelical theology and evolutionary thought*, Grand Rapids, MI: Eerdmans, 1987.

    Adam's ancestors: Race, religion, and the politics of human origins, Baltimore, MD: Johns Hopkins University Press, 2008.

Moore, James R., *The post-Darwinian controversies: A study of the Protestant struggle to come to terms with Darwin in Great Britain and America, 1870–1900*, Cambridge: Cambridge University Press, 1979.

    The Darwin legend, Grand Rapids, MI: Baker Books, 1994.

Numbers, Ronald L., *Darwinism comes to America*, Cambridge, MA: Harvard University Press, 1998.

    The creationists: From scientific creationism to intelligent design, 2nd edn, Cambridge, MA: Harvard University Press, 2006.

    and John Stenhouse (eds.), *Disseminating Darwinism: The role of place, race, religion, and gender*, Cambridge: Cambridge University Press, 1999.

Roberts, Jon H., *Darwinism and the divine in America: Protestant intellectuals and organic evolution, 1859–1900*, Madison: University of Wisconsin Press, 1988.

Ruse, Michael, *Darwin and design: Does evolution have a purpose?*, Cambridge, MA: Harvard University Press, 2003.

Scott, Eugenie C., *Evolution vs creationism: An introduction*, Westport, CT: Greenwood Press, 2004.

Toumey, Christopher, *God's own scientists: Creationists in a secular world*, New Brunswick, NJ: Rutgers University Press, 1994.

Index